FIVE
BLACK WRITERS

ESSAYS ON
WRIGHT, ELLISON,
BALDWIN, HUGHES,
AND LE ROI JONES

FIVE
BLACK WRITERS

ESSAYS ON
WRIGHT, ELLISON,
BALDWIN, HUGHES,
AND LE ROI JONES

Edited with an introduction by
DONALD B. GIBSON

New York · New York University Press
London · University of London Press Ltd
1970

© 1970 by New York University

Library of Congress Catalog Card Number: 70–114760

SBN: 8147–0462–X (cloth)
SBN: 8147–0490–5 (paper)

Manufactured in the United States of America

To Jo Anne and David Marcus

PREFACE

THE FOLLOWING essays were chosen for inclusion in this volume for a variety of reasons—some simply because they are good essays, others because their subjects are particularly pertinent, and still others because they cover some facet of the work of these five authors not covered elsewhere. Hence they are admittedly of uneven quality, as such a wide selection of essays by different writers is bound to be. But I do not consider that a shortcoming. It is possible to learn from a less than brilliant essay as well as from one of the highest quality. Since a primary aim of this volume is to encourage further study of these writers, any ideas expressed about them may well stimulate the mind of a reader, may well serve as a grinding wheel against which he may shape or sharpen his own perceptions about them.

The final section of the volume, "The Writer and Social Responsibility," is intended to elicit further thinking about what constitutes value in literature and about the relation of the writer to his society. There is a good deal more to be said in this area and it is hoped that those essays will encourage critics and readers to go beyond the conventions of the given moment, to break clean from the confines of our current and so very inadequate literary theory. The times are fast changing, but we who love, study, and write about literature are, it seems to me, in many ways very far behind.

The author wishes to thank Mrs. Mary Anne Gluss, Mr. Kevin Keyes, and Mrs. Charlotte Ritchie for their assistance in the preparation of this book. Acknowledgment and thanks are also extended to the libraries of the University of Connecticut and Harvard University, and to the Research Foundation of the University of Connecticut for its support.

Donald B. Gibson

University of Connecticut

CONTENTS

INTRODUCTION*

1

THOUGH the five writers whose work this volume examines are grouped under a single title, it is extremely difficult, without oversimplifying, to consider them as belonging to a category much more specific than "writer." All are Negroes in that they have tacitly admitted to that appellation, and all are identifiable as such by the terms dictated by the society at large. But the meaning of their racial identity is not, insofar as their writing is concerned, easily assessed. Each is unique. Each clearly and markedly differs from the others in most of the meaningful terms in which one might choose to think of them. Politically they differ. Their sense of morality differs. They differ in personality. They come from diverse backgrounds. None of them agrees with the others (at least insofar as their attitudes are definable through their writing) except in the most general terms; no more so, in any case, than any five serious writers are likely to agree. And the terms in which they agree are definable: each is acutely aware in his own way of the condition of the black man in America; each is sensitive to the racial situation. Nonetheless their responses to their observations and experiences are specifically individual, and the particularity of their responses is a measure of their individuality.

This being the case, one should be extremely hesitant about establishing such an artificial and superficial category as "Negro literature." Though the title of this volume implies a relationship among these five writers, it should quickly be pointed out that the common denominator among them is a precise and painful awareness of a situation and a condition, and "Black" in the title means what it is commonly taken to mean and no more than that. The term pretends in no way to describe nor even hint about the quality of the experiences represented by these five. They are Negro writers, but their writing is not "Negro writing." Their racial identity has no necessary relationship to the form or content of their work.

None of them, not even Jones ultimately, considers his blackness to define his *essential* self. In the writing of Wright, Ellison, Baldwin,

* Much of the material contained in the Introduction about Wright was first published in the *CLA Journal*. It appeared in revised form in *CLA Journal*, xii, 344–57 in an article entitled "Richard Wright and the Tyranny of Convention," by Donald B. Gibson, reprinted by permission of the publisher.

Hughes, and Jones, racial identity is a clear fact, but the matter does not end there. If we place their work in the category of "Negro literature," however, we *do* end the matter there. It is clear enough to most black people who have thought about it that "Negro literature" has about it a reductive aura, the same reductive aura that is apparent when Langston Hughes is referred to as "the Shakespeare of Harlem," or when Ralph Ellison is said to be "the best Negro writer of our time." The conception of a "Negro literature" has the effect of removing black writers from the history of our literature (and from American history as well), thus reflecting racism, whether intentional or not, in literary study. "Separate" in this case means "unequal." I have yet to hear someone insist on a "Negro literature" who has not felt literature by black writers to be generally inferior. (I cite for example Robert Bone, who argues for a "Negro literature" in *The Negro Novel in America*.) The following essays should themselves suggest that these five writers do indeed have some things in common, but also such diversity as to preclude their work's forming a distinct black literature. Perhaps a black literature would from several perspectives be desirable, but so far we clearly do not have one.

2

One of the countless ways in which Richard Wright differs from Ellison, Baldwin, and Hughes (but not so much from Jones) is in his obsession with the idea of transgression against convention. Without exception the protagonists of his five novels step outside the boundaries of convention, and the plots of these novels, the progressions and resolutions of the plots, all depend upon the effects resulting from breaches of convention. The same is true of the large majority of the short stories and even of the autobiographical *Black Boy*. Though the characters in Wright's fiction may break laws, their concern is not nearly so much for law as for convention, the customs governing social interaction among individuals of a given social group. None of Wright's central figures ever has the least remorse over breaking a law, nor even of violating the rights of another. Their only guilt stems from fear of reprisal from the protectors of convention, often—in Wright's fiction—the police.

In each of the novels and most of the short stories the protagonist finds himself to have violated convention either through the operation of will or through circumstance, usually circumstance. Once outside the boundaries, he may feel free of restraint, fearful and guilty, or indifferent. The terms in which the plot progresses depend upon which of these responses the act of transgression engenders within him. The resolution of the plot consists in the protagonist's doing one of three things: (1) coming to terms with himself, deciding he is justified in living outside of convention; (2) confessing to the guardians of convention and thereby relieving himself of his burden of guilt; (3) fleeing, hence avoiding consequences. Whatever he does, he faces the possibility of retaliation by the guardians of convention. He will be killed, mutilated, or both unless he escapes them.

The pattern begins with *Uncle Tom's Children*, Wright's first published book. "Big Boy Leaves Home" tells about an innocent young boy, who, because of circumstances, finds himself in a situation in which he must either kill a white man or most likely be killed himself. He does not choose nor will the situation, but once in it, he kills his antagonist, thus violating the convention, so strong in the South, that says a black must never raise his hand against a white. Neither he nor his family reveals the least awareness nor concern with the moral or legal implications of the killing, for all know too well that what is more important is the violation of the convention. His response is to flee, and he is saved to escape to freedom (in his eyes) in a northern city, but not before he strangles a dog that threatens to reveal his hiding place to the pursuing mob and observes his companion of the earlier critical episode horribly mutilated and murdered.

"Long Black Song," the third story in *Uncle Tom's Children*, is indeed puzzling unless viewed in the terms suggested here. The story has two parts; the first creates the circumstances and the second shows the response of the character who, through no will of his own, finds himself required to act. The puzzling aspect of the story involves the tone of the first part of it. If we read the story as racial protest (the second part is clearly that), then it is difficult to account for the attitude that Wright, in telling the tale, expresses toward the Negro wife and the white salesman who engage in sexual relations. Both are described in quite sympathetic terms. The betraying wife has been thinking, before the arrival of the salesman, of the man whom she would have preferred to marry instead of Silas, her husband, and her thoughts have aroused her sexually. The white salesman who later arrives is associated in her mind with Tom, her former boyfriend and the subject of her reminiscence, who left for the army and never returned. The salesman appears to the wife to be "just like a little boy. A little boy selling clocks." It is not precisely a rape that takes place, for the wife finally leads the salesman to her bed. The sexual act between them, in this apparently racial-protest story, is described in the most highly poetic terms. The wife has committed a breach of convention in voluntarily having sexual relations with the white salesman, but Wright is not so very much concerned with her violation for she is not the central character of the tale and is not seen as culpable by the author. He is far more interested in establishing the circumstances to which the husband returns after his absence.

The salesman comes back next day and Silas, who has discovered his wife's infidelity, first horsewhips him and then kills him (or the salesman's partner; the text does not make clear which one is killed). Silas violates the same convention violated by Big Boy; he has killed a white man. Unlike Big Boy, Silas chooses to remain at the house in the face of his certainty that a mob (the guardians of convention) will soon come from town to kill him. He thus boldly defies the convention and accepts the consequences of his own assertion of masculinity:

"Ahm gonna be hard like they is! So hep me, Gawd, Ahm gonna be *hard!* When they come fer me Ahm gonna *be here!* N when they git me outta here theys gonna *know* Ahm gone! Ef Gawd lets me live Ahm gonna make em *feel* it! . . . Yuh die ef yuh fight! Yuh die ef yuh don fight! Either way yuh die n it don mean nothin. . . ."

The wife urges him to flee, but he forces her away and calmly awaits the coming of the mob. His acceptance of his impending doom is not unlike Bigger Thomas's acceptance at the end of *Native Son*. Bigger seems in a more equanimous state, however, because his final awareness stems from a more complex situation and emerges over a long period of time.

Bigger first feels the compulsion to overstep the bounds of convention when he decides with his friends to rob Blum's grocery store. Fear, however, prevents him from committing the robbery, fear so great as to be nearly overwhelming and the same fear, because it is fear of convention, which causes him to smother Mary Dalton. With the death of Mary, accidental as it is, Bigger feels himself free, free of the constraints of convention that have been so threatening. His test, though, is yet to come, for he has not actually rid himself of fear and guilt. The killing itself puts Bigger in the position of having to consider himself and his situation in a completely new light. Bigger is far more conscious of the violation of convention than of law in the death of Mary, a consciousness fore-shadowed in the abortive plan to rob the grocer. He is much more fearful of robbing a *white* man than of the crime of robbery itself, more fearful than his knowledge that the police would look harder for him for committing such a crime accounts for. Once circumstance (the events surrounding Mary's accidental death at his hands) has put him outside the bounds of convention, he has the potential to come to terms with his fear and guilt; only then, however, for before he commits the forbidden act he has no knowledge of himself, of his true identity.

The same theme finds surrealistic expression in one of Wright's best stories, "The Man Who Lived Underground," contained in *Eight Men*.

The central character is a man who escapes from the police after they have forced him to confess to a murder that he did not commit. After his escape he finds his way to an underground grotto in a sewer. Here, free from the restrictions of society, he lives above social convention entirely unrestricted by the values of the society. He takes a large sum of money, jewelry, and precious stones from a vault, papers the walls of his cave with the green bills, hangs the watches and rings on the walls, and strews the stones on the dirt floor where they glitter like lights. He is able to do this only because the symbols of wealth, status, and power have no meaning for him. Among the places he has access to from his sewer is a church, which he peeps into during a Sunday service. He has to fight the nearly overpowering urge to laugh hysterically, for he knows, though unable to articulate the thought, that their ritual observances are meaningless, that viewed from his perspective, with the air from the sewer blowing in upon them, their music, words, and gestures are absurd. His guilt, the guilt he feels simply because he is human, does not allow him to bear the burden of an existence unrestrained by convention. Hence, he emerges, only to be executed by a world that operates exclusively in terms of prescribed value systems. He, a black man, is consciously and purposely murdered by a white policeman (the guardian of convention) not because he is black, but because he threatens the smooth running of the social machine by his lack of obeisance to convention. "You've got to shoot his kind," his murderer says. "They'd wreck things."

Wright's interest in the fate of one who steps outside the limitations imposed by forces external to himself has caused him to be compared with Dostoevski. Those who have made the comparison have probably been thinking primarily of *Crime and Punishment* and "Notes from the Underground." There is, though, an important difference to be noted, especially in relation to the novel. Dostoevski in *Crime and Punishment* was thinking in terms of violations of a moral order, specifically that laid down by Christianity. Wright, on the other hand, was more concerned with violations of convention than of law or morality. Thus in "Big Boy Leaves Home," "Long Black Song," "The Man Who Killed a Shadow," *Native Son, The Long Dream,* and *Savage Holiday*—in most of Wright's fiction for that matter—murder is not treated as a moral issue, but rather as manifesting a breach of convention. The exception to this is *The Outsider,* in which murder becomes a legal and philosophical problem, but not a moral one. At least this is so in the body of the novel. The death of Cross Damon, the central character, may well have moral overtones, but if so, they are imposed by the whim of the author and not inherent within the value scheme implied within the plot of the novel. For Wright convention has strength, force, and value at least equal to that which Dostoevski attributed to Christian morality.

Ellison has frequently been thought of in connection with Wright not only because both are black writers (though the basis of the comparison has often been racial), but because *Invisible Man* is more like *Native Son* than many prefer to admit. Because the emphasis among literary critics in our time is on art, and Ellison himself has stressed the fact that he is an artist in his fiction and not a polemicist nor propagandist, the element of the novel that is indeed polemical and propagandistic has not been sufficiently explored. *Invisible Man* offers great possibilities for discussion of abstractions of many kinds; there is indeed much to be said about its structure and form; it says a good deal about the human condition. Nonetheless, Ellison's novel is not primarily an aesthetic object. It does not support entirely the perspective of most of the published critics who value it. It explains much of what is going on around us at this very moment; it explores many things that we are seeing before our very eyes. Among other things, it shows, even more precisely than *Native Son*, what the true relation of the black man to power is. When the central character dreams of reading a message contained within the briefcase he was given after the "battle royal," a message reading "To whom it may concern: Keep this nigger boy running," we may well conclude that the message is for everybody; the American dream is bankrupt; place your values elsewhere. And so it is. But anyone who does not recognize that the message has a special relevance for Negroes, who with poverty programs, job training, Head Start, Upward Bound, and so on, are indeed being kept running "after that ever-receding horizon," is simply being naïve.

Several other episodes have special relevance to black people in our time. The "battle royal" episode itself, for example, in which blindfolded Negroes battle among themselves for nonexistent prizes, shows that black people are frequently being manipulated by forces over which they do not precisely have control. The long section about the central character's involvement with the Brotherhood is a miniature of the history of the relation of the Negro to the Communist Party. Perhaps one can say that it outlines the relation of all people to the Party, but first and foremost it outlines a specific relation. Likewise the "Liberty Paint" episode has special relevance to black people. When the central character and Lucius Brockway fight, a scene reminiscent of the "battle royal," they are clearly being manipulated by forces beyond themselves. The comment implicit in the description of the central character's job in the paint factory, his first job when he makes pure white paint by adding drops of black dope, is a comment about assimilation and identity and is especially relevant to black people.

Surely the hospital scene too has special relevance, for the very terms in which the questions are asked of the central character and in which he responds pose a question of identity more specifically salient than it is to the white American. This scene says quite clearly that the general society wishes to perform a lobotomy on the Negro, to render him harmless. The machine described is intended to make the central character docile, to take his past from him, to create a nameless automaton. Finally, the dilemma the central character faces in choosing between the ways of Ras and Rinehart is more specifically relevant to the situation of the Negro than to that of whites, though the problem can, if one so chooses, be translated into nonracial terms. Surely the scenes and episodes mentioned above—and many others might well have been chosen—fit any definition of "protest literature."

On the other hand there is an ambivalence and ambiguity in *Invisible Man* which is not in *Native Son*, at least to the same degree, and it is this which appeals most to the literati. The central character of the novel is the true intellectual man in that he has so thoroughly translated his experience into intellectual terms that he is completely paralyzed. He has the capacity—or infirmity—for seeing the opposite of everything he encounters; a virtue, perhaps, under certain circumstances, but it hardly fits him to do anything of significance in the world. For this reason there is no question about what the central character will do after the close of the novel. He will remain in his cellar, for he has no other alternative. He cannot act, and his intimations that he will perhaps emerge are no more straightforward than any of his comments about his experience. (The whole narrative is ironic in that there exists a disparity between the awareness of the narrator and that of the character, himself, whom he describes. The discrepancy between the two perspectives is evident at many points.) Throughout the course of the story he is by turns both Ras and Rinehart, but finally he can be neither. He becomes the "Vet," the character he encounters at the Golden Day and again as he begins his northward journey. Like the "Vet," he is too highly and painfully conscious to live in the world. His final situation is foreshadowed in the novel during the scene in which he first meets the comrades of the Brotherhood. One of the comrades, saying that he knows all Negroes can sing, asks him to sing a spiritual. "The brother *does not sing!*" another comrade replies hotly. Since the central character does indeed know spirituals, yet feels that to sing would be demeaning and humiliating, and since he feels that not admitting he can sing spirituals is a denial of his history and his identity, he can only respond by breaking out into laughter. His consciousness traps him in a position that allows him neither to do nor not to do.

The same unresolvable ambiguity exists in Ellison's handling of the conception of Booker T. Washington. Few have recognized until very recently that the lines appearing at the beginning of the first chapter of

Invisible Man, "In all things purely social, we can be as separate as the fingers, yet one as the hand in all things essential to mutual progress," and the entire speech given at the smoker by the central character, are direct quotations from Booker T. Washington's Atlanta Exposition address of 1895. The lines are clearly ironic in the context of Ellison's novel, and if one reads that address in Washington's autobiography, *Up from Slavery,* they seem there at best cynical. In any case he could not conceivably have believed the sentiments about the attitudes and character of the Negro which he uttered then on the occasion of the first really major address given by a black man to the nation at large. He gave clear sanction to the system of segregation, assuring the nation that Negroes, "the most patient, faithful, and law-abiding people the world has ever known," likewise approved it. Ellison, who attended the school that Washington founded, Tuskegee Institute, does not precisely admire the person described in *Up from Slavery.* He parodies Washington's tale of his admission to Hampton Institute. Washington tells of arriving at the school with no money and nothing to recommend him. A white teacher tells him to clean a room, and when he cleans it so very well he is admitted to the school despite his lack of the minimal fee for admission. Ellison writes in a passage in the novel where the central character is recalling the beginning of Bledsoe's career:

I remembered the legend of how he had come to the college, a barefoot boy who in his fervor for education had trudged with his bundle of ragged clothing across two states. And how he was given a job feeding slop to the hogs but he had made himself the best slop dispenser in the history of the school; and how the Founder had been impressed and made him his office boy.

The other side of the coin, however, reveals Washington as the man who went to Tuskegee, Alabama, to found a school which at that time was hardly more than an idea in the heads of some of the local residents. There was no educational facility of its level for Negroes anywhere in the area. In a relatively short time he and his students built the school, literally, making their own bricks, designing and constructing their own buildings, growing and preparing their own food. From nothing, Washington built up Tuskegee Institute until its endowment was in the hundreds of thousands of dollars. Washington was a very practical person, the archetypal American, the self-made man, who was convinced that by following certain precepts—frugality, industry, resolution—one could achieve the good life. (There are astounding parallels between *Up from Slavery* and Benjamin Franklin's *Autobiography.*) His own experience taught him that anyone who had the drive, will, and ambition that he had could succeed, and the word itself, "success" (or some form of it), appears time and time again in his autobiography.

Now given these contradictory perspectives of Booker T., Ellison splits the man into two persons: he is the Founder, that impeccable, godlike person who founds the university and whose life is exemplary; he is Bledsoe, the cynical opportunist who is so ruthless as to observe no restraint in his quest for personal success and power. The two roles are not reconciled in the novel any more than the roles of Ras and Rinehart are reconciled. Herein lies the crux of a number of things: of the finally unresolved conclusion of *Invisible Man*; of the quarrel between Ellison and Irving Howe (recorded in the last section of essays of this book); and perhaps of Ellison's not having so far published a second novel. These unresolved and unresolvable dilemmas suggest a person in exile, a person who has stated all the possible positions but finds them equally unsatisfactory. It seems to me—and let me admit the highly speculative nature of this conclusion—that Ellison is maintaining his own painful "silence, exile, and cunning."

Invisible Man is a great novel, a novel less captured by the criticism about it than most books. No critic of the novel has done full justice to its irony, ambiguity, and ambivalences, its carefully wrought detail, its political and social relevance. None of us, it seems, can get sufficiently far above it to see it truly and in its entirety. The stringency of the protest element of the novel in the context that Ellison has created proves the falsity, irrelevance, and artificiality of the dichotomy currently established between the aesthetic and social intention, between art and social protest in literature.

It is by now a cliché to say that James Baldwin is a better essayist than novelist. I *feel* I know what that means, but the comparison will not bear very much thought about it. I remember being quite distressed in the third grade when my teacher said that one cannot add oranges and apples because they are of different categories. But it always seemed to me that if you were adding objects or fruits, you could add oranges and apples very well. When we say that Baldwin's essays are better than his fiction, we are comparing oranges and apples in the same way that one can say reasonably that a particular orange is better than a particular apple if he is considering some similar quality in the two such as freshness. But the comparison should not be made if one is thinking of qualities essential to each object. The apple, if the comparison is made in terms of "appleness," or the orange, if of "orangeness," will win out every time. However, when one compares an apple to an orange and says that one is better, he may mean that the one stands higher in its category than the other, though still qualities not essential to the object are being compared. For example, we may say that a fresh, large, juicy California orange is better than a gnarled crab apple. If we say this, we mean that freshness, largeness and juiciness are values we hold, but we must recognize that to the squirrel the gnarled crab apple may be better and also that those desirable qualities are not inherent in the orange, for an old, shriveled, browning orange is no less an orange.

Now whether Baldwin's essays are better than his fiction is no different a judgment from the one that says the California orange is better than the crab apple. The judgment is subjective and relative, far more so than if we were to say that Baldwin is a better essayist than any one of the *Partisan Review* clique. For when we compare two essays, we may compare them in terms belonging to the category "essay." We may compare the organization of ideas, the quality of ideas, the rhetoric or grammar. For the same reasons that we would likely never say that Henry James's prefaces are better (or worse) than his fiction, or that his expository writing is better than the fiction of any other writer, we should not be so willing to say that Baldwin is a better essayist than novelist. I think there are more significant comparisons that can be made between his essays and his fiction.

From Baldwin's first novel, *Go Tell It on the Mountain*, to the most recent, *Tell Me How Long the Train's Been Gone*, there has been an increasing broadness of concern, a movement in his fiction from the purely individual and private toward the social. In this sense his fiction and his social essays of a polemical nature seem to be moving toward some meeting point insofar as their content (rather than style or form) is concerned. By no means has he gone so far as Norman Mailer, who in *The Armies of the Night* has performed a notable marriage between the fictional and essay forms. Such a marriage, an apparent innovation in our time, is not entirely unlike the form achieved in the probing autobiography, *The Education of Henry Adams*. The difference lies in the extent to which Mailer's piece has about it more of the quality of fiction in that the reader gets a greater sense of engagement with a particular personality than with the symbolic figure generated in the pages of *The Education*. It is so very apparent that Henry Adams has left a good deal out; we are likely to feel that Mailer has put everything in. By altering the perspective of the usual autobiography Mailer (and Adams too) has the freedom to probe a "character." The third person permits a distance not possible with the first person. The perspective allows a tension between the reader's sense of actuality (his feeling of some correspondence between the events described and history) and its perception by a discrete human whose vision is determined by his character and circumstances. Baldwin does not go quite this far, yet he seems to have moved in this direction. There seems, for example, far less distance between "Everybody's Protest Novel" and *Tell Me How Long the Train's Been Gone* than between that essay and *Go Tell It on the Mountain*.

Like many first novels, *Go Tell It on the Mountain* is autobiographical, closely personal, and therefore narrow in scope. Though it contains several scenes describing the earlier lives of others, its primary focus is entirely upon the central character, John. The novel has as its aim to describe John's deliverance from the world, the flesh, and the devil and from his father as well. Some attention is given to the role of the society in determining the quality and character of John's life, but that attention is minimal for, given the perspective of the novel, the forces affecting John stem directly from the characters of others in the novel, especially his father and mother, Gabriel and Elizabeth.

Giovanni's Room expands outward. Still the focus is upon the central character, David, but the problem presented by the novel is of such a nature as to involve the question of the responsibility of David to another person. The novel is about the problems of responsibility. Where, it asks, does integrity or simply the desire of the individual to fulfill himself end, and the responsibility to fulfill the obligations of love and friendship begin? In other words the novel expands beyond *Go Tell It on the Mountain* in that the central character's essential problems are, though personal, not exclusively so. David abandons Giovanni and feels that his act of abandonment is responsible ultimately for Giovanni's execution, though he may have needed to abandon Giovanni to save himself. Hence, the personal and private problems of the individual in this case have ramifications beyond the inner workings of his own peculiar psyche. There is a third person involved, David's fiancée, Hella. He must eventually choose between Giovanni and Hella; the salient point, though, is that no matter what his choice, the exigencies of his own predicament impinge upon the lives and fates of others.

Another Country is in two ways an expression of broader social concern than *Giovanni's Room*. It is first of all a kind of general assessment and judgment of the whole of the American society, an attempt to define its character. It is also a further, broader statement of interrelatedness among individuals. The title of the novel subsumes both categories. I believe it might well come from the dialogue in Marlowe's *Jew of Malta*:

FRIAR BARNADINE: Thou hast committed—
BARABAS: Fornication: but that was in another country,
      And, besides, the wench is dead.

The implication here is that the respondent absolves himself from responsibility, but suggests guilt by his reply. The question elicits the need on his part for apology. He clearly feels he has done something wrong, yet he evades responsibility by his obvious excuses, excuses which by their very character are confessions of culpability. By his title, then, Baldwin means to suggest that Americans are not responsible to and for each other; Americans neither accept nor love each other.

When Baldwin wrote *Another Country*, he took a great risk in placing the section on Rufus first for it is undisputably the strongest, most power-ful section of the novel. He took a risk comparable to placing the climax of the traditional plot at the beginning rather than near the end of a work where it usually is. If we were to illustrate the structure of Baldwin's novel graphically, we might best do so by the figure of several concentric circles, the innermost representing that powerful first section. The inten-tion of all that follows the first section is to pinpoint responsibility, to determine the roles that each person has played—and indeed that Rufus himself has played—in the death of Rufus. It is a novel about the respon-sibility of all the characters to each other and about the responsibility the society has in determining the nature and quality of their lives. Some element of the American culture stands in the way of decent relations among people. The statement *Another Country* makes about American society makes it the broadest social comment Baldwin had made in his fiction up to its publication.

Tell Me How Long the Train's Been Gone cannot be described as a protest novel, yet it makes abundantly plain the involvement of the author in problems beyond those having specifically to do with his own individual and private adjustment to the human condition. Here is the most intense and explicit statement Baldwin has so far made in his fiction of his social involvement and concern, and the statement strikes more directly at the racist attitudes of the general society than ever before. Through recount-ing certain experiences of the central character, Leo Proudhammer, and through expression of the attitudes and feelings about race of one of the very sympathetic characters in the novel, Black Christopher, Baldwin protests against the society. When Leo goes into a diner and is subjected to insult because of his race, protest is intended. When he is arrested and feels the possibility of undergoing the torment common among Negroes at the hands of the police, Baldwin protests against the society. He protests in the name of the countless numbers for whom the outcome is not so undamaging as for Leo Proudhammer. Each of the instances in which Leo suffers because of his race is a protest against the condition of black people in America. The very paranoid sensibility that causes Barbara and Leo to ride uptown in a cab because of their fear of riding on a subway is a protest, a protest against a society which does not pro-tect the innocent, provide for the good, nor reward the deserving, espe-cially when these are black.

Christopher is called "Black Christopher" because he is militant in his attitudes and highly conscious and proud of his blackness. It is through him that the most explicit statements of protest are made, statements that Baldwin must somehow believe himself and that Leo Proudhammer thoroughly understands and sympathizes with though unwilling, unable, or perhaps not needing to speak them himself. Such a statement as the following, coming as it does from such a sympathetic character as Black Christopher and proceeding so directly from his personality as delineated in the novel, is as strident a protest as anything Richard Wright ever wrote.

And all these laws and speeches don't mean shit. They do not mean *shit*. It's the spirit of the people, baby, the *spirit* of the people, they don't want us and they don't like us, and you see that spirit in the face of every cop. Them laws they keep passing, shit, they just like the treaties they signed with the Indians. Nothing but lies, they never even *meant* to keep those treaties, baby, they wanted the land and they got it and now they mean to keep it, even if they have to put every black motherfucker in this country behind barbed wire, or shoot him down like a dog.

Statements like this in Baldwin's most recent novel far more closely approximate the language, tone, and meaning of the essays of a political and social character ("Notes from a Region of My Mind," for example) than anything in the fiction heretofore.

Langston Hughes is the least complex of these five writers, and his simplicity, his straightforwardness have been in part responsible for the neglect his work has suffered. It is well enough known that our poets no longer write for people generally, but for academicians and other poets. Langston Hughes, who quite consciously utilized forms and diction that are easily understood, wrote for people, and hence his work lacks that subtle complexity, indirection, and fineness of style characterizing modern poetry.

Hughes had a clear notion, even from the beginning of his career, of what the function of literature is. When in the twenties he seemed to be following the then current vogue of writing of Negroes as primitive exotics, he intended actually to be doing something else. Eugene O'Neill with *The Emperor Jones*, Sherwood Anderson with *Dark Laughter*, Carl Van Vechten with *Nigger Heaven*, and Vachel Lindsay with "Congo" (written in 1914, but influential in establishing the twenties' interest in the Negro as subject matter among writers) expressed the idea that modern civilization is oppressive, and that American Puritanism prevents the expression of true feelings and responses. The Negro, they reasoned, is closer to the primitive and consequently free from the burden imposed by social constraint. They were responding to the Freudian conception of repression, as popularly conceived, and to the general movement toward freedom from social restraint so luxuriantly indulged during the twenties.

Hughes, however, was not following this line of thinking. The general interest in the Negro as subject matter was probably responsible for his work's being published at all, but whereas many of his white contemporaries were treating Negroes in their work with condescension—saying in effect, "Isn't it wonderful that these people can be so natural, so un-sophisticated, so uncivilized?"—Hughes was following a conscious pro-gram that had quite different ends. When, for example, he wrote of the physical beauty of Negroes, his intention was not to entertain whites, but to change the image of the Negro in his own eyes. He felt that, in a society whose standards of beauty exclude him, the Negro for his own self-esteem must see his physical appearance as positive. Hughes was also trying to change the prevailing attitudes of the general society toward Negroes, and a good deal of his poetry about black people has had this end.

"I, Too" (1926) is one of the best known of Hughes' poems and is in many ways typical of the poetry he was to write later. It protests against the condition of the Negro in America and celebrates as well the beauty of blackness. In form it is typical. It derives from the tradition of the dramatic monologue as well as from the blues lyric, a monologue express-ing an individual's lament about his life or some facet of it. Many of Hughes's poems are dramatic monologues, some so close to the blues lyric as to be indistinguishable from it, others more traditional.

Of his forebears in poetry he is closest to Walt Whitman, about whom he wrote a poem, "Old Walt."

> Old Walt Whitman
> Went finding and seeking,
> Finding less than sought
> Seeking more than found,
> Every detail minding
> Of the seeking or the finding.
>
> Pleasured equally
> In seeking as in finding,
> Each detail minding
> Old Walt went seeking
> And finding.

The voice in this poem is the voice of the poet, but usually in Hughes' poetry the speaker is not the poet per se. The speaker is more likely to be a mask for the poet, as is the case so often in Whitman's poetry when he assumes the "persona" so called. Hughes assumes a number of masks, and almost never do his poems reflect what might be inferred to be the subjective and private experience of the poet. Because Hughes desired to be a social, public poet, there is little that reveals anything about the private man.

The same idealism we find in Whitman we find in Hughes, though the latter is too much a pragmatist to participate in the mysticism on which Whitman's celebration of democratic idealism rests. Hughes is idealistic in that he felt strongly the possibility of the realization in America of the full potential of democracy. For this reason there is nothing cynical about his poems. The most strident of his protest writing is tempered by his faith in the ultimate working out of social problems. Whitman was aware of the ways in which democracy was not working out in his time, of the corruption and hypocrisy rampant in the public and private sectors, but he chose to write about these matters outside his poetry. Hughes simply does not make the same division. His intention is to correct social evil by calling attention to it in his poetry.

The subjects and themes of his poetry are paralleled in his fiction and drama. There is indeed a high degree of consistency in his work as a whole. For example, "Cross," which is about a person whose father is white and whose mother is black, parallels in its subject and theme the short story "Father and Son" and the play "Mulatto." The poem "I Dream a World" envisions a world in which freedom, economic and social equality, and brotherhood exist, a theme implicit in the greater part of Hughes's fiction and drama. Even those stories and plays that portray the life and character of Negroes and are not explicitly protest have inherent within them the same faith and hope of a better world.

Hughes often uses humor for the sake of achieving his intentions. *Tambourines to Glory*, though in some sense a tragic drama, utilizes humor extensively. Even *Soul Gone Home*, as sad and depressing as that play is in its implications, is a very funny play on the surface. The poems "High to Low," "Low to High," and "The Ballad of the Landlord" deal with extremely serious problems, the separation of economic classes among Negroes, exploitation by slum landlords, and police brutality. Yet these are among Hughes's most humorous works. Here the humor has about it that bitter-sweet, ironic quality so characteristic of Negro humor, especially that having to do with racial matters.

Hughes would likely not have been able to write so humorously about so many of his subjects if it were not for the breadth and depth of his own humanity. He had the capacity in his work and in his life as well to feel a broad sympathy for the whole race of mankind, a capacity possessed not only by few writers, but by few people. Hughes seemed to those who knew him to accept himself; he did not give the appearance of one who had the least doubt of his own humanity. Hence he could accept others and could "dream a world" in which downtrodden people of all colors and in all countries could share the fruits of the earth.

LeRoi Jones has written some rather "strong stuff," but the interesting thing about his writing *as a whole* is that it will not support the reputation of its author. With the exception of *The Slave*, and that is only a possible exception, it does not seem to me that Jones's work (excluding a few later pieces) can be made out to be racist diatribe or propagandistic attacks upon the general society. On the contrary Jones is more closely related to his fellow litterateurs (the academic writers) of our time and is, hence, far more concerned with examining the inner recesses of his own psyche than with analyzing and commenting on the general social situation in America, especially as this relates to black people. It is extremely difficult for most people to see this, for most people, even the professional literary critics, find it impossible to distinguish between LeRoi Jones the poet, dramatist, and fictionist and LeRoi Jones the social activist and community leader. I am not suggesting any kind of necessary division between art and life; I am suggesting that these two roles have so far not come together in LeRoi Jones's career despite the fact that he would have us all think otherwise. The two roles seem to be merging (see, for example, his poems in his and Larry Neal's anthology, *Black Fire*), but they have not yet come together. Consequently, the major part of his work is personal and private despite rumors to the contrary. *The Slave* and *Dutchman* bear this out, as does practically everything else of a creative nature that he has written.

The Slave would seem the most obvious of the above works to be primarily political and social in character, to have as its end a direct result beyond itself. It is this play that has been used as evidence that Jones is a racist, that he intends to foment hatred between the races, that, indeed, public funds should not be used to support the sentiments put forward in that play. But if we are able for a moment to step back and to observe dispassionately what Jones has put before us, we can see quite clearly that *The Slave* is a grueling, painful examination by the dramatist of himself as a person, as a writer, and as a man.

The degree to which the dramatist is self-critical may be determined by noting the play's tone in relation to the main character, Walker. He is no hero. He does not get off unscathed. The playwright is not in complete sympathy with him. This is not in itself necessarily significant unless we take into account the fact that Walker is a thinly disguised, imagined portrait of the playwright himself. Anyone who knows something about Jones's life will recognize the parallels between the situation of the play and the biography of the playwright.

There is no glory in the world described in the play—no heroism even. We are exposed to a sordid, cruel mess which the hero would have preferred not to participate in had he any control over the forces responsible for the existence of the world he describes. The play is not about the glorious overthrow of the society by black rebels. No black person seeing it would be moved to act, for at the end of the play the playwright obviously intends that the audience should weep. Jones is not so bad a playwright as to present the situation described in the play in unambiguous fashion. It is this ambiguity, this doubt about the rightness and humaneness of Walker's actions, that causes the play to be something more than a simplistic propaganda piece as critics and reviewers have believed it to be. Walker, at the end of the play, is a defeated man; the only thing he has is his life, and that, the prologue makes clear, at great cost.

Dutchman is even more clearly an examination on the part of the playwright of the inner workings of his consciousness. Again the central character is a thinly disguised portrait of the author—or at least of a part of his character as he conceives it. The biographical parallels are to be found here as well—the fact that Clay is from New Jersey, from an upwardly mobile family, an intellectual, a litterateur familiar with Baudelaire and generally conversant about esoteric subjects. The racial theme of the play is obvious and natural. It would have been false to leave it out. But the play is ultimately not about race—or, perhaps more accurately, the play is about race on one level only. Americans are likely to see only that one level and to have obscured from them the vast complexity of *Dutchman*.

First of all, the play is highly symbolic, more symbolic than propaganda plays can afford to be. It draws upon several of the mythologies of the western world and upon a well-known fable as well. Thus it demands interpretation beyond reference to current events. Though I believe symbolic reading should be avoided whenever possible, *Dutchman* is one of those instances demanding symbolic reading. It can hardly be ignored, for example, that the events of the play take place underground. The opening stage direction reads: "In the flying underbelly of the city. Steaming hot, and summer on top, outside. Underground. The subway heaped in modern myth." Without indulging in particular interpretations of the meaning of "underground," let me simply ask the reader to recall some of the myriad encounters and events of mythological characters that have taken place underground or in "bellies" (the analogy Jones makes in the quotation above). We might also be reminded of other writers who have relied upon the mythology of the underground: Dante, Milton, Dostoevski, Wright, and Ellison.

The title itself, *Dutchman*, suggests the legend of the Flying Dutchman, an interpretation borne out by the clear implication at the end that the events of the play transpire again and again eternally. Lula spots another victim—someone like Clay—and she approaches him just as she had approached Clay earlier. The title also suggests reference to a world other than the natural, whether interpreted as meaning simply a bad omen or the ship of the Dutchman (or the man himself) condemned to sail the seas until Judgment Day.

The play may be read as a modern re-enactment of the biblical legend describing original sin, or it can be read as describing the perennial conflict between the sexes. In the former case Lula is Eve; in the latter she represents the negative or evil female principle intent upon destroying the male. In this case her victims are those who are young, sophisticated, intellectual and, in the view of many, unmasculine because they are devotees of the arts. These interpretations related to the nonracial levels of the play are supported by Lula's response after she has stabbed Clay: "Get this man off me!" It is a *man* whom she has destroyed, not a representative of any particular race.

Similar cases could easily be made for *The Toilet, The System of Dante's Hell,* and others of Jones's works. They are all highly sophisticated performances written for the same audience that responds to Robert Lowell, Edward Albee, W. D. Snodgrass, John Berryman, and Denise Levertov. Jones does not write for the masses of the people (as his politics would dictate). Even when he tries to do that, to leave his academic training and sensibility behind him, he can do so only with great difficulty and not nearly so easily as many black poets who do not have his background. His early career clearly indicates that he became a writer out of personal commitment rather than political necessity. He is trying to become the social activist in his poems that he is in his life, but so far the change has not come about—at least insofar as his published works indicate. So in a certain sense LeRoi Jones is the victim his writing so frequently characterizes him as being—a double victim truly, for he is victimized by a society whose guilt prevents it from understanding what he is writing about during the very process of his describing himself as a victim. If literary and political interests want to "get" LeRoi Jones, then let them be honest enough and sensitive enough to "get" him for his political activism and not for his creative efforts. LeRoi Jones the man may or may not have broken the law, but his work is innocent.

Richard Wright

THE ALIEN LAND
OF RICHARD WRIGHT*

Saunders Redding

THE DEDICATION of Richard Wright's posthumous book, *Eight Men*, is more than a curious anomaly. It is an irony. It is addressed to friends in France, "whose kindness made me feel at home in an alien land," and the irony has greater poignancy because the author did not intend it. Wright lacked the ironic cast of mind and heart. Except in intimate privacy and on those rare occasions when he was at ease with his friends, when he was often gay, he had no sport with mockery, especially if it was turned against himself. He had no eye for fun; no ear or tongue for jest. In public—and his books were public—he took the world and all men as he took himself, with grim seriousness.

So the dedication of *Eight Men* was gravely meant as an expression of gratitude to a people who ranked him with the greats of modern fiction, and in this sense it means what it says. But in a more important sense it does not. For if Richard Wright was at home in the "alien land" where he had lived for nearly fifteen years, how could he have written (in *White Man, Listen!*) near the close of those years, "I am a rootless man"? At home and rootless? Surely both were not true. "But," he went on, "I am neither psychologically distraught nor in any wise particularly perturbed because of it." Without exception, directly or by implication, his published works refute him. No modern writer of comparable gifts and reputation has been so mistaken in his judgment of himself, nor understood and valued the sources of his spirit less.

Wright the novelist was first and last an American novelist. He was not at home in France. He never absorbed, nor ever was absorbed in, the strange environment, the Gallic atmosphere. He saw the *mise en scène*, but did not comprehend it, nor did he have the writer's sense of being in it. He was no cosmopolite, like Henry James. France was for him what

* Reprinted from *Soon One Morning: New Writing by American Negroes*, Herbert Hill, ed. (New York: Alfred A. Knopf, 1963), pp. 50–59, by permission of the author and publisher.

pollutions of oppression into their blood and bone. But it had. "Is this us? And is this our America?" It was.

As Richard Wright saw it, redemption lay in revolution; so he became a Communist. He was, he said, at about the time of the publication of *Native Son*, a "card-bearing" member of the Party. He gave his reasons. American democracy isolated him because he was a Negro: the Communist Party offered "the first sustained relationships of my life." He was amazed and immensely gratified to learn "that there did exist in this world an organized search for the truth of the lives of the oppressed and the isolated." He joined the search, he was a member of the revolution because he thought that Negro experience could find "a home, a functioning value and a role" in communism's radical position.

"If you possess enough courage to speak out what you are," Wright wrote, "you will find that you are not alone." He had enough courage, and he spoke out; and this courageous speaking out, it should be remarked, was the only literary creed—it was certainly no aesthetic theory!—he ever went by. Like his mother's face when he once surprised her staring at a particularly lurid cartoon, Wright reflected what he felt in the dark places of his soul—disgust and anger, shame and fear. And these combined with innate honesty to form the main elements of Richard Wright's extraordinary literary power.

He struck with that power in his first published work, *Uncle Tom's Children*, a collection of four *nouvelles*. Three of these are about lynching, and the fourth, "Fire and Cloud," is about revolution, purification, and deliverance, and it ends in exhortation: "Freedom belongs to the strong!" Each is a violent and brutal and shockingly undisguised, *unliterary* comment, not on life, but on a way of having to live and of being forced to live in ignorance, fear, and shame. In his first book Wright is preoccupied with—is, indeed, already beginning to be obsessed by—"the disinherited, the dispossessed," and in Big Boy of the lead story, "Big Boy Leaves Home," he has already created the prototype of all his heroes, who were ever to be angry, bitter, vengeful, violently hurling themselves against the walls that barred them from a life that they knew was a better life than theirs, belonging to people no better than themselves. They knew this from the movies, the picture magazines, and the screaming headlines in the daily press. But while white people were no better, they were different —so different as to seem to Bigger Thomas (*Native Son*) not people at all, but "a sort of great natural force, like a stormy sky looming overhead, or like a deep swirling river stretching suddenly at one's feet in the dark" threatening a death to which one could react "only in fear and shame."

These were Wright's own dominant, empirical emotions. He did not have to create them for his fictional purposes. They were the very substance of his childhood, youth, and manhood, until he moved abroad. He tells us in *Black Boy*, his autobiography, that he learned at an early age "the reality—a Negro's reality—of the white world. . . . I was tense each moment. . . . I did not suspect that the tension I had begun to feel would lift itself into the passion of my life. . . . I was always to be conscious of it, brood over it, carry it in my heart, live with it, sleep with it, fight with it." In a way more direct than is true of most important modern authors of fiction, Wright's heroes were in naked honesty himself, and not imaginary creations that served merely to express his complicated personality.

This is not to say, however, that their adventures and their characterizing quirks and habits, their whims of thought and the compulsive violence of their behavior, were also Wright's. Not by any means. These were the fancied and observed externalizations of what such hero-personalities would do and say and outwardly be—personalities which, unlike Wright's own, were not guided by a moral intelligence, an active social sense, or ethical thought. The tragedy of Wright's heroes is that they lack this direction, and the blunt point of Wright's fiction is that American society denies them the opportunity to acquire it. Speaking in defense of Bigger Thomas, the lawyer of *Native Son* spoke for all Wright's heroes: "Excluded from, and unassimilated in our society, yet longing to gratify impulses akin to our own but denied the objects and channels evolved through long centuries for their socialized expression, every sunrise and sunset make him guilty of subversive actions."

But if the characterizing externalizations are the measure of Wright's imagination, the structure of his heroes' personalities, the patterns of their emotions, and the types of their dreams are the measure of Wright's honesty and of his self-knowledge as a Negro. It is inconceivable that Wright's essay "How Bigger Was Born" is true in fact. It is true only— and the "only" implies no derogation—in spirit. Though the essay declares it, it is hardly to be taken literally—or literally believed that Wright conceived of Bigger Thomas as sometimes Negro and sometimes white. This is an elastic rationalization to justify what the author himself then embraced as a saving *modus vivendi*: the united front of the Communist line—the people's movement, the brotherhood of the oppressed. Bigger Thomas was Negro all the time. And so, of course, was Richard Wright. He made this clear, after he left the Party, in what is probably his most brilliant essay.

This neglected essay—the introduction to a book entitled *Black Metropolis*—is of far greater importance than any one citation indicates. Whether by accident or design, the essay discloses the *central stream* of Wright's entire development both as man and as writer. It reveals the sources of his thoughts and feelings. It takes us into the matrix of his creative conceptions.

He read William James early, at fifteen or sixteen. He got to read him by a subterfuge which involved a denial of his selfhood, and while this was certainly a part of the matter, the greater part was that he found objective philosophical confirmation of what experience had already taught him—that "the lives of the dispossessed are not real to white people." On more than one occasion he had been treated as if he did not exist as a sensate being. As a hotel bellboy in a Southern town he had been summoned to rooms where naked white women lolled about unmoved by any sense of shame at his presence, because "blacks were not considered human beings anyway. . . . I was a non-man, something that knew vaguely that it was human but felt that it was not. . . . I felt doubly cast out."

Then he read James, and James was later supported by the professional social psychologists. It is revealing to quote the passage that Wright quotes: "No more fiendish punishment could be devised . . . than that one should be turned loose in society and remain absolutely unnoticed by the members thereof. If no one turned around when we entered, answered when we spoke, or minded what we did, but if every person we met 'cut us dead,' and acted as if we were nonexistent things, a kind of rage and impotent despair would ere long well up in us, from which the cruelest bodily tortures would be a relief; for these would make us feel that, however bad might be our plight, we had not sunk to such a depth as to be unworthy of attention at all."

This is the ground of all Wright's works, fiction and nonfiction. It is the thought, the theme, and the dramatic design. The passage revealed, as it were, him to himself. It is scarcely to be doubted that from the moment he read it, groping through it toward the knowledge of its empirical truth and listening to its mournful echoes in the still locked chambers of his soul, Wright became a man with a message and a mission. Long before he wrote *White Man, Listen!* the message was addressed to a white audience, and the mission was to bring awareness to that audience and perhaps thereby to save the world.

Both the message and the mission were particularized by Richard Wright's conception of a world where men "still cling to the emotional basis of life that the [old] feudal order gave them," and by his supra-consciousness of being Negro in that world. Translated into creative terms, this necessitated the rendering of Negro life with greater circumstantiality than had ever before been attempted. Oh, what psychological detail, what analysis of external influences, what precise attention to physical minutiae! He was in the naturalistic tradition, but without the naturalistic writer's aesthetic theories, abstract knowledge, and controls. Wright put everything in to arouse an audience which he hoped would be white, as principally it was. Only rarely did he write for Negroes, and only then when he was pressed, and then only on political subjects. He reasoned that Negroes already knew the particulars of what it was to have "uncertainty as a way of life" and "of living within the vivid present moment and letting the meaning of that moment suffice as a rationale for life and death." But whites did not know, so he had to tell them—in the rage of Silas (in "Long Black Song"), in the weakness of Mann (in "Down by the Riverside"), in the despair of Bigger, and in the words of Bigger's Communist lawyer:

I plead with you to see a mode of *life* in our midst, a mode of life stunted and distorted, but possessing its own laws and claims, an existence of men growing out of the soil prepared by the collective but blind will of a hundred million people. I beg you to recognize human life draped in a form and guise alien to ours, but springing from a soil plowed and sown by our own hands. I ask you to recognize the laws and processes flowing from such a condition, understand them, seek to change them. If we do none of these, then we should not pretend horror or surprise when thwarted life expresses itself in fear and hate and crime.

This is life, new and strange. . . . We have kept our eyes turned from it. This is life lived in cramped limits and expressing itself not in terms of our good and bad, but in terms of its own fulfillment. Men are men and life is life, and we must deal with them as they are; and if we want to change them, we must deal with them in the form in which they exist and have their being.

Listen, white folks!

2

Wright's books sold more than a million copies here at home, so there were those who listened, and many of them must have felt as Dorothy Canfield Fisher felt. Still it changed little. What Wright had seen as a possible agent of change, the American Communist Party, disappointed him. He held on for a while, and he remained happy that he had written those stories in which he had "assigned a role of honor and glory" to the Party, but his commitment of faith crumbled. His rejection of the Party early in the war years was only a gesture, for the Party had already rejected him. After the war, when change still did not come, he rejected America.

This, however, was more than a gesture: it was an action of the greatest consequences. Life in France, in Paris, where he went to live, in some ways fulfilled him as a social being. The freedom was good. The "strangeness" was good. The reputation his books had earned him with the French and among Europeans generally was good to savor. He and his family could live where they wished and go where they wanted without the old uncertainties, the fears. It was all good. "I do not expect ever again to live in the States," he said in spring of 1959.

But what was good for him as a social being was bad for his work. He had taken his Negroness with him, but he could not take with him the America that bred and fed his consciousness of Negroness. Perhaps he sought to nourish that consciousness by a kind of forced feeding. He read the American press assiduously, and particularly the American Negro press. He kept up a voluminous correspondence with American friends. He made friends with French Africans—Negroes—in Paris, who conceived, edited, and largely wrote the Negro quarterly publication *Présence Africaine*. He helped them to found the Society of African Culture and was instrumental in establishing an American branch of the Society. But none of these activities was enough. All of them together were not.

When *The Long Dream* was published in 1958, what was happening to Richard Wright—what, indeed, had already happened—seemed obvious to his American readers. The Fishbelly of that book was Big Boy of "Big Boy Leaves Home"; he was the preacher's son of "Fire and Cloud"; and he was Bigger Thomas of *Native Son*—except that now he was an anachronism. The limitations of mood, the restricted inventiveness, and the congeneric characterizations that defined Wright's work were no longer projective of the small, new realities and the big, new *Weltansicht* of the only place and people that could ever be Wright's home. Angry scorn alternating with bleak despair was no longer enough. Violence and brutal physical degradation were still a part of the new reality, but they were no longer all of it. Cowardice, self-abasement, and unmitigated suffering do not now highlight the drama and furnish the big dramatic scenes. *The Outsider* (1953) seemed rather silly; and one is not surprised that the best stories in his posthumous *Eight Men* were written before he left the States.

In going to live abroad Richard Wright had cut the roots that once sustained him; the tight-wound emotional core came unwound; the creative center dissolved; his memory of what Negro life in America *was* lost its relevance to what Negro life in America *is*—and is becoming. The people and the events of his latest books are not true. While Wright remained honest, he was honest only to the memory of things past, to passions spent, to moods gone vapid, and too often these moods found expression in vaporous language:

He peered out of his window and saw vast, wheeling populations of ruled stars swarming in the convened congresses of the skies anchored amidst nations of space and he prayed wordlessly that a bright, bursting tyrant of living sun would soon lay down its golden laws to loosen the locked regions of his heart and cast the shadow of his dream athwart the stretches of time.

Richard Wright had forgotten the tough American idiom. He had been gone from home too long. But he had already earned the right to be judged by his best, and that best was in the moral stance from which he never wavered, and in his courage as a writer, and in his honesty as a man.

THE DARK AND HAUNTED TOWER
OF RICHARD WRIGHT*

Nathan A. Scott, Jr.

THE EXISTENTIALIST overtones and the explicit allusions to Nietzsche and Heidegger in *The Outsider* led some of the reviewers of his book of 1953 to conclude that Richard Wright was misguidedly experimenting with intellectual traditions outside his actual experience and that he had taken a wrong turning. This was a judgment, however, which surely had to require as its basic premise something like the rather incomprehensible mystique about the Negro intellectual which is occasionally invoked by fools and professional obscurantists, that he is somehow ancestrally fated to exclusion from the general Atlantic community of cultural exchange simply because his racial identity does itself, in some ineffable way, consign him to a permanent ghetto of the mind. But, if this mystique is abandoned as the nonsense that it really is, there should have been no occasion for surprise at the expression which *The Outsider* provided of the extent to which Mr. Wright, after several years of residence in France, had been influenced by the secular modes of European existentialism. For here is a philosophical movement which has found its basic subject matter not so much in the history of philosophy as in the crises and distempers of human existence in the twentieth century. The fundamental reality about which it has very often wanted to speak is that of "the extreme situation" —the situation, that is, in which man's essential dignity is radically challenged by an unconscionable subversion of justice and an intolerable distance between master and slave. And this is precisely the reality that stirred Mr. Wright's imagination into life—from the time of his first forays into the literary life, under the sponsorship of the Communist Party, while still a Chicago postal employee in the 'thirties, up to the time of his sudden death in Paris in November of 1960.

So there was nothing at all unnatural in this American Negro writer having responded affirmatively to the *Angst*-ridden accents and idioms of

* Reprinted from *Graduate Comment* (Wayne State University), VII (1964), 93–99. Revised for this printing and reprinted by permission of the author and the editor of *Graduate Comment*.

12

Jean-Paul Sartre and Georges Bataille and Maurice Blanchot. For, among those Negro intellectuals of his time whose gift of expression enabled them to have a "voice," it may well be that there was none for whom the reality of their "extreme situation" constituted so great a burden. The social statisticians today are busy, of course, in their notations of the steadily increasing improvement in what they call "race relations," and it is probably the case that the moral quality of our life is, in this dimension, something less of an embarrassment than it was a decade or so ago. But the tokens of acceptance that the Negro has won here and there are not yet so great as to make it impossible for others to imagine that he, when he is sensitive and discerning, still feels his status to be precarious and undecided. He has only to contemplate the bitter intransigence of the South and the subtle but firmly maintained exclusions of the North to be reminded of how meager and insubstantial is the new ground that he has recently gained. Though it is only in the occasional pockets of Southern depravity that he is still exposed to the nakeder forms of violence and intimidation, he knows that the actuality of the American experience continues to involve for him that most unhinging kind of frustration which is a result of the glitter and promise of life in a great country being near enough for the mind to be dazzled by the sense of their availability, and yet far enough away to exact a sense of defeat more exacerbating than anything a slave could possibly feel. When this bitter irony is explored by a radical imagination, the nature of the human material is surely such as will permit its being seized by way of the image of Tantalus: for all of the bland notations of achieved progress that may be offered by the social scientist, there is still an *agonia* here whose gall partakes of the "extreme situation"—and this was the perspective by which Richard Wright was consistently guided in all his efforts to shape the story of the American Negro into something whose tragic sorrow might quicken the conscience of our time.

Though he had numerous minor predecessors, Mr. Wright was the first American Negro writer of large ambitions to win a major reputation in our literary life. *Uncle Tom's Children*, his first collection of stories, achieved a limited currency in the late 'thirties among readers of leftist social sympathies, but it was not until *Native Son* burst upon the scene in 1940 that he won access to the kind of forum that Sunday Supplement reviewers and a national book club could give. Within a month after its publication tens of thousands of copies were moving across book dealers' counters all over the land; it frequently was being said that nothing so comparable to the great tragic fictions of Dostoevski had yet appeared in our literature; and hordes of Mr. Wright's readers were enjoying that great thrilling shiver of delight that the intellectual middle class in this country during the 'thirties had come to find in what Eric Bentley has called "the fun-world of proletarian legend," particularly when the fun involved the tabooed exoticism of the Negro. The very simplicity and violence of the novel's didacticism did, in a way, permit many people to envisage themselves as in league with Mr. Wright and with Christ in the harrowing of a Hell full of all the forces of reaction and illiberality; and, in this way perhaps, the illusion grew that *Native Son*, by itself and quite suddenly, had very greatly enlarged and deepened our imaginative understanding of a whole dimension of American experience.

This was, however, an illusion, and when one reads today the story of Bigger Thomas, one cannot but be struck by how little the novel gives us of the bite and flavor either of social actuality or of the particular kind of human individual of whom Bigger is offered as an exemplum. To read such a book, for example, as Ralph Ellison's brilliant novel of 1953, *Invisible Man*, is to find, among one's richest satisfactions, the sense of immersion in all the concrete materialities of Negro life. One hears the very buzz and hum of Harlem in the racy, pungent speech of his West Indians and his native hipsters, and all the grotesquerie in his opening account of the dreary little backwater of a remote Southern Negro college has in it a certain kind of empirically absolute rightness. Indeed, the book is packed full of the acutest observations of the manners and idioms and human styles that constitute the ethos of Negro life in the American metropolis; and it gives us such a sense of social fact as can be come by nowhere in the stiffly pedantic manuals of academic sociology.

But, at its center, *Native Son* exhibits nothing other than a socially discarnate and demoniac wraith. In the moments before her "little death," the Negrophile Joanna Burden in *Light in August* cries out to her Negro lover Joe Christmas, "Negro, Negro," as if, in the instant of sexual transport, his human particularity were of no account; and, in the same novel, a lynch mob, Faulkner tells us, "believed aloud that it was an anonymous Negro crime committed not by a Negro but by Negro. . . ." And this is the character whom we find to be the protagonist of Richard Wright's novel of 1940—called, yes, for the sake of the novelistic convention, Bigger Thomas, but really Negro, *Negro*. Thus it is that, for all of the anger the novel directs at the moral imagination that has been poisoned by racism, its own pathos is, finally, a consequence of the degree to which it is overwhelmed by the cancer it wants to cauterize. From the moment, on its first page, when Bigger is awakened by the *Brrriiiinnng!* of his alarm clock, until his "faint, wry, bitter smile" of farewell at Mr. Max on the final page, the novel is controlled by precisely those hopeless assumptions about Negro life which elicited its rage, and its protagonist's sense of his own identity is formed by just that image of himself which, as it lives in the larger culture, has caused his despair. So, in its entirety, the novel moves wholly within the envenomed abstractions of racial myth.

In one of the stories in *Uncle Tom's Children*, "Long Black Song," the husband of a Negro woman who has been seduced by a white salesman says: "The white folks ain never gimme a chance! They ain never give no black man a chance! There ain nothing in yo whole life yuh kin keep from em! . . . Ahm gonna be hard like they is! So hep me Gawd, Ahm gonna be *hard!* When they come fer me Ahm gonna *be here!*" Not only is this the posture of all but one of his protagonists in the stories that make up his first collection, it is also the posture of the young Chicago Negro whose story Mr. Wright tells in *Native Son*. He, too, is one who intends to "be hard"; indeed, as he says, "Every time I think about it I feel like somebody's poking a red-hot iron down my throat." So it is with a sullen suspiciousness that he faces the Chicago philanthropist who takes him off the relief rolls by hiring him as a chauffeur. And it is with an even greater skepticism that he views his employer's daughter and her communist sweetheart who make gestures of fraternity toward him by inviting him to join them in a café as an equal. But this is a relation that never becomes genuinely complicated, for, at the end of their first evening together, the girl is so intoxicated that Bigger, having been entrusted with seeing her home, has to carry her bodily from the family automobile to her bedroom —into which her blind mother comes suddenly, just in the moment when he is contemplating taking Mary sexually. And, in order to prevent the mother's knowing that he and Mary are in the room, he smothers the girl and then, in his panic, stuffs her body into the furnace. This, in turn, leads eventually to his second crime, against his mistress Bessie, to whom he confesses the first deed and whom he must finally remove to prevent her betraying him to the police. But he cannot ultimately avoid his nemesis and is at last captured on a South Side tenement rooftop, as a raging mob clamors for his life in the street below.

Now the engine that Mr. Wright desperately relied upon to whip this lurid fairy tale into some semblance of probability was the courtroom defense of Bigger by his Jewish lawyer, Mr. Max. And here is what we are told, that Bigger

. . . murdered Mary Dalton accidentally, without thinking, without plan, without conscious motive. But, after he murdered, he accepted the crime. And that's the important thing. It was the first full act of his life; it was the most meaningful, exciting and stirring thing that had ever happened to him. He accepted it because it made him free, gave him the possibility of choice, of action, the opportunity to act and to feel that his actions carried weight. . . .

Let me tell you more. Before this trial the newspapers and the prosecution said that this boy had committed other crimes. It is true. He is guilty of numerous crimes. But search until the day of judgment, and you will find not one shred of evidence of them. He has murdered many times, but there are no corpses. Let me explain. This Negro boy's entire attitude toward life is a *crime!* The hate and fear which we have inspired in him, woven by our civilization into the very structure of his consciousness, into his blood and bones, into the hourly functioning of his personality, have become the justification of his existence.

Every time he comes in contact with us, he kills! It is a physiological and psychological reaction, embedded in his being. Every thought he thinks is potential murder. . . . Every desire, every dream, no matter how intimate or personal, is a plot or a conspiracy. Every hope is a plan for insurrection. Every glance of the eye is a threat. *His very existence is a crime.* . . .

And, what is more, we are told that we have only to "multiply Bigger Thomas twelve million times, allowing for environmental and temperamental variations, and for those Negroes who are completely under the influence of the church, and you have the psychology of the Negro people."

Thus it is, I say, that the novel is, paradoxically, controlled by precisely the assumptions about Negro life that elicited its rage, for the astonishing thing that it finally does is to offer a depraved and inhuman beast as the comprehensive archetypal image of the American Negro.

The imagination that we meet here, in other words, is extremist and melodramatic, feeding on the horrific themes of alienation and violence and abysmal fear, and its single occupation is with the racial tragedy. But all the great ones have had what was two hundred years ago called a "ruling passion," and it does indeed seem to be very much a part of the kind of brilliance and assertiveness that we associate with major art. That Mr. Wright should have had his ruling passion is not, therefore, something that we shall hold against him; what was unfortunate in him was his utter defenselessness before it. And here I mean that, despite his cursory tutelage under European existentialism in the late 'forties and 'fifties and despite the attention which he gave to the literature of modern psychology and social science, he never won such a point of purchase in the realm of systematic ideas as might have afforded his mind some protection against the deracinative force of the tragic encounters which it had had with the world. After reading, for example, the heartrendingly poignant story that is told in *Black Boy*, his autobiography of 1945—which is one of the great human testaments in modern American literature—it would surely take an exceedingly sluggish moral imagination for one not to perceive how inevitable it was that this man should bear to his grave the scars of the scalding humiliations that, as a Negro, he was subjected to in his youth in the state of Mississippi. Here, indeed, was a man who knew the insidious day-by-day intimidation, the fear that is in the air, and the atrocious brutality that make up the moral stench of the concentration camp; and, unlike the German Jew under Hitler, he lived this infernal life of the damned and the rejected not just for a few nightmarish years that were known to be absurdly discontinuous with the normal state of things, but he lived it as the historic inheritance of his people; this was all that he knew, from infancy until he was old enough to risk the journey of flight from Memphis to Chicago. So we accept the authenticity of the rage and the anger which were the emotions with which he impulsively faced the world. But, when some such extremity as this constitutes his basic situation, whatever the needs of the existing human being, the artist needs to be equipped with some defense against the intensity of his own experience, for, unless he has some means of supporting or controlling it, the great likelihood is that his work will then express not a coherent ordering of human experience in objective form but only the emotional tics of his own incipient hysteria. And it was just some such vantage point as this that might have enabled him to distance himself from his *agonia* and to be released to the sheer labor of composition itself—it was just this that Mr. Wright never managed. In his famous essay on "Technique as Discovery," Professor Mark Schorer has, of course, proposed that it is in the dynamism of the creative process itself, and through his wrestling with the medium of his language, that the artist comes by those major insights into the meaning of his experience that enable him to take control of it. But the logic whereby *technique* is assigned so decisive a role in the formation of *vision* is something that still escapes me. So mine, therefore, is the older axiom, that an artist needs to know a very great deal *before* he puts pen to paper; and if he does not, he may then, I take it, be expected to provide us with some variety of what the late R. P. Blackmur called "the fallacy of expressive form."

Now this was, I believe, at bottom, Mr. Wright's crucial failure: he simply did not *know* enough about the labyrinthine interiorities of the human soul. His own life-experience conditioned him, of course, to keep a lively awareness that (as W. H. Auden says) "Ubiquitous within the bond / Of one impoverishing sky, / Vast spiritual disorders lie." Yet these were not really *spiritual* disorders, since he made no allowance for human existence having anything other than a purely social-historical dimension. In the *New Year Letter* Mr. Auden suggests that

> There are two atlases: the one
> The public space where acts are done,
> In theory common to us all. . . .
> The other is the inner space
> Of private ownership, the place
> That each of us is forced to own,
> Like his own life from which it's grown,
> The landscape of his will and need. . . .

But so obsessed was Mr. Wright with the demonic aberrations that disfigure "the public space" that he lost any deep sense of what wretchedness there is within "the inner space," within what Mr. Auden calls "our parish of immediacy." T. S. Eliot once said of Ezra Pound's *Cantos* that they posit a Hell for other people, not for Mr. Pound or his readers. It might also be said of the books of Richard Wright that, though theirs is a Hell for most of Mr. Wright's readers (who are white), it is not a Hell for Mr. Wright himself and his racial kinsmen; both he and they bear upon themselves the stigmata of its fury, but both he and they are exempted from that which is generally problematic in the human soul, and from which the fury proceeds. The complex relations between the "two atlases" are not explored. And, in this way, it was possible for Mr. Wright to envisage the human community as though it were split into two opposed camps, the one black and the other white. But, in this way, it was never possible for him even to approximate the Baudelairean astringency— "*Hypocrite lecteur,—mon semblable,—mon frère!*"

And it is also this exclusive and simplistic concentration upon the one atlas, "the public space," which enabled Mr. Wright so disastrously to insist upon racial humiliation as the ultimate suffering, the ultimate indignity. And I speak of the disastrousness of it, because, however thumpingly tautologous it may be to assert that evil is evil, whatever its aspect, this is, nevertheless, the fact of the matter; and to assert that some special evil is the ultimate evil, simply because this is that by which one has oneself been most hurtfully victimized, is merely to indulge in a desperate kind of sentimentality. This was, however, the unpromising position that consistently controlled Mr. Wright's way of performing the act of self-definition as an artist, and, for all of the ardor, it is this sentimentality which makes so humanly impertinent a body of writing than which there is none in our time that ought to have greater pertinence to those like ourselves, who are drenched in the particular American experience that gave to Mr. Wright his ruling passion.

In his review of *Native Son* in March of 1940, Malcolm Cowley, having in mind the consistency with which Mr. Wright's executive design, both in the stories of *Uncle Tom's Children* and in his novel, had been a design of violence, suggested that his "sense of the indignities heaped on his race" might well go so deep as to make it his unconscious tendency in his fiction to revenge himself "by a whole series of symbolic murders." And though Mr. Cowley may at this point have been somewhat overstating things, the propensity for violence cannot, it is true, be gainsaid: Mr. Wright may not have been bent on symbolic murder, but at least it can be asserted that he was eager to sound a hue and a cry and had something of a penchant for "holding a loaded pistol at the head of the white world while he [muttered] between clenched teeth: 'Either you grant us equal rights as human beings or else this is what will happen.'" [1]

[1] Charles I. Glicksberg, "Negro Fiction in America," *The South Atlantic Quarterly*, XLV (October 1946), 482.

But, of course, the unfortunate consequence of his taking this kind of position was that, inevitably, it compelled him to practice a terrible brutalization upon his characters: he had, as in the wronged husband of "Long Black Song," to make them "hard," in order to give dramatic substance to the threat he wanted to utter; and, in thus sweeping them into the raging abysses of violent criminality, he forged an image of *la présence noire* that is in no great way removed from the wild and lickerish nigger who inhabits the demented imagination of the racial paranoiac. For all of the new sophistications that appeared in *The Outsider*, this is as true of his novel of 1953 as it is of his early work of the 'thirties.

Cross Damon is a half-educated intellectual who bears the Negro's ancestral burden of rejection and marginality, but his concern with what is socially problematic in his situation is but one phase of a deeper concern with what is metaphysically problematic in human life. He is a man whose sense of the world has been formed by that tradition of philosophic radicalism that runs from Nietzsche to contemporary existentialists like Heidegger and Sartre, and so he is particularly alert to the religious vacuum which this tradition has asserted to be at the heart of modern experience. He regards the old "myths" as a mischievous and archaistic legacy bequeathed us by the primitive ages of human history in which man,

naked and afraid, found that only one thing could really quiet his terrors: that is *Untruth*. He . . . was afraid of the clamoring world of storms, volcanoes, and heaving waves, and he wanted to change that world. His myths sought to recast that world, tame it, make it more humanly meaningful and endurable. The more abjectly frightened the nation or race of men, the more their myths and religions projected out upon the world another world in *front* of the real world, or, in another way of speaking, they projected another world *behind* the real world they saw, lived, suffered, and died in. Until today almost all of man's worlds have been either pre-worlds or backworlds, *never* the real world. . . .

But in this "real world" in which modern man must live today the nonexistence of God is not to be argued; it is simply to be taken for granted, and the theistic hypothesis is simply to be understood as "something projected compulsively from men's minds in answer to their chronic need to be rid of fear, something to meet the obscure needs of daily lives lived amidst strange and threatening facts." And this means, in Cross Damon's analysis of the modern predicament, that the dreadful burden which man must bear today is the burden of freedom, the burden, as he says, of being "nothing in particular," except what man chooses through his actions to become. This is why panic sometimes drapes the world which Cross looks out upon, for what he knows himself to confront is "the empty possibility of action," the necessity of actually making something of himself, and the knowledge that he can do what he damn well pleases on this earth, that everything is permitted, and that he must discover

good or evil through his own actions, which were more exacting than the edicts of any God because it was he alone who had to bear the brunt of their consequences with a sense of absoluteness made intolerable by knowing that this life was all he had and would ever have. For him there was no grace or mercy if he failed.

He has, in other words, undergone the most expensive denudation that a man can suffer, for to Cross Damon God is dead. And, being thus stripped of that which might alone furnish some objective warrant for the human enterprise, there is nothing else to which he owes any loyalty; he is on his own, a pure *isolé*, and he gives his suffrage to neither family nor tradition nor church nor state; nor does he give it to race. "My hero," said Mr. Wright, "could have been of any race."

When we first meet Cross he is a clerk in a Chicago post office, and his personal life, like that of Sartre's Mathieu in the initial phase of his drama, is in a state of messy disorder. As a result of an early and unsuccessful marriage, he is having to support a wife with whom he no longer lives and three children. And then there is little Dot, his mistress, whom he had supposed to be seventeen years of age but whom he discovers, after the onset of her pregnancy, to be not quite sixteen. Gladys refuses to give him a divorce so that he may marry the girl, and Dot, desperately hoping somehow to trap him into a marriage, intends to seek legal counsel. When Gladys learns of this, she begins to be fearful that Cross may be jailed and that she and the children may be robbed of his support: so she demands that he sign over the house and the car to her. She further demands that he borrow eight hundred dollars from the Postal Union on his salary, so that the titles on both the house and the car may be cleared, and she tells him that, if he refuses, she will go to the police with Dot and assist her in filing charges of rape against him. So Cross has no alternative but to accede to her requests.

But then, on that fateful night when he is returning home after having just received from the Postal Union the eight hundred dollars which he is to deliver to Gladys on the following morning, he is involved in a subway accident in which it is supposed that he has lost his life, the smashed body of another man being identified as his. This is, of course, Cross' great chance, and he is quick to seize it, for it means an opportunity to gain release from the inauthenticity of his existence, an opportunity to escape all those pledges and promises to his wife and his mother and his mistress "which he had not intended to make and whose implied obligations had been slowly smothering his spirit." By this "stroke of freakish good luck" he is able to "rip the viscous strands" of that "vast web of pledges and promises . . . and fling them behind him." Now, for the first time, this young man feels that his life is determined by a really valid project—namely, that of making something of himself and of giving some vital definition to his human identity.

So he takes a train out of Chicago for New York City, where he quickly becomes involved in a phantasmagoric drama of the Communist underworld which culminates in his committing murder three times and in the suicide of Eva Blount, the widow of one of his victims, who, after falling in love with him, cannot bear the truth, when she finally learns of the terrible deeds that he has performed. And Cross at last is destroyed by the Party's assassins.

Now, when the novel is thus summarized, it may appear to be only a rather lurid sort of potboiler; and, to be sure, there is no minimizing the harshness of its violence. Yet, for all of its melodramatic sensationalism, it is an impressive book. Indeed, it is one of the very few American novels of our time that, in admitting into itself a large body of systematic ideas, makes us think that it wants seriously to compete with the major philosophic intelligence of the contemporary period. And it may well be that the strange kind of indifference or even outright denigration that the book elicited at the time of its appearance demands to be understood in terms of the easy assumption which is habitually made in our literary life, that the difference in method and intention between poetry and philosophy ordains the impropriety of a work of fiction being complicated by the dialectical tensions of systematic thought. But this is a kind of finickiness notably unsupported by the European tradition exemplified by such books as Mann's *Doctor Faustus* and Malraux's *La Condition Humaine* and Camus' *La Peste*. And it was toward this tradition that Mr. Wright was reaching in *The Outsider*, which, though it is a very imperfect work, is yet (after *Black Boy*) his finest achievement and, as the one emphatically existentialist novel in contemporary American literature, a book that deserves to have commanded a great deal more attention than it has.

Though Mr. Wright insisted that his hero "could have been of any race" and that his primary quality was the metaphysical horror he felt before the yawning emptiness in things created by the demise of the old "myths," the fact remains, however, that Cross is a Negro. And, as such, he is dubiously privileged to have what the prosecutor Ely Houston calls "a dreadful objectivity," the kind of "double vision," that is, which belongs to one who is "both inside and outside of our culture." But, given the ardency of his commitment to atheistic premises, the actual content of this "double vision" proves to be the conviction of Ivan

Karamazov, that therefore "everything is permitted," not even murder being debarred. And so that night when he walked into the room where the Fascist nigger-hater Herndon and the Communist Blount were fighting and bludgeoned them both to death, he was "not taking sides . . . not preferring the lesser evil," for, in the world as it was apprehended by Cross, there were no sides to be taken; he no longer slept in the old myths of the Greeks and the Jews, and he knew that nothing was to be preferred to anything else. So his act was simply "a sweeping and supreme gesture of disdain and disgust with both of them!" The logic, in other words, is this, that to be a Negro is to be an outsider, not only in a sociological sense but also, and more decisively, in a moral sense as well. And the mission of the outsider, like that of Camus' Caligula, is to reveal to mankind that the human City is really a jungle and that all the disciplines and restraints of civilization are "just screens which men have used" to throw a kind of "veneer of order" over the disorder that still seethes beneath the surface. But since, as it appears, this is a mission that cannot be accomplished apart from terrorism, Mr. Wright's conclusion of 1953 entailed essentially the same mischievousness that had been implicit thirteen years earlier in Native Son, the notion that the natural life-movement of the Negro who bears the full burden of his situation is toward a great blasting moment of supreme destruction. Bigger Thomas is an inarticulate proletarian who enacts his role unthinkingly, whereas Cross Damon, having read his Nietzschean primers, accepts his mission with deliberation and in the spirit of a kind of inverted messianism —but this is the only significant difference between them, for both aim, as it were, at getting outside of history altogether, through an act of consummate violence. Like Conrad's Kurtz, Cross does, to be sure, behold at last "the horror," as he gaspingly admits to Houston a moment before his death; but he has, nevertheless, tasted the terrible joy of his murderous orgasm: he has burst the belt and been "hard" and won through at least to the unhistorical realm of the dream—which is of revenge.

Mr. Wright was always too impatient with what Henry James called the "proving disciplines" of art to win the kind of genuine distinction as a writer for which his talents qualified him. And, like George Orwell, for him the greatest uses of art were not those by which we distance ourselves from the world in order to contemplate more strenuously its pattern and meaning. They were, rather, those by which we seek a more direct entry into the world for the sake of redeeming it from the brutality and the indecencies by which it must otherwise be overwhelmed. So it is rather a sad irony that his own art did in point of fact so often drift toward a definition of man, and particularly of the American Negro, that deeply undercut his conscious intention to make it serve a genuinely humane vision. As James Baldwin has said, the real tragedy of Bigger Thomas "is not that he is cold or black or hungry, not even that he is American, black, but that he has accepted a theology that denies him life, that he admits the possibility of his being subhuman and feels constrained, therefore, to battle for his humanity according to those brutal criteria bequeathed him at his birth." [2] And this is precisely what it is that renders so ambiguous many of the other chief protagonists in Mr. Wright's fiction.

His last years, unhappily, were not, it seems, a period of rich fulfillment and harvest. Mr. Baldwin has reported [3] on some of the asperities that increasingly isolated him from friends and acquaintances and young American Negro and African intellectuals who were living in Paris. And I suspect that his crotchetiness was not unconnected with the fortunes of his reputation in the literary life. Though *The Outsider* won a respectful reception in some quarters, it by no means achieved any large *succès d'estime* in the critical forum; and the novel of 1958, *The Long Dream*, met little more than polite indifference. So it was the publication in 1945 of *Black Boy* which had brought him to the zenith of his success. Thereafter his fiction and his political criticism, though no different in tone and emphasis from his earlier work, seemed to be nettling in their effect, and the reputation of the early 'forties has today become merely a minor datum of that earlier time. This is of course in part, I suspect, but a particular case of the more general demise of the naturalism of the American nineteen-thirties. At the beginning of the decade Edmund Wilson had suggested in *Axel's Castle* that this was an idiom which could survive only by consenting to be complicated by disciplines of intelligence and imagination that he somewhat clumsily denominated as "Symbolism," but this was a challenge that did not begin to be responded to until the early 'fifties, by the generation of Ralph Ellison and Saul Bellow and William Styron. And, however robust our respect may still be for the Dos Passos of the *U.S.A.* trilogy or the Steinbeck of *The Grapes of Wrath* or the Wright of *Native Son*, we find them today to be writers with whom it is virtually impossible any longer to have a genuinely reciprocal relation, for the simple fact is that the rhetoric of what once used to be called "reportage" proves itself, with the passage of time, to be a language lacking in the kind of amplitude and resonance that *lasts*. This may not be the precise judgment which the cunning of history, in its ultimate justice, will sustain, but it is, at any rate, *ours*.

It may, of course, be that this is a kind of verdict on our fiction of twenty-five or thirty years ago that has sometimes been applied with too

[2] *Notes of a Native Son* (Boston: The Beacon Press, 1955), p. 23.

[3] *Nobody Knows My Name* (New York: The Dial Press, 1961), pp. 200–215.

alacritous a facility by the high priests of our present dispensation, and I am prepared even now to confess to the irritation that I recently felt when I came again upon the patrician hauteur of a sentence of the late R. P. Blackmur's in which it is asserted that "*Native Son* is one of those books in which everything is undertaken with seriousness except the writing." But whatever may in turn be history's ultimate verdict on our present way of dealing with the American naturalism of the recent past, there is, quite apart from the line that in this respect we want now to take, a more specific and more cogent reason for the revision that we may want to practice on the accolades of the early 'forties for Mr. Wright's work (the enthusiastic equations of the author of *Native Son* with Dostoevski, etc.), and it is a reason which is clarified by the collection of stories entitled *Eight Men* that appeared a few weeks after his death.

At least three of the stories of which this book is composed were written before 1945, but, since the collection was supervised by the author himself, we are justified in assuming that they do all reflect his final sense of life—and what is most remarkable about the book is the summation that it provides of the consistencies which, throughout his career, formed Richard Wright's personal signature. In each of the eight stories which make up this volume the central figure is a black *isolé* whose crucifixion by a hostile world is offered as type and example of a collective suffering and a collective fate. And all these various statements are marked by an immoderate and melodramatic imagination of the world as "split in two, a white world and a black one, the white one being separated from the black by a million psychological miles." The last of the eight pieces, "The Man Who Went to Chicago"—which is, I take it, autobiographical— ingeniously interweaves narrative and essay, and at one point, in recounting his experience in the early 'thirties "as an orderly to a medical research institute in one of the largest and wealthiest hospitals in Chicago," Mr. Wright says:

Each Saturday morning I assisted a young Jewish doctor in slitting the vocal cords of a fresh batch of dogs from the city pound. The object was to devocalize the dogs so that their howls would not disturb the patients in the other parts of the hospital. I held each dog as the doctor injected Nembutal into its veins to make it unconscious; then I held the dog's jaws open as the doctor inserted the scalpel and severed the vocal cords. Later, when the dogs came to, they would lift their heads to the ceiling and gape in a soundless wail. The sight became lodged in my imagination as a symbol of silent suffering.

And though the image comes toward the close of this collection, once it is encountered it seems then to resonate backward across the entire book, indeed across the entire *œuvre*, and we feel that the human presence at the center of Mr. Wright's dramatic world has itself somehow been converted into a howling dog whose wails are soundless. In one instance, the long story called "The Man Who Lived Underground," this is an extremism which makes for a wonderfully scarifying and improbable piece of Gothicism which is absolutely self-contained and brilliant. And the piece called "Man of All Work" is a beautifully constructed account of a man who, not being able to find any employment, disguises himself as a woman and, in his wife's clothes, hires himself out as a domestic, being certain that, since Negroes are never really looked at anyway, he'll be able to carry the stunt off—a situation which enables Mr. Wright, with a remarkable deftness and irony, to probe the kind of demasculinization of the male and the kind of resulting rupture of the primitive bonds of the family which have often occurred in Negro life; nor does he also fail, with a savage funniness, to suggest what is outrageous in the sexual panic of American whites. But in every other case, as we move throught the stories in *Eight Men*, though we are kept going from page to page and though the writing has the minor virtues of a professionally skillful naturalism, we are dealing with a body of work which totters and collapses under the pressure of a radical imagination unequipped with any defense against its own radicalism; and nowhere else is there a fully achieved work of art.

But, when we have done, it may be that we ought to remember that there are in human experience issues weightier and more exacting than the issues of aesthetics and literary criticism. And it may also be that, in whatever kingdom of the spirit Richard Wright now dwells, as he broods over this uncongenial world of earth, he finds it sufficient merely to say, "I am the man, I suffer'd, I was there." Of this I am reminded, as I glance now at the Dedication of *The Outsider*—"For Rachel, my daughter who was born on alien soil."

THE ORDEAL OF RICHARD WRIGHT[*]

Nick Aaron Ford

IN THEIR BOOK *The Theory of Literature,* Wellek and Warren say that a work of art may embody the *dream* of an author rather than his actual life, or it may be the mask, the antiself, behind which his real self is hiding, or it may be a picture of the life from which the author wants to escape. In the writings of Richard Wright there are glimpses at different times of all three of these purposes. But his dreams are often nightmares, and his masks are designed to reveal more than they hide. Perhaps to a greater extent than any other contemporary American novelist, Wright's authorship is a creature of environment and tortured memories.

Born on a plantation near Natchez, Mississippi, his early life consisted of a series of moves from one unsatisfactory place to another, of gnawing hunger, of parental neglect and misunderstanding, and of incredible humiliation inflicted by white employers. The earliest experience he remembers is one of horror and fear. At the age of four he set fire to his parents' home and barely escaped being burned to death under it. For that act, despite his tender years, his mother beat him into unconsciousness. The effect is summarized in *Black Boy,* his autobiography, in the following manner: "I was beaten out of my senses and later I found myself in bed screaming, determined to run away, tussling with my mother and father who were trying to keep me still. . . . But for a long time I was chastened whenever I remembered that my mother had come close to killing me."

At six he was a drunkard, spending his waking hours begging drinks from patrons of a nearby tavern, while his mother worked in domestic service to support him and his younger brother. At twelve he fought bitterly with his aunt, threatening to cut her throat with a butcher knife which he angrily clutched in his fist. At sixteen he burglarized a neighbor's house and a college storeroom and sold the stolen goods.

Then came the turning point. He stumbled upon A *Book of Prefaces* by H. L. Mencken. Of this experience he says:

[*] Reprinted from *College English,* XV (1953), 87–94, by permission of the author and editors.

26

That night in my rented room, while letting the hot water run over my can of pork and beans in the sink, I opened *A Book of Prefaces* and began to read. I was jarred and shocked by the style, the clear, clean, sweeping sentences. . . . This man was fighting, fighting with words. He was using words as a weapon, using them as one would use a club. Could words be weapons? Well, yes, for there they were. Then, maybe, perhaps, I could use them as weapons?

The next year Richard left the South for Chicago and a new life. The past was dead; only its roots would persist as a memory of the days that had gone. But the memory was bitter. And out of it has flowed the bitter experiences of *Uncle Tom's Children*, of *Native Son*, of *Black Boy*, and of *The Outsider*.

Wright first gained national attention in 1938, when he won the $500 prize, awarded by *Story Magazine*, for his book of short stories entitled *Uncle Tom's Children*. The following year Edward O'Brien, the distinguished anthologist, selected Wright's "Bright and Morning Star" as one of the two best short stories published in 1939 and one of the fifty best stories published in America since 1915.

Although our chief concern is with his novels, *Native Son* (1940) and *The Outsider* (1953), a bare statement of the plots of his prize-winning stories will assist in creating additional background for a better understanding of the major works.

Each of the four stories in *Uncle Tom's Children* portrays the Negro in violent revolt against some phase of his environment. In "Big Boy Leaves Home" the revolt against white suppression and brutality ends in the murder of a white man by two Negro boys, whose companion had been killed without provocation by the white man. In "Down by the Riverside" a long-suffering Negro revolts against conditions that deny his wife an equal chance at medical care and hospitalization; he is lynched after killing a white man who symbolizes that repression. In "Long Black Song" the Negro husband revolts against the idea of a white man's using his wife for sexual purposes and returning the next morning to collect money for a phonograph which he had persuaded the victim to accept. The husband slays the seducer and waits with loaded gun for the lynching mob he knows will come. In "Fire and Cloud" the revolt is against crooked white politicians who try to frighten Negroes into political inactivity by mob violence against their leaders. In these stories Wright is perfecting a technique which reaches its fullest development in *Native Son*.

The main character in *Native Son* is Bigger Thomas, a twenty-year-old Chicago Negro who accidentally kills his wealthy employer's daughter. After he discovers the victim's death, fear drives him to burn her body in the furnace and later kill his frightened Negro girl friend who he thinks might, under police torture, betray his secret.

The murder of the white girl is purely accidental, accomplished by the pressure of a pillow over her mouth to keep her from telling her blind mother that he, the chauffeur, had brought her upstairs in his arms when he discovered she was too intoxicated to walk up under her own power. Although Bigger felt responsible for returning his employer's daughter safely to her room, he was afraid his employers might dismiss him if they should know that he, a Negro, had found it necessary to fulfill this responsibility by carrying the incapacitated girl in his arms.

One of the ironic facts of the story is that although the murder was an accident, it need not have been. For Bigger hated all white folks. He hated them enough to murder without provocation. He felt that he had been cheated out of everything good in life that he had wanted and that white people—all white people—were responsible for his unhappy predicament.

The action of the story is sensational, containing such a ghastly spectacle as the furnace scene, in which Bigger, who has thrust the dead girl's body into the red-hot furnace feet-foremost, discovers that the dangling head cannot be forced in. He takes the long, razor-sharp knife from his pocket and attempts to cut off the head, but the bones are too hard for his small instrument. Then he glances around the room until he sees a hatchet, which he uses to finish the job.

In one of the most pathetic scenes imaginable, the fleeing murderer, completely crazed by the fear of being captured, takes up a brick and beats out the brains of his innocent, trusting sleeping girl friend who has obediently agreed to stay with him until the end.

But the power of this book does not reside in the action or in the portrayal of character. It resides rather in the ethical and sociological implications of the action. The truth of this observation was recently impressed upon me when I saw the motion-picture version of the story, adapted for the screen by Wright himself and produced in Argentina. Without the doctrinal overtones of the novel, it turns out to be just another murder mystery of the kind that bombards the air waves every night from seven to eleven.

Wright's major purpose in this novel was to show that social and economic barriers against race lead to grave injustices toward racial minorities and that those injustices so distort character and personality growth that criminal monstrosities, such as Bigger, are produced. Wright attempted to support his theory by means of testimony presented in the murder trial of Bigger, which takes up approximately one-third of the novel. It is revealed that Mr. Dalton, father of the girl that Bigger killed, has donated large sums of money to Negro charity and that he owns the South Side Real Estate Company in Chicago from which Bigger's family rents the one-room, rat-infested apartment in which the mother, daughter, and two sons live. When the defense attorney asks Mr. Dalton why he does not charge Negro tenants less rent for such uninhabitable accommodations, the philanthropist replies that it would be unethical to undersell his competitors. When he is asked why rent for Negroes is higher than that for whites, he replies that a housing shortage exists in the Negro community. Although he admits that he owns houses in other sections of the city where no shortage exists, he says he will not rent them to Negroes because he thinks Negroes are happier living together in one section. He further admits that, of all the Negroes his philanthropy has helped to educate, he has never employed one in the operation of his vast business enterprises.

The attorney for the defense therefore charges Mr. Dalton with the murder of his own daughter, for it was he who helped to prepare the soil in which a Bigger Thomas could grow. It was he who closed his eyes to the deeper longings of Negroes for justice and equality, attempting to salve his conscience by giving huge sums to racial charities. It was he who had shielded his daughter from all Negro contact, thus leaving her at the crucial moment incapable of wisely dealing with a rebel such as Bigger. If he had provided clean and decent apartments for Negroes as he had for whites; if he had established playgrounds for Negro children as he had for whites; if he had used his influence to open employment opportunities equally to Negroes and whites, a monster like Bigger might not have arisen to take his daughter's life.

It is plain to see that, insofar as this doctrine is philosophy at all, it is a philosophy of social and environmental responsibility. Bigger became what he was, not because he was free to choose his course of action, but because circumstances over which he had no control had driven him to his doom. This is the philosophy of Karl Marx, of whom Wright at that time was a devoted disciple.

According to his own admission in *The God That Failed*, Wright was a member of the American Communist Party from 1934 to 1944. When he wrote *Native Son* he believed that there was "no agency in the world so capable of making men feel the earth and the people on it as the Communist Party."

It is always hazardous to attempt to guess at the motivation for human action. One cannot know with certainty why Wright became a willing dupe for the Communists. His minority status and long history of unemployment, segregation, and physical deprivations undoubtedly contributed to his decision. But, above all, Wright believed then, as now, that the greatest tragedy of mankind lies in the inability of the individual to find satisfactory fellowship in the group. This theme is apparent in *Native Son*, takes on added significance in *Black Boy*, and becomes the underlying assumption of *The Outsider*. It is a theme, however, which Wright was not the first to discover or explore. Hawthorne was gravely concerned with it more than a century ago, and in our own day James Joyce and Thomas Wolfe gave it life. Joyce epitomized it in *Ulysses* when he presented the perplexities and sorrows of Dedalus in search of his father (the symbol of a kindred spirit rather than a blood relationship). Wolfe made it the burden of all his books. In *Of Time and the River* he exclaimed: "We are so lost, so naked and so lonely in America . . . for America has a thousand lights and weathers and we walk the streets, we walk the streets forever, we walk the streets of life alone."

But Hawthorne and Joyce and Wolfe were not Negroes. They knew that this eternal loneliness of the individual is universal, not racial. They knew it could not be remedied by political party or social organization. But perhaps Wright thought the identification of the comrade with the Communist cell, which recognizes no racial distinctions, could be the solution to the problem. Ten years were required to convince him that he was mistaken. And the mental agony which accompanied his awakening was almost unbearable.

Thirteen years after *Native Son*, Wright's second novel, *The Outsider*, was issued by his original publishers. It is more violent than *Native Son*, but it is also more imaginative, more challenging, and more philosophical. Cross Damon, the protagonist, kills four men and drives the woman he loves to commit suicide. But Cross is not motivated by physical fear as was Bigger. He is caught in the crosscurrents of an ideological warfare going on within himself. Except in the first case, he commits his murders to avenge an injured sense of justice, which, he believes, except for his intervention, would continue unchecked and unpunished.

In this novel Wright repudiates with vehemence many of the ideological and philosophical tenets he had espoused in *Native Son*. No longer does he believe that environment and the social milieu create the man. To him now, man is the product of his own free choice, and his destiny cannot be charged to any force or forces outside himself. He illustrates this theory by permitting Cross to become suddenly freed of all previous commitments which may have been entered into by some type of compulsion or by pure chance. He accomplishes this by allowing his hero to emerge from a subway wreck incognito. The newspapers announce that Cross Damon is dead, his body so mutilated in the wreck that it could be identified only by the coat he had been wearing. Cross accepts his freedom and makes plans to leave Chicago for New York and a new life.

From the moment Cross decides to accept the news of his "death" as a reality, he begins deliberately to choose every act which he performs thereafter. His first significant act is the murder of a friend who recognizes him in Chicago. There is no outside compulsion that drives him to this murder. It is purely an act of freedom, performed in the interest of continued freedom. The other three murders are also the result of passionless deliberation, an exercise of the godlike freedom to which man is continually aspiring.

In 1946 Wright moved to Paris, where he has been living with his family ever since. Among his new-found friends is Jean-Paul Sartre, chief promulgator of the philosophy of existentialism. A warm friendship has developed between the two men, and it appears that Wright has been converted to his friend's philosophy. The American admits that he has found it urgently necessary "to search for a new attitude to replace the set of Marxist assumptions which had in the past more or less guided the direction of my writings." Although he asserts that *The Outsider* is the first literary effort of mine projected out of a heart preoccupied with no ideological burden save that of rendering an account of reality as it strikes my sensibilities and imagination, the critical reader cannot escape the conclusion that this book is not only strongly anti-Communist but also markedly existentialist.

Let us examine the first charge. In *Native Son* Jan and Mac, the Communist leaders, were presented as unselfish men who were willing to sacrifice themselves to the cause of racial justice and equality at a time when racial tolerance was much more unpopular than it is today. But in this book he has presented Blount, Hilton, and Blimen as jealous, hypocritical, perverted, unscrupulous, power-crazed puppets dancing to the satanic music of an all-consuming party. He describes the party leaders as follows:

Their aims? Direct and naked power! They know as few others that there is no valid, functioning religion to take the place of the values and creeds of yesterday; and they know that political power, if it is to perform in the minds and emotions of men the role that the idea of God once performed, must be total and absolute.

. . . They will commit any crime, but never in passion. . . . And whatever natural terrors of life there are in the hearts of man, whatever stupid prejudices they harbor in their damp souls, they know how to rouse and sustain those terrors and prejudices and mobilize them for *their* ends.

But in his relentless delineation of the brutality, stupidity, and revolting inhumanity of Communist methods, Wright does not forget to warn his readers that the opponents of these methods are in grave danger of succumbing to the very evils they are attempting to destroy. It seems to be a law of life, Cross discovers, that to fight an enemy means fighting him on his own ground, and that in itself is a defeat. Perhaps he was staring right now at the focal point of history: "If you fought men who tried to conquer you in terms of total power you too had to use total power and in the end you became what you tried to defeat."

Although communism and existentialism have one thing in common— the denial of the existence of God—they are deadly enemies on many other counts. What, then, are the basic principles of existentialism in this novel? I shall limit myself to the discussion of three.

First, the assumption that there is no God is necessary to the development of modern man, who must be self-reliant and self-sufficient and, above all, free.

Sartre explains in his brief treatise on existentialism [1] that if God did exist, man could never be free. He would be forever hemmed in by a priori values already determined before his creation. He could always find excuses for his actions and seek to escape the consequences of them. But if God does not exist, there is no explaining things away by reference to fixed a priori values. Such a position condemns man to complete freedom. Once he enters the world, he *alone* is entirely responsible for everything he does.

When the dying Cross, who had killed four men during the few weeks of his new life and had in turn been shot by his Communist enemies, is asked by the district attorney why he had chosen to live as he had, he replies: "I wanted to be free . . . to feel what I was worth . . . what living meant to me."

On an earlier occasion when Cross is discussing with his Communist acquaintances the backgrounds of modern thought, he says:

All of this brings us to one central, decisive fact: the consequences of the atheistic position of modern man, for most men today are atheists, even though they don't know it or won't admit it.

. . . Now what does this mean—that I don't believe in God? It means that I, and you too, can do what we damn well please on this earth. Many men have been doing just that, of course, for a long time, but they didn't have the courage to admit it.[2]

Second, there is no reality beyond subjectivity. Man can be no more nor less than what he conceives himself to be.

Sartre says: "Subjectivism means, on the one hand, that an individual chooses and makes himself; and on the other, that it is impossible for man to transcend human subjectivity. The second of these is the essential meaning of existentialism."

Wright makes Cross reach the following conclusion as he reasons with himself concerning his predicament: "Every man interprets the world in the light of his habits and desires."

In a more extended discussion with the district attorney, Cross, who speaks for Wright, declares:

[1] *Existentialism* (New York: Philosophical Library, 1947).

[2] "Dostoievsky said, 'If God didn't exist everything would be possible.' That is the very starting point of existentialism. Indeed everything is permissible if God does not exist" (Sartre, *op. cit.*, p. 27).

God, the millions of prisons in this world! Men simply copied the realities of their hearts when they built prisons. They simply extended into objective reality what was already a subjective reality. Only jailers really believe in jails. Only men full of criminal feelings can create a criminal code.

Third, there is no human nature. Each age develops according to dialectical laws, and what men are depends upon the age and not on a human nature.

The existentialists argue that human nature could be the product only of a godlike Creator, who would conceive and create man according to a common specification. Since they deny God, they deny the possibility of the individual man being the product of a general concept in the mind of a Creator. Hence there can be no such thing as human nature.[3]

Wright puts in the mouth of his protagonist the following speech:

We twentieth century Westerners have outlived the faith of our fathers; our minds have grown so skeptical that we cannot accept the old scheme of moral precepts which once guided man's life. In our modern industrial society we try to steer our hearts by improvised, pragmatic rules which are, in the end, no rules at all. If there are people who tell you they live by traditional values and precepts—as the English sometimes pretend—then they are either lying to you or to themselves.

To move from a Marxist position, such as *Native Son* represents, to the nearly opposite philosophy of existentialism in less than eight years is a difficult feat, even for the agile-minded Richard Wright. Consequently, one should not be surprised to find here and there in *The Outsider* undigested and contradictory bits of the new philosophy. For instance, how can an existentialist reconcile the following quotation from *The Outsider* with the atheistic doctrine of his philosophy: "Man is a promise that he must never break"? A *promise to whom?*

In his treatment of race relations Wright has also moved away from the methods of *Native Son*. Although the main character in *The Outsider* is a Negro, the novel cannot be classified as racial literature. It is primarily the presentation of the experiences of a man (race is incidental) who seeks to repudiate his common humanity, a man who, as Wright phrases it, has "wantonly violated every commitment that civilized men owe, in terms of common honesty and sacred honor, to those with whom they live."

Despite the nonracial design, however, Wright does not hesitate to condemn attitudes of racial intolerance and prejudice wherever they appear. But unlike the deadly seriousness of *Native Son*, these attacks are made by light irony and ridicule. For instance, Cross, who is somewhat

[3] Sartre, *op. cit.*, pp. 16–18.

scholarly, having spent two years studying philosophy at the University of Chicago, sets out to obtain a false birth certificate by pretending to be the kind of Negro stereotype that the white clerks appreciate. When his turn comes to present his case, he says to the clerk in a plaintive querulous tone:

"He told me to come up here and get the paper."
The clerk blinked and looked annoyed. "What?"
"The paper, Mister. My boss told me to come and get it."
"What kind of paper are you talking about, boy?"
"The one that say I was born. . . ."
The clerk smiled, then laughed: "Maybe you weren't born, boy. Are you *sure* you were?"
Cross batted his eyes stupidly. He saw that he was making the poorly paid clerk happy; his pretense of dumbness made the clerk feel superior, white.
"Well, they *say* I was born. If I wasn't born I can't keep my job. That's why my boss told me to come here and get the paper."
Two hours later Cross had the duplicate birth certificate . . . and had left in the minds of the clerks a picture of a Negro whom the nation loved and of whom the clerks would speak in the future with contemptuous affection. Maybe someday I could rule the nation with means like this, Cross mused as he rode back to New York.

In the main, Wright appears to have concluded that the problems of racial justice and brotherhood are a part of the larger problems of human relations and that the most successful methods of attack are those directed on the wider front.

Although Wright's philosophical and racial horizons have expanded considerably since *Native Son*, his literary craftsmanship has shown no noticeable improvement. In fact, *The Outsider* is inferior to its predecessor in plot construction, organization, and emotional depth.

In *Native Son* coincidence plays no part in plot construction. Whatever happens is the result of causal relationships generated by the natural consequences of place, time, and environment. But in *The Outsider* the crucial incident (the subway wreck) which enables the protagonist to achieve a new identity is attended by a farfetched coincidence which alone is responsible for the possibility of all later developments.

It just happened that one other Negro who resembled Cross "in color and build" was in the subway car and that this Negro, who was sitting across the aisle, was thrown against him by the force of the collision in such a manner that he (Cross) had to beat the lifeless head into an unrecognizable pulp in order to free himself from the wreckage. It was a coincidence, too, that Cross unconsciously left his overcoat so entangled with the lifeless body of the Negro victim that it became the mark of identification that proved to the world that

Cross was "dead." Later in New York it just happened that Cross was near by when a typical Fascist and a typical Communist (both of whom Cross hated) became engaged in a violent physical battle and that, because of the peculiar situation, Cross was able to slip into the "locked" room unnoticed and administer death blows to each without himself being immediately suspected.

The motivation in *Native Son* is natural and compelling. Bigger's first act of murder is accidental, and the second is the result of overpowering fear. But the motivation for the four murders committed by Cross is neither natural nor compelling. It lies outside the normal pattern of human psychology.

There are some long speeches in *Native Son*, speeches delivered by the attorneys at Bigger's trial. The courtroom is a natural setting in which long-winded, one-sided oratory is customary. The eloquence is appropriate, for a verdict of life or death hangs upon the delicately balanced arguments. But in *The Outsider* the long, learned discussions on the origin, development, and functions of religions, governments, political parties, and economic systems carried on by Cross and District Attorney Houston and by Cross and his Communist antagonists have no natural setting. They seem forced and stagy. They appear to be part of an obvious scheme to drag in irrelevant lectures on special doctrines, whose outcome can have no possible effect on the lives of any of the characters.

The other stylistic qualities which have made all of Wright's books worthy literary experiences have suffered no diminution. The vivid diction, the effective sentence structure, and the pleasing rhythms are still predominant. His emotional control is more apparent than it was in the earlier novel. He declared after the publication of *Uncle Tom's Children* that he was through with sentimentality. He has kept that promise. There is an emotional toughness in *The Outsider* which exceeds the hardness of *Native Son*. One may curse and fume over the harrowing experiences of this book, but never weep.

In conclusion, it is only fair to emphasize that Wright has come a long way in the art of philosophic thought since *Native Son*. It may be that another thirteen years between novels will reduce the groping tension that now beclouds the mind of this talented writer. It may be that his next novel will be a fulfillment of the promise of *Uncle Tom's Children*, of *Native Son*, and of *Black Boy*.

short story: the one affording the thrill of action without genuine insight into character; the other insight into character which aimlessly evaporates. To the literary historian, Wright's importance is that, by bringing both traditions together, he has moulded a type of story superior to either. When detail becomes significant by being significantly associated, the story not only gains direction and climax, but the flimsiness of a melodramatic climax is transformed into the unforgettable power of tragedy.

From the historical perspective, this, I think, is what Wright has accomplished. But I do not mean to imply that he has worked either directly or consciously with either of these traditions. Unimpeded by the requirements of a formal education, his bent for writing appears to have led him directly to authors of current reputation and the writers of the past who influenced them. He has assimilated from them what his developing talent needed, and taking place as it did without external compulsion, the assimilation has sometimes been so complete as to be fairly unrecognizable. I am told that the most powerful influence upon him has been Hemingway, whose pugnacious, independent temper seems to have appealed to him. From Hemingway doubtless came his objective attitude, his direct, unflinching vision, and the short, firm sentences, with their frequent change of grammatical subject, as the appropriate vehicle of expression. Wright's sentences are stript bare of all but the necessary adjectives and connectives. Each is a vigorous self-sufficient unit, which expels its pent-up meaning and willingly gives way to the next in line. But they all retire before the tense authority of dialogue. The dialogue itself is candid, the sort the character would have used in life, or the sort that aims to give such an effect.

He saw the mob close in around the fire. Their faces were hard and sharp in the light of the flames. More men and women were coming over the hill. The long dark spot was smudged out.

"Everybody git back!"

"Look! Hes gotta finger!" [1]

If this passage does not remind one of Hemingway, it is because his style has been assimilated into a quite different personality, and used to such different ends that the relationship is disguised. This is partly owing to the fact that Wright is dealing with Negro dialogue, but mostly because his insights are richer and deeper than Hemingway's. For you will never find the passages of sentimental or sadistic writing in Wright that you will in Hemingway's work. If Wright has emotional conflicts in his short stories, they are dissipated by the act of composition. But Hemingway's emotional blocks are at the basis of his style, which does not resolve them but ex-

[1] Richard Wright, *Native Son* (New York, 1940), by courtesy of Harper and Brothers.

presses them, transformed in various ways, as irony, or sentiment, or brutality, or the inconclusive ending; but always controlled by understatement.

> The world was not wheeling any more. It was just very clear and bright, and inclined to blur at the edges. I washed, brushed my hair. I looked strange to myself in the glass, and went downstairs to the dining-room.
> "Here he is!" said Bill. "Good old Jake! I knew you wouldn't pass out."
> "Hello, you old drunk," Mike said.
> "I got hungry and woke up."
> "Eat some soup," Bill said.
> The three of us sat at the table, and it seemed as though about six people were missing.[2]

Despite the appearance of directness of statement here, the actual emotional meanings are all transformed and controlled, even negated by the conscious surface of the personality. Both writers begin with objective description of the surface. Hemingway gives us only so much of the depth as the surface reveals, which, with his type of character, is very little. But neither does Wright desire nor are his characters sophisticated enough, to conceal from themselves and others what lies deeper within. So the two styles, technically so similar, are used to opposite ends—in Hemingway to distract attention from the confusions beneath, and in Wright to reveal a process that is going on to eradicate what confusion may exist, and therefore to promote a definite resolution of the action at the end of the story.

But Hemingway also did Wright the service of leading him to other authors. Passages, for instance, under the influence of Gertrude Stein are occasionally conspicuous in both writers. They are usually passages, like this from Wright, of interior monologue.

> Never in all her life had she been so much alone as she was now. Days were never so long as these days; and nights were never so empty as these nights.

From such open expression of melancholy Hemingway draws back into his habitual mood of cynical reserve. But Wright proceeds from them further into poetic prose which utilizes contemporary metrical cadences to convey pleasurable emotions, even though they be of hopes as yet unfulfilled. Not from Hemingway but from the Donne-Hopkins tradition came a later wish of this same girl for "white bright days and dark black nights" (to which a rare new element has been added since "dark black" in this context cannot be taken as a sinister but only as a pleasurably mysterious phrase). More

[2] Ernest Hemingway, *The Sun Also Rises* (New York, 1926), by courtesy of Charles Scribner's Sons.

generally, such passages are closer to the fiction of Lawrence and Anderson.

> Again she felt his fingers on the tips of her breasts. She backed away, saying nothing this time. She thrust the gourd out from her. Warm fingers met her cold hands. He had the gourd. She heard him drink; it was the faint, soft music of water going down a dry throat, the music of water in a silent night. She sighed and drank again.

Here the mood and the meaning are close to Sherwood Anderson. But there is wanting the slightly neurotic tempo of his cadences and his interrogative appeals to the reader. The description of drinking offers the enrichment of insight into aspects of the immediate sensation not indispensable to the plot. In Anderson, such sentences are typical, and their overtones accumulate into a general state of narcissistic revery. But in Wright these impressions, though immediately peripheral to the external action, furnish insight into the character that has them, and so, in the long run, they feed into the course of events, to increase the dramatic power and plausibility of the emerging plot. But the most important stylistic influence hardly needs to be mentioned. For idiom, and cadence, and emotional attitude, Wright was fortunate in being able to use the tradition of Negro folk poetry after it had been given polish and flexibility by two generations of sophisticated Negro poets and prose writers. He could thus combine, without embarrassment of fumbling, white and black traditions of craftsmanship of equal maturity.

His employment of these materials, however, to the attainment of a significant plot must be ascribed to nonliterary factors. Fundamental, without question, was the nature of his childhood experiences, which he has described in several autobiographical works. The hardship and cruelty of his childhood set up reactions in him which must be ascribed to the prevalence of a vague awareness of Negro rights in the environment and which led to the personal search for more adequate understanding. He picked his nonliterary studies as unacademically as we have seen him choosing his literary. Here again, he had the good fortune never to have had a formal education with its clutter of useful and useless facts, of tenable and fantastic theories. The sociology he chose substantiated his experiential view that our reactions are conditioned by our environments. His study of psychology, especially as illustrated in the psychological novel, gave him a competence in understanding how complex these reactions to environment actually are. His study of Marxist philosophy, in particular, enabled him to understand that these reactions, however complex, are only variants of class attitudes that are fundamentally the same. By its emphasis upon class conflict it gave him the power to sense the existence of plots in life, just as his psychology had enabled him to develop them with lifelike and probable detail.

The theme, then, was at hand for Wright, as it had not been for either Poe or Katherine Mansfield, and Wright was more fortunate than Hemingway in being so circumstanced that he could pick it up without equivocation and efficiently transform it into art without distortion from any personal limitations. I do not wish to derogate the value of the work of these other writers. But it is all the same true that Poe was so circumstanced that he had only the sensational themes of decadence to build into a short story since his personal neurosis led him to the decaying feudal life of the old South. Similarly, Katherine Mansfield's precise but timid vision was too delicate to penetrate beyond the wisps of sentiment floating over the crumbling fabric of the Victorian heritage. Hemingway, on the other hand, tries to conceal from himself by a pugnacious front his identification with the social distemper he despises in the world of the prosperous around him.

Wright's theme, by contrast, is embedded in the structure of our present society, both north and south, and race riots and lynchings have exposed it uncompromisingly to both Negroes and whites. The conditions of his own life afforded him the capacity to sense its significance more sharply than any white man and many Negroes could. His gift for writing was encouraged by his awareness of this material craving representation. And he came at a time when the illiterate folk literature of the Negroes had already been taken over by educated Negro poets and become the dominant tradition of modern Negro literature. Under these circumstances Wright's application to it of the mechanisms of fiction, as established among white writers, was no longer a possible miscegenation, but deepened his penetration of his theme and enabled him to transfer it into the awareness of his readers.

The illuminating contrast here, where the short stories are concerned, is not with Hemingway who becomes the more resentful the further he gets from his normal association with sophisticated people. It is rather with an author like the Irishman Synge who, when he sympathizes with the tragedy in the life of the poor, turns it not into cynicism but pathos. Once more I cite for the purpose of definition rather than derogation. But, fine as *Riders to the Sea* is as a sad drama of Irish folk life, its sense of gathering doom reminds one more of Maeterlinck than of Wright. The difference that, in the one case, the doom is understood to be imposed by the forces of nature and in the other by men is not a consequence of a difference in intention of sympathy but of insight into the reality of the situation, which was imposed by a difference in the experiential relation to it of the two authors themselves. Synge was a middle-class writer who felt a genuine middle-class sympathy for the poor Irish fisherpeople. He tried to write like one of them, indeed, so genuinely that he lived among them.

Though he had assimilated their dialect, he was unable to assimilate the nuance of psychological meanings this dialect was capable of conveying. Furthermore, unlike Wright's Negroes, these back-country Irish were too benighted to understand the real cause of their misery, which surely lay more in their superstitions, their lack of education and machines, than in the implacable cruelty of the sea. Synge seeks to sympathize not only with their misery but with the superstitions they invoke to explain it, which he would never have accepted to explain anything on his own bourgeois level. Thus, instead of clarifying their psychology through presenting a more valid perspective upon the social factors that determined it than they themselves possessed, he actually increased its ambiguity. These people were too foreign to his habitual attitudes, and as a result his diction has more of vague "atmosphere" than nuance, and his plot becomes dependent upon a mystical naturalism, depicting an ineffectual resistence to obscure irresistible forces, rather than a conflict of recognizable elements which is capable of a solution.

Wright, on the contrary, was born and brought up in the midst of his material. His education, instead of alienating him from his past and its loyalties, was assimilated into already determined attitudes and merely enabled him to express them more adequately than Synge's sincere but external intention of sympathy could do. Nor should it be overlooked that these individual divergences between writers who shared the same general aim, were magnified by the fact that this aim was interpreted differently by the different milieus of which each was a part. Synge's Ireland was witnessing the rise of the bourgeoisie into self-consciousness with the usual trappings of vague proletarian sympathy, whereas Wright was part of a larger context of the rise of the American proletariat into self-consciousness with overtones of hostility towards the middle class. Synge's spontaneous attitude towards the Irish populace is seen in *The Playboy of the Western World*, where the meanings of idioms and plot are quite clear since he makes no pretense of greater sympathy than is involved in the good-natured exposure of shiftlessness and eccentricity.

The difficulties which Synge encountered in *Riders to the Sea* are analogous to Wright's in *Native Son*. But under the changed circumstances, these latter were not such as to be insoluble this side of mysticism, but were solved, rather, with awkwardness and hesitation to the sacrifice of esthetic quality. In *Native Son*, in other words, where Wright took the larger circumference of black and white, bourgeois and proletarian society, as his milieu, he had to comprehend a comparatively unfamiliar and a predominantly hostile environment. But in the short stories, his locus is the black world of the South where he felt completely at home, and where he had only to articulate the misery and revolt of the black man. Both his plot and his style were implicit in his theme, which naturally sought the direct expression of dialogue in the folk idiom. His knowledge of the white literary tradition was necessary only to enable him to evoke the more perfectly what was latent within. At the same time he knows that his particular subjects are not direct representations of his own experience. He follows Eliot's law of the objective emotional correlative. Because he comprehends it so distinctly and feels its validity so genuinely, he appears dominated by his theme. He seems to forget himself in its expression and follow his own story as breathlessly as any reader. He thus, as a stylist, possesses the assurance that is typical of the writer of distinction, who seems to be merely articulating, by means of his craft and his insight, the significant experiences of his fellow men.

Wherefore Wright can take over the *mot juste* of literary tradition, and can use it with an ease forbidden to the inventor of the term, because he is not expressing an alien and supercilious attitude, but only fulfilling the intention of his people in a refinement of their natural cadence and idiom. His selection of words is that normal to the tradition of good writing, not primarily because he is steeped in that tradition, but because good writing, as Eliot's law suggests, recognizes its fealty to the living situation, and uses "traditions" only as tools to achieve its clarification. His choice of diction, dictated by the needs of the situation, therefore, follows a middle course between the underprecision of mystic or romantic escapism and the overprecision of the rationalistic. It maintains a balance between the expository and the emotive aspects of words. It meets the demand for the "right word" because the "ends," since they are adequately understood, can determine the "means." His words are not chosen so that attention is distracted from the theme (the "end") and kept centered on the complexity of the immediate sensation or activity (the "means"). But they are selected, instead, with such judiciousness and economy that suspense is created, and the present scene calls forth its successor until a significant plot has been completely woven. The use of diction in this way is possible only when the social sphere proffers a theme which is not paralyzed by paradox or ambiguity, and which the author's social point of view enables him to recognize.

These comments are applicable to literary forms generally, and their emphasis upon plot does not imply that Wright's stories are virtually one-act plays. They do make use of an unusual amount of dialogue, in order to intensify the validity of the action and the degree of emotional response. But they are not open to the usual objection to the one-act play, that it does not have space enough for significant accomplishment. Because they are short stories, they can employ other mechanisms besides dialogue, and accomplish more in less space. Though Wright never obtrudes obiter dicta, by employing a certain amount of description and a considerable amount of stream of consciousness, he avoids the limitations of the dramatic form.

How Wright achieves these ends can be illustrated by reference to *Long Black Song*. In this story he builds his climax with extraordinary discretion and subtlety. Beginning with a comparatively simple situation, both action and characterization grow more complex as the narrative unfolds. The characters change as a result of the action. They learn through critical experience. There are therefore two aspects of every situation, since each has an effect both upon the nature of the personality and upon the externalization of its nature in the action. For the most part, of course, it is a new facet of a persistent character structure that the new situation discloses. But at moments of climax the personality is dialectically changed, and its outward expression redirected, although this can happen only to the principal character since he alone is principally engaged in the action. Thus in *Long Black Song*, the wife of the poor Negro farmer is the principal character at the start. Her romantic but entirely legitimate longing for a better life follows the familiar American tradition and affords the story a congenial orientation within which the failure can unfold. Her seduction by a white youth only sets the theme into motion. She then retires, keeping the same character structure and the same accompanying ideals. She becomes a chorus upon the action, through which we remain aware that the dream of a better life is frustrated by the inability of men to cooperate, which to her means, first, the conditions of marriage that led her to seek out a Negro lover, then the war that took her lover away, and now the interracial fighting that proceeds under her own eyes. For, after her husband returns and discovers her seduction by a white man, he takes over the story. The external action, though the tension becomes intense, is easily described. The Negro kills the white salesman when he comes back for the Victrola he had left the night before (symbolic both of the wife's dream and of her downfall). A posse gathers to lynch him. But after killing as many of them as possible, he prefers to die in the flames of his own house rather than surrender to their vengeance.

What gives this story its vitality and its individuality is the fact that its action is associated with an inner revolution in the character of the protagonist. It is this element that distinguishes it from the short story of tradition. The poor farmer had been an exceptional type of Negro. He had been neither easygoing after the old manner nor in conscious revolt like so many of the metropolitan Negroes of the present day. On the contrary, to his wife's discomfiture, he had assimilated the practical version of the American way as completely as any respectable poor white farmer. He had believed that if he worked hard, added to his little property by depriving himself and his wife of casual comforts, above all, if he could acquire a hired man, he would have won all the self-respect and social standing a man requires. Thus, as usual in Wright, although his plot is on the surface sheer race conflict, the deeper implications transcend race, apply equally to whites, and only become the clearer through their more intense representation in Negro material. For here, any reader, black or white, conservative or radical, can agree on the diagnosis: that such a belief, though it looks practical, is actually more fantastic than the wife's romantic dream.

Racial feeling becomes the device through which the Negro farmer rejects a point of view that is not racial at all (but bourgeois), and attains a heroism which transcends its racial stimulus (since it is now shared by all those who have a valid belief in democracy). When Silas learns that his wife has been unfaithful with the salesman, he feels at first that she has been traitorous both to him and to their race, and ruined his lifetime of effort. He soon comes to see that her disloyalty to him is permitted by the white bourgeois code he has accepted in other areas. It is the prototype in personal relationships of his stupidity in the economic. Her error has permitted his discovery of an inconsistency in his philosophy of life. So he reorients his attitudes. His hatred turns away from his wife, whose offense he now sees has been imposed upon her by the social system he had accepted and expected to profit by. But instead of letting his hatred turn inward upon himself for having been misguided, his poverty and his race buttress what had been healthy in his bourgeois attitude. His self-reliance guarantees that his energy continue to be directed outward, but towards a new objective. It gives him the courage to kill the white offender and to fight against the posse as long as he can. On the surface this new aim may look like simple uncontrollable desire for revenge. And part of his motivation also is without doubt a continuation of his old ambition for property. But when he retreats within his own house to die there in the flames, he is doing more than protecting his property to the bitter end. His principal motive, I believe, is to withhold from the posse the satisfaction of their sadism in killing him. When dying must be, he wishes to control his own dying and make it an assertion of his new sense of values. To have fought against the posse until the degrading end of their final overpowering him would have been to have continued on another level the old bourgeois fallacy of free competition. His governance of his own death is his application of a new standard for living. In his final act he is already tasting the freedom of the better life of which his wife had dreamed.

Though Silas' revenge is violent, it is based upon a valid conviction and not a fantasy. The conviction is, of course, that men ought to defend themselves when frustrated of their legitimate expectations from life by continual repression. When this defense, though it benefits the personality, results in outward disaster, this conviction has evoked a tragic theme. It is, in fact, the tragic theme of our time. And as such, should be distinguished from the many themes tangential to it, that have flourished in the recent past, and which are, by contrast, the themes of pathos. Negroes, as they became sophisticated, might conceivably have adopted any number of these bourgeois attitudes, which involve irony or pathos in place of tragedy. In the poetry of Robinson Jeffers, after a life of violent inner and outer conflict, death becomes the desired passage into inert anonymity. For Thomas Mann, sin and suffering, through the violence of war, become therapeutic devices of purgation by means of which we automatically recover our lost perception of the virtuous life. As in Dostoevski, the act of violence automatically sets up its opposite; a different consciousness is created spontaneously by the mere course of events. In Wright, a learning process is basic. The reciprocity between developing events and the changing personality involves more than the emergence of different orders of intuition. Part of the reciprocity is between the individual's reason and his emotions. The process, thus conceived, assumes the emerging control of the consciousness, both over one's emotions and the external event. In such a process the end is tragedy when the improved personality, though it deserves to be successful, is defeated by the particular order of events concerned. Wright's characters are, strictly speaking, illiterate. Yet they illustrate better than Mann's characters, for all their rumination, this sort of learning from experience, this growth of a more authentic awareness of the individual's relationship to the outer world. Errors in its verbal statement and vacillations of mood are evidence that the awareness is only forming in the consciousness. But it comes through occasionally, and these occasions are reliable clues by means of which we may understand the unuttered internal meanings behind the hero's overt actions. "Ahm gonna be hard like they is! So hep me, Gawd, Ahm gonna be *hard!* When they come fer me Ahm gonna *be here.* N when they git me outta here theys gonna *know* Ahm gone." The statement is in terms of mere resistance, but it is nevertheless the clue to an inner life, which is expanding on a new basis, with a sense of competence and coordination to a valuable end. Silas is turning against his oppressors the principle they pervert but which, all the same, they taught him: the principle that a man should stand up for his rights. Justified, unperverted as he accepts it, it becomes for him a new ideal of manhood, and death is taken as only the means to achieve it, when there is no other way.

The nature of the theme and the psychology of the heroic personality are the same everywhere in the modern world. The same need to die rather than suffer the inner degradation of slavery and bitter oppression is the note of antifascist literature everywhere. It reappears with only minor changes of emphasis, whether the locus be Spain or China with Malraux, the Soviet Union with Ehrenburg, occupied France with Pozner, fascist Germany with Anna Seghers, or this account at home of *Long Black Song*. Everywhere, also, in Wright's stories, it is the underlying attitude. Other stories more deliberately than *Long Black Song* define its political implications. There is a community of aim and attitude in the opponents of fascism everywhere, which transcends differences of race and class and nation; so that readers sense this community even when members of their own group seem to be attacked. This distinction Wright makes explicit in *Bright and Morning Star*. In this story he makes you hate the lynch mob with a contempt and ferocity only equalled in Soviet stories of the Nazi invaders or American accounts of Japanese atrocities. He makes you hate the white informer within the sharecropper's union. But he is careful to introduce other white members of the union whom the Negroes trust because of their character and their willingness to suffer. But the protagonist is an old Negro mother, and the emphasis of the plot is upon her expiation of her error, which has betrayed her son to the mob. Under her son's eyes, before they are both beaten to death together, she avenges herself and him by taking the life of the stool pigeon she had trusted. But this sequence of external events has been accompanied by changes within her personality. Her awareness of betrayal has been the start of a process of inner development. At first a passive, old-fashioned Negro, with misgivings about her son's union activities, she has learned from error, and now, instead of wailing and submitting, she turns to action. Her intense identification with her son, no longer merely maternal, becomes the greater since she can now in a measure identify with his values in living. Her view of the world has become more complex because she has learned that people are not always what they seem. Though she is not yet certain of the criteria for trust in other people's actions and ideas, she has at length learned to trust herself. Under these circumstances, revenge is only the negative aspect of an awakening self-respect, and the fact of her own dying is driven out of consciousness by the fact of successful action in behalf of her son and the ideals they now hold in common. She has become capable of the same order of heroism as Silas.

The heroic theme in Wright takes the dramatic form of physical conflict. Through the action, the reader becomes aware of changes within the personality of the hero. But the hero's attention is never centered, as it is in Malraux, introspectively upon himself. At the same time, unlike most of the definitely antifascist fiction, unlike *Native Son* as well, the short stories deal with rigidly limited situations. They do not involve any broad picture of social conflict. They are so written that the reader will fit them into the larger frame by himself. Wright's characters are part of that larger frame, but they are too unlettered to be aware of their symbolic roles. They fight generally in isolation, or as a little isolated band, with the intensity and at times the morbidity of those who must fight alone. Somehow, dimly, and quite unverbalized, a faith in democracy animates them so that they seem at times to presage those guerilla fighters so common in Europe during the Second World War. But this isolation of Wright's characters, if it seems politically a proof that the stamina needed to build an organization precedes organization itself, esthetically permits a plot that, by stressing conflict of individual wills in place of social forces, gains in dramatic intensity.

But this conflict of wills can exist only when there is a valid conflict between reaction and democracy within society. The writer who can believe in the progressive extension of democracy will be able to recognize the conflict and squarely face it. Its recognition, by making possible the construction of a plot, both removes the taint of pathos or sentimentality or melodrama (which are the stylistic evidences of the failure to recognize the conflict or to evaluate it), and restores high seriousness to the tragic action. It must not be forgotten that Aristotle's definition of tragedy was determined by his belief in the dominance of clear-cut moral laws, and that our loss of the capacity to create the tragic plot in the modern world is the result of our pluralism and negation of belief. The difference between plot as defined by Aristotle and as Wright uses it is owing to a difference in the nature of the beliefs the plots subsume. In Aristotle it is an eternal proscription which a superior man unwittingly violates. When he becomes aware of his violation, he accepts outward penalty and physical suffering with inward resignation as justified. But in Wright the belief is one created by man, which unfolds, grows richer in content and greater in extension, by the cumulating pressure of man's exercise of his own potentialities. In tragic action under these conditions, it is not the hero who sins, but his opponent. The hero is a common man who is made to suffer because he has got in touch with reality, because his awakened potentialities have brought him into conflict with the forces of reaction. His suffering, consequently, though it is physical as well as mental, is accompanied by an inner state of feeling which is the opposite of submission, one of active, exalted conviction of self-fulfillment.

In these short stories the tragic action ceases to be a mechanism for preserving the status quo by showing what happens to those who violate it. It becomes the price one may have to pay for the satisfaction of living according to one's ever-expanding convictions, of challenging what one has come to know to be evil, and promoting what is for one's own good because it is for the common good. It becomes the present sacrifice men are willing to make for an awareness of the better life within them. A tragedy, then, as a literary form, consists of a conflict in the objective world, through which a contradiction develops, between the external circumstances of the hero's life, which ends in a death imposed by his opponents, and his internal state of feeling, which becomes a sense of fullest living. This contradiction is promoted by his discovery through action of an error of judgment, and ends, through the right use of that discovery, in what is actually the satisfaction of the better integrated personality, even when unlettered Negroes are only aware of the surge of mother love or the obligation their dignity as human beings has laid upon them.

THE EXISTENTIAL DARKNESS:
RICHARD WRIGHT'S
*THE OUTSIDER**

Kingsley Widmer

The Outsider (1953) deserves attention both because of its own merits and because of its role as one of the very few consciously existentialist works in American literature. As an explicitly philosophical novel framed within cogent epigraphs from Kierkegaard and Nietzsche and developed on Sartrean dialectics, it has generally received unphilosophical, puzzled, and negative discussion. An apparently typical dismissal may be found in a pedestrian academic historical study, Robert Bone's *The Negro Novel in America* (Yale University Press, 1958). His one-sentence footnote on *The Outsider* declares it to be "strongly influenced by French existentialism and far inferior to *Native Son*." Yet a disinterested reading of Wright's three novels suggests that, on most artistic and intellectual grounds, *The Outsider* achieves much more than the "naturalistic" and "race problem" *Native Son* (1940) and *The Long Dream* (1958). Except for those with some limiting moral thesis about Negro culture, Wright's existentialist novel would appear to deserve consideration among the few substantial long fictions by Negroes. But our primary concern, like Wright's, must be with *The Outsider* as an American existentialist fable.

As Wright's protagonist insists, his destructively free actions and lucid amorality derive not from "racial consciousness" but from a more universal contemporary state of "dread" which reveals "the horrible truth of the uncertain and enigmatic nature of life." Indeed, it is just this emphasis upon a metaphysical horror—the unbearableness of the truth—which may account for some of the negative response to *The Outsider*. The overwhelming dread of existence provides the characterizing postulate of existentialist literature, and one fundamentally antithetical to the pervasive American optimistic idealism and bland scientism.

Yet Wright's fable itself illustrates the breadth of American anti-

* Reprinted from *Wisconsin Studies in Contemporary Literature*, I (1960), 13–21, by permission of the author and editors.

50

existentialism. In a long set piece of polemic in the latter part of the novel (one of Wright's more unfortunate carry-overs from the didactic Marxist novel of the 'thirties), the barely disguised author surprisingly insists on three quite unexistential pieties. Contrary to the existentialists, Wright argues that science and industrialism are "neutral" in value and, therefore, *might* be transformed into morally good forces. To this he adds that some "unknown" ethical and social *idealism* might be found to provide "a form of discipline for living" in a mass society. And, finally, as such optimistic idealism would suggest, naked man is ultimately benevolent and retains a primal "innocence" which could overcome all guilt and existential dread. Thus the most sustained American existentialist novel, so far, also presents moments of passionate rejection of its own premises and emphasis.

Turning to Wright's dramatization in *The Outsider*, we find what appears to be the gratuitous melodrama generally employed by philosophically insistent literature, as in Marlowe, Dostoevski and Sartre. Wright's ex-philosophy student, Cross Damon, rebels against the humiliations of a middle-class wife, the tedium of a postal clerk's job, a charge of statutory rape by his girl friend, the oppressive "Protestant ethic" of his milieu, and the whole complex of Negro and American "nonidentity." (Many of the details, it becomes obvious, are allegorical, including the demonic crucifixion suggested by the name and the parody of Sören Kierkegaard's use of the postman as archetypal Christian.) A fortuitous subway accident provides the means by which Cross Damon can pretend to be dead and flee his meaningless past. The limbo of freedom brings frenzied destruction, and in a few days he kills a Negro "clown" (his Jim Crow antithesis), tricks several kind people whose pathos would impose obligations on his freedom, and burns a church (the Selective Service office, appropriately, was in the basement). A few days later, having taken on a counterfeit identity (draft card and all), he can act with moral indifference and impartially murder a Fascistic racist (Herndon) and an exploititive Communist (Gil). Soon after, he must logically kill another political functionary (Hilton) to protect his freedom. He finally achieves a sense of purpose by making anguished love to the wife of one of his victims (Eva, the primal sensitive artist). But love also requires authentic identity; Eva, confronted with knowledge of Cross's past and amoral acts, commits suicide, leaving Cross Damon in ultimate loneliness and despair. Such is the dread of truth in others, and the price of truth for the self. His own death, at the hands of bureaucratic functionaries who must destroy him because they cannot understand him, simply closes the absurd rebellion to get "outside history," social morality, and the meaningless self.

Though Cross Damon's destructive acts reflect psychological compulsions and the hostility of the social order, Wright insists repeatedly that they remain gratuitous, i.e., a "free" and random selection of sequences by "a petty god" in a "a Godless world." Wright's Raskolnikov learns, from a Dostoevskian psychological policeman (Ely Houston, the crippled district attorney), that his destructiveness was inhumanely reasonable. The "logic of atheism" can give no meaning to personal desires and promises in a meaningless universe. The truth is not enough. For what Cross has attempted to do, in Wright's words, is to let personal "contingency" become "destiny." He cannot succeed because in a world of dehumanized conflicts, as represented by Communists versus policemen, choices on either side become assertions of nonexistence. Put another way, Cross Damon simply makes demonic crisscrosses, canceling each lie with another lie, each crime with another crime. For example, early in the novel Cross becomes estranged from his wife, Gladys, the epitome of the predatory middle-class virtues:

. . . as he suffered her nagging, he felt increasingly walled off from her; but the more he felt it the more he sought to hide it, and finally there crept into his dealings with her a weird quality of irony. It first manifested itself in an innocent question: How could he help Gladys? And the moment he asked himself that question he knew he did not love her and perhaps had never loved her. . . . She had become for him an object of compassion. He was now haunted by the idea of finding some way to make her hate him. Her hatred would be a way of squaring their relationship, of curing her of her love for him, of setting her free as well as himself.

In the following "complicated psychological attack" which Cross makes upon his wife, he draws upon a previous "accident" of aberrant behavior to suggest a new "accident": ". . . what on earth could that 'accident' be? . . . his self-hate, his aversion for Gladys, his perpetual toying with his own feelings resulted in a sudden, confoundingly luminous idea." His inspiration is to come home from work unexpectedly early, walk in like a mute and mad stranger, hit his wife, walk out, and later return at his usual time as if nothing had happened. The planned "fluke" brings overwhelming consequences: his wife's fear and revenge, and, finally, such a concatenation of impossible pressures that total flight becomes the only possibility. Similarly with the subway accident in which Cross is believed to be dead. He chooses the initial consequences from a random accident as a significant pattern of life, and is driven into fantastically violent circumstances to maintain his choice. Thus "contingency" becomes existential "destiny," destiny as destructive as the circumstances from which it is made. Here, perhaps with more irony than Wright intended, we find a naturalistic delineation of Sartre's maxim that "man chooses himself," i.e., desires to be that which has happened.

Yet a second look at the existential "freedom" in the above passage and episode points up another direction. Wright's deployment of inverse and doubling emotions (love-as-hate, compassion-as-destruction) is a major characteristic of his art. It also seems to be a major characteristic of that long dialectical tradition of which contemporary existentialism is but an emphatic instance. But is Cross Damon's "weird irony" that of "freedom" or simply the compulsions of hatred and self-hatred? Can we not ask the same question of the gratuitous murder by Meursault in *The Stranger?* And of almost every hero of Sartre? And of the works of lesser writers like Genet, Bowles, and Mailer? The ambiguities between existential freedom and the compulsions of hatred appear so recurrent and overwhelming in all of these as to become definitive of existential art. There is, of course, no reason why art, despite the benign analogies of traditional moralists, cannot be based on hatred rather than love.

One of the more astute English exponents of existentialism, Everett Knight, argues that the central method of existential art is to "propound ambiguity" (*Literature Considered as Philosophy*, 1957). Cross Damon is simultaneously the hero and the victim of his existential lucidity. While his choices of action and identity appear free and explicit, he also reveals tortuous "dark compulsions" in the three women he chooses, the betrayals, the acts of violence, the self-confessions, the flights and the self-destruction. He insists, like characteristically modern political leaders, juveniles, and criminals, that "no ideas are necessary to justify his acts." *This* "idea" is but another version of Raskolnikov's final dream.

Curiously enough, the existential freedom in which Wright places his character tends only in one direction, one tonality—an a priori darkness. Wright emphasizes this by having his dark-skinned hero move solely through the dark wintry season, the black ghettos of Chicago and New York, the dark despair of the literature of the irrational (his favorite reading). Even Cross Damon's wildly sardonic levity, which most frightens all those unable to bear the naked truth, displays the qualities characterized by André Breton as "*humour noir.*" At its most literal level, the darkness of the Negro and his resentful self-hatred provides a practical image to embody the darkness of dread. Where Sartre in *Nausea* runs into pathological difficulties in presenting his protagonist's repulsion to the "viscous" corruption of his own body, Wright's protagonist can more readily see, and treat, his dark body as "an alien and despised object" because the white society does just that. To "stand outside the world" in the moral and social darkness, for Wright's hero, depends on an actual as well as a metaphysical alienation of the black man from the white rationalizations of ordinary life.

In his effort to find the "relationship of himself to himself," to escape from his "burden of nonidentity," Cross takes on the "project of deception." Much of this anguished dramatization of self-hatred seems to draw upon Sartre's analysis of *mauvaise foi* (*L'Etre et le Néant*, Ch. 2). In Wright as in Sartre, the systematic bad faith used to hide inner emptiness becomes a harsh parody of the daily compromises and resentments of most men. And, as in Sartre and others, Wright's quest for the authentic takes the path of demonic purgation. Existentialist enlightenment requires a full descent into the darkness of defiance, destruction, hidden desires, and nihilism.

Only thus can one get "outside" history and the deception of "ideas." For Wright's hero, however, very little can be found outside. Cross's repeated existential maxim—"Man is nothing in particular"—shows a greater futility than its source, Sartre's "Man is a useless passion." Carried out fully, the existentialist credo becomes vicious—and this must be a major point of Wright's treatment. Thus his Cross reduces the Kantian irreducible value of the individual in its final defiant assertion, and so ends treating other men, murderously, as "insects," "meaningless obstructions," "nothings."

Wright's ambiguous negation of the existential quest (existential anti-existentialism) reveals, I think, a peculiarly American vantage point. Where Kierkegaard's "single one" could fall back before the horror of the arbitrary absolute on the certitude of a humble moral identity (the postman in Deer Park—*Either/Or*), or more atheistic and antibourgeois European existentialists establish themselves in honorific identities (as traditional artistic and political rebels), Wright shows the American "outsider" without an identity other than the violent cold righteousness of the "inverted idealist." The American either has not or cannot achieve an adequate role for his metaphysical pathos.

For when one is being nothing in particular, passion spent, a fluid society presents no "form or discipline for living." The mobility, the intermittently free access, the fortuitous economic and personal opportunity, the lack of rigorous heroic pattern of America, have eliminated even the negative limits. Unlike the desperate Raskolnikov, Negro Cross can borrow $800, take a Pullman berth, taxi rides, a series of anonymous furnished rooms, bottles of whiskey, and always expect a future somewhere else. He can even make an elliptical confession of his crimes to the inquisitor, and go technically free of punishment. He is, therefore, free to hover within the ambiguities of his metaphysical question: "Could there be a man in whose mind and consciousness all the hopes and inhibitions of the last two thousand years have died?" The Dostoevskian query receives the Nietzschean answer in the final chapter of *The Outsider*: "The real men, the last men are coming." In America, the sloughing off of the old consciousness threatens to show fantastic rapidity and rage, for America, rather than Europe, is the more existential land.

The rage of disbelief in anything, heightened by Wright's feverish heavy prose, whiskeyed and bitter Negro intellectual, and black-and-white winter urban world, climaxes in the long political section of the novel. It may be appropriate to Wright's theme to show the "valueless men," the power-longing amoralists who most fully represent instrumental society, in the vicious political guise of the Communist. But Wright's treatment of this material consists of long didactic speeches and repetitiously obsessive debating. Unlike his French counterparts, the author has no argument for an immediate historical role of political opportunism or oppositionism, but only a total *a*politics. Yet he seems compelled to put his apolitical position in the heavy rhetoric of Communist political exposé. This, certainly, reveals all the personal subjectivity, and dubious art, of existentialist confession.

Oddly enough, Cross Damon's long speech against politics to the Communist functionaries turns on the argument that the existentialist amoralist reveals a fundamental similarity to the political amoralists; both play at being "little gods" seeking the pure "sensuality of power" because they believe in nothing. Even as argument, however, this disenchantment with all ideology and idealism lacks persuasiveness since it insufficiently considers the degree to which many men must rely on dogmas in order to act. In the novel itself, several Marxist and Catholic characters illustrate the common need and pathos of an absolute, organized, and shoddy faith in the order of history and the cosmos. With blind rhetoric, Wright sometimes obscures the dramatic difference he actually creates between his political functionaries and his passionate protagonist. *Their* sensuality of power cannot plausibly be equated with *his* intermittent (even if inadequate) sensual interest in people and feelings. Wright as old-fashioned moralist breaks through the dramatization, and all those "suspending ethical laws" get lumped together. However, the criminal, the Communist, the existentialist philosopher, and the lover move outside the ethical for rather different purposes, and with rather different results. It is the fallacy of the rationalistic moralist to assume that the realms of the amoral (and immoral) lack acute discriminations and distinctive features.

Though Wright's hero "can't believe anything," he believes that a moral order should, somewhere, exist. Lacking alternative meaning, his search for the absolute, by way of crime and dark hatreds, comes back to the social limits of crime and the personal limits of Protestant guilt. Cross's final cry, "I'm *innocent.* . . . That's what made the horror," contains the central attempt at ultimate ambiguity. He is innocent because he is the victim of an inhuman society and ideology. He is also innocent, in contrast, because he is one of the "new men," the amoralists, the vengeful pagans who arrive after the death of all gods and have no values, and therefore no obligations. And, finally, he is intrinsically innocent. All men are. In an essentially meaningless universe, an honest man longs for the guilt which he does not have. Cross achieves the horrible innocence of the existential truth which does not allow man the community of hope.

Wright covertly re-enforces his existential definition, I suspect, with the anxieties derived from the dubious American social order and the vestigial heroic theology of Protestant atheism. It is a rather elaborate negativity for a novel to carry, however profound. While his drama reveals that living by logic, such as killing men who "deserve" to be killed, leads to endless destruction, Wright appears unable to stick to existential qualities rather than arguments and *their* ambiguities. Part of his purpose seems to be the revelation that neither the logic of ideologies (Communist, racist, etc.) nor the logic of circumstance (psychological and social compulsions) can create authentic being. Which is to suggest that both salvational faiths and empirical truths destroy actual life. The author's too simple and halfhearted asides calling for a humanized scientism and benevolent moral idealism appear as another, though unexamined, destructive logic which can neither reveal nor produce vital qualities of existence. But centering on such abstractions tends to defeat the passionate intelligence of the novel. For example, the organizing concept of Kierkegaardian "dread" gets caught within an alliterative pattern of terms rather than within sufficient scenes of tangible life. Thus the book develops around a sectional pentad: Dread, Dream, Descent, Despair, Decision (death)—simply the unfolding of the categories of dread. The crucified atheist criminal—the modern form of the saint—"loved life too much," we are told, but he, like his author, loved (with hatred) moral ambiguities and ideologies even more. Before Cross, saved from ideologies by his outsider's wisdom, can transcend the compulsions which emerge in total freedom, to trust in the other and in the passion and richness of *unjustified* life, he has arrived at his logical end—nothing.

Yet to stray very far from the destructiveness and innocence of the hard existential light would, I take it, result in even greater darkness. Within its rhetorical limitations, *The Outsider* achieves its revelatory end. Contrast it with other American existentialist-demonic fictions, such as Norman Mailer's *Deer Park*. Mailer's Marion Faye (the comparable figure to Wright's protagonist) remains simply an aging juvenile delinquent, and, as with our other juvenile heroes, we suspect his existential truth of being just an exhibitionistic therapy. Wright's monochromatic art of hatred, unfortunately vitiated by repeated turns to abstraction, may be the best of American intentionally existentialist literature. Though the type may well be more worthy of attention than some of the prevailing ersatz-moral novels (such as those of Robert Penn Warren), none of them are eminently satisfactory. For one thing, consciously existentialist fictions are not novels but a more limited form, fables, whether European or

American. And abstract fables mostly about moral ambiguity overriding existence. Perhaps, also, we need to distinguish between the self-consciously existentialist fable, the implicitly existentialist fable (Nathanael West would be a good American example), and those fictions which are fundamentally, but not just, existential (such as the "American" and later tales of D. H. Lawrence, and the Faulkner of *Light in August*, etc.). True existentialism, we are reminded by Wright, is an extreme enquiry into truth, and not a mythos, an ethical system, a science, a religion— or an adequate aesthetic. Explicit existentialism may provide insight, but it is based upon being totally outside life, and maintains its relation to life only by endless self-purging of subjectivity and by demonic catharsis. To be outside reveals the dark truth about those inside, but it is not enough, neither for the hero, the author, nor the reader.

Acceptance of the richness of life—even the possible richness of hatred—enjoys only a dialectical reality in existentialism, and perhaps lacks even that in most positivistic and idealistic views. A heroic negativity, existentialism displays the limits of rebellion, defiance, and perversity. Primarily critical and diagnostic, it exists only by relation to that which it is not. Such a *lebens* philosophy does not equal life itself but only the darkness of evaluation. And that darkness, I have argued (along with Wright) is true but inadequate. The pain of absolute freedom and demonic power may provide an intensification of immediate life, the heroic stance on nothingness. Perhaps more important, existential inquiry can (and does) provide devastating insights into the covert nihilism of most contemporary social, religious, technological, and moral ideologies. But, somewhere, there must be a more joyous acceptance of self, even in Nietzsche's Age of Nihilism, than that of violently guilty knowledge.

REFLECTIONS ON RICHARD WRIGHT:
A SYMPOSIUM ON AN EXILED
NATIVE SON*

Herbert Hill, *moderator*
Horace Cayton, Arna Bontemps,
Saunders Redding, *participants*

HILL: I shall begin by asking Horace Cayton, who knew Richard Wright quite early in his career, to open the discussion. Mr. Cayton first met Dick Wright when Wright came up from the South to Chicago in the 1930's.

CAYTON: It is with great pleasure that I talk about Richard Wright. I think he had more influence on me than anyone else except Dr. Robert Park, who was a great sociologist and a ghost writer for Booker T. Washington. When Dick first came up from Mississippi, he was with his mother.

I was research assistant to the brilliant sociologist, Louis Wirth, at the University of Chicago, and one day there came a tapping on the door of his office. I opened the door and there was a short brown-skinned Negro, and I said, "Hello. What do you want?" He looked like an undergraduate, so I was perhaps condescending in a polite fashion, and, of course, he *was* also colored. He said, "My name is Richard Wright. Mrs. Wirth made an appointment for me to see Dr. Wirth." That made me a little more respectful. I told him to come in. "Mrs. Wirth said that her husband might help me. I want to be a writer."

Well, I thought that was a little pretentious, a brown-skinned boy

* Reprinted from *Anger and Beyond* (New York: Harper & Row, 1966), edited by Herbert Hill, by permision of the publishers.

This symposium took place August 8, 1964, during the seminar "The Negro Writer in the United States" at the Asilomar Conference Center, Monterey Peninsula, California. The seminar was held under the auspices of the University of California (Berkeley).

coming in to the University and saying he wanted to be a writer. Who didn't want to be a writer? But who could write? I began showing him the files in the office—I would not say that we were totally statistically oriented at the University at the time, but we were very empirical. We were going out studying every facet of the city. We were discovering the Italian district, the Polish district, the Irish district, the Negro community. We were studying the vast complex of human beings who make up that monster of Chicago, and Dick said, "You've got all of your facts pointed, pinned to the wall like a collector would pin butterflies." I looked at him. He was a poetic little Negro. I did not see Dick again for some years.

Later, I was running the Community Center on Chicago's South Side, and I got a wire from Dick asking me to meet his plane at the Chicago airport. *Life* magazine was doing a background story on Dick's *Native Son*, which was by then a best seller, and Dick was coming out to Chicago to help them. Excited at the prospect of knowing and working with him, I was waiting at the airport long before the plane got in. The first thing Dick said when he got off the plane was, "Do you know of any Negro who has lost his job because of *Native Son*?"

For a week Dick was my guest. I found him one of the most interesting and fascinating people I had ever known. Born of poor parents in Mississippi, he had gone to a Seventh-day Adventist school where he had received something less than a high school education. When his mother brought the family to Chicago they went on relief (Mary Wirth was their social worker), and Dick joined the Communist party. While working on the Federal Writers' Project of the WPA, he wrote his first book, *Uncle Tom's Children*. Then he moved to New York, where, under incredibly difficult circumstances, he produced *Native Son*. The book was an instantaneous success. It was chosen by the Book-of-the-Month Club, and no other novel by a Negro had ever received such widespread acclaim.

Dick was then in the process of breaking with the party and was as bitter toward them as they were to him. He told me about the party's reaction to *Native Son*. Since the book did not follow the orthodox Marxist line on the Negro question, the Communists were quite hostile. Earl Browder, head of the American Communist party, stated that he saw nothing wrong with *Native Son*, but Dick did not accept this implied invitation to resume his activities in the party. Instead, he published his famous repudiation of the Communist party in the *Atlantic Monthly*.[1] From then on he devoted (and wasted) much of his creative energy in fighting the Communists.

[1] Richard Wright, "I Tried to Be a Communist," *Atlantic Monthly*, August, 1944.

From this first visit on, Dick and I saw each other frequently throughout the years. He would be my guest when he came to Chicago, and I would stay with him, and his wife Ellen, on my trips to New York.

Some years later Dick came to me and said, "I've come to write a picture book [which was later *Twelve Million Black Voices*]. I want to get into your files. I want your sociological concepts." I explained to him the idea of urban versus rural, of culture versus civilization, or a sacred versus a secular society. I talked about the differences between societies in which folkways determine the way of life and those which are governed by contracts rather than promises, and from those two concepts Dick came up with this lovely, poetic formulation: "The Lords of the Land," who characterized the rural, sacred society in the South, and "The Bosses of the Buildings," describing the forces of the cold, impersonal cities of the North.

BONTEMPS: I knew Dick during the same period. I went to Chicago in 1934. At that time Langston Hughes, who had returned from a year abroad in Russia, was living in Carmel, California. In his letters to me he wanted to know who the new writers were after things broke up in Harlem just two or three years earlier. I didn't know any, but Langston had heard about Richard Wright. When he came to Chicago, he said to me, "About this Richard Wright who's writing for *The Masses*, haven't you met him yet? Let's go out and find him." So we went to the phone book to see if there was any Wright in the neighborhood. We telephoned the only Wright we found in the vicinity of Thirty-fifth and State, and said, "Do you know anybody by the name of Richard Wright? He is a young fellow who is apparently a writer." And the voice replied, "Oh, you mean the numbers man."

Finally, we met up with Dick Wright at a party. The interesting thing I remember is that Dick was such a flaming young Communist at the time. He didn't have time to dance or anything like that, though he liked girls and was just at the dancing age, but he had great zeal only for his politics and his writing.

The next time I saw him he was in the Loop. I was standing on the corner waiting for a Cottage Grove streetcar, and he ran across the street and said, "Look here, I have just three cents. I need a nickel to get uptown." This was the Depression and such things were not unusual. I tried to give him a nickel, but he said, "No, I just want two cents." I gave him the two cents, and he said, "I'll bring it to you Friday night."

I thought he was joking, but sure enough, Friday night he came. He walked about two miles to our house and brought the two pennies. After that, every Friday night he used to come over. We'd have dinner and visit together and he'd begin reading us some of the stories he had written which later went into *Uncle Tom's Children*. This was his project then.

I was closely associated with him through that book and through the writing of *Native Son* later on, when he moved to New York. Well, that's just a little sidelight out of the past.

REDDING: I remember Dick from the fall of '43. We met at the Mc-Carter Theatre in Princeton, where Paul Robeson was doing *Othello*. During the course of the performance it was noticeable that Robeson was drooling, spitting really, in the faces of the other actors. At intermission we were standing in a group, Dick, his wife, my wife and several friends, and one of the men criticized Robeson for losing his saliva. Dick got very mad about this and said, "Don't you know that Othello was an epileptic, and that this is a conscious, a purposeful thing; this is part of the role." I don't think his anger had anything to do with the fact that he and Robeson were both Communists at the time.

CAYTON: That reminds me of another story about Dick and acting. When *Native Son* was produced on Broadway with Orson Wells, the show went broke and Dick, although he was tight with a buck, bought up fifty-one percent of that show and put it on the road. Canada Lee played Bigger Thomas, and Dick hated Canada's guts. God, he hated Canada. The reason he did was that he wanted to play Bigger Thomas himself. Hollywood offered him $75,000 and they were going to turn the characters white! As I say, Dick didn't throw away a buck, but he turned this down. He waited for years and went to the Argentine and he had some little blonde white girl play Mary Dalton, the girl Bigger Thomas kills. Ralph Ellison and I went to a preview in New York and there was Dick in the role. He must have been at least thirty-five years old, and what is Bigger, eighteen, nineteen? It was the damnedest thing you've ever seen.

REDDING: I once had an agent named Ann Watkins, and Dick didn't have an agent for his first book, but someone told him that he ought to have an agent and recommended Ann Watkins. Her office was then, and still is—though she herself has retired—at Park Avenue and about Thirty-eighth Street. People always entered her suite of offices from the side street, not from Park Avenue, a fact which Dick did not know. He was taking the manuscript of *Native Son* to her. He went into the Park Avenue entrance, which was the entrance to the plush apartments, and the elevator operator told him, "Boy, if you want to get upstairs, you go to the freight elevator," and of course Dick left there in high dudgeon, and got another agent. Ann Watkins was so mad about it when she heard the story that she had the elevator operator fired. That stupid elevator operator's rudeness cost Ann Watkins in the neighborhood of $25,000.

I have just one more story. Dick owned a farm just outside Paris, and he bought that farm for one reason. He wanted to grow collard greens. He was quite frank about this. Raise some pigs and grow collard greens, because he had been brought up in the South on hog jowl and collard greens and he missed them in Paris. When his farm didn't do right and the greens wouldn't come up, he used to go to LeRoy's, a restaurant catering principally to homesick Negroes in Paris.

BONTEMPS: When I was in Paris, I was anxious to go to French restaurants, but Dick kept taking me over to LeRoy's. He thought I was just as anxious for hog maws as he was. I wasn't.

HILL: I think we should explain that LeRoy's is a little piece of Harlem's Lenox Avenue in Paris. Many of us who go to Paris find it, and Dick took me there, too. LeRoy was a Negro GI who decided he would never come back to the United States and he opened up this little place, on the Right Bank in the Montmartre section, and somehow he managed to get the collard greens, the chitterlings and the ribs and everything else. He was a gentleman whom one might describe as having a high visibility content. It was a kind of joke—you sat at the bar with LeRoy, who presided over the entire enterprise, and you said, "LeRoy, when are you going back?" And LeRoy would turn to the mirror and he'd say, pointing to his face, "When this turns white."

REDDING: I recall asking him when he was coming home, and he said, "Have they built a bridge?"

HILL: I think it would be appropriate here for Arna Bontemps to review, briefly, Richard Wright's work and influence, and perhaps to compare his early books with the ones he wrote later, in Paris.

BONTEMPS: Well, the Depression had sent the Harlem writers scurrying. But I think it more than compensated for this damage by the opportunities it provided for the next wave of literary expression by Negroes. Many old and defeated writers, like the poet Fenton Johnson, wandered into the Writers' Project of the WPA. But the Project also drew the likes of Richard Wright, Ralph Ellison, Frank Yerby, Roi Ottley, Willard Motley and several others, and began to create an environment in which the Negro writer could at last stretch himself to full length.

Wright ascended rapidly to a major rank among American writers, without respect to race. Here was a novelist, powerful enough to break out of the narrow compartment previously occupied by Negro writers. For one thing, he was acutely aware of his prison, and it did not take him long to conclude, as some critics have done, that the novel, as he knew it, was and had been, for generations, a projection of the value system of the dominant class in the society. He took advantage of the panic into which that society had been dumped by the Depression and allied himself with the critics of the basic assumptions of that society and demanded that it hear him out. The consensus of intelligent readers was that he made sense, that he handled his theme with authority, expressed himself with power and eloquence and was entitled to the place he had won in the literary life of the Depression years.

Uncle Tom's Children, the first of his major works, was a collection of four short novels, written while Dick was employed by the Illinois Writers' Project. It was drawn from memories of his Mississippi boyhood. The stories were almost unbearable evocations of cruel realities which the nation and the world had, in the past, been unable or unwilling to face. His purpose, his determination as a prose writer, was to force open closed eyes, to compel America to look at what it had done to the black peasantry in which he was born. Then, in a competition offered by a publisher for the best fiction book submitted by a writer on WPA in 1938, *Uncle Tom's Children*, later published by Harper's, was judged the winner. The critical reception was enthusiastic, and its author was launched. The same critics were more than surprised when *Native Son* appeared two years later and actually, as one of them said, "dwarfed its powerful predecessor." Wright had moved his setting to Chicago, and the narrative vigor, which had impressed readers of the four novellas, had been intensified by a deeper probing into the society that produced the characters. Dick had confirmed his own insight by a new acquaintance with sociology, thanks largely to Horace Cayton. It was seldom disputed, at the time, that Wright's was the most impressive literary talent yet produced by a Negro American. In the next ten years there were nearly fifty translations and foreign editions of his books. His writings became known around the world. His name was bracketed with America's foremost writers and interest in him as a personality began to spread.

Then came *Black Boy*, in 1945. Certainly *Black Boy* gave evidence that the range of its author, like his standing among his contemporaries, was still expanding.

At this point, Dick moved his family to Paris and promptly became one of the most celebrated American expatriates in Europe. He didn't publish another book for eight years, and when he did, *The Outsider*, which appeared in 1953, showed him bringing to bear on his writing the attitudes of French existentialism in the post–World War II era. But *The Outsider* was not quite up to Wright's earlier books. Something was missing. Perhaps it was anger. His new French friends had made the suffering, alienated author feel at home. He had given them his love in return. The anguish and outrage that made his early books memorable faded in the fiction he wrote in the remaining years of his life. *The Long Dream*, 1958, was a dim echo of the Mississippi stories he had written while he was still bleeding. *Savage Holiday*, 1954, was a paperback potboiler. Some of the stories collected in the volume *Eight Men*, in 1961, had been written years earlier and properly belong beside the novellas.

The Paris years, though they added nothing to Richard Wright's stature as a novelist, stimulated considerable writing of another kind, however. In 1941, between *Native Son* and *Black Boy*, Wright had written a deeply

BONTEMPS: Well, I've thought about that a good bit, too. I think he sort of hints at it in the Introduction that he wrote to his collection of short stories, *Eight Men*. There is a story there, and Dick tried to tell it in some detail. Dick did his best writing when he was unhappy, when he was angry, when he was under tremendous tension. And Paris relaxed his tension. It gave him a happy life, but he couldn't write when he was happy.

REDDING: Well, I think that he was alienated from the French culture in ways in which James Joyce and Morley Callaghan and the rest of them were not alienated. I think it had to do with the constant awareness of, well, here I am in Paris, and I can go any darned place I choose to go.

I don't think he ever understood this, really. He was very thoroughly American. James Joyce, Fitzgerald, the others—they were true cosmopolites, and Dick never was. Dick was a small-town boy—a small-town *Mississippi* boy—all of his days. The hog maw and the collard greens. He was fascinated by the existentialist group for a while, but he didn't really understand them.

BONTEMPS: He came to reject them later on, but certainly *The Outsider* was written under their influence; the plot of *The Outsider*, in fact, is almost identical with the plot of Sartre's *The Chips Are Down* [*Les Jeux sont faits*].

Essentially, of course, Wright was and remained not only an American but a Southerner. Negroes have a special fondness for that old saw, "You can take the boy out of the country, but you can't take the country out of the boy." The saying could be paraphrased and pointed up in Dick's case. His deepest roots were in the folk culture of the bottom—not *deep* but *bottom*—South. The lore of that milieu was such an intimate part of his background he sometimes treated it as if it had all originated in his own family.

Take the story of the preacher who came to dinner, which he tells in *Black Boy*. This most familiar of Negro folk tales has stayed alive partly because it helped rural folk, one step removed from slavery, to laugh in the face of their own hunger pains and partly because minstrels and vaudeville comics have used it for laughs ever since. But to Dick the suffering expression of the child who saw the well-fed visiting preacher smacking his lips on the last of the chicken while the parents kept up their show of hospitality, the youngster knowing there was nothing more left for him, seemed so real, he apparently began to imagine himself the primary victim. I have occasionally asked others if they noticed this while reading *Black Boy*. Some had. None indicated having mentioned it to Dick, however, and I certainly had not.

As a product of the South, Wright represented that rare thing we sometimes call a clear case. I recall—thinking of clear cases—the story of John Chavis, of North Carolina, who came along early in the nineteenth century. Two planters in the Oxford area had argued over the question of whether or not Negroes were capable of being educated. The argument was a standoff until they decided to back their opinions with cash. After the bet was made, there was the problem of finding a suitable case in point. It had to be a boy who was free, otherwise his master might not consent to this rather playful use of his time. It had to be a full-blooded Negro or the issue would remain clouded, no matter what the outcome. One party or the other might claim that blood mixture altered the case. So it took them a bit of time before they eventually settled on John Chavis. They sent him to Princeton to see what he could do with the curriculum there, and I have often wondered who paid off after he wrote his dissertation in Latin and got his license as a Presbyterian minister.

In the sense of his being a product of the Southern environment and of the Negro's situation, Dick's case is equally clear. He was untouched by the redeeming influences sometimes present on campuses of colleges for Negroes in the region or even in the high schools. His was a total exposure to the callousness and cruelty of the closed society. Despite these odds, however, a delicate sensitivity survived. A major talent began to grow. There is a rumor that he wrote and published a story in a local Negro newspaper before he left Mississippi. He had completed no more than eight grades—such as they were down there at that time. He was so much an American with very deep roots in Southern Negro life that the effort of the Sartre crowd to take Dick over was bound to fail. Although he was definitely influenced by them over a period of two or three years it was not lasting, it really didn't take.

REDDING: I quite agreed. Existentialism is no philosophy that can be made to accommodate the reality of Negro life, and especially—as Dick Wright comprehended it—of Southern Negro life, which was Dick's major theme. Indeed, his only true theme. Involved Dick certainly was, but not as the existentialist is. Dick's involvement engaged his rational faculties rather more than the existentialist philosophy recommends or permits. The instinct to survive in a hostile world is always there, but Dick knew that the Negro's will to survive was sometimes weak, and he knew, moreover—because the reality of Southern Negro life had taught him well—that survival for the Negro depended upon his not making choices, upon his ability to adapt to choices (the will of others) made for him. He hated this, and it certainly had much to do with his expatriating himself; but it had something to do, too, with his early commitment to Communism, and it had everything to do with his later breaking with it—a break which represented at the time an important choice he could make without greatly threatening his existence.

CAYTON: Let me mention another aspect of Dick that I think may be of interest to young writers. Dick, you know, did not have a college education. He didn't have a high school education. In some respects, the first drafts of his manuscripts looked almost illiterate. He had to rewrite his books many times. He rewrote *Native Son*, to my knowledge, at least four or five times. This was his method, and I trace it directly to his lack of formal education.

HILL: But this is true of many writers. There are many who have to write and rewrite—despite a college education.

CAYTON: But Dick's problem was rather elementary, a problem of grammar and the like. He was a genuine self-man man.

The only person I ever met who was a better conversationalist—no, as good a conversationalist—was Sinclair Lewis. Dick read constantly and in many fields. I remember one time I had a tooth pulled in Brooklyn. I was in great pain. Dick and I were riding on the subway, and he was describing the nerve endings. I was quite angry. "How did you learn all this stuff?" I asked. And he said, "Well, there's nothing to it. I just picked up a book on dentistry." Then he went on to describe the functions of the body, and I said, "What are you, a doctor?" He said, "Anybody can be a doctor. You just sit down and read." And I said, "Please shut up, you son of a bitch."

Dick talked to me over a period of five years about a story he was working on. It was about a Negro woman who was just about light enough to pass, but she had bleaching cream, which was supposed to lighten her. This bleaching cream had arsenic in it, so that while she was committing sociological suicide, she was also committing biological suicide. And this is no exaggeration, because Dick actually bought up any number of bleaching creams and had chemical analyses made of them.

But more directly, Dick could move with any group. I remember the time I took him to Marshall Field, III, at that time the fifth most wealthy man in the world. He'd just come into a vast sum of money and Dick and I were going to start a magazine. We entered Field's office, and I must say I was a little intimidated. The man had about $500 million. I looked for Dick to be a little intimidated, too, but here was this little Mississippi Negro sitting up, talking to this white gentleman, and he wasn't intimidated at all.

REDDING: No, I suppose he never was intimidated by people, but certain attitudes could intimidate him. Or maybe that's not the right word. The word is probably daunt, or dismay.

A little while back, Arna, in describing the Wright of the 1930's, used the expression "flaming," I believe it was, and said that he—Dick—was "burning with zeal and enthusiasm"; and this touches upon something I'd like to say, something pertinent. I'll be brief.

Dick did burn with zeal, but it was always zeal for a cause, and he tended to be chary and a little suspicious of people who didn't. He never seemed to believe that an attitude toward life that was lighted by the faintest ray of hedonism could be quite real and legitimate. The gods within him were saturnine, gloomy, of tragic bent. It was not that Dick wanted people to be enthusiastic over his cause of the moment, but he could only just tolerate the indifferent and dispassionate, the come-day, go-day people one is likely to meet in any sizable company, and the people to whom life is a joke, and not an ironic joke. Look at the groups toward which he gravitated in Paris: the existentialist; the black nationalist of *Présence Africaine* (which, incidentally, he helped to found); African exiles; Algerian expatriates, and the like—people with causes which he could embrace with whatever enthusiasm was left over from his own cause. A cause he never realized he abandoned—or did it abandon him?—the moment he took up residence in France.

I think it was this quality of his zeal that accounts for the almost total absence of humor in his books. Dick did not recognize the truly comic. The closest he could come to it was irony. But look at his irony, for heaven's sake! It seldom causes laughter. It is grim, sardonic, and never mirthful. It is the irony of the discovery that the rat-infested, vermin-ridden flat in which Bigger Thomas lives is the property of the "helpful," "generous," "sympathetic" Mr. Dalton. It is the irony of the young Negro who must disguise himself (unman himself!) as a woman in order to get a job, and of his being so completely mistaken for what he is *not* that the consequences, which might have been merely comical, are inevitable. There is instance after instance in Dick's work.

This humorlessness was Dick's greatest flaw, both as an artist and as a man. His best books, like those of Dostoevski and Tolstoi, who were also writers without humor, compensate for it with their moral integrity, their social force, their truth; and I would like to think that *Native Son*, *Black Boy* and a half dozen of Dick's short stories will stand the test of time. But I also think that we're all agreed that less than ten years after the death of the man is too soon for final judgments of the still-living artist.

Ralph Ellison

NIGHTMARE OF A NATIVE SON:
INVISIBLE MAN, BY
RALPH ELLISON*

Jonathan Baumbach

Who knows but that, on the lower frequencies, I speak for
you?
—Invisible Man

I HESITATE to call Ralph Ellison's *Invisible Man* (1952) a Negro novel,
though of course it is written by a Negro and is centrally concerned with
the experiences of a Negro. The appellation is not so much inaccurate as
it is misleading. A novelist treating the invisibility and phantasmagoria of
the Negro's life in this "democracy" is, if he tells the truth, necessarily
writing a very special kind of book. Yet if his novel is interesting only
because of its specialness, he has not violated the surface of his subject;
he has not, after all, been serious. Despite the differences in their external
concerns, Ellison has more in common as a novelist with Joyce, Melville,
Camus, Kafka, West, and Faulkner than he does with other serious Negro
writers like James Baldwin and Richard Wright. To concentrate on the
idiom of a serious novel, no matter how distinctive its peculiarities, is to
depreciate it, to minimize the universality of its implications. Though the
protagonist of *Invisible Man* is a southern Negro, he is, in Ellison's rendering, profoundly all of us.

Despite its obvious social implications, Ellison's novel is a modern
gothic, a Candide-like picaresque set in a dimly familiar nightmare landscape called the United States. Like *The Catcher in the Rye*, *A Member
of the Wedding*, and *The Adventures of Augie March*, Ellison's novel
chronicles a series of initiatory experiences through which its naïve hero
learns, to his disillusion and horror, the way of the world. However, unlike
these other novels of passage, *Invisible Man* takes place, for the most part,
in the uncharted spaces between the conscious and the unconscious, in

* Reprinted from *The Landscape of Nightmare* (New York: New York
University Press, 1965), by permission of the publishers.

73

the semilit darkness where nightmare verges on reality and the external world has all the aspects of a disturbing dream. Refracted by satire, at times, cartooned, Ellison's world is at once surreal and real, comic and tragic, grotesque and normal—our world viewed in its essentials rather than its externals.

The Negro's life in our white land and time is, as Ellison knows it, a relentless unreality, unreal in that the Negro as a group is loved, hated, persecuted, feared, and envied, while as an individual he is unfelt, unheard, unseen—to all intents and purposes invisible. The narrator, who is also the novel's central participant, never identifies himself by name. Though he experiences several changes of identity in the course of the novel, Ellison's hero exists to the reader as a man without an identity, an invisible "I." In taking on a succession of identities, the invisible hero undergoes an increasingly intense succession of disillusioning experiences, each one paralleling and anticipating the one following it. The hero's final loss of illusion forces him underground into the coffin (and womb) of the earth to be either finally buried or finally reborn.

The narrator's grandfather, whom he resembles (identity is one of the major concerns of the novel), is the first to define the terms of existence for him. An apparently meek man all his life, on his deathbed the grandfather reveals:

Son, after I'm gone I want you to keep up the good fight. I never told you, but our life is a war and I have been a traitor all my born days, a spy in the enemy's country ever since I give up my gun back in the Reconstruction. Live with your head in the lion's mouth. I want you to overcome 'em with yesses, undermine 'em with grins, agree 'em to death and destruction, let 'em swoller you till they vomit or bust wide open.[1]

Though at the time he understands his grandfather's ambiguous creed only imperfectly, the hero recognizes that it is somehow his heritage. In a sense, the old man's code of acquiescent resistance is an involved justification of his nonresistance; it is a parody on itself, yet the possibility always remains that it is, in some profound, mysterious way, a meaningful ethic. On a succession of occasions, the hero applies his grandfather's advice, "agreeing 'em to death," in order to understand its import through discovering its efficacy. On each occasion, however, it is he, not " 'em," who is victimized. Consequently, the hero suffers a sense of guilt—not for having compromised himself but for failing somehow to effect his grandfather's ends. Ironically, he also feels guilty for deceiving the white "enemy," though he has "agreed them" not to death or destruction, only to renewed complacency. For example:

[1] Ralph Ellison, *Invisible Man* (New York: New American Library, 1953), p. 19. All quotations are from this edition.

When I was praised for my conduct I felt a guilt that in some way I was doing something that was really against the wishes of the white folks, that if they had understood they would have desired me to act just the opposite, that I should have been sulky and mean, and that really would have been what they wanted, even though they were fooled and thought they wanted me to act as I did. [p. 20]

The hero's cynical obsequiousness has self-destructive consequences. Having delivered a high school graduation speech advocating humility as the essence of progress, he is invited to deliver his agreeable oration to a meeting of the town's leading white citizens. Before he is allowed to speak, however, he is subjected to a series of brutal degradations, which teach him, in effect, the horror of the humility he advocates. In this episode, the first of his initiatory experiences, the invisible man's role is symbolically prophesied. The hero, along with nine other Negro boys, is put into a prize ring, then is blindfolded and coerced into battling his compatriots. Duped by the whites, the Negro unwittingly fights himself; his potency, which the white man envies and fears, is mocked and turned against him to satisfy the brutal whims of his persecutor. That the bout is preceded by a nude, blond belly dancer whom the boys are forced to watch suggests the prurience underlying the victimizer's treatment of his victim. The degrading prizefight, a demonstration of potency to titillate the impotent, in which the Negro boys blindly flail one another to entertain the sexually aroused stag audience, parallels the riot in Harlem at the end of the novel, which is induced by another institution of white civilization, the Brotherhood (a fictional guise for the Communist party). Once again Negro fights against Negro (Ras the Destroyer against the hero), although this time it is for the sake of "Brotherhood," a euphemism for the same inhumanity. In both cases, the Negro unwittingly performs the obscene demands of his enemy. In magnification, Harlem is the prize ring where the Negroes, blindfolded this time by demagoguery, flail at each other with misdirected violence. The context has changed from South to North, from white citizens to the Brotherhood, from a hired ballroom to all of Harlem, but the implication remains the same: the Negro is victimized by having his potency turned against himself by his impotent persecutor.

After the boxing match, what appears to be gold is placed on a rug in the center of the room and the boys are told to scramble for their rewards. The hero reacts: "I trembled with excitement, forgetting my pain. I would get the gold and the bills, I thought. I would use both hands. I would throw my body against the boys nearest me to block them from the gold." [p. 29]

He is, on the rug as in the boxing ring, degraded by self-interest. Though his reaction is unpleasant, it is, given the provocation, the normal, calculable one. He has been tempted and, unaware of any practicable ethical alternative, has succumbed in innocence. When the temptation recurs in more complex guises later in the novel and Ellison's nameless hero as adult falls victim to his self-interest, he is, despite his larger moral purposes, culpable and must assume responsibility for the terrible consequences of his deeds. In each of the various analogous episodes, the hero is torn between his implicit commitment to his grandfather's position—subversive acquiescence—and his will to identify—the primal instinct of self-assertion. Both commitments dictate pragmatic, as opposed to purely ethical, action, with, inevitably, immoral and impractical consequences. The rug becomes electrified, the gold coins turn out to be brass—a means, like the bout, of mocking the Negro's envied potency. That the fight and electrification follow in sequence the naked belly dancer in the course of an evening of stag entertainment for tired white businessmen indicates the obscene prurience behind the white citizen's hatred of the Negro. By debasing and manipulating the Negro's potency, the white mutes its threat and at the same time experiences it vicariously. It is in all a mordant evocation, satiric in its rendering and frightening in its implications. The white man's fascination with the Negro as a source of power (potency) is another of the thematic threads that holds together what might otherwise be a picaresque succession of disparate episodes. The ballroom humiliation serves as a gloss on the following scene, in which the hero is expelled from the Negro state college for, ironically, the consequence of his obedience to a white trustee.

The president of the Negro college, Dr. Bledsoe (all of Ellison's names characterize their bearers), entrusts the hero, up to then a model student, with the responsibility of chauffeuring a philanthropic white trustee, Mr. Norton, on a tour of the manicured country surrounding the campus. Driving aimlessly—or perhaps with more aim than he knows—the hero suddenly discovers that he has taken the trustee to the backwoods homestead of Jim Trueblood, the area's black sheep, an "unenlightened" Negro whose sharecropper existence (and incestuous, child-producing, accident with his daughter) is a source of continued embarrassment to the "progressive" community of the college. The hero would like to leave, but Norton, curiously fascinated by the fact that Trueblood has committed incest (and survived), insists on talking with the sharecropper. At Norton's prodding, Trueblood tells his story, an extended and graphically detailed account of how he was induced by a dream into having physical relations with his daughter. The story itself is a masterpiece of narrative invention and perhaps the single most brilliant scene in the novel.

As Trueblood finishes his story, we discover in a moment of ironic revelation that the bloodless Norton is a kind of euphemistic alter ego—a secret sharer—of the atavistic Trueblood. Earlier, while being driven deeper into the backwoods country—the reality behind the ivy league facade of the college—Norton had rhapsodized to the narrator about the unearthly charms of his own daughter, for whose death he feels unaccountably guilty:

> Her beauty was a well-spring of purest water-of-life, and to look upon her was to drink and drink and drink again. . . . She was rare, a perfect creation, a work of purest art. . . . I found it difficult to believe her my own. . . . I have never forgiven myself. Everything I've done since her passing has been a monument to her memory. [pp. 43–44]

Trueblood, then, has committed the very sin that Norton has, in the dark places of his spirit, impotently coveted. Upon hearing Trueblood's story, Norton participates vicariously in his experience, has his own quiescent desires fulfilled while exempted, since Trueblood has acted for him, from the stigma of the act. Underlying Norton's recurrent platitude that "the Negro is my fate" (he means that they are his potency) is the same prurience that motivates the sadism of the white citizens in the preceding scene. However, in an ironic way, Trueblood *is* Norton's fate. When Trueblood finishes his story, Norton feels compelled to pay him, as the white citizens reward the Negro boxers, in exchange for, in a double sense, having performed for him. When Norton (who exists here really as idea rather than character) leaves Trueblood's farm, he is exhausted and colorless, as if he had in fact just committed incest with his own daughter.

Having exposed Norton to the horror of his own philanthropic motives, after a further misadventure among inmates of a Negro insane asylum, the hero is expelled from school by Bledsoe because "any act that endangered the continuity of the dream is an act of treason." The boy, sensing his innocence, feels haunted by his grandfather's curse. Through Ellison's surrealistic rendering, we sense the nightmare reality of the hero's experience (as we do not with Norton's comparable nightmare):

> How had I come to this? I had kept unswervingly to the path before me, had tried to be exactly what I was expected to be, had done exactly what I was expected to do—yet, instead of winning the expected reward, here I was stumbling along, holding on desperately to one of my eyes in order to keep from bursting out my brain against some familiar object swerved into my path by my distorted vision. And now to drive me wild I felt suddenly that my grandfather was hovering over me, grinning triumphantly out of the dark. [p. 131]

Accepting responsibility for the sins of his innocence, the hero goes to New York, armed with several letters of "identification" which Bledsoe has addressed to various trustees for the ostensible purpose of finding him a job. When the hero discovers that the letters have been written "to hope him to death, and keep him running," that the renowned Negro educator Bledsoe has betrayed him treacherously, has in effect ordered him killed as an almost gratuitous display of power, he experiences a moment of terrible disillusion. At the same time he senses that this betrayal is in some way a reenactment of the past: "Twenty-five years seemed to have lapsed between his handing me the letter and my grasping its message. I could not believe it, yet I had a feeling that it all had happened before. I rubbed my eyes, and they felt sandy as though all the fluids had suddenly dried." [p. 168]

In a way, it *has* happened before; for Bledsoe's act of victimization (the beating of Negro by Negro) is analogous to the punishment the hero received in the prize ring at the hands of the largest of the other Negro boys. Bledsoe's deceit, like its analog, is motivated by the desire to ingratiate himself with the white society which dispenses rewards—which provides, or so he believes, the source of his power.

As one episode parallels another, each vignette in itself has allegorical extensions. Employed by Liberty Paints, a factory "the size of a small city," the narrator is ordered to put ten drops of "black dope" into buckets of optic white paint in order, he is told, to make it whiter. The mixing of the black into the white is, of course, symbolic: the ten drops are analogous to the ten boys in the prize ring, and in each case the white becomes whiter by absorbing the Negro's virility, by using the black to increase the strength of the white. Yet the name "optic white" suggests it is all some kind of visual illusion. When the black dope runs out, the hero as apprentice paint mixer is ordered by his boss, "the terrible Mr. Kimbro," to replace it, without being told which of seven possible vats has the right substance. Left to his own discretion, the hero chooses the wrong black liquid, concentrated paint remover, which makes the white paint transparent and grayish; this act symbolizes the implicit threat of Negro potency left to its own devices. The paint-mixing scene is paralleled by the violence of the insane Negro veterans at the bar (the Golden Day) in which they beat their white attendant Supercargo into grayness and terrorize the already depleted Norton. It anticipates the antiwhite violence of Ras the exhorter-turned-destroyer, the only alternative to invisibility the white man has left the Negro.

Yet there is the illusion of another alternative: when the narrator adds the black drops to the paint which already contains the black remover, though the mixture appears gray to him, it passes for white in Kimbro's eyes. This is, in symbol, the role of subterfuge and infiltration—his grandfather's legacy and curse.

I looked at the painted slab. It appeared the same: a gray tinge glowed through the whiteness, and Kimbro had failed to detect it. I stared for a minute, wondering if I were seeing things, inspected another and another. All were the same, a brilliant white diffused with gray. I closed my eyes for a moment and looked again and still no change. Well, I thought as long as he's satisfied. . . . [p. 180]

Kimbro permits the gray-tinged paint to be shipped out and the hero wonders whether, after all, he has been the deceiver or the deceived. He suspects, when Kimbro dismisses him, that he somehow has been the dupe. That the paint passes for white in Kimbro's eyes suggests that the black with which it was mixed was, like the hero's existence, to all intents and purposes, invisible.

Essentially invisible, the narrator undergoes a succession of superficial changes of identity—in a sense, changes of mask—each entailing a symbolic, though illusory, death and rebirth. Knocked unconscious by the explosion of a machine which makes the base of a white paint, a machine that he was unable to control, the hero is placed in another machine, a coffin-like electrified box, in order to be "started again." The shock treatments sur-realistically rendered recall the electrification from the rug, however magni-fied in intensity. Like most of the episodes in the novel, it is on the surface a comic scene, though in its implications (lobotomy and castration) it is a singularly unpleasant nightmare. The hero's first awareness upon awakening is that he is enclosed in a glass box with an electric cap attached to his head, a combination coffin-womb and electrocutor. When he is blasted with a charge of electricity, he instinctively screams in agonized protest, only to be told in response as if he were indeed a piece of equip-ment, " 'Hush goddamit . . . We're trying to get you started again. Now shut up!' " [p. 203] After a while he is unable to remember who he is or whether he has in fact existed before his present moment of consciousness: "My mind was blank, as though I'd just begun to live." Like the charged rug, though considerably more cruel, the shock treatments are intended to neutralize him, in effect to castrate him. In his moments of confused consciousness he hears two voices arguing over the proper method to treat his case. One is in favor of surgery, the other in favor of the machine.

"The machine will produce the results of a prefrontal lobotomy without the negative effect of the knife," the voice said. "You see, instead of severing the prefrontal lobe, a single lobe, that is, we apply pressure in the proper degrees to the major centers of nerve control—our concept is Gestalt—and the result is as complete a change of personality as you'll find in your famous fairy-tale cases of criminals transformed into amiable fellows after all that bloody business of a brain operation. And what's more," the voice went on trium-phantly, "the patient is both physically and neurally whole."

"But what of his psychology?"

"Absolutely of no importance!" the voice said. "The patient will live as he has to live, with absolute integrity. Who could ask more? He'll experience no major conflict of motives, and what is even better, society will suffer no traumata on his account."

There was a pause. A pen scratched upon paper. Then, "Why not castration doctor?" a voice asked waggishly, causing me to start, a pain tearing through me.

"There goes your love of blood again," the first voice laughed. "What's that definition of a surgeon, 'A butcher with a bad conscience'?"

They laughed. [pp. 206–207]

I quote this passage at length to suggest the high-voltage charge of Ellison's satire, capable at once of being mordantly comic and profoundly terrifying. The clinical attitude of the psychologist ("society will suffer no traumata on his account") suggests the northern white position toward the Negro, as opposed to the butcher-surgeon who represents the more overtly violent southern position. The ends of both, however, are approximately the same —emasculation; the difference is essentially one of means.

The narrator is, in this scene, almost visibly invisible, discussed impersonally in his presence as if he were not there. When he is unable to recall his name, his mother's name, any form of his identity, any form of his past, the doctors seem pleased and deliver him from the machine, the only mother he knows.

I felt a tug at my belly and looked down to see one of the physicians pull the cord which was attached to the stomach node, jerking me forward. . . .

"Get the shears," he said. "Let's not waste time."

"Sure," the other said. "Let's not waste time."

I recoiled inwardly as though the cord were part of me. Then they had it free and the nurse clipped through the belly band and removed the heavy node. [p. 213]

In describing the birth from the machine, Ellison suggests through evocation that it is also a kind of castration. Insofar as it leaves the hero without the potency of self, it is, in implication, just that.

Aside from the Prologue and parts of the Epilogue, which have an enlightened madness all their own, the experience of the machine birth is the least realistic, the most surrealistic, in the novel. And this brings us to what I think is the novel's crucial flaw, its inconsistency of method, its often violent transformations from a kind of detailed surface realism in which probability is limited to the context of ordinary, everyday experiences to an allegorical world of almost endless imaginative possibilities. Often the shift is dramatically effective, as when the hero and Norton enter the insane world of the Golden Day (here the truth is illuminated by a nominal madman who has the insane virtue of pure sight) and Norton is forced into a frightening moment of self-recognition. On other occasions, the visional shifts jar us away from the novel's amazing world into an awareness of the ingenuity of its creator. Since Ellison is at once prodigiously talented and prodigiously reckless, *Invisible Man* is astonishingly good at its best. By the same token the book is uneven; on occasion it is very bad as only very good novels can be. Given the nature of his vision, Ellison's world seems real—or alive—when it is surrealistically distorted, and for the most part made-up or abstract—when it imitates the real world. Largely recounted in the manner of traditional realism, the hero's adventures in the Brotherhood up until the Harlem riot constitute the least interesting section of the novel.

In joining the Brotherhood, the narrator gives up his past to assume a new identity or rather new nonidentity, Brother ————. Because of his remarkable speech-making abilities, as well as his conscious ambition to be some kind of savior, he becomes one of the leading figures of the Harlem Brotherhood. Finally, his controversial activities make it necessary for him to disguise himself in order to get through Harlem safely. Brother ————'s disguise—dark glasses and a wide-brimmed hat—which he has hoped would make him inconspicuous in Harlem, creates for him still another identity, which is, in effect, just a new aspect of nonidentity. Wearing the hat and glasses, Brother ———— is unrecognized as his Brotherhood self, but is mistaken for a man named Rinehart, a charlatan of incredible diversification. Rinehart, whose identities include numbers runner, police briber, lover, pimp, and Reverend, is, the hero discovers, a kind of alter ego to his invisibility. If you are no one, you are at the same time potentially everyone. The hero has disguised himself in order to avoid the consequences of his acts and instead finds himself held responsible for Rinehart's inordinate sins—for all sins—which are, in the Dostoevskian sense, his own. When the Brotherhood's theoretician Hambro informs the hero that, with the alteration of the larger plan, his role has changed from exhorter to pacifier, he senses his likeness to his dazzling alter ego:

". . . Besides I'd feel like Rinehart. . . ." It slipped out and he looked at me.
   "Like who?"
   "Like a charlatan," I said.
   Hambro laughed. "I thought you learned about that, Brother."
   I looked at him quickly. "Learned what?"
   "That it's impossible *not* to take advantage of the people."
   "That's Rinehartism—cynicism. . . . " [p. 436]

In following the dictates of the Brotherhood, the hero has hurt, he discovers to his pain, the very people he has intended to help. Without benefit of glasses and hat, he has been a Rinehart in disguise all the time. He has been, paradoxically, an unwitting cynic. Duped by his self-conscious, romantic ambitions to be another Booker T. Washington, the hero has let the Brotherhood use him for their cynical "historic" purposes. As a Brotherhood agent, he demagogically incites the Harlem Negroes to potential action only to leave them prey to the misdirected violence of Ras, their violence ultimately turned, like that of the boys in the prize ring, against themselves. With awareness comes responsibility, and the hero recognizes that he alone must bear the guilt for the Brotherhood's betrayal of the Negro. The ramifications of his awful responsibility are manifested generally in the hellish Harlem riot at the end of the novel and particularly in the disillusion and death of the most admirable of the Brotherhood, Tod Clifton (the name suggests a kind of Promethean entrapment), whose career prophesies and parallels that of the hero.

Earlier in the novel, Ras, after sparing Tod's life, has exhorted his adversary to leave the Brotherhood and join his racist movement (a fictionalized version of the Black Muslims). Their confrontation, an objectification of the hero's interior struggle, anticipates Tod's defection from the Brotherhood.

"Come with us, mahn. We build a glorious movement of black people. *Black people!* What do they do, give you money? who wahnt the damn stuff? Their money bleed black blood, mahn. It's unclean! Taking their money is shit, mahn. Money without dignity—that's *bahd* shit!"

Clifton lunged toward him. I held him, shaking my head. "Come on, the man's crazy," I said, pulling on his arm.

Ras struck his thighs with his fists. "Me crazy, mahn? You call me crazy? Look at you two and look at me—is this sanity? Standing here in three shades of blackness! Three black men fighting in the street because of the white enslaver? Is that sanity? Is that consciousness, scientific understanding? Is that the modern black mahn of the twentieth century? Hell, mahn! Is it self-respect—black against black? What they give you to betray—their women? You fall for that?"

"Let's go," I repeated. He stood there, looking.

"Sure, you go," Ras said, "but not him. You contahminated but he the real black mahn. In Africa this mahn be a chief, a black king!" [pp. 322–23]

In this eloquent scene, Clifton finally rejects Ras, but he is undeniably moved by his enemy's crude exhortation. Ras—the name suggests an amalgam of race and rash—is a fanatic, but given his basic premise, that the white man is the Negro's natural enemy, his arguments are not easily refutable. Unable to answer Ras, Clifton, out of a sense of shame or guilt, knocks the Exhorter down, committing an act of Rasian violence. The punch is an acknowledgment, a communion, an act of love. As they leave, the hero discovers that Clifton has tears in his eyes. Clifton says, referring to Ras, " 'That poor misguided son of a bitch.' 'He thinks a lot of you, too,' I said." [p. 326]

Clifton is sympathetic to Ras's motives, but he is nevertheless too civilized to accept his methods. The Brotherhood, then, with its cant of "historic necessity," represents to Clifton the enlightened alternative to racist violence through which the Negro can effect his protest. Entrapped by the Brotherhood through the commitment imposed by his integrity, Clifton becomes, even more than the narrator, a victim of the Brotherhood's betrayal. Like the implicit suicide of Conrad's Lord Jim, Clifton's death (he provokes a policeman into shooting him) is a sacrifice to a culpability too egregious to be redeemed in any other way, and, at the same time, a final if gratuitous act of heroism. In giving himself up to be murdered, Clifton takes on the whole responsibility for the Brotherhood's betrayal of the Negro. If by his sacrifice he does not redeem the hero from his own culpability, he at least through his example sets up the possibility of Brother ———'s redemption. If the various characters with whom the "invisible" hero is confronted represent possible states of being, Clifton symbolizes the nearest thing to an idea.

Clifton's death, because it permits the hero to organize the Negroes around a common cause (the narrator's funeral oration is a magnificent parody of Antony's), is potentially an agent of good, for Clifton can be considered in a meaningful sense a sacrifice. However, even that is denied him. At the last minute the Brotherhood withdraws its support from the hero, and, left to their own devices and the exhortation of Ras, the aroused Negroes perform arbitrary acts of plunder and violence. That Clifton's death initiates the Harlem riots, which serve the Brotherhood's new purpose of pacifying the Negro by exhausting his hate-charged energies in meaningless self-conflict, is a last terrible mockery of his decent intentions.

In hawking the chauvinistic "Sambo dolls" which dance at the tug of an invisible string, Clifton was not so much mocking the Brotherhood's attitude toward the Negro as he was parodying himself. His own comment about Ras suggests in a way the impulse of his nihilistic act:

"I don't know," he said. "I suppose sometimes a man *has* to plunge outside history. . . ."
"What?"
"Plunge outside, turn his back. . . . Otherwise, he might kill somebody, go nuts." [p. 328]

Deceived by the bogus historians of the Brotherhood, Clifton has "plunged outside history," though in punching the white policeman he demonstrated that he had not quite "turned his back." As an alternative

to violent reprisal—Clifton was an essentially gentle man racked by rage—
he became a heckler of the Brotherhood, of the Negro, of the white man's
treatment of the Negro, of himself, of the universe. Though he is one of
the few noble characters in Ellison's world, his destruction is less than
tragic. A man of tragic stature, Clifton is a captive participant in an absurd world which derogates him and mocks the significance of his death
as it did his life. Clifton's sacrificial act, its intention perverted, is mostly
invisible. The others of the Brotherhood—Wrestrum (rest room), Tobitt
(two bit), Jack (money, masturbation)—who in their commitment to
"science" have become as dehumanized and corrupt as those they oppose,
survive the shift in tactical policy.

When the hero discovers that it is through him that the Brotherhood
has betrayed Clifton, he feels responsible for his friend's death. Earlier,
in outrage he spat at one of Clifton's dancing puppets, knocking it "lifeless," performing symbolically what the policeman does actually—the
murder of Clifton. When the hero knocks over the doll, an outsider
laughs at what he thinks is the likeness between the spitter and the spat-on
doll. Just as Clifton in selling the obscene doll has been mocking himself,
the hero in spitting at the doll has been attacking himself as well as
Clifton, though without benefit of awareness. Only after his showdown
with the Brotherhood, and even then incompletely, does the hero become aware that he has been performing all along as if he were, in life size,
the dancing puppet doll.

At his moment of greatest self-awareness, the hero suffers his most
intense sense of guilt. Watching two nuns in the subway (one black, one
white), he remembers a ritual verse he had once heard.

> Bread and wine,
> Bread and wine,
>   Your cross ain't nearly so
>   Heavy as mine. . . . [p. 382]

The rhyme comes to him as an automatic response, its singsong at first
overriding its sense. Momentarily, almost without awareness, as the pain
of wound travels from flesh to brain, he comes to assume its implications.
As he watches some Negroes maltreat a white shopkeeper, he experiences
a terrible revelation:

A pressure of guilt came over me. I stood on the edge of the walk watching
the crowd threatening to attack the man until a policeman appeared and dis-
persed them. And although I knew no one could do much about it, I felt
responsible. All our work had been very little, no great change had been made.
And it was all my fault. I'd been so fascinated by the motion that I'd forgotten to measure what it was bringing forth. I'd been asleep, dreaming.
[p. 384]

A sleepwalker in a world never real enough for him to believe in, the hero experiences a succession of awakenings, only to find himself participating in still another level of nightmare. In accepting Clifton's role as martyr-saint, in taking on the responsibility for all of Harlem, all of Brotherhood, in extension, *all*, he succeeds only in setting himself up for a final, self-destroying victimization. Aware of the futility of all his past acts and, in implication, all acts in the absurd context of his world, the hero commits an act of meaningless violence. Entrapped by a situation for which he is at least partly responsible, with his neck quite literally at stake (Ras wants to hang him), he impales the demonic innocent, Ras, through the jaw with his own spear.

That Jack, the leader of the Brotherhood, has one eye (as earlier the euphemistic preacher Barbee is revealed as blind) is symbolic of the distorted perspective of the Brotherhood's "scientifically objective view" of society, in which the human being is a casual puppet in the service of the "historic" strings that manipulate him. Clifton makes only *paper* Negroes dance; it is Jack and Tobitt who treat flesh-and-blood Negroes as if they were puppet Sambo dolls. (By having Clifton charge a "brotherly two bits" for the puppet dolls, Ellison, through suggestion, transfers the onus of traitor to Tobitt and in extension to the Brotherhood itself.) When the hero discovers that the Brotherhood has betrayed him, he consciously resolves to impersonate the puppet doll he has so long mimicked unwittingly—to, as his grandfather advised, "overcome 'em with yeses . . . agree 'em to death and destruction." For all his Rinehartian machinations, he manages, however, only to abet the scheme of the Brotherhood.

Seeking redemption from his compounded guilt, he is sucked into the maelstrom of the Harlem riot for which he suffers a sense of limitless, unreclaimable responsibility. He realizes that "By pretending to agree I had indeed agreed, had made myself responsible for that huddled form lighted by flame and gunfire in the street, and all others whom now the night was making ripe for death." [p. 478] The flaming buildings and streets, the burnt tar stench, the black figures moving shadowlike through the eerily illumined night become an evocation of Hell, a mirror for the hero's raging interior guilt. At the center of the riot—at the very seat of Hell—he experiences the deaths of his various corrupted identities, shedding the false skins to get at the pure invisibility underneath. As Ras approaches, the hero searches for his "Rineharts," his dark glasses, only to "see the crushed lenses fall to the street. 'Rinehart, I thought, Rinehart!' " as if he had just witnessed Rinehart himself—his Rinehart self—collapse in death before him. To propitiate Ras and stop the riots, the hero disavows allegiance to the Brotherhood, killing in effect his Brotherhood self. But as he is invisible, he is unheard, his words as always not communicating his meanings. Struck by the absurdity of the demonic Ras on horseback, of the senseless pillage and murder around him, and, after all, of existence itself, the hero is for the moment willing to relinquish his life if it will make the white man see him and consequently see himself. But the example of Clifton's meaningless sacrifice dissuades him. The hero, faced with death, decides that it is "better to live out one's own absurdity than to die for that of others, whether for Ras's or Jack's." When in self-protection he impales Ras, who is in a sense the deepest of his identities, he experiences the illusion of death and rebirth: "It was as though for a moment I had surrendered my life and begun to live again." [p. 484]

Newly baptized by an exploded water main, like the birth from the machine, a somewhat illusory (and comic) resurrection, the hero seeks to return to Mary, his ex-landlady, who has become a symbolic mother to him. But as he is unable to imitate Christ, he is unable to reach Mary. Instead, chased by two white looters, he falls through an open manhole. Unable to find the exit to his coffinlike cell, he burns various papers of his past (high school diploma, Sambo doll, Brotherhood card) for torches to light his way out, only to discover in a moment of terrible realization that the Jacks and Nortons have left him no exit, that without his paper symbols he has no past and consequently no home, no identity. With this knowledge he relaxes in the carrion comfort of his dank hole, having returned at last to the womb of the earth. It is, as he puts it, a "death alive," from which emergence will be rebirth, his victimization transcended, his guilt perhaps purged, his soul if possible redeemed. A nonparticipant in existence, an invisible man by choice, the hero continues to live in his private cellar, which he has illumined by 1,369 lights (a symbolic attempt at transcending his invisibility—at seeing himself), the electricity supplied gratuitously in spite of themselves by Monopolated Light and Power. As the whites had mocked his potency and used it for their own ends, he is now paying them back in kind. Though he is protected from the pain of disillusion while isolated from the brutal, absurd world he hates and, in spite of himself, loves, the hero plans some day to emerge into the outside world because, a son of God and man, one of us, he is willing to believe that "even the invisible victim is responsible for the fate of all." [p. 487]

Much of the experience in Ellison's novel is externally imposed; that is, each scene, through allusive reference, is made to carry a burden of implication beyond that generated by its particular experience. Consequently the weight of the novel, its profound moral seriousness, resides primarily in conception rather than rendering. Given the problem of transforming large abstractions into evocative experiences, Ellison is nevertheless able more often than not to create occasions resonant enough to accommodate his allegorical purposes. Finally, one senses that the novel, for all its picaresque variety of incident, has a curiously static quality. This is not because the episodes are the same or even similar—on the contrary, one is compelled to admire the range and resourcefulness of Ellison's imaginative constructions—but because they are all extensions of the same externally imposed idea; they all *mean* approximately the same thing.

Like so many of our serious writers, Ellison is not prolific. It took him, by his own testimony, some seven years to write *Invisible Man,* and now eleven years after its publication his second novel is still not completed. If Ellison's reputation had to rest, as it does at the time of this writing, on his one impressive if uneven novel, *Invisible Man* is, I suspect, vital and profound enough to survive its faults—to endure the erosions of time. As a satirist and surrealist, Ellison excels among his contemporaries and can bear comparison with his mentors—Kafka, Joyce, and Faulkner. As a realist, he is less adept: talky, didactic, even at times, if the term is possible for so otherwise exciting a writer, tedious. For all that, Ellison has written a major novel, perhaps one of the three or four most considerable American novels of the past two decades.

An excerpt from his forthcoming novel, "And Hickman Arrives," published in the first issue of *The Noble Savage,* exhibits some of the same evangelical rhetoric that gives *Invisible Man* its terrible impact. Still, it is idle from a fifty-page fragment to prophesy what kind of novel it will make. Moreover, "And Hickman Arrives" has many of the damaging excesses of the first novel. Ellison has a penchant for letting good things go on past their maximum effectiveness. Yet his excesses are also his strength; like Faulkner before him, Ellison is a writer of amazing verbal energy and at his best he creates experiences that touch our deepest selves, that haunt us with the suffocating wisdom of nightmare. American novelists have often had a predilection for large, protracted books, as if great length were a virtue in itself. Ellison is no exception. However, he is one of the few novelists on the scene today who seems capable of producing a large, serious novel, justified by the size of its experience and the depth of its informing intelligence. On the lowest (and highest) frequencies, he speaks for us.

RALPH ELLISON'S *INVISIBLE MAN**

Marcus Klein

RAPLH ELLISON's invisible man speaks first of all for himself, a Negro whose career, because he is a Negro, has been a search for a primary, existential sense of himself. The existential question, as a critic says, "lies waiting around the corner for any introspective person, but it straddles the main highway for a thoughtful Negro." [1] And despite the statement of faith with which *Invisible Man* ends, that the hero can accomplish visibility, this invisible man speaks in the conviction of utter failure.

In fact, the only way in which he might exist is in an enormous act of vengeance, a mechanics which Bigger Thomas had discovered before him. But the world is nothing so simple for him as it was for Bigger. Simple murder won't do, and anyway he sees the contradiction in vengeance. He accomplishes revenge and existence only at a remove, in a nightmare underground. He is removed into nightmare not because it may be that in the ordinary ways of being, men are inevitably determined, nor because there may be no such thing as the existential self, nor because the gratuitous act may be really gratuitous and without sense except in dreams. That would be certainly to open the universal theme. And he is condemned not because of cowardice or lack of maturity—despite the fact Ellison has once commented on his hero's "refusal to run the risk of his own humanity, which involves guilt." [2] He is not a coward and he is very little guilty. And he is thrust into a nightmare not, despite the fact that Ellison has said it, because the frustration of identity is pe-

[1] F. Cudworth Flint, "Fiction Chronicle," *Sewanee Review*, LXII (Winter, 1954), 176.

[2] Ralph Ellison in an interview by Alfred Chester and Vilma Howard in *Paris Review*, No. 8 (Spring, 1955), p. 68. See also Ellison's statement to Rochelle Girson ("Sidelights on Invisibility," *Saturday Review*, XXXVI [March 14, 1953], 49): "Invisibility has to do with the failure of most of us to regard the individual we contact as a human being. . . . On the other hand, you have the failure of the individual to exert himself to be mature, to run the risk of humanity. . . ."

* Reprinted from Marcus Klein, "Ralph Ellison," *After Alienation* (Cleveland and New York: World Publishing Company, 1964), pp. 71–146, by permission of the publisher.

culiarly the American theme. He is condemned first of all because he is black. The novel is glued to the fact. . . .

Out of the world and apart from ordinary defined experience is just where, in fact, the hero of the novel always finds himself. The large action of *Invisible Man* is all a circular voyage, consisting of four prominent adventures. It begins with a ritual of the hero's initiation, a test of his bravery, of his knowledge of caste, and of his sexuality, and it ends in failure, with the hero castrated, presented with proofs of his cowardice and ignorance, in a condition prior to his initiation. He is at the end back in the underworld from which he had tried to emerge, with this difference only, that he has illuminated his underworld and he now knows where he is.

That is the great irony the novel deliberately plays on itself—the world moves, the hero tells us in almost the first words of the Prologue, not like an arrow, nor in a spiral, but like a boomerang; his end, he says, is in his beginning. And it should be said immediately, the novel's great fault is in the fact that its end *is* its beginning. The novel is a furious picaresque which plunges the hero forward through a series of violences. Moreover, it is *all* an initiation rite. The hero moves from childhood to the age of manhood, and from the South to the North, and he is one of those heroes who move from the provinces to the capital, to the center of power, from innocence to experience. He moves, moreover, through what seems at all points a linear exploration of the "Negro problem," through ideologies by which it might be approached, and beyond that, through what one of the symbolic structures of the novel suggests is an exploration of some one hundred years of American history. But for all that multiplicity of parallel actions, the novel has no real progress except that at each stage it clarifies and reinforces the hero's dilemma.

" 'Ah,' I can hear you say," the hero says in almost the last words of the Epilogue,

"so it was all a build-up to bore us with his buggy jiving. He only wanted us to listen to him rave!" But only partially true: Being invisible and without substance, a disembodied voice, as it were, what else could I do? What else but try to tell you what was really happening when your eyes were looking through?

But the witness is not here being responsive to the witness against him. This appeal is a last-ditch attempt to rescue the book from what must have seemed to Ellison its strategic error. The amount of clarity the novel finally comes to is enormous, and so much clarity is shocking, but still it is a clarity without any further effect. The novel doesn't finally go anywhere.

It is a fault that apparently led Ellison to the desperate, empty, un-reasonable, and programmatic optimism of the last few pages of the novel: ". . . we [Negroes] were to affirm the principle on which the coun-try was built. . . ." We "were linked to all others in the loud, clamoring semi-visible world. . . ." "I've overstayed my hibernation, since there's a possibility that even an invisible man has a socially responsible role to play." One asks this hero how he is to come out and be socially re-sponsible? Upon what ground in reality can he affirm *any* positive principle? Just what is he going to do? Everything in the novel has clarified this point: that the bizarre accident that has led him to take up residence in an abandoned coal cellar is no accident at all, that the underworld is his in-evitable home, that given the social facts of America, both invisibility and what he now calls his "hibernation" are his permanent condition. And really his only extension into the upper world can be in negative acts and fantasies of vengeance—which do indeed make up another ending to the novel.

And it is just another consequence of its circularity that *Invisible Man* has many endings. The novel sets out to gain clarity but no new dis-covery. Its ending is in its beginning. Therefore, with every gain in illumination, the novel concludes. There is a constant increase of wattage, but what is to be seen remains the same. And then the consequence of that fact is that—except in the Prologue and the Epilogue to the novel, where the hero speaks in time present and out of all his experience—the hero is fitted with a perceptiveness that is far inferior to Ellison's. Or, if not always, that becomes a fault. He is sometimes an *ingénu*, sometimes a naïve Gulliver when gullibility should be impossible, sometimes, suddenly, the author. There is a constant struggle between the two, Ellison strain-ing not to let his protagonist know too much because that will give the book away, and sometimes failing. And finally the consequence of this latter fact is that a great deal of the novel is in a great density of symbols and puns. They don't, as the danger is, clog the action. They do contain the material. But they don't always contribute to the material. Because the hero can't know too much, because every discovery risks being the last discovery, because Ellison knows very well what each of his hero's experiences comes to, much of the hero's experience is converted into tantalizing hieroglyphics. The puns, which should be devices of com-pression, mount on each other and, like the major episodes of the novel, they tend each of them to tell the same and the whole story.

But then if at the end Ellison cops a plea—"what else could I do? What else but try to tell you what was really happening when your eyes were looking through?"—his plea is in every way valid. The novel's task is just the perception of obvious, repeated facts which no one sees. The task itself must be constantly emphasized and repeated in a great variety of ironic symbols, because that is a dramatic necessity in the nature of the task. The repetition is the proof that the task is authentic. The hero is first a high-school boy in a Southern town, then a college student at a Negro university, then, briefly, a laborer in a Northern factory, then a leader in what in the novel is called the Brotherhood, and finally an underground man. That is his whole story, all of it devoted to one struggle which is perpetual and obsessive because all his experience does really come to the same thing, an unremitting and fruitless attempt to achieve visibility. The book is filled by a lifetime of events, all of them leading back to the same meaning.

So in the Prologue, speaking of his invisibility in his coal cellar, the hero says he needs light because without it he is not only invisible but formless, and it is part of the joke he intends that he is, what someone calls him later, a nigger in a coal pile, that black can't be seen in the dark. The obvious is not obvious. The need is for illumination. And a series of leaders with whom the hero becomes engaged and who promise perception turn out to be blind. A Negro minister at his college, the Reverend Homer (Blind Homer) A. Barbee, preaches a sermon of hope, faith, and endurance, and falls flat on his face. Brother Jack, the local leader of the Brotherhood, sees salvation in the dialectic of historical necessity and can't see a thing because he has a glass eye, just because he has given his eye to the Brotherhood's vision. The Founder of the hero's Negro college, a great leader of his people and a thin disguise for the hero's first hero, Booker T. Washington, is presented to him first in an ambiguous statue in which the Founder is either lifting a veil from the face of a slave or lowering it.

And the task the novel sets for itself, perception of the obvious that is not seen, is reiterated in constant talk and punning, which jumps out everywhere, on eyes, vision, and visions. The hero is troubled by a burning eye within. His one current friend, in the Prologue, time present, is "a junk man I know, a man of vision," who has supplied him with wire and sockets with which to illuminate his underground—the double joke in that being that electricity is light and power and therefore vision, and that a "junk man" is a narcotics peddler, one who has visions to sell. A moment later in a marijuana sleep the hero has his first, this time surreal, vision of the facts of Negro experience. And there is more around every corner. All the novel's purpose is reiterated constantly, in fact, as its basic metaphor is elaborated: the hero is invisible because no one sees him, and it is the function of every episode to confirm the fact that this black man is condemned to a hopeless struggle to be seen.

The hero's end, then, is in his beginning. Quite literally. The novel happens between the Prologue and the Epilogue and those episodes constitute a single dramatic action: the hero, now, in his cellar, is doing sums in his career, writing his memoirs. And except for its burst of optimism, the Epilogue goes nowhere that the Prologue hasn't already been.[3] The novel, apparently, owes much to *Notes from the Underground*, and not least an ending that it does not clearly earn. Moreover, between the Prologue and the Epilogue, the novel moves in a series of circles—concentric planes of meaning, each traveling right back to its beginning, each mode of adventure confirming the circularity of the hero's voyaging. Each adventure is itself a repetition of each of the others and all the hero's experiences come to the same thing, but from a variety of ways of experiencing. His adventures are of a political order, and then they also have personal significances for him, having to do with his search for a personal identity, and then they are historical, marking a journey through a history of America since Emancipation which comes out where it entered, and finally they are adventures in a metaphysics, and each plane of adventuring rounds back to where it began.

It all began, the hero says, with his grandfather, an odd old guy. He has been told he takes after him. On his deathbed his grandfather had passed on advice which, the hero says, has become a curse.

Son, after I'm gone I want you to keep up the good fight. I never told you, but our life is a war and I have been a traitor all my born days, a spy in the enemy's country ever since I give up my gun back in the Reconstruction. Live with your head in the lion's mouth. I want you to overcome 'em with yesses, undermine 'em with grins, agree 'em to death and destruction, let 'em swoller you till they vomit or bust wide open.

By the end of the novel the hero comes to see in his grandfather's "Yes" a greater affirmation than anything in the novel suggests his grandfather meant. He discovers in it assent to the great principles on which the country was built. But in any event, between the beginning and the ending, his grandfather's riddle defines his every gambit. The grandfather's incantatory phrases contain, Ellison has said, "a rejection of a current code and a denial become metaphysical." The hero is set earnestly to wish his way out of the curse, and the curse composes his being, his actions, and his purpose. He comes to each adventure saying Yes and he learns, or in every adventure but the last he almost learns, at the same time to say No. In the last adventure he goes underground, and it is one of the many puns brought together in that development that his "underground" is a post of constant subversion.

Between, then, his grandfather's curse in the beginning and his acceptance of it in the Epilogue, the novel moves the hero through ad-

[3] Ellison says that he wrote the Prologue after he had finished the action proper of the novel.

ventures in the typical ways Negroes and whites manage, or don't manage, to live together in America. He is moved in each case to the point where all relationships disappear in an explosion, from the way of the caste system of a Southern town to that of the subtler caste system of the Negro college created and endowed by whites, the caste inherent in latter-day abolition, to that of the factory in the industrial North, to that of the dogmatic brotherliness of the Brotherhood, finally to the ultimate extension of all these ways: the race riot with which the action proper of the novel ends. And the issue of each of these adventures is a race riot of one dimension or another, and that is the point of them all. An earnest, yea-saying young man reluctant to be a saboteur explores the typical relationships between Negroes and whites and finds them charged with incipient violence, needing but the slightest accident to set them off. The hero moves from one episode to another because in every one an accident happens.

The accident is always just a slight and unavoidable lapse from the propriety he struggles to maintain. In the first episode he delivers his high-school valedictory address. It is a speech on the proper subject—humility is the secret and the essence of progress for the Negro—addressed to the Southern town's most prominent white citizens, who are drunk at this moment and who pay no attention to him. Benumbed by the noise, the smoke, and the reek of the stag dinner for which he is a part of the entertainment, he speaks the words "social equality" for "social responsibility," and by his slip he springs from the crowd a moment of sudden, terrifying silence. In this moment of his triumph, he is crowded suddenly back into the dark, the dark from which, by his academic prowess and his show of humility, he has thought to escape. Humility is not a technique of progress, but the means of his subjugation, and he dare not *not* be humble. That is something his grandfather had known.

At college, next, with all proper respect he chauffeurs a visiting Northern trustee, Mr. Norton. He takes Mr. Norton to a place Mr. Norton wants to visit, the cabin of a local sharecropper, and discovers himself in a double accident. The sharecropper tells a story of incest and Mr. Norton suffers a heart attack. Still properly deferential, the hero takes Mr. Norton to a local saloon, which unfortunately this day is entertaining the Negro veterans from the local madhouse, and he deposits him into the middle of a riot. The adventure ends with his being expelled from college because, so the college president tells him, he has actually obeyed the wishes of a white man and not merely seemed to. Then in the North, as a laborerer in a paint factory, he stumbles into a union meeting and, earnest to please everyone, he finds that because he is a Negro, he is a scab, and as such a catalyst to violence. Then as a favored recruit in the Brotherhood, he takes a single step on his own authority: he organizes a public funeral for a Brother shot by the police, which results in the riot in Harlem that is his last adventure. It is his one lucky accident that in that riot he tumbles into an open manhole, leading to his coal cellar.

The lesson in his accidents is, of course, the instability in all typical relationships between Negroes and whites in America, and the impossibility for a Negro of propriety enough. There is always a boomerang somewhere. Beyond that, these accidents function to reveal to the hero that he is not a person in his relations with whites, but a role, and furthermore they serve to reveal to him the kind of role he plays. It is always the same. The end of the novel is finally his ironic acceptance of his role along with his acceptance of his grandfather's curse.

His whole fate is present, though the hero is not allowed to know it, in that first adventure the climax of which is his dreadful slip of the tongue. A great part of the novel, indeed, is in that initial episode. What is revealed here is what is going to be revealed to the hero, in different circumstances, but with not much modification, in his every subsequent adventure.

In fact, in this first adventure he is clearly threatened but not actually punished for his slip of the tongue. The townsmen allow him to continue his speech, on the condition that he never forget his place. But it is his place, precisely, that the episode fixes. The scene of the speech which the hero supposes to be his valediction is itself a race riot. With some of his schoolmates, he has been made to participate in a prior entertainment for this town smoker. He and his friends are to stage a battle royal.

We were a small tight group, clustered together, our bare upper bodies touching and shining with anticipatory sweat; while up front the big shots were becoming increasingly excited over something we still could not see. Suddenly I heard the school superintendent, who had told me to come, yell, "Bring up the shines, gentlemen! Bring up the little shines!"

They are herded before a magnificent, stark-naked blonde, and threatened if they look and threatened by the crowd if they don't. They are held there, made to suffer sexual embarrassment becoming sexual torture, and made to participate then vicariously in the lurching obscenities of the town's ranking citizens. They are goaded, threatened, tantalized, tickled, promised money, beaten, degraded and insulted, worked to the hysteria which is that of their audience, and then thrown blindfold into their battle royal where, in blind passion, they punch and kick at each other while the white mob howls around them. After the battle, at the end of their strength, they are forced to another frenzy by being made to scramble for coins on an electrified rug.

It is to this crapulous mob, in this coliseum, that the hero then talks about "social equality." The episode is a sustained orgy. It not only mocks the hero's earnest dogma of pacific humility, and it not only baptizes him in the terror that, he will find, lurks in all adventures of Negroes among American whites. There is no telling what craziness and what brutish violence lie at any next step. More than that, the episode concentrates, brilliantly, and it exposes at the pitch of a ritualistic frenzy the interior facts of caste, not only its mechanism of economic exploitation (the hero tries to make a deal with one of his schoolmates and is rebuffed, division has been effectively imposed upon them), but all its deeper exploitation of the Negro as a ritualistic scapegoat.

The hero is not only discriminated against. The politics of this system goes much deeper. In fact, he is coddled by that white man, the school superintendent, who has most immediate authority over him—the school superintendent presents him for his speech with a pat on the back, a brief case, and a scholarship. He and his schoolmates are not without honor. These whites use them in ways curiously like love. It is the function of this caste system to suppress a great deal more than the Negro, and it is the lesson of this episode that these Negroes incarnate for these whites everything that they suppress. The Negroes are made by them into the bacchants they themselves dare not be. They are made agents of, and at the same time sacrifices to, the forbidden, everything that is dark, their irrational craving for cruelty, their greed and their sex and their itch for self-destruction, the swoon of the id. These Negroes become for them, then, underground men, irrational, sinful, Satanic, the embodiment of the urgent dark, the pressing power of blackness. And beyond that, they act out for them the whole violent struggle for civilization, by first becoming the dark powers and then by exorcising themselves in violent self-punishment. And then again, in a way to triple the irony, in the same moment the Negroes justify the usage that has in the first place made them scapegoats by performing the whole of this ritual for money.

The battle royal is an extraordinarily compressed piece of work, and its one fault is that it is both more intensely maintained and more exhaustive than anything else in the novel, and so the hero's adventures hereafter become more or less adequate echoes of it. But in any event it does contain, both in its significances and in its form, the most of the hero's career. The same chaos of appetites and guilt that is the real, hidden nature of Negro and white relations is exploded at the hero in each of his subsequent accidents.

That same chaos is what is revealed in the double accident of the Mr. Norton episode. The sharecropper, upon command, *lures* Mr. Norton to a heart attack. His story of incest has a truth of blood in it—his name is Trueblood—a truth that Mr. Norton, a New England gentleman and a latter-day, declined Calvinist, cannot in any other way accept. He is fascinated, as it were, into a heart attack which is the equivalent of the townsmen's orgiastic smoker. Trueblood plays out the amoral role assigned to the Negro boys of the battle royal. He does what Norton cannot do. His incest has been with his daughter, and Norton, too, has a daughter. " 'You did and are unharmed!' " Norton shouts. " 'You have looked upon chaos and are not destroyed!' " He acts out a scapegoat ritual with Trueblood and then he gives Trueblood money. Trueblood has done him some service. And the saloon episode contains the same implications, only now reversed: the Negroes use Norton for their purposes of vengeance. When he enters, the madmen go mad, and overwhelm him with the madness of blood. . . .

His reconstruction in the South having failed, having in fact collapsed into riot, the hero participates in that next epochal event of his racial history, the Great Migration—a migration from the South to the North, the traditional road of freedom, from the country to the city, from agrarianism to industry. The Great Migration is to be another promise of progress in freedom which is not redeemed. Its end, too, is chaos bared, because it is just the same promise as that which was implicit in the liberalism of the golden day. Now that liberalism is even more distant from its source, and it has been progressively emasculated.

Fresh from his engagement with Mr. Norton, the hero comes to New York and falls upon the mercies of a young Mr. Emerson, the son of a Mr. Emerson who has himself now become a rich New York businessman. Young, psychoanalyzed Mr. Emerson, a reader of *Totem and Taboo*, some of whose best friends are Negroes, offers the hero conspicuous kindness. He knows something about tyranny too. He considers himself his father's prisoner. He offers himself up as Huck Finn to the hero's Nigger Jim (a gesture which makes full sense, it happens, only when it is assumed that young Emerson knows about Leslie Fiedler's discovery of a homosexual theme in *Huckleberry Finn*). And young Emerson invites the hero to a party at the Club Calamus—another pale progeny, apparently, of the Golden Day.

When the hero enters industry, his paint factory, it is, as is historically appropriate, by using "Emerson's name without his permission." (Though there would seem as well to be a private joke in the event. Ralph Ellison's middle name is Waldo.) Come to industry, he discovers that the promise in the Great Migration was just a device of industrial capitalism, that he is an unwitting and certainly an unwilling weapon wielded against labor unionism, and he discovers that his coming to terms with this technological society will be nothing if not violent. The industrial war is, so far as he is concerned, just another, though a more complicated, version of the same war. The Great Migration leads him back to chaos. Specifically, the factory explosion sends him to the hospital, into, perhaps, the systematic persecutions that after World War I followed the Great Migration. It is the hospital's intent to put the hero in a glass box and render him docile. He is submitted to the equivalent of a lobotomy, which is in its turn the equivalent of another operation waggishly suggested by one of the doctors—castration. The point of the operation, a doctor explains, is that "society will suffer no traumata on his account."

The operation does not secure the intended results, and the hero is plunged then into the final one of the great events of his racial career, the Great Depression. He discovers his whereabouts by coming on what may be taken as the Great Depression's most conspicuously typical event, a tenement eviction. It is an event that provides him with another punning metaphor for his history, "dispossession," and it provides him at the same time, as is historically appropriate, with a seeming opportunity. The event is his introduction to the promising radical politics that could flourish because of such events—he makes a speech to the crowd and is on the spot recruited by the Brotherhood. There is seeming opportunity in the Brotherhood, of course, because it seems brotherly, because it is active, because it seems to make the Negro's cause its own. Beyond that, it imposes on the hero a version of his racial history that unites him with the majority, thereby eliminating the war that he has borne in his secret consciousness. The evictees for whom the hero has just spoken are, Brother Jack tells him, "agrarian types" who are being "ground up by industrial conditions," and so, all Brotherhood doctrine would seem to say, the race war is subsumed by and solved by the class war.

To wage the class war instead is not only the way toward freedom, but it is freedom itself. Like other Negro intellectuals during the Great Depression, the hero accepts this unique promise provided by the Great Depression. There is an alternative only in the futile nationalism of Marcus Garvey, for whom, in the novel, Ras the Exhorter-Destroyer stands. But then the Communist Party did not secure its promise, and so neither does the Brotherhood. It abruptly withdraws its concerns for Harlem—and the hero comes on the fact that the race and the class wars are not identical. Furthermore, he discovers that he is bound to maintain the race war within the ranks of the Brotherhood. Brother Jack is one-eyed and cannot see him. The hero, after his first revelation of Jack's duplicity, looks around a corner of his mind and sees "Jack and Norton and Emerson merge into one single white figure." The Brotherhood's version of history is arbitrary and does not include his history. And therefore the hero is forced back to the version of reality that at bottom he knows—which is, it turns out, Rinehart's, and which is in the image of chaos.

Rinehart is what this history comes to, and he is its hero. He is the climax of the progress up from slavery. Chaos is his freedom. He moves easily in it. He secures his living from it, and if he has been condemned to it, he takes from it also the implements of his revenge. He has made chaos a base of political action. He is a thief, a rascal, an underground man engaged in the subversion of society. Like Melville's hero, he undermines confidence, and thereby the very foundation of society.

The hero's last adventure, in the Epilogue, in his hole in the ground, serves to confirm and to deepen Rinehart, and Rinehart, the underworld man, is the last of a series of puns for the "underground" which now, in a last shift, is to become actual. The hero's progress has been a series of boomeranging reversals, and he returns now to the most final reversal of all. In every instance when he has thought he has been moving upward, he has been moving down. Especially as he has neared his last adventure there has been a play of punning foreshadowings about him all unwary. He attends the Brotherhood's social events at an apartment house named the Chthonian. He attempts to secure secret information about the Brotherhood from a girl named Sybil—as Aeneas consulted the sibyl before he entered the underworld. From the beginning his grandfather had spoken to him from the grave. The technically accommodated Negro of the paint plant had been an underground man. The Brotherhood itself is a secret, underground organization. The hero's progress has all along been a descent.

He has gone out into life repeatedly, he has been frustrated repeatedly, and at the end he descends into death. That is one implication of his drop into his underground. He has looked for definition, and found chaos. He has made a series of voyages into the world which is a white world, and he ends in the pit of darkness. He has sought rationality, and he ends in the heart of the irrational. He has looked for tranquillity, and he ends in hell. There are all these suggestions brought together in his fall. His search for an adequate politics, for a technique of accommodation, his search for a personal identity, his adventuring through his own racial history, have all led him to this complete negation. The hero in his hole in the ground is back to where he began.

But his descent into the underground is the climax to still another set of implications in his adventures, and his return now to his beginnings is a full and stable resolution to all his adventures. With this final reversal, his reverses have come to an end because, like Rinehart before him, he now accepts reversal as the positive law of his being. It is his metaphysics. He is an invisible man in a world without form—but that, his underground adventure, like the Rinehart episode, goes to prove, is something. He does have an identity and a place, only they are contrary. There is a paradox in the fact that the hero's place in the world is underneath the ground, out of the world, but then the paradox is twisted again when the hero converts his hole in the ground into a home. His coal cellar, Ellison has himself pointed out, is not a sewer, but a source of heat and light and power. The hero converts all his losses to assertion. In fact he has found his politics and his person, and he has made sense out of his history, and so in his fall there is finally an ascension—which Ellison ultimately blurs by his promise that the hero will someday rise to do good among men.

His adventures have gone to prove to the hero, simply, that he is black, and, not so simply, that blackness is equivalent to the reverse of things. Now he asserts his blackness, accepting and using all its qualities and associations. The "Blackness of Blackness," the text offered by the preacher of the Prologue, has been, in effect, the text he has had to learn. In the Prologue he had said that he had to illuminate the blackness of his invisibility. Blackness is the cause of his persecution, of the deprivation of his individual humanity, of his apartness. But blackness is also the dark secrets in his persecution, all the totems and taboos that have been thrust upon him. His adventures in light and dark, in what amounts to the Manicheism of the American racial situation, have provided him with the lesson that he is Satan, whose residence should be in the underground, or as he incorporates lawlessness and irrationality he is Dionysus, or he is the darkness just behind consciousness. He is that which is hidden and deceptive and destructive, that which in nature is alien to man, invisible but present, the shadow upon the world. And he is the very principle of the boomerang which scatters all progress, all history, and all the enlightened ethics of civilization.

He embraces the *blackness* of blackness and thereby becomes an underground man—like Dostoevski's hero, an incarnation of that which is just beneath the surface of things, that is treacherous, irresponsible, and mad.[4] He embraces that fate to which he was "before of old ordained," and thereby inherits that "power of blackness" which Melville said "derives its force from its appeals to that Calvinistic sense of Innate Depravity and Original Sin, from whose visitations, in some shape or other, no deeply thinking mind is always and wholly free."

The invisible man's end is in the embrace of his diabolism—diabolism is his politics, his identity, his history, and his metaphysics. And his future is to be Satan's—treason, violence, revenge. These are the normal activities now of his underground life. Most of the time he walks softly, he says in

[4] As important a source of the hero's underground adventure would seem to be a novella by Richard Wright, "The Man Who Lived Underground," *Cross Section*, ed. Edwin Seaver (New York: L. B. Fischer, 1944), pp. 58–102. In Wright's novella, too, a Negro protagonist stumbles into an abandoned underground room which he converts to a home. Ellison's hero illuminates his cellar with 1,369 lights and he plans to have in it five radio-phonographs. Wright's hero papers the walls of his cellar with one-hundred dollar bills, hangs the walls with gold watches and rings, and strews the floor with diamonds. Like Ellison's hero, he arranges for light by stealing electricity. Like Ellison's hero, he finds his freedom underground.

the Prologue, so as not to awaken the sleeping ones. He restricts himself to the subversion of Monopolated Light & Power. And he dines on his favorite dessert of vanilla ice cream and sloe gin—white, presumably, seeping blood. But once, with little direct provocation, he had beaten and almost killed a white man. An invisible man tries to make himself felt.

And the true end of the invisible man's proper adventures is in a dream of gigantic vengeance. Fallen into his coal cellar, he dreams of Jack and Emerson and Bledsoe and Norton and Ras and the school superintendent. They demand that he return to them, and when he refuses, they castrate him—they do, that is to say, what they have done. They throw his bloody parts over a bridge, but now his sex catches there, beneath the apex of the curving arch of the bridge, and drips blood into the red water. The hero laughs and tells his torturers that it is their own sun hanging there, and their moon and their world, and that dripping upon the water is all the history they are ever going to make. And then the great bridge itself gathers itself together and slowly moves off, "striding like a robot, an iron man, whose iron legs clanged doomfully as it moved." The hero, full of sorrow and pain, shouts that it must be stopped, but that terrifying figure is his own metamorphosis. And the great dark threat in it is his resolution.

After that all messages would seem to measure Ellison's desperate reluctances. But the hero is turned, in any event, at the very end, to a staccato of abrupt affirmations—of democracy (". . . we, most of all, had to affirm the principle, the plan in whose name we had been brutalized and sacrificed"), of love (". . . in spite of all I find that I love. . . . I *have* to love"), of the mind, of social responsibility, and of the immediate prospect of his emergence. It must be said that Ellison is to be seen at the very last moment trying to take back the book he has written, or at the very least muffling all its severities, and that is unfortunate. But then it should be said as well that lacking some such attempt, there will be nothing more for Ellison ever to say.

The constant technical flaw in *Invisible Man* is that it so frequently comes to an end, and Ellison is put at every point to a greater muscularity to make the next scene more intense, more thoroughly revealing of what has already been largely revealed. It is the concomitant of that flaw that *Invisible Man* is a death-driven novel. Its movement is to confirm again and again that the hero doesn't exist, and Ellison's difficulty, to put it another way, is to resurrect the hero for each subsequent adventure. The novel's series of ironic negations is, after all, a series of negatives. It can and does reach its last possibility. Ellison will be left with only stale repetitions of the act of dying unless he can in fact assert social responsibility and mind and love—and, because the "Negro problem" is entirely an American problem, democracy. That is the only way he can keep possibility open.

That is to say that the end of *Invisible Man* is the beginning of another novel, one that will draw the complicated positive engagement of the hero in this life, specifically this American life. It is the huge achievement of *Invisible Man*, meanwhile, that it has got a vastness of experience as Negroes particularly must know it—there can be very little that it has left out—into a single meaning. The novel creates a negative metaphor, invisibility, that is fully analytic and fully inclusive, that does hold together for a moment the long experience of chaos that has met Ellison's vision.

THE IMAGE OF MAN AS
PORTRAYED BY RALPH ELLISON[*]

Therman B. O'Daniel

IN 1952, Ralph Ellison published his first and only novel, *Invisible Man*. Immediately, the critics rather generally acclaimed it to be an important book, and a significant achievement. One critic hailed it as "the most impressive work of fiction by an American Negro which I have ever read . . .";[1] while two others considered it to be "an exceptionally good book . . .";[2] and "a resolutely honest, tormented, profoundly American book . . .";[3] and still another was moved to state that "the language of literary criticism seems shallow and patronizing when one has to speak of a book like this."[4] On the basis of the high critical approval, of which these statements are samples, *Invisible Man* proceeded to win the National Book Award as the best American novel of that year.

Since then, articles upon articles on Ellison's novel have appeared in the scholarly journals, in general magazines, and in books; until, at the present time, the body of critical literature on the work and its author is tremendous.

Several things, perhaps, may account for the unusual amount of attention which Ellison's book has received. First of all, it is actually a remarkably good book, an interesting and exciting work of fiction which, beginning with the Prologue, immediately catches the reader's attention and holds on to it tenaciously as the story unfolds. Secondly, it is a complicated and highly involved novel which employs a combination of several techniques—realism, impressionism, and surrealism. And being a creative work of this type, it is sprinkled throughout with dreams and symbols—some resolved and some unresolved—and nothing pleases the modern critic more than to come upon a work like this in which he can sink his interpretive teeth and gnaw away at possible solutions.

[1] Orville Prescott, *The New York Times* (April 16, 1952), p. 25.
[2] Anthony West, "Ralph Ellison," *Principles and Persuasions* (New York, 1957), p. 212.
[3] Wright Morris, *The New York Times Book Review* (April 13, 1952), p. 5.
[4] Delmore Schwartz, *Partisan Review*, XIX (May–June, 1952), 359.
[*] Reprinted from the *CLA Journal*, X (1967), 272–84, by permission of the author and editors.

One critic, for instance, considers Trueblood, Ellison's peasant farmer who has an incestuous relationship with his daughter, to be a modern incest hero, "a man who rises above the myth by acknowledging the unconscious motive." By refusing "the refuge of the myth, the refuge of *not knowing*, and by undeceiving [himself he reverses] the prophecy. We are left to conclude that it is the myth that destroys and that the heroic act for modern man is the casting off of pretense." [5]

Another critic, in the September (1966) issue of the *Walt Whitman Review*, has found in Homer A. Barbee's eulogy to the Founder and First President of Ellison's unnamed Southern Negro college all of the symbols of Walt Whitman's "When Lilacs Last in the Dooryard Bloom'd."

All the Whitman symbols [he writes] are there: the lilac, the star, and the thrush—the bells and the funeral train—but, and I do not think that this point can be emphasized too heavily, Ellison employs them for almost entirely opposite reasons than did the bard of American poetry. I feel such a critic as Charles Feidelson, Jr. to be correct when he concludes that Whitman was attempting in his poem to measure the potential of the poetic mind within the framework of the death of the great emancipator, Abraham Lincoln. But Ellison is much less concerned with poetic potential than with more pessimistic ideas, for the reader is quick to recognize that he uses these same symbols of the lilac, star, and thrush to measure the great irony and bitter disillusion of racial betrayal brought about after the death of another great fighter for emancipation, the beloved Founder—Ellison's picture of a black and mythical Lincoln.[6]

These few illustrations partially indicate the kind of modern allegorical and symbolical novel *Invisible Man* is, but it is more—much more. Basically, Ellison's book is an extended, complicated piece of plotted prose fiction designed, like most novels, to present as vividly as possible the image of its protagonist, or main character. In Ellison's case, the main character in his novel is a male American—specifically, an American Negro man. Now, in order to make his image as full and as rounded as possible, the author pulls out, as it were, all of the stops on his mighty fictional organ, permitting all of the pipes to blast out their eclectic sounds upon the American scene.

Hence, *Invisible Man* is many things in one. It has been described as a modern picaresque novel, owing some debt to Mark Twain.[7] Readers acquainted with Melville's works might be quick to notice some parts of Ellison's book which remind them, in a peculiar way, of *The Confidence-*

[5] Selma Fraiberg, "Two Modern Incest Heroes," *Partisan Review*, XXVIII (May–June, 1961), 660–661.

[6] Marvin E. Mengeling, "Whitman and Ellison: Older Symbols in a Modern Mainstream," *Walt Whitman Review*, XII (September, 1966), 68.

[7] Robert A. Bone, "Ralph Ellison and the Uses of Imagination," *Anger and Beyond*, ed. Herbert Hill (New York, 1966), p. 94.

Man. On the other hand, *Invisible Man* is certainly a devastating satire after the manner—in its own distinctive way, of course—of the eighteenth century English tradition, and it is as bitter in parts—but certainly not throughout—as Swift's *Gulliver's Travels,* but with the satire being handled in a cleverly deceptive, indirect manner in order to lessen the harshness of its impact. Then too, possessing both prologue and epilogue, Ellison's work suggests its structural kinship with the classical drama; and opening at the point in the protagonist's life when he has just completed high school—*in medias res,* so to speak—a young black Ulysses about to be launched on his American odyssey—the novel is seen to possess much of the machinery of an epic in prose. In addition, there is its educational content, the treatment of which links it with the educational novel—but again, in a peculiarly modern and American way.

But there have been many novels in which an American Negro protagonist has been vividly portrayed, and many of these have been written by Negro authors. In what way, then, is Ellison's book different?

The answer to this question partly lies, I think, in what the very perceptive critic, the late Alain Locke, said about the book some years ago, soon after it was published. After stating that: "Ralph Ellison is a protégé of Wright, who predicted for him a bright literary future"; and after criticizing Ellison for some blemishes found in his work, namely his "verbosity and [excessive use of] hyperbole," he said that *Invisible Man* was "written in a style of great force and originality," and that the novel represented "both in style and conception a new height of literary achievement." Then continuing at some further length, he added:

The life story of its hero, obviously semi-autobiographic, ranges from the typical South of a few years back to the metropolitan North of New York and vicinity. Conceptually it runs also almost the whole gamut of class in American society and is interracial at all stages, even in the deep South from the benefactor patron of the college visiting for Founders Day to the sinister "crackers" of the rural backwoods. It is in fact one of the best integrated accounts of interaction between whites and Negroes in American society that has yet been presented, with all characters portrayed in the same balance and perspective. Ellison's philosophy of characterization, incisive, realistic, unsparing of physical and psychological detail—all his major characters are stripped bare to the skin and bone, so to speak—is close to the best European realism in that it is so three-dimensional. We see a grand caravan of types, all registered first person on the sensitive but rather cynical retina of the young Negro protagonist. In the South, the patronizing but well-intentioned school trustee, the piously hypocritical Negro school principal, the gauche, naïve but not too honest students, the disillusioned, institutionalized war veterans, the townsfolk, the peasants of the countryside, white and black, and most particularly the unforgettable earthy peasant character of Jim Trueblood.

In the North, the pageant resumes with all sorts and manner of men and women: the financiers of Wall Street and their decadent jazz-loving sons, factory workers, pro and anti-union varieties, the urban peasants and their homely oddities, parlor-pinks and hard inner-core communists, race leaders, educated and illiterate, each after his kind—and the Harlem community generally displayed finally at frenetic tension in its one big authentic riot. Stylistically all this unrolls in a volcanic flow of vivid, sometimes livid imagery, a tour de force of psychological realism. A double symbolic meaning piled on top of this realism gives the book its distinctive and most original tone and flavor: *Invisible Man* is actually a surrealistic novel because of this, and but for its lack of restraint would rank among the very best of the genre. But the unrestrained bravado of treatment, riding loose rein at full gallop most of the time and the overprecious bravura of phrase and diction weight it down where otherwise it would soar in well-controlled virtuosity. Many readers will be shocked at Ellison's daring franknesses and dazed by his emotional intensity but these are an integral part of the book's great merit. For once, too, here is a Negro writer capable of real and sustained irony.[8]

The fact that Ellison, as Locke points out, is a "writer capable of real and sustained irony" is another reason why *Invisible Man* is an unusually distinctive novel. Considering the fact that the American Negro has been subjected to two major types of prejudice—racial prejudice and color prejudice—the mere title of this work is pregnant with ironic implications. What it ironically implies is that the Negro, whose color can be seen from afar, and whose blackness is often directly the cause of his being subjected to the most humiliating experiences, cannot be seen at all because he is *invisible!*

And when we remember what the narrator, who is the Invisible Man of the story, has told us in the very first paragraph of the Prologue, namely, that he is really not invisible at all; that he is "a man of substance, of flesh and bone, fiber and liquids—and" that he "might even be said to possess a mind"; and when we remember his telling us: "I am invisible, understand, simply because people refuse to see me. . . . When they approach me they see only my surroundings, themselves, or figments of their imagination—indeed, everything and anything except me"; the irony instead of decreasing mounts a hundredfold. For what more humiliating experience is there for a man to have than to be ignored.

Critic Locke mentioned two other things in his excellent analysis of *Invisible Man* which its author, Ralph Ellison, has gone to some lengths to deny. Locke stated that the life story of the novel's hero was "obviously semi-autobiographic," and taking all things into consideration, including the critic's use of the prefix *semi* which stresses the fact that he meant

[8] Alain Locke, "From *Native Son* to *Invisible Man*: A Review of the Literature of the Negro for 1952," *Phylon*, XIV (First Quarter, 1953), 34-35.

that the author made imaginative use—and not necessarily literal use—of some autobiographical facts, this would seem to be a reasonably sound assertion to make.

Author Ellison's statement on this point, however, is an emphatic No. In an interview on "The Art of Fiction" with Alfred Chester and Vilma Howard, his very first statement is the following: "Let me say right now that my book [*Invisible Man*] is not an autobiographical work." [9]

Except for a curious interest in the truth, whether this answer or another had been given on this particular point, is relatively unimportant as far as the artistry of the novel is concerned. But Locke's other statement: "Ralph Ellison is a protégé of Wright," because it is much more pertinent, might engage our attention for a moment, and lead to the conclusion of this brief discussion.

Ellison was an admirer of Richard Wright; was encouraged by Wright to study and learn the technique of the literary craft; and had his first piece of writing, a book review, published in Wright's magazine, *New Challenge*; but, in several of the essays in *Shadow and Act*, he denied that his relationship to Wright was ever that of a protégé.

Here again, the interested and careful reader might wonder whether Ellison did not consciously learn more from Wright than he cares to admit; or whether, unconsciously, he did not learn more from him than he realized. One thing is certain, both Baldwin and Ellison—though Ellison, not quite to the unreasonable extent as Baldwin—go to a considerable amount of unnecessary trouble to set very restricted limitations upon their debt to the author of *Native Son* and *Black Boy*.

On the other hand, it is true that Wright and Ellison—though both Negroes—are products of different backgrounds. Wright's early experiences were unforgettably bitter, and he possessed the talent—unaided by hardly any formal education—to describe them in prose that is so realistically vivid and powerful that it is sometimes frightening and painful to read. Ellison, although his family was poor, is from the Negro middle class. He was educated in a fairly good high school where the fine arts were taught; studied music formally and later became a professional musician; knew about symphonies and wanted to write one; had three years of college study; knew about sculpture and wanted to be a sculptor; and, as a matter of fact, he knew what being a Renaissance Man meant, and wanted to be one of those too. He came to think seriously of writing last, and when he was encouraged by Richard Wright, he wanted to be a writer also. But, as we have said, the backgrounds of the two men were decidedly different. Wherein Ellison might delight in having learned from Hemingway the sportsmanly art of "wing-shooting," [10] Black Boy Wright, no doubt, must often have come dangerously close to being shot.

[9] Ralph Ellison, *Shadow and Act* (New York, 1964), p. 167.
[10] *Ibid.*, p. 168.

"And yet, from the very beginning," states Ellison, when he seriously considered becoming a writer, "I wanted to write about American Negro experience and I suspected that what was important, what made the difference lay in the perspective from which it was viewed." [11]

It is this difference between the two men—a difference in their backgrounds which led to a difference in the perspective from which each viewed American Negro life—that makes their writings different. Richard Wright's experiences as an American Negro caused him to write tragedies; Ralph Ellison's experiences, which he readily admits were never "too uncomfortable," [12] caused him to write, in his *Invisible Man*, a tragicomedy. In several of its parts, *Invisible Man* is a bitterly ironic, tragic book, but like all tragicomedies it has an incongruously happy ending.

Richard Wright's Black Boy possessed no powers of legerdemain which enabled him to disguise himself at will, as Ellison's Rinehart, or to become, at other times, completely invisible. For him there was no hiding place in a symbolic subterranean coal bin. He had to face up to the cruel and excruciatingly brutal forces of reality.

But Ralph Ellison, who presents a different image of man in his *Invisible Man*, continues to insist that:

For better or worse, whatever there is of value in Negro life is an American heritage and as such it must be preserved. Besides, I am unwilling to see those values which I would celebrate in fiction as existing sheerly through terror; they are a result of a tragicomic confrontation of life. [13]

It is then this attitude, this philosophy of life, that enabled Ellison to portray in his novel perhaps the best balanced and most complete and comprehensive image of the American Negro that has yet been presented by any contemporary writer. Some realism, some pessimism, a considerable amount of disillusionment, some bitter irony and satire, and even some hate are all found in this unusual novel. But since Ellison is definitely a romanticist and an optimist, some humor, some hope, and some love are also found in it. In the final pages of the Epilogue of *Invisible Man* he writes: "I have been hurt to the point of abysmal pain, hurt to the point of invisibility. And I defend because in spite of all I find that I love. In order to get some of it down I *have* to love. I sell you no phony forgiveness, I'm a desperate man—but too much of your life will be lost, its meaning lost, unless you approach it as much through love as through hate." [14]

[11] *Ibid.*, p. 16.
[12] *Ibid.*, p. 142.
[13] *Ibid.*, p. 22.
[14] Ralph Ellison, *Invisible Man* (New York, 1952), pp. 437–38.

RALPH ELLISON AND THE
AMERICAN COMIC TRADITION[*]

Earl H. Rovit

THE MOST OBVIOUS comment one can make about Ralph Ellison's *Invisible Man* is that it is a profoundly comic work. But the obvious is not necessarily either simple or self-explanatory, and it seems to me that the comic implications of Ellison's novel are elusive and provocative enough to warrant careful examination both in relation to the total effect of the novel itself and the American cultural pattern from which it derives. It is generally recognized that Ellison's novel is a highly conscious attempt to embody a particular kind of experience—the experience of the "outsider" (in this case, a Negro) who manages to come to some sort of temporary acceptance, and thus, definition, of his status in the universe; it is not so generally recognized that *Invisible Man* is an integral link in a cumulative chain of great American creations, bearing an unmistakable brand of kinship to such seemingly incongruous works as *The Divinity School Address*, *Song of Myself*, *Moby-Dick*, and *The Education of Henry Adams*. But the later proposition is, I think, at least as valid as the former, and unless it is given proper recognition, a good deal of the value of the novel will be ignored.

First it should be noted that Ellison's commitment to what Henry James has termed "the American joke" has been thoroughly deliberate and undisguised. Ellison once described penetratingly the ambiguous *locus* of conflicting forces within which the American artist has had always to work: "For the ex-colonials, the declaration of an American identity meant the assumption of a mask, and it imposed not only the discipline of national self-consciousness, it gave Americans an ironic awareness of the joke that always lies between appearance and reality, between the discontinuity of social tradition and that sense of the past which clings to the mind. And perhaps even an awareness of the joke that society is man's creation, not God's." This kind of ironic awareness may contain bitterness and may even become susceptible to the heavy shadow of despair, but the art which it

* Reprinted from *Wisconsin Studies in Contemporary Literature*, I (1960), 34–42, by permission of the author and editors.

produces has been ultimately comic. It will inevitably probe the masks of identity and value searching relentlessly for some deeper buried reality, but it will do this while accepting the fundamental necessity for masks and the impossibility of ever discovering an essential face beneath a mask. That is to say, this comic stance will accept with the same triumphant gesture both the basic absurdity of all attempts to impose meaning on the chaos of life, and the necessary converse of this, the ultimate significance of absurdity itself.

Ellison's *Invisible Man* is comic in this sense almost in spite of its overtly satirical interests and its excursions into the broadly farcical. Humorous as many of its episodes are in themselves—the surreal hysteria of the scene at the Golden Day, the hero's employment at the Liberty Paint Company, or the expert dissection of political entanglements in Harlem—these are the materials which clothe Ellison's joke and which, in turn, suggest the shape by which the joke can be comprehended. The pith of Ellison's comedy reverberates on a level much deeper than these incidents, and as in all true humor, the joke affirms and denies simultaneously—accepts and rejects with the same uncompromising passion, leaving not a self-cancelling neutralization of momentum, but a sphere of moral conquest, a humanized cone of light at the very heart of the heart of darkness. *Invisible Man*, as Ellison has needlessly insisted in rebuttal to those critics who would treat the novel as fictionalized sociology or as a dramatization of archetypal images, is an artist's attempt to create a *form*. And fortunately Ellison has been quite explicit in describing what he means by *form*; in specific reference to the improvisation of the jazz-musician he suggests that form represents "a definition of his identity: as an individual, as a member of the collectivity, and as a link in the chain of tradition." But note that each of these definitions of identity must be individually exclusive and mutually contradictory on any logical terms. Because of its very pursuit after the uniqueness of individuality, the successful definition of an individual must define out the possibilities of generalization into "collectivity" or "tradition." But herein for Ellison in his embrace of a notion of fluid amorphous identity lies the real morality and humor in mankind's art and men's lives—neither of which have much respect for the laws of formal logic.

At one time during the novel when Ellison's protagonist is enthusiastically convinced that his membership in the Brotherhood is the only effective means to individual and social salvation, he recalls these words from a college lecture on Stephen Dedalus: "Stephen's problem, like ours, was not actually one of creating the uncreated conscience of his race, but of creating the *uncreated features of his face*. Our task is that of making ourselves individuals. The conscience of a race is the gift of its individuals who see, evaluate, record. . . . We create the race by creating ourselves and then to our great astonishment we will have created something far more important: We will have created a culture. Why waste time creating a conscience for something that doesn't exist? For, you see, blood and skin do not think!" This is one of the most significant passages in the novel, and one which must be appreciated within the context of the total form if the subtle pressure of that form is to be adequately weighed. And this can be done only if the Prologue and the Epilogue are viewed as functional elements in the novel which set the tempo for its moral action and modulate ironically upon its emergent meanings.

The Prologue introduces the narrator in his underground hibernation musing upon the events of his life, eating vanilla ice cream and sloe gin, listening to Louis Armstrong's recording, "What Did I Do to Be so Black and Blue?" and trying to wrest out of the confusions of his experiences some pattern of meaning and/or resilient core of identity. The next twenty-five chapters are a first-person narrative flashback which covers some twenty years of the protagonist's life ending with the beginning, the hero's descent into the underground hole. The concluding Epilogue picks up the tonal patterns of the Prologue, implies that both meaning and identity have been discovered, and dramatically forces a direct identification between the narrator and the reader. Ostensibly this is another novel of the initiation of a boy into manhood—a *Bildungsroman* in the episodic picaresque tradition. The advice of the literature teacher has been realized; the hero has created the features of his face from the malleable stuff of his experience. He who accepts himself as "invisible" has ironically achieved a concrete tangibility, while those characters in the novel who seemed to be "visible" and substantial men (Norton, Brother Jack, and even Tod Clifton) are discovered to be really "invisible" since they are self-imprisoned captives of their own capacities to see and be seen in stereotyped images. However, to read the novel in this way and to go no further is to miss the cream of the jest and the total significance of the whole form which pivots on the ironic fulcrum of the blues theme introduced in the Prologue and given resolution in the Epilogue. As in all seriously comic works the reader is left not with an answer, but with a challenging question—a question which soars beyond the novel on the unanswered notes of Armstrong's trumpet: "What did I do to be so black and blue?"

For the protagonist *is* finally and most comically *invisible* at the end of the novel; he has learned that to create the uncreated features of his face is at best a half-value, and at worst, potentially more self-destructive than not to strive after identity at all. For Ellison ours is a time when "you prepare a face to meet the faces that you meet"—a time when we have learned to shuffle and deal our personalities with a protean dexterity that, as is characterized through Rinehart, is a wholesale exploitation of and surrender to chaos. After the narrator's fall into the coalpit he discovers that his arrogantly naïve construction of personality is nothing more than the accumulated fragments in his briefcase: the high-school diploma, Bledsoe's letter, Clifton's dancing doll, Mary's bank, Brother Tarp's iron. And most ironically, even these meager artifacts—the fragments he has shored against his ruin—represent not him, but the world's variegated projections of him. The narrator learns then that his educational romance is a farcical melodrama of the most garish variety; the successive births and rebirths of his life (his Caesarean delivery from college, his birth by electronics at the factory hospital, the christening by the Brotherhood) were not the organic gestations of personality that he idealized so much as they were the cold manipulations of artificial insemination. His final acceptance of his invisibility reminds us of the demand of the Zen Master: "Show me the face you had before you were born."

However, we must note also that this acceptance of invisibility, of amorphous nonidentity, is far from a resignation to chaos. The protagonist has successfully rebelled against the imposition of social masks whether externally (like Clifton's) or internally (like Brother Tarp's) bestowed; his is not a surrender of personality so much as a descent to a deeper level of personality where the accent is heavier on possibilities than on limitations. The 1,369 glowing light bulbs in his cellar retreat attest to the increased power and enlightenment which are positive gains from his experience, as well as to the strategic advantages of his recourse to invisibility. The literature teacher unwittingly pointed out the flaw in his exhortation even as he declaimed it: "Blood and skin do not think!" For to think is to be as much concerned with analysis as it is with synthesis; the ironic mind tears radiant unities apart even as it forges them. Accordingly Ellison's narrator assumes the ultimate mask of facelessness and emphasizes the fluid chaos which is the secret substance of form, the dynamic interplay of possibilities which creates limitations. The narrator is backed into the blank corner where he must realize that "the mind that has conceived a plan of living must never lose sight of the chaos against which that pattern was conceived." In accepting himself as the Invisible Man he assumes the historic role which Emerson unerringly assigned to the American poet; he becomes "the world's eye"—something through which one sees, even though it cannot itself be seen.

And here it may be fruitful to investigate briefly the peculiar relationship of Emerson's work to Ellison (whose middle name is propitiously Waldo). In the recently published excerpt from a novel in progress, "And Hickman Arrives," Ellison has his main character, Alonzo Zuber, Daddy Hickman, make some complimentary remarks about Emerson, "a preacher . . . who knew that every tub has to sit on its own bottom." Daddy Hickman, a Negro preacher ("Better known as GOD'S TROM-BONE"), is vividly characterized as a wise and shrewd virtuoso of the evangelical circuit who might not unfairly be taken as a modern-day Emerson, preaching eloquently the gospel of humanity. These facts may be significant when we remember that Emerson's work is given short shrift as rhetorical nonsense in *Invisible Man* and his name is bestowed upon a character whose minor function in the novel is to be a self-righteous hypocrite. This shift in attitude may indicate that Ellison has come to realize that there are some major affinities binding him to his famous namesake, and, more important, it may enable us to understand more clearly the remarkable consistency of the American struggle to create art and the relatively harmonious visions which these unique struggles have attained.

Superficially there would seem to be little to link the two men beyond the somewhat labored pun of their names and Ellison's awareness of the pun. The one, an ex-Unitarian minister of respectable, if modest, Yankee background, whose orotund explorations in autobiography gave fullest form to the American dream—whose public pose attained an Olympian serenity and optimistic faith which have caused him to be associated with a wide range of sentimentalities from Mary Baker Eddy to Norman Vincent Peale; the other, an Oklahoma City Negro, born in 1914, ex-Leftist propagandist and editor, who would seem to have belied the Emersonian prophecy of individualism and self-reliance by the very title of his novel, *Invisible Man*. The one, nurtured by the most classical education that America had to offer; the other, a rapt disciple of jazzmen like Charlie Christian and Jimmy Rushing who has attributed to their lyric improvisations his deepest understanding of aesthetic form. The one, white and given to the Delphic utterance; the other, black and adept in the cautery of bitter humor. But in their respective searches for identity, in their mutual concern with defining the possibilities and limitations which give form and shape to that which is human, the poet who called man "a golden impossibility" and the novelist who teaches his protagonist that life is a latent hive of infinite possibilities draw close together in their attempts to find an artistic resolution of the contrarieties of existence.

"Only he can give, who has," wrote Emerson; "he only can create, who is." Experience is the fluxional material from which these all-important values and identities are created, and Emerson's great essays are processive incantations whose ultimate function is to bring identity into being, even as they chant the fundamental fluidity of all forms spontaneously and eternally merging into other forms. When we remember that Emerson once wrote: "A believer in Unity, a seer of Unity, I yet behold two," it may be worth a speculation that the Emerson behind the triumphant artifices of the *Essays* was not a terribly different person from the Invisible Man in the coalpit whose submersion into the lower frequencies had given him an entree to the consciousnesses of all men. This awareness of the absurdity of meaning (and the potential meaningfulness of chaos) is at the heart of Emerson's delight in paradox, his seeming inconsistencies, his "dialogistic" techniques, his highly functional approach to language. "All symbols are fluxional," he declaimed; "all language is vehicular and transitive and is good for conveyance not for homestead." Thus Melville's attempted criticism of Emerson in *The Confidence-Man* misses widely the mark; Emerson isn't there when the satire strikes home. Melville, who above all of Emerson's contemporaries should have known better, mistook the Olympian pasteboard mask for a reality and misread the eloquent quest for identity as a pretentious melodrama. For, as Constance Rourke recognized, Emerson is one of our most deft practitioners of the American joke, and the magnitude of his success may be measured by the continued effectiveness of his disguises after more than a hundred years.

But again we must return to the *form* of *Invisible Man* to appreciate how deeply involved Ellison's work is with the most basic American vision of reality. Although it is probably true as some critics have pointed out that the dominating metaphor of the novel—the "underground man" theme—was suggested by Dostoevski and Richard Wright, it is for our purposes more interesting to note a similar metaphor in Hart Crane's poem, "Black Tambourine":

> The interests of a black man in a cellar
> Mark tardy judgment on the world's closed door.
> Gnats toss in the shadow of a bottle,
> And a roach spans a crevice in the floor.
>
> .   .   .   .   .
>
> The black man, forlorn in the cellar,
> Wanders in some mid-kingdom, dark, that lies,
> Between his tambourine, stuck on the wall,
> And, in Africa, a carcass quick with flies.

Invisible Man achieves an expert evocation of that "mid-kingdom," that demimonde of constant metamorphosis where good and evil, appearance and reality, pattern and chaos are continually shifting their shapes even as the eye strains to focus and the imagination to comprehend. The Kafkaesque surrealism of the novel's action, the thematic entwinement of black-white and dark-light, and the psychic distance from the plot-development which the use of the Prologue and the Epilogue achieves posit the moral center of the novel in that fluid area where experience is in the very process of being transformed into value. The narrator, the author, and the reader as well are caught in the "mid-kingdom" which seems to me to be the characteristic and unavoidable focus of American literature. For this mid-kingdom, this unutterable silence which is "zero at the bone," seems to me to be the one really inalienable birthright of being an American.

Some Americans following Swedenborg named it "vastation"; others gave it no name and lamented the dearth of an American tradition within which the artist could work; at least one commissioned the sculptor, St. Gaudens, to incarnate it in a statue. One way of attempting to describe the sense of being within this mid-kingdom can be most dramatically seen in "The Castaway" chapter of *Moby-Dick* where Pip is left floundering in the boundless Pacific. And although the techniques of approaching the experience have been richly various, the experience itself, an incontrovertible sense of absolute metaphysical isolation, can be found at the core of the most vital American creations.

"American history," writes James Baldwin in *Notes of a Native Son*, is "the history of the total, and willing, alienation of entire peoples from their forbears. What is overwhelmingly clear . . . is that this history has created an entirely unprecedented people, with a unique and individual past." The alienation, of course, is more than sociological and ideological; it seeps down into the very depths whence the sureties of identity and value are wrought; and it imprisons the American in this mid-kingdom where the boundaries—the distance from the tambourine on the wall to the carcass quick with flies—cannot be measured in either years or miles. The American seeking himself—as an individual, a member of the collectivity, a link in the chain of tradition—can never discover or create that identity in fixed restrictive terms. The past is dead and yet it lives: note Ellison's use of the narrator's grandfather, the yams, the techniques of the evangelical sermon. Individuals are frozen in mute isolation, and yet communication is possible between them: the Harlem riot, the way the narrator listens to music. Ellison's novel is the unique metaphor of his own thoroughly personal experience, and yet it makes a fitting link in the chain of the American tradition.

That Ellison and his narrator are Negroes both is and is not important. From the severe standpoint of art the racial fact is negligible, although there are doubtless areas of meaning and influence in *Invisible Man* which sociological examination might fruitfully develop. From the viewpoint of cultural history, however, the racial fact is enormously provocative. It is strikingly clear that contemporary American writing, particularly the writing of fiction, is dominated by two categories of writers: members of religious and racial minorities, and writers who possess powerful regional heritages. Both groups have an instinctive leasehold within the boundaries of the "mid-kingdom"; the Negro, the Catholic, the Jew, and the Southerner share the immediate experience of living on the razor's edge of time, at the very point where traditions come into desperate conflict with the human need to adapt to change. And, of equal importance, both groups—in varying degrees—are marked out on the contemporary scene as being "different"; both groups cannot avoid the terrible problem of identity, because it is ever thrust upon them whether they like it or not. These are the conditions which in the American past have nourished our spasmodic exfoliations of significant literary activity: the great "Renaissance" of the 1840's and '50's, the Twain-James-Adams "alliance" of the late nineteenth century, the post–World War One literary fluorescence from which we have just begun to break away. But the Lost Generation was the last generation which could practice the necessary expatriation or "fugitivism" in which these factors—the disseverance from the past and the search for identity—could operate on nonminority or nonregional American writers. Thus Ralph Ellison—and contemporaries like Saul Bellow, Flannery O'Connor, and William Styron—are *inside* the heart of the American experience by the very virtue of their being in some way "outsiders." Like Emerson, himself a royal inhabitant of the mid-kingdom over a century ago, they are challenged to create form, or else succumb to the enveloping chaos within and without.

And the answers which they arrive at—again as with Emerson—are answers which cannot be taken out of the context of their individually achieved forms without being reduced to platitude or nonsense. Form, the creation of a radical, self-defining metaphor, is the one rational technique which human beings have developed to deal adequately with the basic irrationality of existence. The answer which *Invisible Man* gives to the unanswerable demands which life imposes on the human being has something to do with human limitation and a good deal to do with freedom; it has something to do with hatred, and a good deal more to do with love. It defines the human distance between the tambourine and the carcass and it accepts with wonder and dignity the immeasurable gift of life. The black man in the cellar transforms his isolation into elevation without denying the brute facts of existence and without losing his ironic grip on the transiency of the moment. The amorphous ambiguity of the mid-kingdom is for a timeless instant conquered and made fit for habitation. Perhaps tragedy teaches man to become divine, but before man can aspire to divinity, he must first accept completely the responsibilities and limitations of being human. The American experience, cutting away the bonds of tradition which assure man of his humanity, has not allowed a tragic art to develop. But there has developed a rich and vigorous comic tradition to which *Invisible Man* is a welcome embellishment, and it is this art which promises most as a healthy direction into the future.

James Baldwin

DARK ANGEL: THE WRITINGS OF
JAMES BALDWIN*

Colin MacInnes

I ENVY whoever writes of James Baldwin a century from now. That his work will then be discussed I have no doubt, since of all writers in English of our era his style is most classic, his theme one of the most relevant. But it is because of this theme, precisely, that it is so hard to criticize his writing now.

Baldwin's essential theme is life-death-passion-honor-beauty-horror . . . the perpetual theme since the Greeks and long before, the only one worthy of a great artist and of which, as writer and man, he has proved himself so worthy. But the particular raw material from which Baldwin derives his underlying attitudes is the "racial question"; and to hear those words is to make any white heart sink. For we all agree about the "racial question," do we not? Most of us by ignoring it, so that it is not a "question" at all, and those of us whom it harasses, by the expedient of adopting "liberal" attitudes towards it. Of course all men are equal, or ought to be! Of course we are for the freedom of our black brothers! But in this liberal posture there are fatal flaws. The first is that, in respect to the "color question," no white can ever possibly know what he is being "liberal" about. It can never enough be emphasized: no white, not even of an oppressed minority, nor however strong his sense of justice and imagination, can ever know, *in his skin*, what it is to be a colored man in a white racist society. I had a glimpse of this once when, in the late 'forties, I was attacked, alone, by an Arab throng in the old city of Cairo. I shall never forget those blindly piercing eyes: staring in mindless hatred not at me but at a *thing* totally detestable. Such looks are everyday experiences to Negroes in the African and American South, and we who are white simply cannot know them.

The other flaw becomes apparent when one imagines what the liberal vision of the Negro in the white world really consists of. On objective examination, it turns out to be what one might call the Eleanor Roosevelt

* Reprinted from *Encounter*, XXI (1963), 22–23, by permission of the author and editors.

vision. Things have not changed much save in one essential respect: the Negro is loved, nay respected, not rejected any longer. But has he *power?* Is he employing whites, telling them what to do, ordering their destinies— even choosing to reject them altogether? No, most certainly he is not! He must still be an inferior, albeit one cherished and accepted. ("The African is my brother, but I am his elder brother," as Albert Schweitzer has said).

What can this vision mean to any Negro—or to any who is not a cordial imbecile? I imagine, absolutely nothing. Negroes do not want equality on white men's terms: they want the only equality worth having, and which is real, namely one which can be *demanded* from a position of authentic strength. To any thinking, feeling Negro, a white man will thus be a racist who is a declared enemy, or a liberal who is a false friend. And that is why no white man, however brave and well-intentioned, can ever sing the Negro song. Even if what he says is true in every aspect, and even if he accepts in his heart without reserve not "liberal" equality—the kindly dole—but the equality born of power and possible danger to himself, his voice will be the wrong voice. No man can ever really speak for women; no Gentile for a Jew; no white man ever for a man of color.

So the singer of the blues must be a black man, but the paradox is that his audience must still be white. This is partly because there is no point in telling Negroes of the racial situation: it would be like lecturing convicts on conditions inside a jail; though certainly a colored writer can *define* their situation to his people, and thus help them to confront their past the better to win their future. The next reason is that the Negro readership of "serious" writing is still insufficient to sustain a major writer; the audience is there all right, but because of enforced illiteracy the form of communication will be the wrong one. But the final reason why James Baldwin speaks to us of another race is that he still believes us worthy of a warning: he has not yet despaired of making us *feel* the dilemma we all chat about so glibly, of forcing us to see it is our problem, not the Negroes', and of trying to save us from the agonies that we too will suffer if the Negro people are driven beyond the ultimate point of desperation.

How long he will or can maintain this posture of entreaty one cannot tell. For no Negro writer is less interested than he in the condescending praises that the white literate shower on what they suppose to be a cultural curiosity; and like all Negro artists, he must be painfully aware of his people's call, in time of acutest crisis, to a total loyalty, an absolute closing of the ranks. And in his latest book, as we shall see, he is standing as if on a lonely precipice, still crying to white hearts and brains, but making what seems to be a last desperate appeal—anguished if not yet utterly bereft of hope.

Baldwin has seemed both novelist and essayist (also one of the extraordinarily rare TV performers who are entirely convincing), but in reality he is neither: he is a premonitory prophet, a fallible sage, a soothsayer, a bardic voice falling on deaf and delighted ears. These qualities emerge best in his "essays" (for such one must call them, though they are so agonized and hortatory that the word hardly fits), and far less decisively in his novels. If I say I do not think his novels convey his intentions so effectively—if I say in fact that he is "not a novelist"—no doubt this will vex him but, if so, I think mistakenly. To begin with, to be a novelist seems to me something that, with the rarest exceptions, is so lacking in glamor or compulsion. The novel, today, is a hold-all you can throw any old literary garments into, and I am sure few who use this form—if it is still a form—are much dedicated to it: the motives for its use, even by deft practitioners, are in part commercial, since novels can make money, and in part because the public likes its intellectual meals served up in that kind of dish. Then, to achieve a world-wide reputation by the force of three collections of magazine articles, as Baldwin has so far done, seems to me a more astonishing achievement than to be a novelist of note. But most of all it is because I see—or hear—James Baldwin as a voice, a presence, a singer almost, that I feel the mode of direct address—to us in his own person, and not through invented "characters"—expresses his talent and his message best.

Yet before I try to describe these essays (a superfluous task, really, since their subject and form are pared down to an almost painful lucidity), I shall remind the reader of the novels, and say what I feel to be their limitations and their strengths.

GO TELL IT ON THE MOUNTAIN (1953)

This is a densely-packed, ominous, sensual, doom-ridden story, lit by rare beauty, love and human penetration. The theme is life and religion and how both, wonderful and terrible, can create and destroy. The scene is the Temple of the Fire Baptized in Harlem during two days and a long night; from which place the writer leads us back and forth in time among the lives of worshippers in the congregation.

The prime figures are Gabriel the deacon, proud, passionate, violent and unforgiving as Satan, yet taking none of Satan's sweets (unless perhaps the love of power), and still wrestling inexorably with his God; and his adoptive son John, aged 14 (who believes Gabriel to be his father), torn between hatred of his parent and the wish to love him, and between the force of his own animal and mental life, and the hope of submission to salvation.

Gabriel, who is from the South, is twice married: first to Deborah, a sad sterile saint who was once raped by whites, and then to Elizabeth, whose bitter and beautiful lover Richard has killed himself leaving her the infant John. Gabriel has thus taken two "fallen" women—and is, we learn, responsible himself for yet another "fall"—that of Esther, a southern beauty who gives him a son, Royal, whom he rejects with shame and yearning.

By Elizabeth, his second wife, Gabriel has three children, the first-born being the defiant and irreligious Roy whom he beats and secretly adores. Gabriel's sister Florence who is, so to speak, the deacon's human—if not religious—conscience, has also lost her charming wastrel husband Frank. The chief remaining character is Brother Elisha, a sweet-natured, fervent young pastor of the church who stands in relation to young John as a true brother.

All this may seem something of a mouthful—as indeed it sometimes does even in the novel, where the author makes severe demands on our attention. We may also notice that, among these blasted and determined lives, there are three disastrous marriages, two tragic love affairs, three rapes or seductions, and that four of the most adjusted and potentially happy characters meet violent ends; also that the sole other unself-torturing personage in the book, the young pastor Elisha, is the only one who is not, as all the others are, related.

This bald synopsis may conjure up the notion of a melodrama, but the book is not like that at all. In the first place Baldwin never makes his characters suffer—or even die—unless they, so to say, "have to": unless, that is, the tragedy both arises from their inner natures and explains them. (A sure sign, incidentally, of an able writer is that he will never do violence to his creations unless this is, artistically, quite inevitable; whereas inferior writers strike their characters arbitrarily down for superficial effect—thereby throwing the whole story out of human balance.) The next reality about this misery and drama is that these are, by implication, a consequence of the Negro situation in the United States. For though this novel is less overtly a declaration of the doom that haunts Negro lives than other books of Baldwin's are, the social pressures impelling to destruction are suspended over almost every page. The third redeeming feature lies in the interplay of the obsessive religious instincts of the characters—or the lack of these—with their spiritual and even physical lives. Religion, whatever its quality, is not for them a mere matter of "worship" detached from normal daily existence: it is a fierce and constant compulsion that never abandons them a second.

To give a clue to the nature and omnipresence of this religious feeling, one might mention books entirely different from it—*Pilgrim's Progress*, say, or *The Scarlet Letter*. The point is that this is not a religious book in the sense of religion being an accessory theme grafted on to the plot—as so often turns out to be the case with the Roman Catholic novelists—but a story saturated with religious feeling, and which simply would not exist at all without it. As for the quality of this religious instinct that inexorably impels the characters, one might describe it as that of early prehierarchical Christianity, but transformed in three ways by its Negro nature. In the first place, it is *sensual* as white Christian religion so rarely has been, even to the extent of physical paroxysms in the church amounting to a kind of holy orgasm—not so much hysterical, as in equivalent white ecstasies, as in the sense of the flesh made spirit. Bodily sin may be rejected, but by no means the body (the fervent Elisha, we notice, is an accomplished and graceful athlete). Next, their faith is the characters' chief form of *social* life, as well as religious: most of them only begin to operate, or to do so intensely, as social beings, in the religious context of their lives. And last, their religion is unquestionably—though the author does not stress this fact unduly—one of moral protest. We know at once who the Egyptians are, and who the Israelites that their God will lead out of bondage.

As for the effects of their religion on their lives, these are, in human terms, usually repellent. One may admire the pride and utter devotion to their faith of the devouter characters; but scarcely the cruelties to themselves and others to which their beliefs command them. To meet, the "sinners" (as Esther, Royal, Frank or Richard) would certainly be more endearing; and even Gabriel's sister Florence, who comes to God in the end by fear of death, not by devotion, or his second wife Elizabeth, who refuses to deny the earlier joy of her "sinful" fondness for her dead lover Richard, are infinitely more humane—and, one may say, Christian—than the relentless deacon or his coldly saintly first wife Deborah. Yet I should make it clear Baldwin is far too subtle an artist to reverse the conventional roles and make the good bad, and the bad good. For there is a lack of profundity in some of the "good" sinners, and the author can equally suggest that the holy Elisha is, in human terms, most lovable.

What Baldwin's own views on all this are—I mean his views as James Baldwin, and not as the creator of these persons—it is difficult to tell, and indeed it is scarcely our business to try to guess. All one can say with certainty is that he has been marked forever by his own early religious experience, and that he understands this theme as do few writers of our day. Also that his understanding is informed throughout with hope and pity; two qualities, I would like to add, that few writers are entitled to make manifest, since one must earn one's right to bestow them on mankind. (We are surely all tired by now of reviewers who tell us the most commonplace authors are "compassionate": you must be a fine kind of man or woman to be worthy to show compassion.)

We see this best in his portraits of the two chief characters of the book—in the Lear-like Gabriel, and in young John, reaching eagerly his whole being out to life from what imprisons it. Gabriel, like Lear, is in most senses a monster; and, tougher in spirit than the mad king, he does not even crack when his will comes close to madness. He has sinned with Esther, yes, but no man—still less any woman—may tell him so: God has forgiven him, for God is Gabriel's god, and to mankind he is unrepentant. Even when young John bends, at the book's end, to his overpowering will (or seems to), Gabriel cannot love John: his inexorable suspicion in fact redoubles. To those who have served him, or his body—Deborah, Esther and Elizabeth—he remains a demanding tyrant. Because he is God's elect, his hatred for any of God's creatures who do not bow before him is vengefully malevolent.

And yet . . . how is it that it is impossible to loathe—even to despise— Gabriel? Firstly, because he suffers and—worst of all suffering—endures its agonies without enlightenment. And then, though pride in a general way may be detestable (and spiritual pride, as Gabriel never knows, the ultimate of sins), one cannot but respect—if not admire—his pride: it is so total and so terrible in its effects on him. Most touching of all, this puritan who denies the flesh is hopelessly attached to it: his agony at the death of his bastard son Royal, and his love for the son Roy who denies him, give to this grim prophet feet of common clay.

But Gabriel's love for his own flesh makes him hate the son John who is not of his flesh. It is not that John is illegitimate, for so was his own loved son Royal—but that he, Gabriel, did not create him. And John, whose infant will is no less violent than his adoptive father's—and whose intelligent introspection is incomparably greater—knows this, curses Gabriel in his heart, and even hopes, when his half-brother Roy is stabbed,[1] "that Roy, to bring his father down, would die."

But John is also possessed, partly by example and partly by inner light, of religious yearnings. I am not quite sure how authentic James Baldwin intends us to believe John's religious instinct may be—for John's is not, for instance, a "natural" religious temperament like Elisha's or

[1] Roy is stabbed, in a gang fight, by whites. This is an echo of the insult that was done to Gabriel's first wife Deborah, and of the white police violence that led to the suicide of Elizabeth's first lover, Richard. But notice that the author makes clear, through the mouth of Roy's mother Elizabeth, that Roy's black gang has provoked the whites as much as they were provoked; also that the murder of Gabriel's cherished illegitimate son Royal resulted from a quarrel between blacks.
I mention these complications to show that Baldwin never denies the possibility of black villainy, as much as white; though what he does show— and one cannot but think rightly—is that the black-white situation in the States *must* lead to murder.

even, in terms of charity, his mother Elizabeth's. And since John is but fourteen, and undergoes, in the final pages of the book, an ecstatically terrifying conversion, my feeling is the writer intends this to be a reality for an adolescent boy but not, perhaps, an ultimate, enduring reality. Indeed, the final cryptic sentences of the book suggest this, when John says to his mother: "I'm ready . . . I'm coming. I'm on my way." This "way," one can feel, will never cease to be in some sense religious, but surely not as the Temple of the Fire Baptized—let alone the deacon—would understand this term.

The description, in the last chapter, of young John wrestling with religion, beholding eternity and death, plummeting into darkness, soaring to the dazzling light, is one of the most convincing accounts of a conversion I have read. It is unbearably harrowing, profoundly imaginative, and psychologically exact. The reader's sensation of being physically present in the Temple—and of entering John's soul stretched out on the spiritual rack—is so compelling as to make one wish to flee this holy place. And curiously, one has a strong sensation of *noise*—of hectic music, rushing winds, agonized hosannahs, tortured hallelujahs: so much so that, at this moment of the book, Baldwin seems suddenly to become a blues or gospel singer.

Among what are known as "technical" felicities of the novel, I would mention first the language. Of possible influences on his style Baldwin himself has written, "I hazard the King James Bible, the rhetoric of the store-front church, something ironic and violent and perpetually understated in Negro speech . . ." and all this is accurate; though I would especially insist on the last item as opposed to the first, since any Semitic floridity that may linger in the Authorized Version is attenuated by that chiselled, *lethal* quality of prose which, as we shall see later on, is one of the glories of Baldwin's essays: words of a measured passion, like a healing knife. Though most of the book is in "author's narrative," rather than in dialogue, I would add that speech, when it does come, is marvellously economical, accurate and revealing. The scene, for instance, in which Gabriel tries to extricate himself from responsibility for his own and Esther's child makes me suppose that Baldwin will one day be a playwright—if he is not, as I suspect, already one.

As for the "flashback" device—so immediately effective and comprehensible in the cinema, but often troublesome in print—this does sometimes leave the reader rather up in the air but, in compensation, it permits of horribly effective ironies when the past abruptly clicks back to the present whose actions it has determined. In final praise, I would mention Baldwin's consummate gift for evoking what I believe to be the most elusive of emotions to any writer—that of pure animal love; and not of mere "sex," but a tender, erotic passion. And deeply as the dramatic and religious elements of the book impress me, I find even more wonderful his gift for persuading me beyond possibility of doubt that Elizabeth adored Richard, Elisha does love John—and even that poor Gabriel yearns for dead Royal and for living Roy.

GIOVANNI'S ROOM (1956)

As if the "color question" were not enough, we now plunge into yet another "social problem," namely the homosexual dilemma.

Before describing Baldwin's treatment of this theme, I may say (for what, coming from me, it's worth) what I think about this tiresome topic. In brief, I believe that heterosexuals, bisexuals, and homosexuals of both genders have existed in the world since Eden, and will continue to do so till the last trump sounds. That homosexuality is an aberration cannot be denied: not at all for "moral" reasons, but because it denies one of nature's prime laws, which is the reproduction of our kind. On the other hand nature, in her infinite wisdom, could surely not have constructed the male and female bodies as she did without anticipating that these deviations would occur—and also, I would guess, without worrying a bit as to whether they would ever be sufficiently widespread to interfere with her eternal plan.

Now all this is realized, and is lived, in many countries I have visited but in the nations of Anglo-Saxon puritan tradition—that is to say, principally England and the United States—this simple reality is ferociously denied. In these sad lands the heterosexual, fearing perhaps to be mistaken for anything else (which no man or woman who fully is such need ever fear a second), beat on their hairy chests or fertile bosoms in fervently anxious rejections of the homosexual. Conversely, the Anglo-Saxon puritan queer—who must surely be one of the most unpleasant and tedious of creatures the globe has yet inflicted on itself—seeks to make out of his deviation a grotesquely vainglorious cult of total boredom and stupidity.

That moral and social problems do arise from homosexuality cannot be questioned; that they also do from heterosexuality cannot either. And I would advance as an absolute maxim that the greater the degree of obsession with this matter in any society, the greater will be the social frustration and torment it engenders. Now if this be true, we may see a parallel—which I hope any colored reader will excuse—between the "homosexual problem" and the "Negro problem." The plain fact about both is that neither is: the Negro is not a problem to himself, but to the racialist; the "problem" of queerdom resides in the hearts of queer-haters and of those who, being queers, either glorify the commonplace or deny their own inner natures. And in general I would add that, whenever human beings call anything whatever a "problem," you may be almost certain that it is not one, but man-made and soluble. The only true problems in our world are poverty and pain, and their alleviation; but blinding our willful eyes to these cruel and perilous anxieties, we seek for substitute "problems" with horrible success.

One further prefatory remark to *Giovanni's Room*. In it, James Baldwin, who is a Negro, writes exclusively of whites—so successfully that anyone who did not know what race he has the honor to belong to could never guess, from any internal evidence whatever, that he was other than a white himself. I do not insist on this feat as being extraordinary, since any writer of competence and imagination *must* be able to enter minds and spirits entirely different from his own. For after all, male writers —unless they be the authors of *Billy Budd* or *Robinson Crusoe*—must devise convincing characters of the other sex, and vice versa; and this is frequently achieved triumphantly. No one, for instance, can doubt that Manon Lescaut really is a girl although she was created by a man; or that Chéri is a boy, despite Colette's having invented him. And if you can manage this initial bit of legerdemain, why should you not, in imagination, change your race successfully? Othello, to anyone who knows Africans, unmistakably is one (there were hundreds of Africans in England in Shakespeare's day, and I do not doubt he chatted with them for hours in taverns round Wapping or elsewhere). The white characters in Chinua Achebe's Nigerian novels are, just as pertinently, Englishmen.

Yet Baldwin's choice of a white setting for his second novel does raise two thoughts about it. The first is that the switch of mood, from *Go Tell It on the Mountain* to *Giovanni's Room*, is so astonishing. Even a white with no knowledge—or better, love—of Negroes, will instantly, on reading the first novel, feel himself plunged into a different racial world. Conversely, I imagine no Negro, reading the second book, would suppose himself, for a moment, in a colored one. The next thought is—why did Baldwin set his homosexual theme in a white society? Was it because this aberration is more characteristic of our race than his? With all respect, I do not think this can be the reason. Was it because he feared an unfavorable reaction by his race had he portrayed a colored gay society? This cannot be the reason either since, as we shall see, this situation is confronted in the third novel, *Another Country*. My own belief is that the true explanation is the simplest one. Baldwin had lived in Paris, and wanted to write a novel in this décor. Despite a Negro presence, what is characteristic of Paris is that it is, among so many things, a cosmopolitan white city. Therefore Giovanni is an Italian, and the "I" of the book a white American. What, at all events, is positive is this: there is no "getting at" white Americans because the fallen hero of the book is what he is; for James Baldwin's reasons for criticizing white Americans are infinitely profounder than this one could ever be.

The "plot," then, of *Giovanni's Room* is, by comparison with that of the earlier book, a simple one; indeed, the work is more a *nouvelle* than a novel and, in certain nonrealistic passages, more in the nature of a prose poem than a work of fiction. David, the young American son of an amiable but characterless and boozy father, and whose mother died in his infancy, has had, in adolescence, a homosexual experience—which attracts and frightens him—and is now an expatriate in Paris engaged to Hella, who is away travelling in Spain. Through his acquaintance Jacques, an elderly queen from whom he is obliged to borrow money, he is introduced to Guillaume's queer bar where the new and splendiferous barman is Giovanni. A drunken night culminating in a hectically romantic early breakfast at the Halles brings David to Giovanni's lodgings in the outer suburbs. There David remains for several months, falling out of love with Giovanni even to the extent of engineering a loveless affair with the rich American girl Sue. When Hella returns from Spain, David returns to her entirely, to Giovanni's consternation. But when Giovanni murders the odious bar owner Guillaume, and is to be guillotined for this, David feels himself responsible for Giovanni's death and turns against Hella who, finding David is now reverting to a homosexual pattern, leaves him in detestation.

I must say at once I think the realistic passages of the book are admirable, and its more important psychological conclusions much less so. In a nutshell, the flaw seems to me to be that *Giovanni's Room* is— whereas the earlier book only seemed at first to be—a melodrama. In tone, the work has a sort of Edgar Allen Poe fatality, and one cannot but feel the writer has fallen into the fatal trap (the Thomas Hardy fallacy, one might say) of manipulating fate for a predetermined purpose, instead of making it—in the manner of the Greeks—appear as an inevitable force arising from the logic of event and character. And I would go on to suggest that this defect arises from an ambiguity in the writer's own attitude to homosexuality. The "moral" of the work is that homosexuality is doomed, and brings doom. This may very well in fact be true, but the trouble is Baldwin makes it seem less true to life as he describes it than to a preconception that his characters must be condemned.

The book's title, and the room itself are, I suppose, a symbol: that of the sterility and self-destruction of homosexual love. Giovanni's lodging is in a grim street far from the centers of Parisian life, it is squalid and disorganized in appearance, and it looks out on a wall—or rather, does not, for Giovanni has painted the window over. It is their first meeting, and Giovanni is speaking:

Look at the garbage of this city . . . where do they take it? I don't know where they take it—but it might very well be my room.

And David reflects:

This was not the garbage of Paris, which would have been anonymous: this was Giovanni's regurgitated life . . . for this was not a matter of habit or circumstance or temperament; it was a matter of punishment and grief.

Giovanni and David are both by experience bisexuals with the important difference that Giovanni is a true one (that is to say, his loves for both women and men have hitherto been instinctive and unclouded), whereas David fears and regrets his own homosexuality however strongly it impels him. This is in one sense simply a distinction between the Latin-pagan and the Anglo-Saxon-puritan temperaments, but it also involves a contradiction that I find hard to accept in the characters of these two men as Baldwin evokes them. For that David would turn against the homosexual element in his nature is entirely credible; but that Giovanni, as the writer had revealed him, would be destroyed by David's leaving him, I find hard to believe. And when the author tells us

Beneath the joy, of course, was anguish, and beneath the amazement was fear [which] had become the surface on which we slipped and slid, losing balance, dignity and pride. . . .

I am bound to feel that when the author says "we" it is a case of Baldwin-David, so to speak, imposing reactions on Baldwin-Giovanni that are alien to the nature of the latter. Nor can I credit that a—to put it crudely—proud bisexual butch Italian—albeit one lonely, poor, emotional and without strong will—which Giovanni is shown to be in the earlier part of the book, should become, in a mere matter of months, and as the result of *any* happening, the venal hysterical fairy that he does. The "room," and its fatality, exist in David's imagination from the start, and rightly so, he being divided in his heart; but that it should be, for Giovanni, a potential prison cell—the analogy is actually made with a real cell by the author later on—is far less credible. And when Baldwin tells us

I do not think I will ever love anyone like that again. And this might be a great relief if I did not also know that, when the knife has fallen, Giovanni, if he feels anything will feel relief. . . .

I really lose touch with him altogether, because I simply don't believe anyone feels "relief" when being guillotined.

But when we come to realistic descriptions of the cosmopolitan homo-sexual world, the writer cannot be faulted: he catches exactly its odious and exciting elements and also—a far more difficult feat—the beauty, in which no dogmatic heterosexual will ever believe, of the rare homosexual affection. Among the horrors:

There were the usual paunchy, bespectacled gentlemen with avid, sometimes despairing eyes, the usual knife-blade, lean, tight-trousered boys. One could never be sure, as concerns these latter, whether they were after money or blood or love.

And:

This lewdness was particularly revolting in that it not only failed of wit, it was so clearly an expression of contempt and self-contempt; it bubbled upward out of them like a fountain of black water.

And more subtly still,

. . . for affection, for the boys I was doomed to look at, was vastly more frightening than lust.

Nor is the writer—ever a moralist, and here a true one—for a moment un-aware that loveless heterosexual "love" is just as horrible as any other. For when David uses the girl Sue to escape from Giovanni, he reflects

But I was thinking that what I did with Giovanni could not possibly be more immoral than what I was about to do with Sue.

Nor does it escape the writer that old women chasing boys can be just as revolting as the old men he has shown us doing so. Correctly, he gives this observation to the girl Hella:

The way these old hags guzzle and make eyes at anything in pants, especially anything about eighteen—well, I said to myself, Hella, my girl, take a good look. You may be looking at your future.

Nevertheless, we must take it that, in general terms, the author's con-clusion is that homosexuality is the greater destruction:

And at moments like this I felt that we were merely enduring and committing the longer and lesser and more perpetual murder.[2]

[2] For anyone interested in the disputed question of the origins in child-hood of homosexual inclination we may notice that Baldwin does not give

Technically, the book is somewhat disturbing. Once again we are submitted to the "flashback" device, but with less assurance than in the earlier work, and at one point the reader may be rather confused by a "flash-forward" to a moment ahead in time of the pivotal period that is initially established. The author also handles the "I" narrative device a little erratically by suddenly presenting us with detailed "he" scenes (for instance in the death cell) which the supposed "I" narrator could not possibly have witnessed.

But to set against these weaknesses I must mention passages not, perhaps, always relevant to the main story, but which reveal yet another aspect of Baldwin's talent, or temperament, which is his wisdom; for deft analysis of human nature, and aphorisms about our lives, abound. For instance:

Perhaps, as we say in America, I wanted to find myself. This is an interesting phrase, not current so far as I know in the language of any other people, which certainly does not mean what it says, but betrays a nagging suspicion that something has been misplaced.

Or:

People who remember court madness through pain, the pain of the perpetually recurring death of their innocence; people who forget court another kind of madness, the madness of the denial of pain and the hatred of innocence; and the world is most divided between madmen who remember and madmen who forget.

There are also splendid descriptions of Parisian personages and seasons, of which I would specially mention the evocation of that eternal and formidable figure, the French lady behind the cash register, and of the summer and autumn which are the metaphor of Giovanni-David's rapture and destruction.

I hope I don't sound patronizing if I say I think *Giovanni's Room* is a brave try, however beautiful in parts. It was not all that easy for any writer in English to confront this theme in 1956 and, more particularly, a Negro writer who was already vulnerable on so many other grounds to mean and hostile criticism. One difficulty, of course, is that the Anglo-Saxon reading public is not yet ready, even today, for a book on this subject which can take it straight without the writer having to look over six shoulders at once to avoid all kinds of misinterpretation.

David the conventional over-loving mother—since she is long dead—but a weakly affectionate father and a hard foster-mother . . . to my own mind just as likely an explanation.

ANOTHER COUNTRY (1962)

This is the least overtly personal of James Baldwin's novels, the most ambitious and, I regret to have to say, the least successful. The theme is most promising, for Baldwin here unites the two races and examines the relations between whites and blacks in contemporary New York.

Rufus, a dazzling, self-torturing colored jazz musician, is the friend of Vivaldo, a "good liberal" white writer of Italian-Irish descent. Vivaldo, between bouts of whoring up in Harlem, is attached to a slatternly white Greenwich Village painter called Jane; and, when the book begins, Rufus has begun an affair with a poor-white expatriate from the South named Leona. This affair, which begins on a high note of sexual excitement, ends in Leona's madness and Rufus' suicide, for the black and white pasts of the two lovers rise up and drive them both to hatred and destruction.

Ida, Rufus' younger sister, and soon to be a successful jazz singer, now starts a love affair with Vivaldo which is the central topic of the book. Throughout its tempestuous progress the author examines, in immensely painful detail, all the forces, personal and racial, that make love between black and white almost impossible. Vivaldo and Ida finally survive their ordeal by the self-knowledge, and knowledge of each other, they acquire through it—which chiefly involves the white liberal man rejecting facile "solutions" and learning to live, as Ida must, with the racial problem haunting every moment of his life. "I don't want you to be *understanding*," Ida says to him in a final scene. "I don't want you to be kind . . ." and at their last embrace, the author describes the black girl "stroking his innocence out of him."

Subsidiary characters are Eric, a rich white actor who has escaped from Alabama, a former lover of Rufus, and now of a French ex–male prostitute called Yves. Also Cass, a white woman of "good family" who is married to the ex-Polish Richard, a bad but successful novelist—this being a "white racial" tangle that enables Baldwin to echo the profounder conflicts of Rufus-Leona and of Vivaldo-Ida. To this one must add that since all the principal male characters (except Richard) turn out to be bisexual, there is a good deal of homosexual bed-switching—as well as liaisons between some of the characters of a more orthodox kind.

To begin with the book's virtues, one may say it is a wonderful, if scarifying, portrait of New York, about which great agglomeration the writer makes us feel that all Manhattan Island ("the world's most bewildered city"), and not just Harlem, is a ghetto of imprisoned and self-imprisoned human victims. The author both implies this constantly and states it at times overtly:

It might, almost, for strange barbarity of manner and custom, for the sense of danger and horror barely sleeping beneath the rough, gregarious surface, have been some impenetrably exotic city of the East.

And on New Yorkers:

They seemed . . . to be at home with, accustomed to, brutality and indifference, and to be terrified of human affection. In some strange way they did not seem to feel that they were worthy of it.

As most of the scenes take place in the depths of winter, we are made to feel the harsh climate reflects the cruel spirit of the city; but even when summer comes things aren't much better:

The heat and the noise began their destruction of nerves and sanity and private lives and love affairs. The air was full of baseball scores and bad news and treacly songs; and the streets and the bars were full of hostile people, made more hostile by the heat.

The evocations of the blighted love of Rufus for Leona, and of the ultimately successful one of Vivaldo for Rufus' sister Ida—and even more, perhaps, of the male black-white friendship of Rufus and Vivaldo—are often most touching, as well as profoundly revealing of the huge obstacles to interracial affections. And though the writer places most of the blame for this frustration upon the whites—which in one sense is only just, since the overall racial situation in the U. S. is white-created—he is very ready to allow that blacks have been equally distorted by these circumstances. Thus, Rufus excuses his cruelty to Leona by accusing her of loving only his sex (which is untrue), Vivaldo sees that his friend Rufus hates him because, though white, he *is* nevertheless his only true friend, and Leona is made to realize that Rufus' hatred for her is really because, being black, he can't believe he's "good enough" for her. The author is also just in showing that there are far blinder white liberals than Vivaldo—who is at least *trying*, at the cost of pain—and introduces us to a hideous gallery of these spiritual eunuchs. But his final conclusion seems to be that, save in the rarest and most agony-racked of unions, true illumination and equality between the races will be rare. Rufus and Vivaldo, for example, may at first seem to us, for a black and white, to be unusually intimate. But:

And yet how much, as it turned out, had each kept hidden in his heart from the other!

And when he gives the ensuing terrible speech to Ida, one cannot but feel his own message is that almost all whites, however well-intentioned, still have everything to learn:

"What you people don't know," she said, "is that life is a *bitch*, baby. It's the biggest hype going. You don't have any experience in paying your dues and it's going to be rough on you, baby, when the deal goes down. There's lots of back dues to be collected, and I know damn well you haven't got a penny saved."

Interspersed throughout the novel one may also find many of those acute observations of life and character that have the unmistakable Baldwin terseness and penetration:

The waiter entered the room, looking as though he wondered where on earth he could be. . . .

.   .   .   .

They shook hands and murmured salutations in a silence that began to stiffen like the beaten white of an egg.

.   .   .   .

Strangers' faces hold no secrets because the imagination does not invest them with any. But the face of a lover is an unknown precisely because it is invested with so much of oneself.

The trouble with a secret life is that it is very frequently a secret from the person who lives it and not at all a secret for the people he encounters.

For the act of love is a confession. One lies about the body but the body does not lie about itself; it cannot lie about the force which drives it.

Then what has gone wrong with the book? In a general way, I would say that *Another Country* is much too bulky for what it has to say. The passages in which Baldwin makes his points, and makes them splendidly, are buried amid vast wastelands that neither add to nor prepare for the declaration of his essential themes. There is an immense amount of dialogue, but a great deal of it is what I would never have believed possible in any page Baldwin wrote, which is simply dull. It is not just a matter of "cutting"—though even this, I think, would have often been a help. For example, I ask myself (turning rather niggly) what on earth this can add to anything?

She turned to Jane and Vivaldo. "So long, kids. See you soon."
"Sure," Jane said.

"I'm expecting you," Richard said, "don't fail me. So long, Jane."
"So long."
"So long."

It is true that, in his record of white speech, the author is excellent at catching the ominous facetiousness, the tone of menace combined with frenetic optimism, that characterizes so much American conversation: the note of *battle* underlying the "friendliest" remark. But too often the dialogue is not human speech at all, but a case of the writer, somewhat languidly, using his characters' voices as mere vehicles for his own not very astringent thoughts.

As for sexual episodes, although there are glorious moments (and let no one imagine the author of *Giovanni's Room* cannot evoke the passions of men and women), the effect is frequently turgid and high-flown: the worst passages being almost like inflated set-piece parodies of the best. The obscenities given to the characters are sometimes disturbing not because of themselves, but because they add little to any effect, so that it is almost as if the author is writing them out of his system at the unfortunate reader's expense. As for the bisexual element, although I personally would be the last to deny its validity in general (since I believe it to be far more widespread than homosexuality), its introduction does sometimes seem to me frankly improbable. For instance, I just can't believe that Eric, who is presented to us as a dedicated queer from childhood, would suddenly have had an affair with Cass (Clarissa) for which nothing in his character prepares us. And although I know Americans drink a lot (so do we, but we don't drink against ourselves as they do), I do wish the bourbon bottles and ice cubes had clinked rather less frequently throughout the volume. (The trouble about making your characters drunk too often is that you must then either make them talk drunk and be bores, or talk sober and be incredible.)

Structurally, the book is weak. Not only does our old friend (or enemy to clarity), the flashback, make once more its fell appearance—and here, I feel, for no valid artistic reason—but the ending is inconclusive in the extreme. The author has already resolved his principal theme—the Ida-Vivaldo triumph over race—in the penultimate chapter, when, lo and behold, young Yves descends from the skies at Idlewild—which episode, though excellently described, leaves the reader, so to speak, up in the air. Perhaps a minor obstacle to enjoyment of the book is that with the exception of the two chief colored characters, Rufus and Ida—and just possibly their friend Vivaldo—the personages are, in themselves, so uninteresting. This need not, of course, exclude the possibility of the author's making them so—most of the cast of *War and Peace*, for instance (particularly the entire Rostov family) would, in reality, have been terrible bores to meet—and would anyone in his senses wish to spend even five minutes with anybody whatever in *A Passage to India*? But the trouble is that, artistically speaking, so many of the persons in this book seem dingy; and that in it, Baldwin is really too much of a realist. Life may indeed be like that, but it is to avoid its tedium, and seek after enlightenment, that we read novels. One explanation of this defect may be that Greenwich Village, with more frauds to the square foot than even in Islington or Chelsea, is a most unpromising décor for a writer of James Baldwin's caliber.

But Rufus and Ida do redeem the book: Ida, "haughty and free," and her wonderful doomed brother, who recalls the seductive Richard of the first novel. Baldwin has a superb instinct for brushing aside the clichés about his people and showing us all their majesty—and their failings. His conclusions about their relations with ourselves may be pessimistic, but—until better days, pray God, soon dawn—one must feel rightly so. Here we all are at present, in a New York subway, on our journey to superfluous perdition:

Many white people and many black people, chained together in time and in space, and by history, and all of them in a hurry. In a hurry to get away from each other, he thought, but we ain't never going to make it.

THE COLLECTED ESSAYS

There are three books of these, *Notes of a Native Son* (1955), *Nobody Knows My Name* (1961), and *The Fire Next Time* of the present year [1963]; and since certain themes recur in each collection, I shall consider these essays all together.

The first quality in these essays is their extraordinary *tone*. Baldwin was just over thirty when the first collection appeared—and many of the essays were of course written when he was even younger—but already the note of authority is as unmistakable as it is unforced. As to the style, if I may borrow his own description of jazz and gospel songs—"taut, ironic, authoritative, and double-edged"—these fit exactly. To them I would add a natural dignity, a sadly acid wit, and an enormous, quite uncondescending—if exigently demanding—humanity.

Their chief theme is race, and all I can say about Baldwin's analysis of this ghastly topic is that if there is anything conceivable to add, I cannot imagine what it may be. Hearing him is not always a pleasurable experience—it is, in fact, apart from the beauty of his prose, usually an embarrassing one—but at least, having read him, you can no longer feel you do not *know*, if only at second hand. In a final section I shall describe his analysis of the racial dilemma; but before doing so—and perhaps somewhat absurdly, since almost all the essays return inevitably to this focal point—I shall consider their subjects in a more general "literary" way.

AUTOBIOGRAPHICAL SOURCES OF HIS OWN NOVELS

These are to be found in minute detail in many of the essays, and are of great interest to readers who may wish to relate the experience of life to the creation of art. There are vivid descriptions of the New York (and Parisian) setting of the books, and a most touching portrait of the writer's father who, one may guess, was the original of Gabriel in the first novel. Forays into the deep South—the "Old Country" to northern Negroes, yet a foreign land in any human sense—are eloquently and painfully described.

LITERARY AND ARTISTIC CRITICISM

Among artists and their creations that are analyzed are *Uncle Tom's Cabin* (devastatingly); the "colored" film, *Carmen Jones* (even more so); a critique of Faulkner's racial theories (which sink without a trace, despite Baldwin's respect for Faulkner as an artist); André Gide; the films of Bergman; and the affectionate quarrel of the writer with Norman Mailer. No less than three essays are devoted to the life and work of Richard Wright, in relation to whom Baldwin was both extremely close, and as distant as any two writers could be. But although his criticism of Wright's art and social ideas is unremitting, it is equally generous, for Baldwin is the first to allow the huge debt he owes to his precursor.

U. S. NEGROES AND AFRICANS

Just as Baldwin is haunted by the black-white relationship in general, so he is—as all U. S. Negroes must be—by the contact that can be made with the African descendants of their same ancestors. This theme recurs in several essays, and is chiefly developed in *Princes and Powers,* an account of the Conference of Negro-African Writers and Artists at the Sorbonne (published in *Encounter,* January 1957). His most striking reaction to the strangers is, "The Africans seemed at once simpler and more devious, more directly erotic and at the same time more subtle, and they were proud."

U. S. NEGROES AND EUROPEANS

Among this group of essays the most memorable—and tragicomic—is the harrowing account of the author's imprisonment in Paris, one Christmas, on the false charge of being a receiver of stolen goods (the "goods" in question being a bed sheet). There is a revealing account also of the amazement with which Baldwin's presence was greeted in an Alpine village where no colored man had ever been seen before.

The remaining essays—about one-half in all—deal directly with the color theme. Of these the most famous and remarkable is "Down at the Cross," which appeared originally in *The New Yorker* earlier this year [1962] under the title "Letter from a Region of My Mind"; and which (accompanying a heartfelt "Letter to My Nephew") constitutes the most recent book, with its ominous title of *The Fire Next Time*. I suppose almost everyone has now read this essay—Mr. Robert Kennedy surely has— and it deals, among many things, with Baldwin's reaction to an encounter with Elijah Muhammad, leader of the Black Muslims, and with his followers including his heir apparent, Malcolm X.

The white liberal reaction to the news that James Baldwin had met Elijah Muhammad would of course be, "But naturally, he will see this man is no more than a dangerous black racist imposter!" But if anyone does think that, they understand neither Baldwin, nor the Black Muslims, nor the Negro people as a whole. One has only to read some of the detailed interviews with Malcolm X to see that this zealot is no colored Alfred Rosenberg, but a lucid, passionate, and highly intelligent prophet whose declarations, however detestable, are unanswerable within their own terms of reference. That is to say, given what Negroes were promised 100 years ago at the Emancipation, and given the massive betrayal of these promises, the extreme position Malcolm X adopts has a horrible logic and, despite the atrocity of his conclusions, an austerely undeniable truth.

That Baldwin has much sympathy for the Muslim position cannot be doubted (who *can* fail to have sympathy for it in some measure?), yet he is too fine a human being, as well as a black human being, to accept it. But I must insist that it would be folly for us whites to take it for granted that Negro artists and intellectuals, simply because we somewhat patronizingly admire them, will all automatically deny the Muslim message and its perils to ourselves. Let it not be forgotten that, in Europe of the 'thirties, the fascists claimed many an intellectual. And the only way we can hope to ensure that Malcolm X does not win the Negro intellectuals' loyalty is by hearkening to their warnings—and even to those of Malcolm X—and *acting* upon these without any more delay.

What, then, is the racial message these alarming essays leave us with? If liberalism is not enough, what does Baldwin ask of us? And ask of all whites, not only white Americans (though his message is, of course, directed most particularly to them), because we Britons, for example, have a profound responsibility in this matter. We, not Americans, took the first black slaves to the Americas; we have a black colonial past and, even today, a black colonial present; we too have a colored minority in our midst; and most of all, we are part of that internationally *white minority* (for whites are now a minute, almost eccentric, fraction of the global population) that must learn how to come to human terms with the multitude of colored races if only to avoid our own destruction by them.

First, we can try to follow Baldwin's analysis of the predicament, and extract from it the following propositions:

We must not expect the impossible of Negroes, but realize what they are.

I can conceive of no Negro native to this country who has not, by the age of puberty, been irreplaceably scarred by the conditions of his life.

I am not one of the people who believes that oppression imbues a people with wisdom or insight or sweet charity, though the survival of the Negro in this country would simply not have been possible if this bitterness had been all he felt.

The African before him has endured privation, injustice, medieval cruelty; but the African has not yet endured the utter alienation of himself from his people and his past.

I am proud of these people not because of their color but because of their intelligence and their spiritual force and their beauty.

A ghetto can be improved in only one way: out of existence.

We must see estrangement from Negroes is estrangement from ourselves.

The ways in which the Negro has affected the American psychology are betrayed in our popular culture and in our morality; in our estrangement from him is the depth of our estrangement from ourselves.

Hatred, which could destroy so much, never failed to destroy the man who hated and this was an immutable law.

At the root of the American Negro problem is the necessity of the American white man to find a way of living with the Negro in order to be able to live with himself.

It is a terrible, an inexorable, law that one cannot deny the humanity of another without diminishing one's own: in the face of one's victim, one sees oneself.

We must understand the real roots of the problem.

But the dispute has actually nothing to do with education, as some among the eminently uneducated know. It has to do with political power and it has to do with sex. And this is a nation which, most unluckily, knows very little about either.

We would never, never allow Negroes to starve, to grow bitter, and to die in ghettos all over the country if we were not driven by some nameless fear that has nothing to do with Negroes.

It is only too clear that even with the most malevolent will in the world Negroes can never manage to achieve one-tenth of the harm which we fear.

And this reason, this fear, suggests to me one of the real reasons for the status of the Negro in this country. In a way, the Negro tells us where the bottom is: *because he is there,* and *where* he is, beneath us, we know where the limits are and how far we must not fall.

It is still true, alas, that to be an American Negro male is also to be a kind of walking phallic symbol: which means that one pays, in one's own personality, for the sexual insecurity of others.

White Americans find it as difficult as white people elsewhere to divest themselves of the notion that they are in possession of some intrinsic value that black people need, or want.

Therefore, a vast amount of the energy that goes into what we call the Negro problem is produced by the white man's profound desire not to be judged by those who are not white, not to be seen as he is, and at the same time a vast amount of the white anguish is rooted in the white man's equally profound need to be seen as he is, to be released from the tyranny of his mirror.

Color is not a human or a personal reality: it is a political reality.

We must realize what all human creatures really are.

Let us say, then, that truth, as used here, is meant to imply a devotion to the human being, his freedom and fulfilment; freedom which cannot be legislated, fulfilment which cannot be charted.

But our humanity is our burden, our life; we need not battle for it; we need only to do what is infinitely more difficult—that is, accept it.

I imagine that one of the reasons people cling to their hates so stubbornly is because they sense, once hate is gone, that they will be forced to deal with pain.

It is really quite impossible to be affirmative about anything which one refuses to question; one is doomed to remain inarticulate about anything which one hasn't, by an act of the imagination, made one's own.

What, in sum, black men held in common was their ache to come into the world as men.

We must overcome the wish to save, and learn to be saved.

. . . it is we, who, every hour that we live, re-invest the black face with our guilt; and we do this—by a further paradox, no less ferocious—helplessly, passionately, out of an unrealized need to suffer absolution.

"I am not at all sure," states one prominent Negro, who is *not* a Muslim, "that I *want* to be integrated into a burning house."

Love does not begin and end the way we seem to think it does. Love is a battle, love is war; love is growing up.

There is no reason for you to try to become like white people and there is no basis whatever for their impertinent assumption that *they* must accept *you.*

We must realize the time is now.

And if the word *integration* means anything, this is what it means: that we, with love, shall force our brothers to see themselves as they are, to cease fleeing from reality and begin to change it.

It is galling indeed to have stood so long, hat in hand, waiting for Americans to grow up enough to realize that you do not threaten them.

He [the Negro] is *the* key figure in this country, and the American future is precisely as bright or as dark as his.

The price of the liberation of the white people is the liberation of the blacks—the total liberation, in the cities, in the towns, before the law, and in the mind.

The challenge is in the moment, the time is always now.

If I have called this study, rather romantically, *Dark Angel*, this is not simply because its subject is a Negro, and his temperament and character one of the most lovable of any I have yet encountered ("a very tight, tense, lean, abnormally ambitious, abnormally intelligent, and hungry black cat"). It is because my words have also a double meaning: *dark* being not only colored, but used in the sense of "dark irony" (*humour noir*)—an insidious, mocking, dangerous, challenging, seriously subversive tone that may be felt in all Baldwin's writings. And when I think of *angels* I think, certainly, of guardian ones, and of visitants from heaven who bring tidings of joy and comfort to mankind, but also remember that angels are perilous creatures, often appearing with a sword to warn, admonish, even scarify and scourge.

Yet may one offer counsel even to an angel? First, I do not believe Baldwin, despite his intense consciousness of us, and his personal friendships with so many white people since he became a writer, knows at all what the white man's, or woman's, predicament is in relation to the problem that so constantly harasses his spirit. It may seem a hypocritical impertinence for any white to say to any Negro, "We have suffered more than you," yet I believe that there is much truth in this. For if you are wronged that is horrible, but your spirit, though tortured, can remain pure; but if you have wronged, and know it, you know also not just desperation, but pangs of remorse that nothing—not even atonement—can ever alleviate.

My other admonition (turning at long last the tables!) is this one. Baldwin has told us, in the essays, how Richard Wright, his mentor, reached the point at which, on the "color question," he had said his say but did not realize it. Might not now—though in an entirely different context—an identical danger threaten the hero of this essay? It is not that anyone could wish he should change his ideas by one iota, nor be less faithful to the cause which he has made his own—and one which has nourished and ennobled him, as he has it. It is not either, I do hope, that I am being here a crafty white, trying to seduce, by a "sophisticated" argument, the black man from his essential devotion. It is rather that one must wonder what, *as a writer*, James Baldwin is going to tell us now? Could it not be the same tale told, even more profoundly, in an entirely different form? For after all, Bessie Smith, whom Baldwin so much admires, made her message about the colored situation all the more specific and eternal by dint of never singing precisely what this message was.

IN DEFENSE OF JAMES BALDWIN *

Norman Podhoretz

OVERPRAISING mediocre or merely passable or positively bad novels is a regular habit with American reviewers—so much so that anyone who takes literature seriously is forever finding himself in the tiresome position of having to cry Fraud at the latest masterpiece to be discovered by the papers. Yet when a truly important novel is either neglected (as was originally the case in this country with William Golding's *Lord of the Flies*) or gets a bad press (as, say, Norman Mailer's *The Deer Park* did), the process of correction seems to require an unconscionable length of time. The sooner the process begins, however, the sooner it is bound to end, and I would therefore like to venture a step or two in the direction of literary justice to a new novel that seems to me to have been maltreated in an appalling way: James Baldwin's *Another Country*.

In speaking of maltreatment, let me make it clear that I do not mean to introduce a note of pathos into the discussion. Mr. Baldwin is certainly a victim of injustice at the moment, but he is not a pathetic victim. For one thing, his two earlier novels, *Go Tell It on the Mountain* and *Giovanni's Room*, were both praised beyond their proper deserts (especially the second), so that the general failure to appreciate *Another Country* can be taken as an ironic rectification of the balance. In addition to that, *Another Country* has been on the best-seller lists since it came out several months ago, so that Mr. Baldwin can at least read his bad reviews in comfort. Thirdly, far from being a perfect novel, *Another Country* is faulty to a degree that would wreck a work of lesser force and intensity and truthfulness, so that many of the charges that have been made against it are in themselves quite justified. Finally, the reviews were by no means uniformly hostile. Several pieces in scattered papers and magazines throughout the country—most notably Granville Hicks's moving and intelligent account in *The Saturday Review*—were enthusiastic, and many others, while finding fault with Baldwin's "lack of restraint," or his overly candid descriptions of sexual activity, or his use of dialogue, or his treatment of character, or his handling of plot, nevertheless acknowledged the novel's "power." All the

* Reprinted from *Doings and Undoings* (New York: Farrar, Straus and Co., 1964), by permission of the publisher.

reviewers, moreover (including those who detested the book), made sure to reserve enough space for an earnest tribute to Mr. Baldwin's talents, calling him one of our very best writers and voicing a pious confidence in his ability to do better in future.

But in spite of all this, I will stand by the word *maltreatment*. With few exceptions, the major reviewing media were very hard on *Another Country*. It was patronized by Paul Goodman in *The New York Times Book Review*, ridiculed by Stanley Edgar Hyman in *The New Leader*, worried over (with, it must be said, genuine distress) by Elizabeth Hardwick in *Harper's*, summarily dismissed by *Time's* anonymous critic, loftily pitied by Whitney Balliett in *The New Yorker*, and indignantly attacked by Saul Maloff in *The Nation*.

Three of these reviewers—Goodman, Hardwick, and Hyman—are first-rate critics, and I therefore find it hard to believe that their wrong-headed appraisals of *Another Country* can be ascribed to a simple lapse of literary judgment. How could anyone as sensitive and knowledgeable as Elizabeth Hardwick have been so led astray by Baldwin's occasional lapses into sentimentality in writing about love and sex as to call the book "conventional" and "uninspired"? How could a man of Stanley Edgar Hyman's sophistication have been so fooled by the large quantity of explicit erotic detail in *Another Country* as to accuse Baldwin of having cynically set out to fabricate a best seller? How could Paul Goodman, who most assuredly knows better, have taken the fact that all the characters are cut off from the main world of the city as a sign that this novel is a typical commercial product? My own guess is that all these critics disliked *Another Country* not because it suffers from this or that literary failing, but because they were repelled by the militancy and the cruelty of its vision of life. Granville Hicks was right when he called the book "an act of violence," and since it is the reader upon whom this violence is being committed, perhaps one ought to have expected that many reviewers would respond with something less than gratitude.

Another Country is about a crucial year in the lives of a group of people who inhabit a kind of underworld (for the most part physically located in Greenwich Village) of interracial and intersexual relations. Of the five main characters, two are Negroes—a famous jazz drummer, Rufus Scott, and his younger sister Ida, an aspiring singer—and the other three are white—Rufus's closest friend, a young, unpublished, and unmarried writer (Vivaldo Moore); a woman whose marriage is beginning to fail (Cass Silenski); and a homosexual actor who comes originally from the South (Eric Jones). Rufus—by far the most impressive character Baldwin has ever created—has a love affair with a pathetic white Southern girl named Leona which ends for him in suicide and for her in insanity. After Rufus's death, his sister Ida falls in love with Vivaldo, and while they are living together (less stormily than Rufus and Leona had, but stormily enough), Ida is unfaithful to him with a television producer who promises to further her career, and he, though not a homosexual, spends a night in bed with Eric by whom, as Stanley Edgar Hyman delicately put it, he permits himself to be "rectally violated." By this time, we have already learned that Rufus, although not a homosexual either, had also had an affair with Eric. As for Eric, he too crosses over the line and enters into an affair with Cass, who is fed up with the kind of man her husband has become since producing a successful but trivial novel.

Whites coupled with Negroes, heterosexuals coupled with homosexuals, homosexuals coupled with women, none of it involving casual lust or the suggestion of neurotic perversity, and all of it accompanied by the most serious emotions and resulting in the most intense attachments—it is easy enough to see even from so crude a summary that Baldwin's intention is to deny any moral significance whatever to the categories white and Negro, heterosexual and homosexual. He is saying that the terms white and Negro refer to two different conditions under which individuals live, but they are still individuals and their lives are still governed by the same fundamental laws of being. And he is saying, similarly, that the terms homosexuality and heterosexuality refer to two different conditions under which individuals pursue love, but they are still individuals and their pursuit of love is still governed by the same fundamental laws of being. Putting the two propositions together, he is saying, finally, that the only significant realities are individuals and love, and that anything which is permitted to interfere with the free operation of this fact is evil and should be done away with.

Now, one might suppose that there is nothing particularly startling in this view of the world; it is, after all, only a form of the standard liberal attitude toward life. And indeed, stated as I have just stated it, and held with the mild attachment by which most liberal and enlightened Americans hold it, it is scarcely more shocking than the usual speech made at every convention of the American Society of Social Workers. But that is not the way James Baldwin holds it, and it is not the way he states it. He holds these attitudes with a puritanical ferocity, and he spells them out in such brutal and naked detail that one scarcely recognizes them any longer —and one is frightened by them, almost as though they implied a totally new, totally revolutionary, conception of the universe. And in a sense, of course, they do. For by taking these liberal pieties literally and by translating them into simple English, he puts the voltage back into them and they burn to the touch. Do you believe, he demands of you, that racial prejudice is wrong, that all men are created equal, that individuals must be judged on their own merits? Then you must dare to surrender the objections you are surely still harboring in your soul against miscegenation. You must acknowledge that there is no reason why whites and Negroes should not sleep together and marry and produce children with as little interference as members of the same race now encounter. And that this is impossible you must recognize as a momentous fact about American life, signifying a moral sickness that may end by destroying our capacity for any kind of human contact whatever. Do you believe, he demands of you again, that love is the supreme value and that sex is the most natural expression of love? Then you must dare to realize that the stifling of your own impulses toward a sexual articulation of the love you feel for members of your own sex is unnatural, signifying a warping of the instincts and of the body that may end by destroying your capacity for any kind of sexual experience whatever.

Another Country, then, is informed by a remorseless insistence on a truth which, however partial we may finally judge it to be, is nevertheless compelling as a perspective on the way we live now. It is a cruel truth, and a demanding one, but it is not without an element of sweet spiritual generosity. For implicit in it is the idea that everyone carries his own burden, that every burden is ultimately as heavy as every other, and that a man is either brave enough or strong enough to stand up straight under the weight on his back or he isn't; and if he isn't, he will pay the price and no one else has the right to judge him harshly; and if enough people are found to be lacking in enough bravery or enough strength, then there must be something wrong with the conditions they are being forced to endure and the values these conditions have bred.

Wherever Baldwin manages to remain true to this vision—as in the magnificent opening section about Rufus, the account of the relations between Vivaldo and Ida, and scattered passages in every other part of the book—he is at his very best, achieving a unique blend of subtlety and forcefulness, anger and understanding. But there are situations and characters that tax Baldwin's power to sustain the burden of his moral attitudes to the breaking point. Thus, he is merciless on Cass Silenski's husband Richard, who is a bad writer and a success, while remaining infinitely charitable toward Vivaldo, who is also a bad writer but a failure; he inclines toward sentimentality in most of the erotic passages involving either a white and a Negro, or two men, or a homosexual and a woman, whereas he is visibly skeptical of the validity of the more standard varieties of sex; he can trace every nuance in the relations of an unmarried couple, but in writing about marriage he falls into something very close to philistinism; and in general he judges white characters (with the exception of the homosexual Eric) by more rigorous criteria than he is willing to apply to the Negroes in the book. All of which means that Baldwin, who speaks so passionately of the white man's need for the courage to know the Negro and the heterosexual's need to know the homosexual, is himself unable to summon the courage to know and respect those who live in that other country usually designated as normal.

But I do not wish to end on a negative note. Despite the lapses of which he is guilty here, what Baldwin has accomplished in *Another Country* is impressive and important. Within the context of his own development as a writer, I believe that *Another Country* will come to be seen as the book in which for the first time the superb intelligence of Baldwin the essayist became fully available to Baldwin the novelist, in which for the first time he attempted to speak his mind with complete candor and with a minimum of polite rhetorical elegance, and in which for the first time he dared to reveal himself as someone to be feared for how deeply he sees, how much he demands of the world, and how powerfully he can hate. Is that why so many of the reviewers disliked *Another Country*? The question is worth pondering.

BALDWIN AND THE
PROBLEM OF BEING*

George E. Kent

In a *New York Times Book Review* essay, James Baldwin has stated that the effort to become a great novelist "involves attempting to tell as much of the truth as one can bear, and then a little more." [1] It is likely in our time to mean attacking much that Americans tend to hold sacred, in order that reality be confronted and constructively altered. As stated in "Everybody's Protest Novel," it means devotion to the "human being, his freedom and fulfillment; freedom which cannot be legislated, fulfillment which cannot be charted." [2] Baldwin then wishes to confront and affect the human consciousness and conscience. He rejects the tradition of the protest novel because he feels that it denies life, "the human being . . . his beauty, dread, power," and insists "that it is categorization alone which is real and which cannot be transcended." [3] He tries to write the way jazz musicians sound, to reflect their compassion, [4] and it is noteworthy that Baldwin's tendency in *Go Tell It on the Mountain* and *Another Country* is to focus upon the individual characters' experiences in a way similar to Ralph Ellison's description of Jazz:

> For true jazz is an art of individual assertion within and against the group. Each true jazz moment (as distinct from the uninspired commercial performance) springs from a contest in which each artist challenges all the rest; each solo flight or improvisation, represents . . . a definition of his identity, as member of the collectivity, and as a link in the chain of tradition. [5]

[1] James Baldwin, "As Much Truth as One Can Bear," *The New York Times Book Review* (January 14, 1962), p. 1.

[2] *Notes of a Native Son* (Boston, 1955), p. 15.

[3] *Ibid.*, p. 23.

[4] "What's the Reason Why: A Symposium by Best Selling Authors," *The New York Times Book Review* (December 2, 1962), p. 3.

[5] Ralph Ellison, "The Charlie Christian Story," *Saturday Review of Literature* (May 17, 1958), p. 42.

* Reprinted from the *CLA Journal*, VII (1964), 202–14, by permission of the author and editors.

It should be generally observed that Baldwin's writings owe much to Negro folk tradition (the blues, jazz, spirituals, and folk literature), and to the chief experimental practitioners of modernist fiction, with especial emphasis upon Henry James.

The moral vision that emerges is one primarily concerned with man as he relates to good and evil and to society. For there is evil in human nature and evil abroad in the world to be confronted, not through Christianity whose doctrine tends to be the perverted tool of the ruling classes and groups whose bankruptcy was registered by the slaughter of the Jews during the Third Reich,[6] but through the love and involvement available from those able to eat of the tree of the knowledge of good and evil and live. Within the breast of each individual, then, rages a universe of forces with which he must become acquainted, often through the help of an initiated person, in order to direct them for the positive growth of himself and others. The foregoing achievement is what Baldwin means by *identity*. To achieve it, one must not be hindered by the detritus of society and one must learn to know detritus when one sees it.

Perhaps the question which throws most light upon Baldwin's works is simply: How can one achieve, amid the dislocations and disintegrations of the modern world, true, functional being? For Baldwin, the Western concept of reality, with its naïve rationalism, its ignoring of unrational forces that abound within and without man, its reductivist activities wherein it ignores the uniqueness of the individual and sees reality in terms of its simplifications and categorizations, is simply impoverishing. He who follows it fails to get into his awareness the richness and complexity of experience—he fails to be. And freedom is unattainable, since paradoxically, freedom is discovery and recognition of limitations, one's own and that of one's society;[7] to deny complexity is to paralyze the ability to get at such knowledge—it is to strangle freedom.

Groping unsteadily amidst the reductivist forces is an America which does not achieve, therefore, its primitive and essential moral identity. For the great vision that motivated the American adventure, there has been substituted a quest for spurious glory in mass production and consumption. And yet, ". . . there is so much more than Cadillacs, Frigidaires, and IBM machines. . . . One of the things wrong with this country is this notion that IBM machines *prove* something."[8] Still until America achieves its moral identity, its people, whether white or black, can fulfill nothing.

The struggle for identity, i.e., for functional being, is the major issue of Baldwin's first novel, *Go Tell It on the Mountain*. Attempting to tell

[6] James Baldwin, *The Fire Next Time* (New York, 1963), p. 66.
[7] "James Baldwin: An Interview," *WMFT Perspective* (December 1961), p. 37.
[8] *Ibid.*

part of the story found in the Negro's music, which "Americans are able to admire because a protective sentimentality limits their understanding of it," [9] Baldwin examines three generations of a Negro family whose life span extends from slavery to the present day. The novel investigates, with warmth and perception, the Negro's possibility of achieving identity through the discipline of Christianity. The style is richly evocative, and one hears echoes of Joyce and Faulkner, the rhythms of the old-time Negro sermon and the King James Bible. Unfolding in a series of major movements, the story proceeds as follows: the first movement introducing the reach of fourteen-year-old John Grimes for identity, a fearful, faltering reach, from a boy filled with guilt, hatred, fear, love, amidst the stern, religious frustrations of his elders and the pagan rebelliousness of his brother, Roy; the second presenting the tragedy of Florence, unable to overcome, among other things, the concept of the Negro she has internalized from the dominant culture—and therefore on insecure terms with herself and others; the third presenting Gabriel Grimes, stepfather of John, blocked from complete fulfillment by his attempts to escape his pagan drives in a fierce, frustrated embrace of Christianity; the fourth presenting Elizabeth, mother of John, who after brief fulfillment in illicit love, retreats, frightened and awestricken, into the frustrated and frustrating arms of Gabriel Grimes. The final movement is the questionable flight of John Grimes from the quest for identity into the ostensible safety of religious ecstasy.

Vitally represented through a series of scenes occurring on his fourteenth birthday, reflected through images of poetic intensity, are the conflicts of young John. He stands upon a hill in New York's Central Park and feels "like a giant who might crumble this city with his anger . . . like a tyrant who might crush this city with his heel . . . like a long awaited conqueror at whose feet flowers would be strewn, and before whom multitudes cried, Hosanna!" [10] Or concerning the rewards to be inherited from his preacher father: ". . . a house like his father's, a church like his father's, and a job like his father's, where he would grow old and black with hunger and toil. The way of the cross had given him a belly filled with wind and had bent his mother's back . . . ." [11] Mixed with his vision and perverting it is John's guilt over his sexual drives, the religious concept of the city as evil and the fatal tempter of the soul, and his parents' feeling that the city (New York) is filled with antagonistic whites who will block the worldly aspirations of Negroes. Over such obstacles John peers, enveloped in a solitude that seems well nigh unbreakable.

[9] Notes of a Native Son, p. 24.
[10] Go Tell It on the Mountain (New York, 1953), p. 35.
[11] Ibid., p. 37.

Part II, containing the stories of the adult members of the family who came to manhood and womanhood at the time of Emancipation, begins powerfully. Passionate scenes reveal the problems with which each character struggles. For Florence, the sister of the minister Gabriel, the central problem is to achieve an identity that excludes the concubinage already offered by her white Southern employer, the general sexual opportunism, or the image of the toil-blasted bearer of children with its attendant heritage—a cabin like her mother's. In addition, Florence is one of a long line of Baldwin's characters who have absorbed from the dominant culture the concept of blackness as low, contemptible, evil. Baldwin has said, "The American image of the Negro lives also in the Negro's heart; and when he has surrendered to this image life has no other possible reality." [12] Controlled by such an image, Florence founders in a mixture of self-hatred, self-righteousness, sadism, and guilt feelings. Married to a ne'er-do-well she succeeds merely in outraging herself and him, and in driving him away. She bows to religious ecstasy. Baldwin's point, of course, is that she was unable to achieve a life affirming love or her potential identity, and that her ecstatic surrender to Christianity as she nears the end of life is a gesture of desperation.

A man of titanic drives, Gabriel is a sufficient metaphor for man in a grim struggle with the forces of the universe; he stops just short of evoking the sense of tragedy, since self-recognition is not clearly confessed. What is available for articulating the self amid these forces, however, is a version of St. Paul's Christianity which assures the self a Pyhrric victory by a repression that carries the mere coloring of a humanistic morality. Since sex, for Baldwin, is obviously a metaphor for the act of breaking one's isolation and, properly experienced, responsibly entering into the complexity of another human being, Gabriel's evasion of it by marrying the sexless Deborah (symbolically enough, mass raped by Southern whites and sterile) is his flight from dealing with his humanity. Baldwin contrasts him well with the pagan Esther, by whom a temporarily backsliding Gabriel begets a child he does not acknowledge. Esther has a firm concept of her dignity and humanity, and what is life-affirming and what is life-negating, and some of his fellow ministers, too, show that they do not take their fundamentalist concepts to rigid conclusions. Gabriel's response is to retreat more fiercely into religion, marry, after the death of Deborah, the fallen Elizabeth, and harden in his grotesqueness.

Elizabeth is the ethical and moral center of the book. It is through her attachment to her father and reaction against her mother and aunt that she gains the sense of a love that is life giving. She knows that love's imprisonment is not a "bribe, a threat, an indecent will to power";

[12] *Notes*, p. 38.

it is "mysteriously, a freedom for the soul and spirit . . . water in the dry places." [13] It seems to me, however, that Baldwin's hand falters in his analysis and presentation of her as a young woman. Her important relationship with her father, to the extent that it is at all rendered, is simply that of the conventional petting and "spoiling" afforded by a loose-living man who does not take his fatherhood very seriously. That is to say that the father's free-loving nature binds him to nothing, and, after cautioning Elizabeth (as we learn through a summary) never to let the world see her suffering, he returns to his job of running a house of prostitution. Amidst the religious illusions of the other characters, however, she retains a strong, quiet sense of her integrity, despite a relative commitment to religious passion.

Her fall came through her common-law husband, Richard, to whom she gave a self-sacrificial, life-creating love. Although the portrayal of Richard as victimized by society and as a man whose being cannot fulfill its hunger is moving, the explanation of his curiosity and hunger seems oversimplified, if not, indeed, dehumanized: ". . . that I was going to get to know everything them white bastards knew . . . so could no white-son-of-bitch nowhere never talk me down, and never make me feel like I was dirt. . . ." [14] Although the statement well reflects Richard's sensitivity and insecurity under the racial system of America, it hardly explains "his great adoration for things dead."

After the proud young Richard kills himself in reaction to extreme humiliation by the police who have imposed upon his consciousness the image of the low bestial Negro that he has tried to escape, Elizabeth gives birth to the bastard John, whose quest for identity forms the central movement of the book. As the second wife of Gabriel, she emerges as a person of complexity, and is sensitively involved in John's reach for life.

By a series of flashbacks, the author keeps us mindful that the present involves John Grimes's search for identity, the achievement of which is to be understood within the context of the lives of his elders. In the last section of the story, he is in crisis, and with the help of his friend Elisha, in a religious ecstasy, commits himself to the Cross. At various points, Baldwin uses a character by whose views the reality witnessed is to be qualified. In addition to the foreshadowings scattered throughout the story, there is Gabriel to point out that the ecstatic conversion is still to be tested by the long, complex journey of life. So quite without surprise, we encounter in a later short story, "The Death of the Prophet," an apostate Johnny who returns guiltily from some place of estrangement almost to collapse in the presence of his dying father.

[13] *Go Tell It on the Mountain*, p. 210.
[14] *Ibid.*, pp. 225–226.

That Baldwin in *Go Tell It on the Mountain* has drawn heavily upon autobiographical experiences is obvious, and those who like the pursuit can make interesting parallels with autobiographical situations reported in the essay collections: *Notes of a Native Son, Nobody Knows My Name,* and *The Fire Next Time.* But, from the artistic point of view, what is more interesting is their transmutation, their representation as organized energies that carry mythic force in their reflection of man attempting to deal with destiny. Much power derives from the confrontation of the ambiguity of life. That ambiguity carries into the various attitudes suggested toward the version of Christianity that his characters relate themselves to. The relatively nonreligious characters do not deny the relevance of God but seem to feel as Esther, the spurned mother of Gabriel's illegitimate child, puts it: ". . . that [the Lord's] spirit ain't got to work in everybody the same, seems to me." [15] Of the religiously engrossed characters, only Elizabeth achieves a relatively selfless being. However, the religion sustained the slave mother of Gabriel. Even for the twisted, it is a place of refuge, an articulation of the complexity of the mysterious forces of a demanding universe. But finally, the religion only partially illuminates, and the characters must grope in its light and bump against forces within and without that the religion has merely hidden or dammed.

With some admitted oversimplifications inescapable in tracing thematic lines, it may be said that in his two succeeding novels Baldwin is preoccupied with sex and love as instruments in the achievement of full being. As a novelist still under forty, he is no doubt creating works important to his total development, but in neither of these novels—*Giovanni's Room* and the best seller *Another Country*—does he seem to fully create his fictional worlds and characters; in short, he does not seem to have found characters who release his very real ability to create.

In an essay "Preservation of Innocence," Baldwin explicitly makes his criticism of popular concepts of sexuality. His chief point is that our rational classifications of sexual characteristics and our efforts to preserve conventional norms tell us little about what it means to be a man or a woman. Our classifications are not definitive, and therefore we panic and set up safeguards that do nothing more than guard against sexual activities between members of the same sex. But such reductive simplicity, he argues, guarantees ignorance merely, or worse the probability that the bride and groom will not be able to add to the sum of love or know each other since they do not know themselves. Whatever position one takes regarding the argument, the following statements shed uncomfortable light upon the relationship between the sexes in much of American fiction:

[15] *Go Tell It on the Mountain,* p. 161.

In the truly awesome attempt of the American to at once preserve his inno-cence and arrive at man's estate, that mindless monster, the tough guy, has been created and perfected, whose masculinity is found in the most infantile and elementary externals and whose attitude towards women is the wedding of the most abysmal romanticism and the most implacable distrust.[16]

Further complaint of the reductive approach to sexuality is contained in a review of André Gide's *Madeline*, in which he describes the possibility of communing with another sex as "the door to life and air and freedom from the tyranny of one's own personality. . . ."[17] And he describes our present day as one in which communion between the sexes "has become so sorely threatened that we depend more and more on the strident ex-ploitation of externals, as, for example, the breasts of Hollywood glamor girls and the mindless grunting and swaggering of Hollywood he-men."[18] Despite our claim to knowledge, Baldwin implies, sex is a mystery that each person must find a way to live with.

In the light of the foregoing, it seems to me, Baldwin's intention in the novel *Giovanni's Room* is more easily understood. The main line of the story portrays the way youth's inherited definitions of sexuality fail him in his attempts to come to terms with his own, and adds to the sum of evil in his relationship with others. The chief character David repre-sents the rational Westerner, who has absorbed the simplified, compart-mentalized thinking of his background. Falling first in a romantic homo-sexual experience with a fellow adolescent, Joey, he experiences that escape from isolation and the heightened spiritual awareness which love is sup-posed to bring. However, "A cavern opened in my mind, black, full of rumor, suggestion . . . I could have cried, cried for shame and terror, cried for not understanding how this could have happened to me, how this could have happened in me."[19] Unresolved oedipal conflicts are hinted, and just when he needs spiritual sustenance from a father, his father, who knows nothing of the son's experience, insists upon retaining the simplified concept of himself as his son's "buddy." In flight from Joey, David repeats the mishap in the army, then takes flight to France to "find himself," but once there tentatively enters into a similar relation-ship with Giovanni. David expects Giovanni to be but an interval in life, since David has also a girl friend, Hella, a very rational-minded girl who has gone to Spain to think out whether she is in love. But, moving just one step ahead of the predatory homosexual underworld, Giovanni's life de-

---

[16] "Preservation of Innocence," *Zero* (Summer, 1949), pp. 18–19.
[17] *Nobody Knows My Name* (New York, 1961), p. 161.
[18] *Ibid.*, p. 162.
[19] *Giovanni's Room* (New York, 1956), p. 12.

mands David's love as its only hope for transcendence. Irresponsibly, and in a way that denies their complexity as human beings, David disappoints the hopes of Giovanni and disillusions Hella.

What Baldwin registers well is the desperate need for love that brings transcendence. The homosexual's problem is shown to be the threat of being forced into the underworld where bought love of the body, without transcendence, is simply productive of desperation. The women pictured face a similar problem on a heterosexual level. The world portrayed is nightmarish, but hardly, in any sense, really vital. One of its serious problems though is that the reader is not allowed to escape the feeling, in the bad sense, of staginess and theatricality. The characters are in hell all right, but the reader never is, and I do not think that this is so simply because the approach to sex is unconventional. The characters do not root themselves deeply enough to become momentous in fictional terms, nor do they stand with intensity for elemental forces which we are forced to consider an inescapable part of our lives. So that, despite claims for complexity, the characters are too easily defined with relationship to a thesis.

Before coming to a consideration of *Another Country*, I should point out that Baldwin is the author of several stories of distinction, though there is hardly space for more than a brief mentioning of them. "Previous Condition" is the intense story of a young Negro's attempt to secure his being from its alienated condition within and the forces of prejudice without. It appeared in *Commentary*, October, 1948, as Baldwin's first story. "The Death of the Prophet," *Commentary*, March, 1950, was mentioned in connection with *Go Tell It on the Mountain*. "Come Out the Wilderness," *Mademoiselle*, March, 1958, reprinted in *Best Short Stories from Mademoiselle*, New York, 1961, explores the lostness of a Negro girl who has been alienated from her original racial environment. "Sonny's Blues," *Partisan Review*, Summer, 1957, reprinted in *Best Short Stories of 1958* and Herbert Gold's *Fiction of the Fifties*, New York, 1959, carries the venture of a Negro boy through narcotics to music where he finally gains a sense of identity expressed. "This Morning, This Evening, So Soon," *The Atlantic Monthly*, September 1960, reprinted in Martha Foley, *The Best Short Stories of 1961*, New York, 1961, an issue dedicated to Baldwin, explores the necessity of a successful young Negro actor to come to terms with his place in history. Each story shows a sure sense of the short story form, a moment of illumination that has significance for the total life of the character. Baldwin's greatest indebtedness in the short story is to Henry James.

Another Country, New York, 1962, Baldwin's latest novel, is a serious and ambitious attempt, a fact which should be recognized despite the fact that to make it a serious novel of the first rank would demand severe cutting and some intensive rewriting. The problem is still that of arriving at a definition of one's being which will be adequately sustaining in the face of the evils of life, and to support another's complexity through love. Both heterosexual and homosexual scenes abound, but, as stated in the discussion of *Giovanni's Room*, these are the instruments for the exploration of being, the metaphors for self-definition and for responsibly entering the complexity of another. They have, therefore, a serious purpose, and Baldwin is too concerned about whether the sex experience provides a transcending love to make distinctions between the heterosexual and homosexual experience. Most of the men have engaged in a homosexual act, and have from it defined their sex for the future; that is, they decide whether the homosexual experience is or is not for their being, with most deciding in favor of heterosexuality.

The first story is that of Rufus, the Negro musician, who is fighting within himself both the real and the imaginary aspects of the race problem, and therefore cannot communicate with Leona, the Southern poor white girl that he picks up with the conscious purpose of sexual exploitation and of getting rid of her before she can "bug" him with her story (i.e., involve him in her complexity as a person). Rufus has suffered real racial persecution, so that even harmless remarks by Leona send him into a rage, and he finally drives her into a nervous breakdown and succumbs to his own frustrations by committing suicide. The horror of their experience is communicated with considerable skill. Rufus's failure in *being* is then retested in the lives of other characters who were, in varying degrees, associated with him.

Vivaldo Moore, the Irish-Italian, attracted to Rufus's sister, at first, partly through being a "liberal," and partly because of his sense of having failed her brother, must be made to confront her as a complex human conundrum, capable of ruthless exploitation and high-level prostitution: that is, he must lose his innocence. Cass and Richard Silenski must abandon their oversimplified classifications of each other and achieve a sense of reality in their marriage. Eric, the homosexual, must overthrow his Southern background and come to terms with himself in France. Everybody, indeed, must learn his own name. Thus the lives of successive sets of people must come against the problems of being, love, and involvement.

One trouble with the scheme is that so few of the characters exemplify the complexity contended for them. Rufus, Ida, and Eric are the more adequately developed characters. The rest are not projected far enough beyond the level of nice, erring people. Thus the central problem of the book lacks momentousness. Ralph Ellison has said of the novel that ". . . it operates by amplifying and giving resonance to a specific complex of experience until, through the eloquence of its statement, that specific part of life speaks metaphorically for the whole." [20] It is precisely the fore-going illusion that *Another Country* in its totality is unable to create. The section concerned with the discovery of Rufus's death and the at-tendance at his funeral is excessive reportorial detail, sometimes theatri-cal, sometimes written at the level of the women's magazine. And the social criticism is inert, for the most part, a part of the chatty reflections of a particular character or of long clinical discussions.

On the other hand, there are some penetrating scenes that reflect the fine talent of Baldwin. In addition to the story of Rufus, I should cite most of the scenes where Ida is present and some of the scenes between Cass Silenski and Eric. In such scenes, the bold use of naturalistic devices—the sex scenes and four letter words—project meaning well be-yond surface communication. What else could so well convey Rufus's horrified retching at his dilemma or the terrible exasperation of Ida and Vivaldo? Still, scenes abound in which naturalistic detail simply thickens the book and the four-letter words provide a spurious emphasis, galvaniz-ing the reader's attention to no end. And yet *Another Country* is a book that has much to say, and, as I have tried to indicate, sometimes does.

It is not too much to assert then that Baldwin's novels since *Go Tell It on the Mountain,* though fine in segments, tend to reflect a hiatus in his artistic development. In *Go Tell It on the Mountain,* he was working with a body of understood, crystallized and only partially rejected re-ligious and racial mythology that, therefore, carried coiled within it the wires of communication. It is not to say that the artist's challenge and task were simply to point out that he had primarily to manipulate the myth, to steep it in deliberate ambiguity, in order to reflect its Sphinx-like be-trayal of those who uncritically absorbed it. The religious interpretation, after all, is within touching distance of the over-all idea of Matthew Arnold's famous essay, "Hebraism and Hellenism." His autobiographical intimacy with such material required and received artistic skill and dis-tance. Creating against such a background Baldwin effected a novel which transcended racial and religious categories—became an evoked image of man facing the mysterious universal forces.

On the other hand, the Baldwin of the last two novels confronts the modern consciousness amidst fluxions more talked about than crystallized, and moving at considerable speed: elements of modern man connoting fragmenting certainties eroded at the base, the succor for which has been sought mainly in the vague horizons of the backward look. The workings of sex amidst those fluxions are certainly, in the modern awareness, one major element in the choppy sea of our minds, in which definable shapes seem to appear for the purpose of disappearing. To define them artistically

[20] Granville Hicks, editor, *The Living Novel* (New York, 1957), p. 61.

would seem to demand extraordinary effort indeed, whether in traditional or experimental terms.

The conclusion, therefore, to which a full reading of Baldwin seems inescapably to lead is that since his first novel he has not evolved the artistic form that will fully release and articulate his obviously complex awareness. And that to do so may require an abandonment of safety in the use of form equal to that which he has manifested in approach to subject, an act which may concomitantly involve estranging many of the multitude of readers which he has acquired. For an artist of Baldwin's fictional resources, talent, and courage, or his obvious knowledge of evolved fictional techniques, the challenge should hardly be overwhelming.

JAMES BALDWIN: THE BLACK
AND THE RED-WHITE-AND-BLUE*

John V. Hagopian

JAMES BALDWIN is one of the most accomplished and sophisticated American writers of today, and from a strictly literary point of view it is unfortunate that he expends so much of his energy on nonfiction. To be sure, his essays are sensitive accounts of the complex spiritual and moral predicament of the Negro intellectual, but as Baldwin himself once said (in *Notes of a Native Son*) he does not want to be a Negro—he wants to be a writer. Yet we find him still expending his creative energies on the genre of the protest essay, which he no doubt finds more satisfactory than the protest novel but which is nevertheless a way of being a Negro rather than a writer. That he has gained enormously in skill since *Giovanni's Room* is clear from his latest story, "This Morning, This Evening, So Soon" (*Atlantic Monthly*, Sept., 1960). It is a work which deserves to take its place as one of the most important short stories written since the war, not only because the theme of the Negro girding himself to take his rightful place in American society is significant in our postwar cultural history, but because *as literature* it is a very fine piece of work.

"This Morning, This Evening, So Soon" appears to be a relatively simple story, but it is full of subtle and surprising complexities. A young American Negro, who has for twelve years been living in Paris, where he has established a family (a Swedish wife and a seven-year-old son) and has found fame as a singer and actor, has decided to return to America. He is full of anxiety, especially for his son, who may suffer the spiritually crippling effects of American anti-Negro prejudice. But the experiences and reminiscences of his last twenty-four hours in Paris make him feel "very cheerful, I do not know why" and he finds himself smiling at the prospect of taking his son "all the way to the new world."

The story is divided into three sections which might have been subtitled: I. Family, II. Friend, III. Strangers; hence, it moves from the intimate center of the unnamed narrator's experiences outward into public

* Reprinted from the *CLA Journal*, VII (1964), 133–40, by permission of the editors.

life and society. Simultaneously, the narrator—and the reader—gains more and more insight into the complexities and changes in the current of his emotions, although much happens that he does not fully understand. The "I" narrator tells us (in the present tense) about the events as they happen and (in the past tense) about his reminiscences, together with his own interpretations which are often too explicit:

Everyone's life begins on a level where races, armies, and churches stop. And yet everyone's life is always shaped by races, churches, and armies; races, churches, and armies menace, and have taken, many lives.

Such comments give the reader the false notion that he is getting the meaning as well as the action from the narrator. Intelligent as the narrator is, and trained as he is to be wary, observant, and critical, such observations are appropriate to his character and are often apt and to the point. But he has had prejudices of his own ("I had always thought of Sweden as being populated entirely by blondes"), is supersensitive to every act and gesture by a white man that might conceivably be interpreted as anti-Negro ("was it my imagination or was it true that they seemed to avoid my eyes?"), and often speaks ("she is only an American like me") and feels ("I feel very cheerful, I do not know why") in ways that he does not fully understand. Hence the narrator does not, however much he may seem to, do all the reader's interpretive work for him. In fact, the fundamental meaning of the story remains implicit.

In the opening lines of the story, the narrator cites the members of the family circle: his wife Harriet; his sister Louisa, who has come to Paris for a brief holiday before accompanying him and his family back to America; his son Paul, to whom America is "only a glamorous word"; and "the director of the film," who remains unnamed at this point because he is not important until we reach the second section of the story. The strangers of the third section are, of course, not mentioned because the narrator is speculating on events as they occur and does not know what is going to happen. Many of the undercurrents of the opening section will not have much impact on the first reading because Baldwin holds back the vital information that the narrator and his sister are Negroes until after he has established his characters as a family unit. Only on second reading can he realize the tactfulness of Harriet when she explains to their son that his father's crankiness at breakfast "is because he is afraid they will not like his songs in New York. Your father is an *artiste, mon chou,* and they are very mysterious people, *les artistes.*" The Negro question is avoided because "Harriet does not so much believe in protecting children as she does in helping them to build a foundation on which they can build again, each time life's high-flying steel ball knocks down everything they have built." And only on second reading can we understand the reason why Louisa must seem to Paul "peculiarly uncertain of herself, peculiarly hostile and embattled," or the sinister significances of her insistence to Harriet that "We have *got* some expressions, believe me. Don't let anybody ever tell you America hasn't got a culture. Our culture is as thick as clabber milk." It is in this atmosphere of family love that the narrator's fears emerge: "Paul has never been called any names before"; in America he and Harriet would never have been able to love each other; he fears "all the threats it holds for me and mine." And he shrewdly observes that "Harriet is really trying to learn from Louisa how best to protect her husband and her son." The sum total of this first section is an image of a family group full of love and good will facing a threatening experience in which each is eager to help and protect the other.

After Harriet and Louisa leave to spend an evening in Paris and after Paul has been delivered to the safekeeping of the concierge, the narrator returns to his apartment to await the visit of Vidal, the director of the film which has made him famous. On the balcony he smokes, looks at Paris, where he has "always felt at home," meditates and reminisces: "I love Paris, I will always love it, it is the city which has saved my life . . . by allowing me to find out who I am." It was in Paris eight years before that he fell in love with Harriet just before returning to America for the funeral of his mother—"I felt . . . for the first time that the woman was not, in her own eyes or in the eyes of the world, degraded by my presence." He was afraid of America and eager to return to her. New York seemed like "some enormous, cunning and murderous beast, ready to devour, impossible to escape," and he was especially vulnerable because he "had forgotten all the tricks [of appearing subservient to the whites] on which my life had once depended." There are few subtleties in this transitional part of the story. The narrator is ambivalent about America, fears it but is attracted to it: "I was home." There is a fine little sketch of the noise and power of New York, capped with the observation that "the human voices distinguish themselves from the roar by their note of strain and hostility." When his sister Louisa, who met him at the ship, directed the cab driver to the New Yorker Hotel, the narrator was surprised, for Negroes had always been discriminated against there. Obviously the country was changing, but Louisa's optimism was cautious: ". . . this place really hasn't changed very much. You still can't hear yourself talk."

The second section of the story begins with the arrival of Jean Luc Vidal, a "tough, cynical, crafty old Frenchman," a former Gaullist whose wife and son were lost in the war and who had spent time in a Nazi prison. This man is very fond of the young Negro whom he has made into an international star in a film significantly entitled *Les Fauves Nous Attendent*. But Vidal had done more for him than that; he had taught him to express and thus to relive his deep-felt hatreds through his art and had exposed the self-pitying antiwhite prejudice that prevented him from responding to any white man as an individual just as effectively as anti-Negro prejudice blinded white people to the individuality of Negroes: "I am a French Director and I have never been in your country and I have never done you any harm—but . . . you are not talking to Jean Luc Vidal, but to some other white man, whom you remember, who has nothing to do with me." To Vidal the narrator can speak openly of his fears at returning to a country where "I always feel that I don't exist, except in someone else's—usually dirty—mind . . . I don't want to put Harriet through that and I don't want to raise Paul there." Vidal reassures him that his return needn't be permanent, that his new status and the prospects of great wealth are worth the risk. At the end of this dialogue, the two leave for their evening out.

Section three begins with their arrival at a discotheque where they encounter a group of American Negro students, two girls and two young men. The most attractive of the girls approaches them, astonished at her luck "because it's in the papers that you're coming home." These Negroes, like the narrator, obviously regard America as "home" despite the conditions of their life there. Their dialogue reveals their fear and hatred of the whites, but also their belligerent determination to fight back. One says, "I fear you are in for some surprises, my friend. There has been some changes made." Then "Are you afraid?"

"A little."
"We all are," says another, "that's why I was so glad to get away *for a little while.*"

As the group goes bar-hopping, they are joined by an Arab named Boona, an erstwhile prizefighter from Tunis and an acquaintance of the narrator. Though he is a disreputable fellow and obviously does not fit with the group, the narrator cannot send him away for fear of appearing to display prejudice against Arabs. One of the Negro girls asks Boona, "Wouldn't you like to go back [to Tunis]?" and he replies, "That is not so easy." (The significance of this will be dealt with in a moment.) During the course of the night, Boona steals money from the purse of one of the girls; he is confronted, denies it—"Why she blame me? Because I come from Africa?" In this section of the story the narrator makes no commentaries on the action, and when the girl decides not to press the point ("I'm sure I lost it. . . . It isn't worth hurting your feelings") we can only assume that she has observed the Arab's desperation and is therefore willing to endure the loss of the money. The party breaks up at dawn, and the narrator goes home, stopping at the concierge's apartment to pick

up his son: "I feel very cheerful, I do not know why." The concierge, referring to their trip to America, says, "What a journey! *Jusqu'au nouveau
monde!*"

I open the cage [of the elevator] and we step inside. "Yes," I say, "all the
way to the new world." I press the button and the cage, holding my son and
me, goes up.

The symbolism of the ending is clear. Although this Negro and his
son are in the cage of their Negro skins, they are rising in the world. But
what, exactly, has happened to explain or justify this optimism? The answer is that as the story moves in wider and wider orbits around the central character, we see that his original feeling that everything was divided
into his oppressed self and the hostile world was false, that he is part of
a history and a humanity that is far more complex than that. The narrator
cannot identify himself simply as an oppressed person, for much of the
world does *not* oppress him. He finds love not only from his Negro sister,
but from a Swedish woman who marries him and gives him a son and
from a French film director who teaches him some hard truths about
life. In the film he had been obliged to portray a mulatto boy who hated
"all dark women and all white men" and he had not been throwing himself fully and honestly into the role. Vidal had goaded him:

"Have you never, yourself, been in a similar position?"
I hated him for asking the question because I knew he had the answer to it.
"I would have had to be a very lucky black man not to have been in such a
position."
"You would have had to be a very lucky *man*."
"Oh, God," I said, "please don't give me any of this equality-in-anguish
business."
"It is perfectly possible," he said sharply, "that there is not another kind."

Vidal then gave him a stern lecture on history, pointing out that the
white men—especially the French—are paying for their history of abuse
of the colored peoples and that if revenge is what the Negro wants he
will certainly have it. He then strikes home with a telling blow: "How
will you raise your son? Will you teach him never to tell the truth to
anyone?" The narrator then recalled how he had held his own father in
pity and contempt for not being able to prevent or even to prepare for
humiliation and the anguish of Negro life in Alabama. "But for Paul . . .
I swore I would make it impossible for the world to treat Paul as it had
treated my father and me." But since the story does not end at that
point, this must be taken as a temporary and transient stage in the nar-

rator's development. And Vidal's wisdom, too, is by no means the last word.

The last word apparently has to do with Boona, i.e., with the contrast between the Arab from Tunis and the Negro from America, neither of whom wishes to go home. But their situations are not quite the same, as the narrator comes to realize; there is a profound difference in their racial histories. The Arabs do not identify themselves as Frenchmen, but the Negroes are Americans. In his balcony meditation the narrator had mused on the plight of the Arabs in Paris and how their treatment had caused such a degeneration among them. "I once thought of the North Africans as my brothers" and responded to "their rage, the only note in all their music which I could not fail to recognize." Yet because "they were perfectly prepared to drive all Frenchmen into the sea and to level the city of Paris" he could not identify with them—partly because he owed his spiritual life to France and partly because his own rage against America is the anger one feels against the wrongs of a country he loves ("waiting for the first glimpse of America, my apprehension began to give way to a secret joy, a checked anticipation"). Furthermore, he had discovered aboard ship during his first voyage home that the white Americans "who had never treated me with any respect, had no respect for each other." True, they quickly came to call each other by their first names, but their friendliness "did not suggest and was not intended to suggest any possibility of friendship." And earlier in the story he had observed that the whites "could not afford to hear a truth which would shatter, irrevocably, their image of themselves." But he shares with his sister Louisa the conviction that if the whites could be brought to confront the Negro honestly and to accept him for what he was—not only a fellow human being but a permanent and unshakable part of his American culture—the entire culture could be made whole and healthy. Louisa had said that even the Negro must be brought to realize this truth:

That's what I keep trying to tell those dirty bastards down South. They get their own experience into the language, we'll have a great language. But, no, they all want to talk like white folks. . . . I tell them, honey, white folks ain't saying *nothing*. Not a thing are they saying—and *some* of them know it— they *need* what you got, the whole world needs it.

It is this kind of racial pride that the Arabs in France do not share with the Negroes in America, that has been buttressed by the narrator's observation of the understanding and kindness displayed by the Negro tourists toward Boona. That is what makes him cheerful at the end. It is an achievement that he has come to feel a whole man in France; it is a greater achievement that he can face with pride the prospect of being a Negro in America.

Langston Hughes

These essays, except for Blyden Jackson's, were written prior to the death of Langston Hughes, and the editor has chosen to let them stand as originally published rather than to edit them with respect to Mr. Hughes's death.

THE TRAGIC MULATTO THEME IN SIX WORKS OF LANGSTON HUGHES[*]

Arthur P. Davis

The Weary Blues (1925), the first publication of Langston Hughes, contained a provocative twelve-line poem entitled "Cross," which dealt with the tragic mulatto theme. Two years later when Mr. Hughes brought out Fine Clothes to the Jew (1927), he included another poem on racial intermixture which he named "Mulatto." During the summer of 1928 when Hughes was working with the Hedgerow Theatre at Moylan Rose Valley, Pennsylvania, he completed a full-length drama on the tragic mulatto theme, which he also called Mulatto. This play was produced on Broadway in 1935 where it ran for a full year, followed by an eight months' tour across the nation. From the play, the poet composed a short story, "Father and Son," which though written later than the play, appeared in The Ways of White Folks (1934), a year before the drama was produced. Returning once more to the theme, Hughes in 1949 reworked the play Mulatto into an opera, The Barrier, the music for which was written by the modern composer, Jan Meyerowitz. The opera was first produced at Columbia University in 1950. And finally in 1952, Hughes published another short story on the tragic mulatto theme entitled "African Morning." This sketch appears in Laughing to Keep from Crying, a second collection of short stories. In short, for over a quarter of a century, the author has been concerned with this theme; returning to it again and again, he has presented the thesis in four different genres, in treatments varying in length from a twelve-line poem to a full-length Broadway play.[1]

Before discussing Mr. Hughes' several presentations of the theme,

[1] I must point out that the six works chosen for this study are not the only ones by Hughes treating the subject. These six, however, are the most typical and therefore serve my purpose best. See "Red Headed Baby" (The Ways of White Folks) and "New Cabaret Girl" (Fine Clothes to the Jew) for other examples of Hughes' concern with the problem of mixed blood.

[*] Reprinted from Phylon, XVI (1955), 195–204, by permission of the editors.

however, let us understand the term "tragic mulatto." As commonly used in American fiction and drama, it denotes a light-colored, mixed-blood character (possessing in most cases a white father and a colored mother), who suffers because of difficulties arising from his biracial background. In our literature there are, of course, valid and convincing portrayals of this type; but as it is a character which easily lends itself to sensational exaggeration and distortion, there are also many stereotypes of the tragic mulatto to be found. And these stereotypes, as Professor Brown has so ably pointed out, are not only marked by "exaggeration and omission," they often embody racial myths and shibboleths.[2] In them "the mulatto is a victim of divided inheritance; from his white blood come his intellectual strivings, his unwillingness to be a slave; from his Negro blood come his baser emotional urges, his indolence, his savagery."[3] Whether any given character is a true flesh and blood portrait or a stereotype depends, of course, upon the knowledge, the skill, and the integrity of the artist; and this is true whether the author be Negro or white. But it would not be unfair to state that though both are guilty, the white writer tends to use the stereotype more often than the Negro.

Regardless of the approach, however—valid portrayal or stereotype—the tragic mulatto, because of our racial situation, has been popular with the American writer from the very beginnings of our literature. In fiction and in drama, we have a long line of tragic mixed-blood characters, extending from Cooper's Cora Munro (*Last of the Mohicans*) and Boucicault's Zoe (*The Octoroon*) down to the present day creations of William Faulkner and Fannie Hurst. Considering its popularity, we are not surprised that Langston Hughes has made use of the theme, but we are intrigued by the persistency with which he has clung to it over the years.

Why then has he been so deeply concerned with the tragic mulatto? Has he given us a deeper and more realistic analysis of the mixed-blood character? Are his central figures different from the stereotypes created by other writers? Or, does Hughes, perhaps unconsciously, employ the theme of the tragic mulatto to express vicariously and symbolically some basic inner conflict in his own personality? It will be the purpose of this paper to seek an answer to these questions through an analysis of six of Mr. Hughes' works.

Let us turn first to "Cross," the original statement of the theme and the "germ-idea" from which the Mulatto group was derived. Surprisingly stark and unadorned, the poem begins with ballad-like abruptness:

[2] Sterling A Brown, "Negro Characters as Seen by White Authors," *Journal of Negro Education*, II, No. 2 (1933) 179 ff. This is a full and excellent discussion of the Negro stereotype in American fiction.
[3] *Ibid.*, 194–95.

My old man's a white old man
And my old mother's black,
If ever I cursed my white old man
I take my curses back.

If I ever cursed my black old mother
And wished she were in hell,
I am sorry for that evil wish
And now I wish her well.

My old man died in a fine big house,
My ma died in a shack,
I wonder where I'm gonna die,
Being neither white nor black?

Through suggestion and implication rather than by direct narrative, the poet has given us in three quatrains the whole tragic story of a mulatto's bitter resentment against his "mixed" background and his failure in life which he seems to attribute to that background. We are told specifically that the mulatto at first blamed both parents for his plight; that subsequently, for some unstated reason, he forgives his father and mother; and finally that he pities himself because of a sense of not-belonging. These are the stated facts of the piece, but a close reading of the poem suggests other implications as important as the facts themselves.

There is first of all the idea of desertion on the part of the white father indicated in the two separate death places—one in "a fine big house," the other in a shack. There is also rejection implied in that we assume the mulatto lived with his mother. We therefore detect a hint of envy and regret when he speaks of his father's inaccessible fine big house. Perhaps there is a bit of fondness on the part of the mulatto unconsciously expressed in the phrase "my old man." We know that he forgave his father, and we sense a feeling of regret on his part even for the death of a parent who had rejected him and whom he could not know. In the final analysis, the poem boils down to a fruitless search for a father and a home, and it is this pattern which Langston Hughes has followed in all of the subsequent works on the tragic mulatto theme.

In contrast to the classic restraint and economy of phrase we find in "Cross," Mr. Hughes in "Mulatto" [4] writes with an exuberance which is almost hysterical in quality. We feel immediately the passion and violence, and we somehow get the impression that all of the speakers in the poem

[4] In the following version of "Mulatto," I have omitted several lines because of limited space.

(it is a dramatic dialogue) are either shouting or screaming. The clash between white father and rejected son is driven home from the very first line:

I am your Son, White Man!

Georgia dusk
And the turpentine woods,
One of the pillars of the temple fell.

> *You are my son!*
> *Like hell!*

The moon over the turpentine woods.
The southern night
Full of stars,
Great big yellow stars.
>Juicy bodies
>Of nigger wenches
>Blue black
>Against black fences.
>O, you little bastard boy,
>What's a body but a toy?

The scent of pine wood stings the soft night air.
>*What's the body of your mother?*

Silver moonlight everywhere.
>*What's the body of your mother?*

Sharp pine scent in the evening air.
>A nigger night,
>A nigger joy,
>A little yellow
>Bastard boy.
>*Naw, you ain't my brother.*
>*Niggers ain't my brother.*
>*Not ever.*
>*Niggers ain't my brother.*
>*Git on back there in the night,*
>*You ain't white . . .*

I am your son, white man . . .

We note at once that the rejection theme so vaguely suggested in "Cross" has become the central theme of this poem. All other issues are subordinate to it; and all of the images, symbols, incidents, and background scenery serve but to accentuate and dramatize the basic thesis of rejection. For example, Hughes intensifies the denial of kinship by making it now into a two-generation refusal: both half-brother and father brutally rebuff the mulatto. The poem also makes use of ironic contrast to degrade the mulatto's circumstances of birth. Stressing the stinging scent of the pine wood—a smell associated with cleanliness, purity, and idyllic lovemaking— he creates of it an inverted and distorted symbol of the sordid act of copulation between "blue black" nigger wenches and fallen white pillars of the temple. The idea of ironic contrast is further implied when he associates the clean and crystal-like brilliance of the innumerable "great big yellow stars" with the many "yellow bastards" so carelessly conceived beneath their sparkling splendor. The slurring reference on the part of the whites to this kind of evening's fun as "nigger joy" and the whole barbecue-like abandon of the scene both stress and dramatize the irresponsible casualness of this type of frolicking in the Negro section "against black fences." The use of the preposition "against" heightens the insult. All of these things serve not only to highlight the rejection of the mulatto but in effect to furnish a rationale for it.

The most insulting of these slurring expressions in the mouths of the white speakers is the line thrice repeated in the poem: "What's the body of your mother?" This slur, the rankest form of "the dozens," degrades the rejection of the yellow bastard past all hope of reconcilement. Hence there is no hint of fondness or forgiveness here. The mulatto, no longer a vaguely unhappy misfit as in "Cross," has become in the eyes of the whites a pariah, a mongrel cur who can never be "recognized." The rejection here is sadistically final and decisive.

We note one curious approach in "Mulatto." Hughes seems to place no blame at all on the dusky women who take part in these "nigger nights." He seems to ignore entirely their burden of guilt. All of his castigation is aimed at the white pillars of the temple who can indulge in such orgies and then callously reject the issue of their evening's pleasure. Is the poet suggesting that the black women are helpless victims? That would be too unrealistic. What he probably implies here is simply this: that the nocturnal interracial love-making itself is not the essential evil. It is the rejection of parenthood on the part of the father which is the unforgivable crime. And in other works on this theme, as we shall see later, he recognizes the economic pressures which motivate these black-white liaisons.

The next three versions of the tragic mulatto theme—the play, *Mulatto*, the short story, "Father and Son," and the opera libretto, *The Barrier*— may be treated together because they are one story presented in three different forms. Although there are minor differences among the three—differences occasioned largely by the nature of the form used—it is surprising how closely each follows the other. Unfortunately, the only one of the three published in English is "Father and Son" (there is an Italian version of *Mulatto* in print). My quotations from the play and the opera, therefore, will come from manuscript copies of these works. May I say in passing that the opera libretto is artistically the most finished version of the story. Much of the violence and sensationalism of the original play is toned down in the poetry of the libretto. I know that it is impossible to evaluate an opera apart from its music, but the libretto for *The Barrier* stands well alone as poetic drama. Since the play *Mulatto* is the original version of the three, I shall use that as a point of departure, quoting from "Father and Son" and *The Barrier* whenever necessary.

Mulatto tells the story of Colonel Thomas Norwood, a Georgia plantation owner, and his bastard son, Bert, a mulatto who insisted on being not just another "yard-nigger," but Colonel Norwood's son. The child of Cora Lewis, Norwood's colored mistress, Bert, unlike the other children of this alliance, looks like his father, has his father's eyes and height, and above all else, possesses the colonel's fiery spirit. When the story opens, we find that Bert has returned home for the summer. For the past six years he had been kept in school in Atlanta and is back now only because of his mother's pleading. At home Bert refuses to work as a field hand, ignores the colonel's rule about Negroes using his front door, talks back to white folks in the town, and violates in every way the mores of the community. Most shocking of all, Bert publicly announces that he is not "all-nigger," that he is Colonel Norwood's son and heir. Appalled by this conduct, Norwood calls Bert in and brutally attempts to make him "see his place." A violent scene between father and son takes place. Taunted by insults to his and to his mother's status, Bert in anger—and really something deeper than anger—kills his father and then commits suicide symbolically in his father's house before the mob can get him. This barest of outlines is the plot of all three versions of the story. Let us look now at several pertinent details.

Again, as in the poem "Mulatto," the central theme here is violent rejection. As a little tot, Bert used to trail at the colonel's heels, and the latter seemed to like this mark of affection until one day Bert made the mistake of calling Norwood "papa" in front of white visitors. The child received a vicious slap from his father for this *faux pas*. That was the first denial, and it left an indelible impression on the boy. In the last violent scene with Norwood, Bert tells the old man: "I used to like you when I first knew you were my father . . . before that time you beat me under the feet of your horses." (Slowly) "I liked you until then."

The second denial came when Bert returned from school that summer. In utter forgetfulness of Southern custom, he had attempted to shake his white father's hand and had been cruelly rebuffed. In the third encounter between the two, Norwood raises his cane to strike the boy but is restrained by the latter's unflinching belligerency. And in the final tragic meeting of the two, we have the supreme rejection: Colonel Norwood denying, not the physical but the spiritual kinship between the two:

NORWOOD: . . . Now, I'm going to let you talk to me, but I want you to talk right.
BERT (*still standing*): What do you mean, "talk right?"
NORWOOD: I mean talk like a nigger should to a white man.
BERT: Oh! But I'm not a nigger, Colonel Tom. I'm your son.
NORWOOD (*testily*): You're Cora's boy.
BERT: Women don't have children by themselves.
NORWOOD: Nigger women don't know the fathers. You're a bastard.

After this taunting and degrading denial, Bert loses all control. Screaming hysterically, "Why don't you shoot?" he wrests a gun from the old man's hands and then chokes him to death. The fact that his father wanted to kill him is too much for the young boy's strained emotions. He cannot get the old man's intention out of his mind. "Why didn't he shoot, mama?" he asks wildly. "He didn't want *me* to live, why didn't he shoot?" The subsequent suicide is not only a way of cheating the mob. We sense that with the death of the colonel, the bottom has really dropped out of Bert's world, and he kills himself proudly.

One notes that throughout the play Bert seems to feel no shame for being a bastard; on the contrary, he seems almost proud that he is Norwood's son. On one occasion he tells his mother: "I'm no nigger anyhow, am I, ma? I'm half-white. The colonel's my father—the richest man in the country—and I am not going to take a lot of stuff from nobody. . . ."

It was not that Bert was living unhappily between two worlds—he had made an excellent adjustment in Atlanta Negro society. Nor did he want to be white. Bert simply wanted a home and a father; and with the unprejudiced viewpoint of youth, he could not understand why the colonel would not accept him as a son. His mother tries to reason with him on the matter (and I use here a quotation from *The Barrier*):

CORA: You don't seem to know that here in Georgia
　　　You are not your father's son.
BERT: Mama, I love you . . .
　　　But I can't understand now
　　　What you're saying.
　　　All I know is I am his son—
　　　And not in Georgia nor anywhere else,
　　　Should a man deny his son.

This is Bert's position; it is also that of Langston Hughes. In spite of racial background and regional traditions, the problem, looked at objectively, is a personal one: the rejection of his son by a father.

Before we leave these three versions of the Bert–Colonel Norwood story, let us consider Cora. Again, as in the poems, Hughes attached no blame or condemnation to Cora's status as a white man's mistress. Except for the troubles which Bert caused—troubles which she understands better than anyone else in the play—Cora leads a fairly happy life; and more significant, she considers herself a good woman. Note her reaction when the tragedy comes to her loved ones:

> I lived right, Lawd!
> I tried to live right!
> Lawd! Lawd!
> And this is what you give me!
> What is the matter, Lawd,
> Ain't you with me?

There is no feeling of guilt here because Cora, motivated by economic pressures, had taken honest advantage of a relationship which gave her and her family a fuller and more secure life. Note again the position she takes in Act II (Scene 2) of *Mulatto* as she recalls hysterically her first affair with the Colonel:

". . . then I cried and cried and told my mother about it, but she didn't take it hard like I thought she'd take it. She said fine white mens like de young Colonel always take good care of their colored womens. She said it was better than marryin' some black field hand and workin' all your life in the cotton and cane. . . ."

The last version of the tragic mulatto theme in Langston Hughes' works is found in "African Morning," a short story appearing in *Laughing to Keep from Crying* (1952). The scene of this little sketch is laid in the delta country of the River Niger. The story depicts a day in the life of Maurai, a lonely, twelve-year-old, half-white, half-native boy, the only mixed-blood person in his seaport village. Son of the English local bank president and his native mistress, Maurai had been reared inside the European enclosure in the home of his father. Having lost his mother, Maurai had been rejected by her people and left with his father's new African mistress. He was also rejected by his father who tolerated him, used him for running errands, but who wasted no love or affection on the little half-caste child. For example, when white visitors came, the father made Maurai eat in the kitchen with the black mistress.

When the story opens we find Maurai changing from his native to

European dress in order to go on an errand for his father. (Note that even in dress he has no fixed world.) Going to the bank, he walked into his father's office where whites were counting gold. "Wait outside, Maurai," said his father sharply, covering the gold with his hands. Natives were not allowed to possess gold; it was the white man's jealously guarded prerogative to do so, and because of this proscription gold became a symbol of the whites' power and control. "Maybe that's why the black people hate me," Maurai mused, "because I am the color of gold." (Langston Hughes here and elsewhere uses "yellow" as a symbol for the degradation and unhappiness which supposedly come from mixed-blood situations.)

After delivering his father's message to a sea captain, Maurai is taken for a native "guide boy" by one of the white sailors; but as soon as he reaches the docks he is taunted and beaten by the native black boys and the black women because of his color and his European clothes. He runs to the jungle with the sound of their "yellow bastard" ringing in his ears. In a jungle lagoon, he finds solace for both bruised body and lacerated spirit. Maurai was not afraid of the jungle or of the crocodiles or snakes that could be in the lagoon. Maurai was afraid of only three things: "white people and black people—and gold." As he floated in the pool, he began to pity himself and his sad lot: "Suppose I were to stay here forever," he thought, "in the dark at the bottom of the pool." But Maurai was only twelve, and these morbid thoughts soon passed. He got out of the pool, dressed, and returned to his home inside the European enclosure. As lonely as his present existence was, he realized that it would be much worse when his father returned to England, "leaving him in Africa where nobody wanted him."

Artistically, "African Morning" ranks with *The Barrier*. Probably because of its African background, it seems more convincing than the other versions of the tragic mulatto theme. It is also more touching because it concerns a defenseless child. All in all "African Morning" is a restrained, finished, and effectively written sketch. Possessing none of the sensationalism of the *Mulatto* trio, it nevertheless tells once more the same basic story—that of a mixed-blood boy, hungry for recognition, being rejected by a father.

On the surface, Langston Hughes' tragic mulattoes do not seem to be essentially different from the stereotypes of other writers. Their violence, as in the case of Bert, their loneliness, their divided loyalty, their frustrations, their maladjustments, and their tendency to destroy themselves—all of these characteristics, typical of the stereotype, are found (or suggested) in Hughes' central figures. But there are at least two vital differences in the latter's approach. In the first place, many—not all but many—white writers state or imply that the effect of mixed blood per se has something to do with the mulatto's supposedly confused personality; note, for example, the following passage from Paul Green's *In Abraham's Bosom*:

BUD: White and black make bad mixtry.
LIJE: Do dat. (*Thumping his chest*) Nigger down heah. (*Thumping his head*) White mens up here. Heart say do one thing, head say 'nudder. Bad, bad.

As a Negro, Hughes is never guilty of this kind of nonsense. Knowing, as do all intelligent persons, that heredity works along individual rather than racial patterns, he has avoided this aspect of the stereotype, and that in itself is a difference of some importance.

The outstanding contribution, however, which Hughes has made in his delineation of the tragic mulatto, it seems to me, is to point out that at bottom the problem of the mixed-blood character is basically a personal problem. Bert and Maurai, for example, would have been satisfied just to have the recognition of their respective fathers. They were apparently not interested in the larger sociological aspects of divided inheritance. They were not trying to create racial issues. They wanted two very simple but fundamental things: a home and a father. In short, Hughes reduces his tragic mulatto problem to a father-and-son conflict, and for him the single all-important and transcending issue is rejection—personal rejection on the part of the father.

I am convinced that Langston Hughes felt very keenly on this whole matter of rejection, and I believe that a most revealing postscript to this discussion of father-son relationships may be found in his autobiography, *The Big Sea* (1940). In this work there is a chapter entitled simply "Father," in which Hughes has accounted for, it seems to me, several of the attitudes he portrays in his tragic mulattoes.

Coming from a split home, Langston Hughes did not get to know his father until he was seventeen, the latter having moved to Mexico after the family breakup. During all of his early years of frequent removals and hand-to-mouth living with his mother and other relatives, Hughes came to look upon his father, living "permanently" in Mexico, as the "one stable factor" in his life. "He at least stayed put," and to the young Langston this was an impressive achievement. Although his mother had told him that the senior Hughes was a "devil on wheels," he did not believe her. On the contrary, he created in his mind a heroic image of his father, picturing him as a "strong bronze cowboy in a big Mexican hat," living free in a country where there was no race prejudice.

And then at seventeen, Hughes met his father and went to live with him in Mexico. Disillusionment came quickly, followed by a reaction far more serious. He found that the elder Hughes was neither kind nor understanding. "As weeks went by," he writes, "I could think of less and less to say to my father. His whole way of living was so different from mine. . . ." For the first time, the boy began to understand why his mother had left her husband; he wondered why she had married him in the first place; and most important of all he wondered why they had chosen to have him. "Now at seventeen," Langston Hughes tells us, "I began to be very sorry for myself. . . . I began to wish that I had never been born —not under such circumstances."

And then this unhappy, seventeen-year-old boy, like Maurai in "African Morning," contemplated suicide: "One day, when there was no one in the house but me," he writes, "I put the pistol to my head and held it there, loaded, a long time, and wondered if I would be any happier if I were to pull the trigger."

Subsequently, during a spell of serious illness, Langston Hughes' dislike of his father crystallized into something dangerously approaching fixation. "And when I thought of my father," he tells us, "I got sicker and sicker. I hated my father."

That last short sentence helps to explain for me Hughes' persistent concern with the tragic mulatto theme. In his handling of the theme he has found an opportunity to write out of his system, as it were, the deep feelings of disappointment and resentment that he himself felt as a "rejected" son.

ISOLATION IN LANGSTON HUGHES'
SOUL GONE HOME

William Miles

FEW WRITERS have been as prolific in their attempt to describe and interpret Negro American life as Langston Hughes. Poet, novelist, short story writer, and dramatist, "he writes to express those truths he feels need expressing about characters he believes need to be recognized." [1] One such truth is the forced isolation of the majority of black people by the culture within which they are forced by circumstance to exist. The intensity and repressiveness of such isolation alienates the black person not only from the culture at large, but frequently from his own brothers as well. [2] This is the theme of Hughes' powerful one-act play, *Soul Gone Home*. In less than four pages of text he presents a tragic and poignant picture of a people so isolated from each other that the establishment of meaningful emotional relationship is no longer possible.

The theme of isolation is not, of course, original with Hughes. What is original in *Soul Gone Home*, however, is the manner in which this theme is treated. The play is a fantasy in both situation and structure. Reality as we commonly experience it is replaced by the unreal, the dreamlike; the usual physical laws governing life and death are suspended. Yet the emphasis of the play is clearly on things as they exist in actuality. The play is about a situation resulting from the condition of black people in America. The immediate situation explored within the fantastic world of the play is itself unreal: a conflict between an uncaring mother and the ghost of her dead son in which the latter condemns his mother ("You been a hell of a mama! . . . I say you been a no-good mama.") [3] because

---

[1] *Langston Hughes: Five Plays*, edited with an introduction by Webster Smalley (Bloomington: Indiana University Press, 1963), p. vii.

[2] This phenomenon is explored at length and in great depth by Richard Wright in *Black Boy*. There it is made explicitly clear that the relationships within the author's family are directly determined by the condition of the black person in the society.

[3] Hughes, p. 39. All subsequent quotations from the play will be taken from this edition and noted directly within the text of the essay.

she failed to provide him with the necessities of life, food, clothing, "manners and morals."

This internal conflict in the realm of fantasy forms the center of the drama, but the structural limits are defined by reality. *Soul Gone Home* begins with the mother grieving over her son's body and concludes with his removal by the ambulance drivers. However, Hughes has constructed even these two apparently real incidents in such a way as to render them unreal. For example, the opening stage direction informs us that the mother is "loudly simulating grief" (p. 39) and the play ends on the same note with her again feigning grief in the presence of the indifferent ambulance drivers.

The importance of both this underlying structure and the unreality of the situation is that they immediately establish the fact of the isolated condition of the mother and son. The boy is, of course, apart from the real world in the sense that he is dead, and, likewise, the mother is removed by the very fact that she can openly converse with him. Indeed, the mother is actually doubly removed: her "real" life, or what glimpses we get of it, is characterized by a sense of unreality. Symbolically, therefore, she is not a part of the reality defined by the general society, and her being outside in large part is the result of her race. To emphasize this fact, Hughes underlines the isolated condition of both mother and son through their lack of relatedness to the white ambulance drivers.[4] Both are completely oblivious and indifferent to the dead boy and the tears of the "grieving" mother, and their lack of responsiveness to the situation is a measure of the vast gulf separating black and white.

Structurally, therefore, fantasy functions to establish the complete physical isolation of the two main characters from the real world. The focal point of the play, the inability of mother and son to relate on the emotional level, exists in a cause-and-effect relationship with their isolation from the society: forced and repressive physical isolation of one group by another results in severe emotional alienation among members of the persecuted group. In developing and emphasizing this emotional element, Hughes superimposes upon his fantasy clear implications of stark reality. Thus the total effect of *Soul Gone Home* is realism, and while the central conflict may be internal, the implied commentary relates wholly to the external world.[5]

[4] We are never told directly that the drivers are white, but we must assume them to be if simply because the mother thinks they are.

[5] At this point I should like to make it clear that the interpretation of the play as a study of what happens emotionally to victims of a white culture which has isolated them depends wholly upon implications which abound in the work. As Smalley points out, "That which is unsaid becomes almost more important than that which is put into the dialogue." Certainly one could in-

The conflict itself takes place in appropriate surroundings: it is night and the scene is "a tenement room, bare, ugly and dirty." (p. 39) Such a setting is explicitly illustrative of the type of life which the dead boy was forced to live and with keen insight into his once human condition, he attacks his mother for her lack of concern. Always in need of food, he had grown up "all bowlegged and stunted from undernourishment," and had died at sixteen of tuberculosis brought on by a lack of "milk and eggs" in his diet. Furthermore, he has come to realize that his "home" totally lacked an atmosphere of love and failed to provide him with examples of proper "manners and morals." Sickly and treated as nothing more than a burdensome bastard, he was forced out on the streets to grub out whatever money he could find. However, refusing to recognize her existence for what it really is, the mother sadly defends her actions and is quick to point out that the boy *was* nothing more than a burden to her. As this argument is developed, one can easily see that the gulf between white and black is as great and unbridgeable as the one existing between this mother and son.

Hughes does not explicitly explore the causes of such a situation nor the reasons it is permitted to persist. Why should a sixteen-year-old boy have to die from the lack of necessary foods; why should a mother be forced to view her child in terms of how much monetary help he can be; and, indeed, why should a mother herself be forced to turn to prostitution in order to scratch out an existence? Such questions are left unanswered, but Hughes does indicate responsibility. All the implications of Soul Gone Home point directly to the white world as the source of the problems of the majority of Negro Americans. Two incidents in the play illustrate this fact: the complete indifference of the white ambulance drivers, and the mother's symbolic whitening of her face before she goes out to prostitute her body.

It is interesting to note that the son, ironically, gains his great insight into the essential condition of life and his true relationship with his mother only upon dying. When the mother demands to know where he learned "all them big words" such as "manners and morals," he replies, "I learn't 'em just now in the spirit world." "But you ain't been dead no more'n an hour," the mother counters. "That's long enough to learn a lot," he says. (p. 40) In less than an hour of death the son has learned more about life than he did in sixteen years of real existence on earth. This new insight into and knowledge of what his and his mother's life has been is symbolically represented by the throwing off of the pennies (the material world) which cover his eyes.

terpret the boy's death as resulting simply from the character of an irresponsible mother, but even a cursory reading of Hughes' work reveals an almost total concern for and awareness of the social implications of themes and characters.

Son: I'm dead now—and I can say what I want to say. (*Stirring*) You done called on me to talk, ain't you? Lemme take these pennies off my eyes so I can see. (p. 39)

Hughes' implicit comment that only death (or some type of escape from existing conditions) can provide true insight into the human condition of the black American in a closed white society is closely paralleled in the work of Richard Wright. When Bigger Thomas commits the accidental murder of Mary Dalton in *Native Son*,

he blossoms into full consciousness as a personality. He is at once free of the society in which he lives. He can now analyze the relationship between the Negro and white world. He can probe into his own personality reactions and those of the people around him. For the first time in his life he lives as a whole human being.[6]

Likewise, the son in the play is able truly to see and assess his situation only when he is free from the constraints of the white-dominated physical and material world; only then can he "see" and "talk." Only in death has he found a home and a "real" life; he is a "soul gone home."

It is also an ironical but poignant consequence of the conflict between the mother and son that the mother utterly fails to comprehend what her son is talking about. Always on the defensive, she not only justifies her own position and actions, but even attempts to shift the blame for them to the boy.

Mother: (*Proudly*) Sure, I could of let you die, but I didn't. Naw, I kept you with me—off and on. And I lost the chance to marry many a good man, too —if it weren't for you. No man wants to take care o' nobody else's child. (*Self-pityingly*) You been a burden to me, Randolph.
Son: (*Angrily*) What did you have me for then, in the first place?
Mother: How could I help havin' you, you little bastard? Your father ruint me—and you's the result. And I been worried with you for sixteen years. (*Disgustedly*) Now, just when you get big enough to work and do me some good, you have to go and die. (p. 41)

The mother's complete isolation from her son is firmly implanted in the minds of the audience by her final gestures. She again feigns grief over the loss of her son; she smooths out the bed where he lay, thus seemingly blotting out any signs of his former existence; and she makes a final statement which indicates that her love for her son is less than complete.

[6] Constance Webb, "What Next for Richard Wright?" *Phylon*, X (1949), 161.

MOTHER: Tomorrow, Randolph, I'll buy you some flowers—if I can pick up a dollar tonight. You was a hell of a no-good son, I swear! (p. 42)

Through the skillful combination of situation, structure, character and symbol, Hughes has produced a compact and powerful play of a people so isolated that even the ordinarily secure relationship between mother and son is impossible. And while this thematic consideration is immediately relevant to the Negro American, *Soul Gone Home* does achieve a sense of universality in that its social commentary relates to any oppressed minority. Furthermore, the play also fulfills the criteria for "high art" laid down by LeRoi Jones.

High art, first of all, must reflect the experience, the emotional predicament of the man, as he exists, in the defined world of his being. It must be produced from the legitimate emotional resources of the soul in the world. It can *never* be produced by evading these resources or pretending that they do not exist. It can never be produced by appropriating the withered emotional responses of some strictly social idea of humanity. It must issue from *real* categories of human activity, *truthful* accounts of human life, and not fancied accounts of the attainment of cultural privilege by some willingly preposterous apologists for one social "order" or another.[7]

As Jones would have it, *Soul Gone Home* "tells it like it is," but in such a way as to create an impact and effect not soon nor easily forgotten.

[7] "Problems of the Negro Writer," *Saturday Review*, XLVI (April 20, 1963), 20.

A WORD ABOUT SIMPLE[*]

Blyden Jackson

It is highly probable that Langston Hughes reached his most appreciative, as well as his widest, audience with a character whom he named, eponymously and with obvious relish, Jesse B. Semple. The *Jesse*, not too incidentally, clearly invited an abbreviation to Jess.

Simple made his bow to the world in the columns of the *Chicago Defender*, the Negro weekly which, in its heyday from early in World War I through the whole of World War II, circulated into virtually every nook and cranny of Negro America and, indeed, functioned as a sort of bible to many Negroes in every walk of Negro life. Via the columns of the *Defender*, then, Hughes addressed not so much the Negro elite, cultural or otherwise. Rather, thus he spoke, powerfully and directly, to the very Negro of whom Simple was supposed to constitute an almost perfect replica. He spoke, that is, in great part to the black rank and file of our industrial Babylon, who may not be nearly so illiterate as their slave forebears, but who even now are still a far cry in their rapport with the world of books from the proverbial Harvard graduate.

Illiterate or not, however, these Negroes, a twentieth-century equivalent of Chaucer's fair field full of folk, seem to have taken Simple to their hearts. They followed Simple week after week in the columns of the *Defender*. They gossiped about him with their associates of their own kind. They found Simple understandable and comfortably convincing. True, they had not created Simple from an impulse originating in their own minds, nor made him what he became through arts which they had learned to practice, as, for instance, an earlier epoch of folk Negroes had created, and then, in effect, composed the Negro spiritual. In these senses, but only in these senses, Simple lacks the full authenticity of folk material. He was an adopted child, not a native son. Yet the attitude of his foster parents, the often so-called "common, ordinary" Negroes, toward him, their ready identification with him, suggests a special status of importance for his significance. Whether or not he is truly like most ordinary Negroes, he is certainly, in both form and substance, what many ordinary Negroes were

* Reprinted from *CLA Journal*, XI (June, 1968), 310–18, by permission of the editor.

at least once prepared to concede without rancor they thought they were. At least, to that extent, Simple must be accounted a folk Negro's concept of the folk Negro. Thus, too, he must be seriously considered a valuable specimen of Americana.

As such, it may well be noted first of Simple that he is a colored man, a highly visible Negro with a skin too dark, facial features too African, and hair too anything but lank, to be mistaken for an Aryan. He comes from Virginia, although in the days of his youth, when the Solid South (an admirable figure of speech) was still intact, there could be localities in Virginia as dismaying to Negroes as the worst counties in the heartland of the Old Confederacy. After a childhood in which he was, in his own words, "passed around" among his relatives—for, of his actual parents, he clearly never had much knowledge—he has gravitated to Harlem, with intermediate stops, during one of which he has married and "separated," that have qualified him for a true insider's view of a big-city Negro ghetto. Under the perspective of *multum in parvo*, indeed, his personal history typifies in several vital respects the sociological Negro of his class. He is the product of a broken home, out-migration from the South, and a disillusioning experience as a young and naïvely hopeful husband.

Put in the context of the environment forced upon him, Simple's efforts to express himself through the spoken word could hardly be expected to emanate from a well of English undefiled. As a matter of inescapable fact, he speaks a dialect. It is not that curious idiom, in which pronouns converted into "dises" and "dats" play a conspicuous role, so long associated with the synthetic Negro of blackface minstrelsy and the, until most recently, orthodox American dogmas about Negro behavior. That idiom, it probably should be observed, seemed determined to maintain the proposition that Negroes could not master the approved pronunciations of some English sounds either (or both) because of innate biological inadequacies in the organs of speech solely and irremediably attributable to the Negro's African blood, or (if not and) because the Negro ear, in its neurological inferiorities, simply could not properly hear the nuances of sound imparted to speech by a white tongue. But Simple talks as he does plainly because he has not had the benefit of living during his formative years where the people closest around him would have provided him with models of impeccable utterance. Nor has he had later much institutionalized linguistic aid that could have served as a corrective. In his own superbly succinct solecism, he has not been "colleged." He says usually (although puzzlingly enough, not invariably) "I were" for "I was." It is as if he has somehow established in his mind both an awareness of the interesting intelligence that verbs should be conjugated and an inclination so special to show his eagerness to comply with civilized procedures that he overdoes his willingness to inflect. Moreover, as with his peers whom one may encounter in such fictive haunts as those of *Invisible Man,* he has also a taste, as well as a positive knack, for either coining, or remembering, locutions that rhyme as they quip and that, in addition, are great fun to be savored as they are paraded over, and rolled around, the tongue.

He spends, for instance, the infrequent freest of his free time with a party-loving voluptuous vixen who is "loose as a goose," [1] strictly an "after-hours gal," [2] and "great when the hour is late, the wine is fine, and mellow whiskey has made you frisky." [3] His Cousin Minnie, who explodes upon him from an obscurity into which, once he is forced to contemplate her face and physiognomy, he would gladly consign her again at least until the Resurrection, seems to him to have taken as her motto what she has, incidentally, once proclaimed to him in no uncertain terms as the first principle of her existence, "beg, borrow and ball till you get it all." [4] Reflecting mournfully on the course of young love as he has often observed it in the ghetto, he intones, "Midsummer madness brings winter sadness, so curb your badness." [5] Yet, in a moment of his own ebullience he can, with a vulgarity unusual for him, although speaking really in an aside and not to the lady in question, command a passing female whom he does not know, but whose figure agreeably astonishes him, "Baby, if you must walk away, walk straight—and don't shake your tail-gate." [6]

Simple, in short, is a character who would clearly be something of a bull in a china shop in those purlieus of America frequented by the so-called best people. Nevertheless, even at his very worst he represents a great departure from the stereotypes of the Negro traditionally afloat in the common lore of the American mass intelligence. He is not Little Black Sambo grown up and existing half-wittedly in an urban setting beyond his resources to cope with, nor is he a brute, a demented apeman with a fearful affinity for lust and pillage, especially apropos the bodies and properties of persons more Nordic than himself. Indeed, quite to the contrary, he is an *ingénu* with very decent instincts, and a ruffian only in the sense that he is, underneath his gaucheries and his shortcomings, a diamond, unpolished and sometimes uncut.

He has, as has already been implied, reached maturity with little guidance after a childhood in humble circumstances. He did sojourn, as we have also seen, on his travels, in Baltimore long enough to have become

[1] Hughes, *Simple Takes a Wife* (New York, 1953), p. 221.
[2] *Ibid.,* p. 47.
[3] *Ibid.*
[4] Hughes, *Simple Stakes a Claim* (New York, 1953), p. 90.
[5] *Simple Takes a Wife,* p. 92.
[6] *Ibid.,* p. 101.

involved with the wife from whom he has been estranged for a considerable time. His serious and sustained interest in the likable nice girl whom he
is determined to wed, once he has secured the divorce the cost of which
somewhat appalls him, testifies to his fundamental kinship with the Tom
Joneses, rather than the Blifils, of this world. His vices might perturb
an Anthony Comstock. They would hardly perturb an apostle of sweet
reasonableness. He drinks a nightly beer. When he can get it, he is not
averse to stronger stimulant. But he is, except on the rarest of occasions,
only a mild inebriate, his addiction being controlled, indeed, both by his
disposition and his purse. On the other hand, to speak the utter truth, he
is also a great cadger of drinks, principally from the college-bred associate who is his boon companion at Simple's most accessible version of
the Mermaid Tavern.

Even so, however, his addiction to the bottle, such as it is, is actually
only the indulgence of a comradely spirit. At the bar, with the excuse of a
slowly diminishing glass in his hand, and an attendant ear at his side,
he assumes the role of genial philosopher which is his métier. For bitterness has not corroded him as it has a Bigger Thomas or a Rufus Scott. It
is a human comedy which Simple passes in review in his castle of indolence at his Harlem rendezvous, not an unrelieved panorama of hopeless gloom and horrors. Things happen in Simple's world sometimes for
the best, all too often for the worst, although there is a tendency for the
good things to come to good people just when the bad things are about
to become unbearable, and, always, for the common lot of man, the good
and the bad are tempered, and their deviations in any direction mediated
toward a neutral ground, by laughter, the superb and therapeutic acknowledgment by the human intellect that frailties of many kinds are endemic
to the human condition.

Nor is Simple's laughter an assault on others. It is, like his petty
bibulousness, companionable. He laughs with his fellows, at their foibles,
and at his own. When he recounts his wooing of his wife and the subsequent gradual disintegration of his marriage, he is at least as much
the target of his own satirical thrusts as anyone else. When his young
cousin just out of high school, Franklin D. Roosevelt Brown, as much a
bolt from the blue as is to be later the Cousin Minnie to whom reference
has already been made, appears, to discomfit him momentarily, and then
to win his only apparently grudging approval, it is his own slack habits
which he reviews for exposure to good-humored ridicule as much as his
young cousin's impetuosities. Moreover, as it does develop that he rather
likes playing the role of a father, or an older uncle, to his young kinsman,
and, even, that he plays both roles rather well, the sardonic self-depreca-
tions with which he dismisses his virtuous behavior confirm the verdict
of his relations with the girl who is his intended, that he is essentially made

of the salt of the earth, that his deeper instincts substantiate democracy's trust in the average man, that he even has dreams, big dreams of a noble nature, which, if he cannot always articulate them, or even admit publicly to their possession without some self-embarrassment, still are, after all is said and done, the things to which he truly clings.

Hughes with Simple is not, as is well known, the first Negro writer to write about the Negro folk. Long before Simple, to take a justly conspicuous example, James Weldon Johnson in his *God's Trombones* renders old-time folk-Negro preaching into verse, a medium which he may well have chosen in the hope that it would impart to his black divines a longer and happier literary life, especially since the verse is not in dialect. Johnson probably wanted his preachers to be admired. For, just as Johnson expressly felt that the great wide world of conscious cultural recognition had failed to give due credit to the Negro spiritual, so he was correspondingly distressed at this same world's neglect of the art of the old-fashioned Negro preacher; an art which, moreover, he could see very clearly and surely was being contained within an epoch in Negro history which would not, and, indeed, could not, last. Johnson, then, with his preachers, was an advocate, not so much of the mere existence of a phenomenon, as of a theory maintaining its special worth. But Hughes wanted Simple merely to be known. At the very heart of American racism there seems to be an assumption of the most dangerous import: to wit, that there are no Negroes who are average people. Moreover, this assumption for a long time exercised great sway over virtually all the American contemplation of Negro life. All Negroes were exceptional. A few, like Booker T. Washington in his time, and Ralph Bunche, later on, were exceptionally intelligent, usually because, probably, of an admixture of white blood. Also beneficent, as well as more understandable, since intellect is not the decisive factor for performing artists, but rather, some strange and peculiar organic or neurological accidents, were freaks like Blind Tom and Marian Anderson, Negroes who could play and sing not only their own simple Negro songs, but even compositions from the classical literature of serious music. But whether Negroes were tragic mulattoes or curious developments from their usually in some way defective African genes, in the final analysis, they were all freaks, even when of a beneficent kind.

Most Negroes, however, were not freaks of a beneficent kind. They were departures from nature in their lack of normal human attributes. So read, and still reads, the holy writ of American racism. Moreover, by an unfortunate coincidence, so read, in effect, the pronouncements of most Negro writers on Negro subjects. In all of Negro fiction the Negro who is unabashedly and simply an average man is as rare as once, in that same fiction, octoroons were disturbingly numerous. The best-known Negro novels, even *Invisible Man* (as, however, it must be admitted, its title implies) abound with grotesques, with people who do not act normally and whose distinctive stigma is failure, so that the prevailing conclusion to a Negro's tale of Negro life is catastrophe—Bigger Thomas awaiting execution, Lutie Johnson fleeing the corpse of the would-be seducer she has just murdered, Bob Jones on his way to enforced military service, the Invisible Man submerged, and lost, in his hole in the ground.

The motives of the Negro writer, of course, have not been those of the white supremacists, nor has been the chain of reasoning by which he has arrived at his conclusions. Negroes have been maimed, the Negro writer has contended, by their environment. The Negro characters of the Negro writer are freaks, pitiably and depressingly so, say their Negro creators, because the superimposed conditions of Negro life make them what they are. Their environment is freakish. How can they be otherwise? Yet, the plain truth is that men have never conclusively resolved the conundrum of the true influence of adversity upon the human psyche and that, moreover, most Negroes in actual life are not awaiting execution, fleeing murdered corpses, or living in subbasements either for ritual or fiscal reasons of an imperative nature.

What, then, are Negroes really like? This is the question which Langston Hughes seems to ask with his portrait of Simple. And his reply seems to be altogether different from many of the chilling responses to that same question provided by the apostles of a belief in the Negro manqué. Thus, in Hughes' warm and sane definition of an average Negro, Simple is no freak of any kind. He adores Jackie Robinson and respects Ralph Bunche, but he is no superman like either of them. Simple is an ordinary person who happens to be a Negro. He has an understandable distaste for white people who abuse him merely because he is a Negro or who commit acts which contribute to the system that exists solely to perpetrate a continuing series of such abuses. On the other hand, he takes also a dim view of the nastiness often observable in Negroes. His landlady, he has noted, is no angel of sweetness and light and, indeed, he scathes a Negro girl who is clerking in a white chain store for her rudeness and incompetence quite as much as he does President Eisenhower for spending so much time playing segregated golf in segregated Georgia.

To Simple, quite obviously, the millennium is far, far in a distant future. His vision of the good life is a modest conception only remotely related to the heady doctrine of the perfectability of man, as articulated, let us say, by such an evangelist of a New Order as a Shelley or a Fourier. It is based upon a soberly realistic acceptance of human society in which due allowance is made for man's limitations as well as his potential for self-improvement. Nor is Simple unique in the art of Langston Hughes. Rather he is representative. He belongs to the same world as the Negro characters, more memorable for their ordinariness than anything else, in

Hughes' one novel, *Not Without Laughter*. For Hughes never succumbed to the monstrous error of arguing that, because race prejudice is itself monstrous, it has made Negroes monsters.

American history proves Hughes right. In the 1860's there were some prophets who debated only the probable length of the period during which Negroes, freed to use their own resources, could manage even physical survival in the complex American environment. Some of these critics wondered, indeed, if the American Negro might not even be extinct by the end of the nineteenth century. The nineteenth century has been gone almost seventy years. At Emancipation, speaking generously, there were less than five and a half million Negroes in America. In the 1960's speaking cautiously, there are at least four Negroes extant for every Negro alive when President Lincoln issued his history-making Proclamation. Moreover, gradually, and in spite of an occasional setback here and there, it has become unmistakably clear that the general direction of Negro welfare in America is up. The Negro has survived, multiplied, and improved his American status in every respect.

He will never, however, be perfect. Nor will America. Most Americans, moreover, in the twenty-first century, as now, heretofore and forever hereafter, will continue to be average personalities. They will still, to an extent, get divorces, waste time with light women, drink beverages stronger than tea, lose an occasional job, mistreat their fellows, shirk responsibilities, and commit crimes against the state and nature. But they will also, and probably to a relatively greater degree, sometimes fall ecstatically, beautifully, and nobly in love, aid their relatives, do good turns for friends and, now and then, even for strangers, and, at some rare, unforeseen and, to them, unavoidable moments, even rise above themselves to perform ·prodigies of heroism and gracious feats magnificent in their altruism. Black and white, that is, they will be like Simple. Thus, they will justify, as they demonstrate, Langston Hughes' faith in human nature and illustrate the soundness of his affirmations about Negroes, America and humanity in general. These future Americans, that is, will join the Negro readers who, when Simple did appear in the *Defender*, rallied round him in such a manner as to indicate their conviction of his reality. They will give further incontrovertible proof, in their sentiments as well as their conduct, of the validity of Hughes' judgments on his chosen subject, the true character of the Negro Everyman. They will vindicate, in fact, the basic implications of our political and social creeds in America which argue that governments and communities exist not for the privileged few, but in the interest of everyone—even, and indeed most, for the Simples of this earth.

LeRoi Jones

LE ROI JONES OR,
POETICS & POLICEMEN OR,
TRYING HEART, BLEEDING HEART *

Stephen Schneck

1. OF HIS CHECKERED CAREER

IN 1965, LeRoi Jones was a young, black, literary lion. His play, "Dutch-man," had been awarded the Obie for the best American play of 1963–64. Grove Press had published a book of his poems, *The Dead Lecturer*, and was bringing out a novel, *The System of Dante's Hell*; two of his one-act plays, "The Baptism" and "The Toilet," were playing to enthusiastic houses. Another play, "The Slave," had just closed a successful run, and Jones was much in demand on the lecture and poetry-reading circuit. He was thirty-one years old, well reviewed by critics, constantly referred to in conjunction with "Negro writing," and that bible of commercial mas-turbation, Playboy magazine, described him as "the most discussed—and admired—Negro writer since James Baldwin." Blah-blah.

Jones was a novelty, one of the first black voices crying out in the white wilderness. The lectures he gave, the panel discussions he partici-pated in—all were utilized as platforms for launching attacks upon white America whose bullshit Jones, like many black men, had loved too well, from which he had expected too much, by which he had been cuckolded, and about which he was now bitter. Many of these attacks were ill-con-ceived, barely logical, too shrill, often grossly unfair, and always aimed at the crotch of the soft, white, good, liberal, WASP-Jewish intellectual. (Universal Honkie hate came later.)

The response was predictable. "White philanthropy runs amuck again," Jones wrote in a story called "Unfinished."

What he meant was that while in 1965 and into 1966 he kept cursing, ranting and raving and writing about himself, about beautiful black and hateful white America, for his efforts he received the John Hay Whitney

* Reprinted from *Ramparts*, VI (June 29, 1968), 14–19, by permission of the editors.

Award, became a Guggenheim Fellow, taught classes at the New School for Social Research and at Columbia University. He was laved with cocktail party love and lionized with literary laurels and cash monies.

At first, the blasé New York culture scene was titillated by his maledictions. He was invited to all the enchanted-circle beautiful-people parties, literary events, show business orgies, and hip gatherings. The more he attacked white society, the more white society patronized him. Who'd have suspected that there was so much money to be made from flagellation? Whitey seemed insatiable; the masochistic vein was a source of hitherto untapped appeal, big box office stuff, and LeRoi Jones was one of the very first to exploit it.

Naturally the smart money crowd, the commercial-intellectual establishment, decided he was running a game, that he was into a gimmick, a commercial pose, a successful device. After all, LeRoi had been around the Village for years, had run with the white beatniks in the early '50s, had married a white Jewish girl. So how could he really mean what he was saying? Actually *mean* it . . . ?

That was 1965. It is now three years later, and the score has changed. Currently, Jones is out of jail on $25,000 bail.

"Bail, hell! $25,000 isn't bail, it's a goddamned ransom," Jones snorted. He has an appeal pending for a conviction of illegal possession of firearms, for which he received a two-and-a-half to three-year prison sentence and a $1000 fine. That's the score these days. LeRoi Jones, like the rest of America, has changed since 1965.

2. GOING UPTOWN

We were all such innocents back then and so much more corrupt. (Violence may be monstrous, but self-deception is moral corruption.) In 1965, black and white men of good will were integrating the South together. Civil rights was still a possibility. So how could LeRoi be so serious? He was *ours*. Wasn't he?

He wasn't, and he *was* serious. He demonstrated this fact by an act that not even the cynical New York art world could pass off as a publicity bit or another tasteless tantrum. Jones, on the very brink of the American dream of fame and fortune, withdrew from the magic circle and went uptown. All the way uptown—to Harlem—leaving the high art scene to his white colleagues. The intellectual establishment could and did take the insults, obscenities, bad manners and name calling. But what was unforgivable, the one thing they couldn't take, was to be deserted, stood up. LeRoi Jones left them.

He traded in his successful-writer's suit for an Afro-American costume.

He stopped speaking to his old white friends and rarely came down from the black ghetto. Said one of these ex-friends, "Maybe Roi is a racist, but he sure as hell is no opportunist." He sure as hell wasn't. Not only did he withdraw his person, but he took his art along with him. A three-act, four-hour play optioned for Broadway was not produced. He withdrew *Black Magic*, a complete collection of his poetry, from Grove Press. The white world could stay where it was, but LeRoi Jones wasn't staying with it. Opportunity was white and Jones stayed black. Further, he was a poet, and poets are notorious natural revolutionaries. "Poetry is revolution," many, including Jones, have written.

Usually it starts as a personal revolution, evolving, if the poet and the times are right, into a broader, more comprehensive social revolution. Jones, the right man at the right time, made the passage with more expediency than most.

"Now that the old world has crashed around me, and it's raining in early summer, I live in Harlem . . . and suffer for my decadence which kept me away so long," he wrote in the fall of 1965. He was hard at work putting together the Black Arts Repertory Theatre School, which was to present theatricals that were cruder, more offensive, and even more anti-white than his previous downtown neocommercial plays.

Then he created a scandal by spending some antipoverty HARYOU (Harlem Youth) funds. Imagine Jones using federal money to finance his war on white America! When *that* got out there was an end to the project. And some of his own people, Harlem sharks, began hustling him. So he left Harlem and moved back to the old home town, Newark, New Jersey.

3. SPIRIT HOUSE

Let me rework a tired old dirge for your reading pleasure. Let us all concentrate on a mental image of the Newark slums. Let's conjure up images of urban decay, generations of decay presided over by generations of white politicians. Let's picture the tenements, the grey sidewalks, the sagging storefronts. The doorways and the broken windows mended with cardboard and Scotch tape. The walls of Newark's slums stained with soot, caked with grime, pock-marked with some of the 10,414 rounds of automatic ammunition the New Jersey National Guard sprayed into the black ghetto last July [1967].

Smell the dark, fragrant stairwells and the stinking hall toilets and odorous hallways of the tenements of black Newark. Smell the piss and the poverty in the public housing projects. Smell the back seats of the patrol cars and the precinct house, smell the Lysol and leather, the black skin and dried blood. Smell the garbage strewn in the empty lots and the soulfood cooking behind the doors.

See the patrol car turn the corner and the black faces staring from the sidewalk. See other black faces duck inside. See the younger kids playing in the gutters. See the older kids scoring in the poolrooms and luncheonettes. See the grown men passing the brown paper sack, keeping an eye out for that patrol car. See that patrol car come sliding around the corner again. Look out.

See LeRoi Jones. In the middle of Newark's ghetto where he took over a three-story building, called it Spirit House, and went on with the work he had started in Harlem—his *community services.*

His what? LeRoi Jones, the rabid, racist, separatist, militant black poet/playwright doing community service? The New York theatre and literary gang sneered. The hip faggots tittered. Just what community was LeRoi serving . . . ?

"Spirit House," Jones says, is a black community theatre owned by the people of the community. . . . We present whatever the community wants. Movies, plays, lectures, sports. . . . We have a permanent ensemble of actors. . . . We use lots of kids from the neighborhood. We put on plays for children. . . ."

One of these children's plays, written, directed and produced by Spirit House, was presented at the memorial services for Malcolm X, held at Harlem's controversial Intermediate School 201 at the end of February this year [1968]. There was much hullabaloo over that service. Teachers were suspended, then reinstated, then resuspended for bringing their classes. Lots of little black children sat in the public school's auditorium and listened to speakers like former vice-principal Herman Fergusen, at the time under indictment on a charge of plotting to assassinate Whitney M. Young and Roy Wilkins, two moderate civil rights figures. Fergusen delivered a talk advising black people to get themselves ready for the "hunting season." Not only kids were present. But there were lots of black school children attending the Malcolm X Memorial and watching a one-act pantomine by LeRoi Jones and his Spirit House players. Not Peter Pan but agit-prop.

Jones' pantomime made the point that the white race existed on the labor, creativity and vitality of the blacks.

Call *that* a play for children? Call *that* a community service? Depends on what community you live in, I suppose.

"When I die, the consciousness I carry I will to black people. May they pick me apart and take the useful parts, the sweet-meat of my feelings. And leave the bitter, bullshit rotten white parts alone," Jones wrote, declaring his dedication to his community.

4. HISTORY

At 2:30 in the morning of July 14th of last year [1967], a Volkswagen camper was touring the Newark battlefield. At the intersection of South Orange Avenue and South Seventh Street, the bus was stopped by two units of the Newark Police Department, and the occupants—Barry Wynn, an actor; Charles McCray, an accountant; and LeRoi Jones, poet, playwright and owner of the vehicle—were pulled out of the bus. That much is agreed upon. The rest is a mixture of truth, lies, distortions, misrepresentations and imprecise reportage, all blending into that fictive reality which eventually passes for history.

According to a statement that Jones prepared for his lawyer:

> After midnight on July 14th, 1967, I and my companions were driving in my station wagon, talking and listening to the radio. As we reached the corner of South Orange Avenue, which was on our direct route home, we were stopped by at least two carloads of white-helmeted police with shotguns and several detectives.
>
> We were told to come out of the car. When I opened the door and stepped down, one detective, whom I recognized as having once attended Barringer High School while I was there, preached to me, screaming that "we were the bastards" who'd been shooting at them. "Yes," he said, "a blue panel truck." (My station wagon is an olive green camper bus.) I said that we had not been shooting at anyone. I told the officer that I thought I remembered him from high school—whereupon he hit me in the face and threw me up against the side of the truck. (The others had also been taken from the truck.)
>
> The detective then began to jab me as hard as he could with his pistol in my stomach, asking, "Where are the guns?" I told him that there were no guns. Suddenly it seemed that five or six officers surrounded me and began to beat me. I was hit perhaps five times on top of my head by night sticks, and when I fell, some of the officers went about methodically trying to break my hands, elbows and shoulders. One officer tried to kick me in the groin—and there were many punches thrown. As they beat me they kept calling me "animal" and asking me, "Where are the guns?" Inside the wagon, the beating continued. They took us from the wagon, and as I was pushed up the stairs at Police Headquarters, an officer called out, "Wait a minute" and then punched me in the pit of the stomach. I fell to the ground clutching my stomach.
>
> Inside the station, Mr. Spina (the police director) was standing behind the desk. I asked him had he ordered me beaten. He replied, "They got you, didn't they?"—smiling. . . .
>
> We were then taken to City Hospital; I was dragged in and handcuffed in a wheelchair. The "doctors" put in eight or nine stitches, and one doctor shouted at me, "You're a poet, huh? Well, you won't be writing any poems for a long time now."

We were then taken to police headquarters on Franklin Street, fingerprinted and brought into the courtroom and arraigned. The prosecutor asked for $25,-000 bail for me, which the judge allowed. I was taken to the Essex County jail and put into solitary confinement, where I remained until I was released. (All motions for lowering the bail were denied.)

Seven months later, in January 1968, LeRoi Jones and his two codefendants went on trial for unlawful possession of two loaded, pearl-handled revolvers and a box of ammunition.

Judge Leon W. Kapp and an all-white jury heard half-a-dozen policemen swear that the revolvers had been found in Jones' station wagon. The officers all swore that they had not struck Jones nor had they seen anyone else strike him. His head injuries, they said, had been caused by a bottle flying through the air. They had no idea from whence it came.

Jones swore that he didn't know where the guns came from. He suspected that they came from the officers who had stopped, beaten and arrested him and then needed some justification for their actions.

"They weren't my guns. I don't keep guns," Jones says. "And I surely wouldn't be so stupid as to carry any guns into the middle of a riot." Which seems obvious enough. Jones is very well known in Newark.

"Sure, he's a famous nigger," one member of the Newark Police Department told me. "Sure, we all know who LeRoi Jones is."

Not that it really matters any more whether the guns were his or whether they were planted by the officers who'd worked him over. The painful point has been made. Jones is very guilty. Of something. Of poetry, probably. Of speaking in persuasive tongues to that part of the heart that is better left unaroused. So even if we give LeRoi the benefit of the doubt, it still comes down to the fact that at worst, they got the right man on the wrong charge.

Gruet, having writ the word "nonsense" in Calvin's book, was executed for having committed blasphemy and treason. Artus, having writ the words "solemn conspiracy" in his own book, was broken for telling the truth and committing treason.

The Essex County court where Jones and his codefendants were tried was presided over by the Hon. Leon W. Kapp. Whatever else he lacks, Judge Kapp has proper respect for the power of poets. Perhaps *respect* is not quite the right word. Say simply that Judge Kapp holds poets responsible for their poems. And that he does not grant poetic license frivolously.

The average sentence meted out to those arrested during the Newark riots for illegal possession of firearms was six months, and half of that

was on probation. McCray and Wynn, Jones' codefendants, received, re-
spectively, 12 months in jail, six months on probation and a $500 fine; and
nine months in jail, nine months' probation and a $250 fine.

When it was Roi's turn to be sentenced, Judge Kapp produced the
latest issue of *Evergreen Review* (December 1967). In it was a poem by
Jones, and Judge Kapp read it aloud to the all-white jury. A man of
grotesque niceties, he substituted the prurient *blank* for certain words.
In abridged version, this was the poem he read:

BLACK PEOPLE!
    What about that bad short you saw last week
on Frelinghuysen, or those stoves and
    refrigerators, record players, shotguns,
in Sears, Bambergers, Klein's, Hahnes',
    Chase, and the smaller joosh
enterprises? What about that bad jewelry, on
    Washington Street, and
those couple of shops on Springfield? You
    know how to get it, you can
get it, no money down, no money never,
    money dont grow on trees no
way, only whitey's got it, makes it with a
    machine, to control you
you cant steal nothin from a white man, he's
    already stole it he owes
you anything you want, even his life. All the
    stores will open if you
will say the magic words. The magic words
    are: Up against the wall mother
fucker this is a stick up! Or: Smash the
    window at night (these are magic
actions) smash the windows daytime,
    anytime, together, lets smash the
window drag the shit from in there. No
    money down. No time to pay. Just
take what you want. The magic dance in the
    street. Run up and down Broad
Street niggers, take the shit you want. Take
    their lives if need be, but
get what you want what you need. Dance up
    and down the streets, turn all
the music up, run through the streets with
    music, beautiful radios on
Market Street, they are brought here
    especially for you. Our brothers

are moving all over, smashing at jellywhite
    faces. We must make our own
World, man, our own world, and we can not
    do this unless the white man
is dead. Let's get together and kill him my
    man, lets get to gather the fruit
of the sun, let's make a world we want black
    children to grow and learn in
do not let your children when they grow
    look in your face and curse you by
pitying your tomish ways.

Then Judge Kapp laid the magazine down and began his critique. He characterized the poem as a ". . . diabolical prescription to commit murder and to steal and plunder . . . causing one to suspect that you were a participant in formulating a plot to ignite the spark . . . to burn the city of Newark!" His honor had a flair for the fantastic; yet the man was closer to the truth than most. He was also an example of the paranoid reality, the state of mind that has annexed America. "It is my considered opinion that you are sick and require medical attention."

"Not as sick as you are!" the poet called out.

Unrepentant. Definitely unrepentant. Throughout the trial, Jones made no effort to cop a Famous Writer's plea which usually allows the celebrity to walk out with a suspended sentence and a reasonable fine. Not only did he talk out of turn, LeRoi was dressed to offend. No traditional blue suit and white shirt (standard dress, advised by all attorneys) but a striped *dashike*, the tunic-like garb of the currently popular Afro-American mode. On his head he wore a red cap. And the outfit was strikingly set off by the enormous contempt the poet obviously felt for the proceedings, which he wore on his sleeve in place of his heart.

Judge Kapp went on to say, "Your talents have been misdirected. You have the ability to make a wholesome contribution to ameliorate existing tensions . . . but instead we find you in the vanguard of extreme radicals who advocate the destruction of—"

"*The destruction of the unrighteous!*" Jones wrote himself into what was intended to be the judge's soliloquy.

"—of our democratic way of life," the inexorable judge kept capping himself. "On the basis of your conviction for unlawful possession of two revolvers—"

"And one poem!"

"—judgment that you be confined to the New Jersey State Prison to serve a term of *not less than two years and six months*, and not more than three years, and that you pay a fine of $1000."

LeRoi Jones, handcuffed between two deputies, paused at the courtroom door and called back over his shoulder, "The black people will judge me. . . . *History will absolve me.* . . ."

Hopefully, Jones will be judged not only by his own people, but by a more immediate court. He has appealed his conviction, and his appeal should be sustained. In any event, he has written his own higher appeal to reason in a short story called "Words":

I make these documents for some heart who will recognize me truthfully. Who will know what I am and what I wanted beneath the maze of meanings and attitudes that shape the reality of everything. Beneath the necessity of talking or the necessity for being angry. . . . The purpose of myself has not yet been fulfilled.

5. INTERLUDE

But what is the purpose of Jones? Obviously, not what it seems, for LeRoi Jones is obviously not what he seems. He is no martyr, unless we martyr him. Neither is he a black bogey-man, a Mau-Mau monster or, as several of his former white friends have described him, a bad-talking clown. He is a poet, a playwright, a conscience, a consciousness.

Probably Norman Mailer's characterization of Jones at a recent benefit is the best explanation of Jones's purpose, his *raison*, and a fair description of his true talents. That night at New York's Town Hall, Mailer said that Jones had written the best one-act play in America ("Dutchman") and went on to say, "Who is this man, why are we here, will we survive? Thank you."

Therefore, if we wish to allow Jones to fulfill himself, if we desire to turn black militancy into a *wholesome contribution*, we have only to alter those elements in our society which thwart the Negro, frustrate the poet and menace our survival.

We have merely to tear down the ghettos and build up decent, integrated communities; re-educate our police departments to value life above property; destroy racial prejudice on both sides of the black and white picket fence dividing the cities; provide equal educational and employment opportunities for all; impeach Judge Kapp and others who have no conception of or respect for the law; share the wealth; and make a few other alterations in the shape and style of our society.

To exorcise LeRoi Jones and his black devils and save ourselves from the summers to come, we need only follow the above suggestions. Then we won't have to worry about Black Power, white backlash, civil insurrection, police brutality or anything else. For by that time, surely, the Messiah will have come.

6. WHAT AMERICA IS ALL ABOUT

In January of this year [1968], LeRoi Jones was convicted and sentenced to not less than two and a half and not more than three years in the New Jersey State Prison for illegal possession of firearms. On March 5th, an appeal to set aside this conviction was rejected by the U. S. Supreme Court. To date, Jones has another appeal pending; when it will be heard is not yet known.

On the 10th of April 1968, at 7:40 in the evening, CBS News in N. Y. released a taped interview with Charles Kinney, representing the Newark Police Department; Anthony Imperiale, leader of the local white vigilantes; and LeRoi Jones, representing an organization called the United Brothers.

The joint press conference was held to clear up "some misunderstandings" between Mr. Imperiale's organization—a group of armed, white Newark citizens who formed after the July riots to protect their property and themselves from black rioters; the Newark Police Department; and LeRoi Jones, representing not only himself, but the United Brothers, which may or may not represent the Newark ghetto.

Among the "misunderstandings" that apparently got cleared up was the central question of guilt—just who was responsible for last summer's rebellion and for the rash of incidents and arson cases that have taken place since. You'll never guess.

Captain Kinney announced that "the Reds in Newark, who are part of an international left-wing conspiracy financed by Peking" were responsible.

Shockingly, LeRoi sat right there and agreed with the police official. Negro members of these left-wing groups were, in Jones' words, "black lackeys of the white radicals."

Mr. Imperiale, who teaches karate and the use of firearms to his Northward Citizens Committee, was also in agreement. "We believe that the communists and the Trotskyite persons who have no interest in the city of Newark, except to cause a distraction on behalf of possibly Moscow or Peking, came in here and helped out on those riots."

Jones picked up the theme and improvised a chorus: "We, the Black Nationals in Newark, believe that we can gain power in Newark through political means, and there are white-led, so-called radical groups that are exploiting the black people's legitimate desire for power. Exploiting it and actually using black people as a kind of shock troops to further their own designs."

Now just what are you saying, Mr. Jones? A man as wry, as sophisticated, as hip as LeRoi Jones, a man who has already denounced the national bullshit and put the high art and expensive culture scene down, down, down, reduced to baiting Reds at this stage in his career? What is that all about?

About two and a half to three years in the New Jersey State Prison, that's what it's all about, the cynics of all colors quickly piped up when they first heard the news. *That man, LeRoi, he's facing serious time and they got a gun to his head.*

Well, maybe. That would seem the most logical explanation for Jones' cooperation with what he had previously characterized as the "twin evils of racism and fascism." (Not to mention the monster, CBS.) Yes, maybe they offered Jones a deal. Apparently the question also occurred to the networks' interviewer who, rather circuitously, put it to Jones:

"Do you mean was I promised something for doing it?"

"Precisely," said the CBS man.

"Well," said LeRoi, "I told you before that they promised to make me Secretary of State, and so when you see that happen, you know that's what it was."

The same question was asked of Captain Kinney, and the captain's answer was appropriately uptight. "There certainly have been no promises on any law enforcement agency's part. LeRoi has been found guilty. His trial is subject to appeal. He is getting all the rights of every American citizen, but there's certainly been no promises made to him in any fashion whatsoever."

"Captain Kinney," asked the CBS man, "Some of these charges obviously are very serious. We are now having our first public airing of them. Is there any legal action pending?"

Said the captain, "Yes. I have submitted a complete report to my superiors with recommendations that my findings go before a county grand jury and/or a federal grand jury." The captain, in fact, had recently returned from testifying before HUAC [House Un-American Activities Committee] and while in Washington Captain Kinney had named *names*. *Real people's* names were offered in testimony as persons responsible for Newark's burnt-out slums.

With the exception of one—Tom Hayden, head of a local community organizing group and resident of the ghetto—they were all black leaders, some militant and some moderate. And all faced possible indictment for God knows what Kinney was prepared to charge them with. Was LeRoi Jones ready to go along with this crap? Was he helping send his people to a grand jury?

Who knows. Maybe that was part of the deal that might have been made. Maybe they promised him that no one would be hurt. The grand jury stuff was just conversation. Just something to get the heat off the Newark police and off the black men of the Newark ghetto, off Jones himself. So maybe he was just pretending . . . of course he was. Just playing. Playing politics. And talking that square American jive about outside agitators and orders from Peking and Moscow. (Still, it must have left a rotten taste in his mouth. Still, there are worse things than a rotten taste in your mouth.)

But, by cooperating, Jones did (hopefully) himself a favor, and maybe he did the black community a favor as well. I suspect that he was trying to. He was trying *something*, that is pretty obvious.

Another Newark resident, a friend of both Jones and Hayden, felt very badly but didn't think that LeRoi had sold himself or anyone else. "LeRoi was talking about certain white extremist groups. And what he was attempting to do, it seems to me, was to get the heat off the black militants, because that is who the Newark police were trying to blame for the fires."

You get the not-too-subtle point? We already know that Jones had jumped off the rising escalator to fame and fortune, so why should anyone be surprised when he quit the "white extremists," leaving them to swim or drown in the treacherous ghetto tides? As for the blacks named and charged by Captain Kinney, so what? There are some black men, or rather certain *types* of Negroes (Jones pronounces the word "Knee-grows") that Jones dislikes as much as whites.

Like all black militants this season, Jones is preaching separation of the races, black political power, black control over black communities and racial pride above all. God bless black. No wonder Tony Imperiale, in the course of the CBS interview, was able to say, "We're all just Americans, concerned for our people and for our lives. . . ." Just plain folks, just frightened Americans. Just wily politicians and racist cops and poets who have lost their poetry trying to save their lives and their people. . . .

Therefore, I surely would have enjoyed a peek at LeRoi's face, not his mask but at the face behind that mask, when, later on in the interview, the CBS man asked him, "Well, Mr. Jones, these disclosures about this alleged conspiracy, will this mean that you and Mr. Imperiale are going to work hand-in-hand from here on in to keep the peace in Newark?"

"Well, I don't know about hand-in-hand," was what Jones answered, but what was Jones thinking? What was he feeling? Was he laughing, was he crying, was he burning, was he sick to his stomach or was he just sitting there *jiving*?

And Tony Imperiale, sitting right next to him, said into the microphone, "Like LeRoi says, it doesn't mean that we're going to be working hand-in-hand, but it's a start."

And that's what America is all about, isn't it folks? The similarities between Jones, Imperiale and the cooperation of the Newark Police Department; the services of CBS, and one day, maybe, the apples of paradise;

an American Dream in every pot, be that pot white or black. Power and wealth and security for all concerned.

Except, of course, for the dirty Commie agents with their orders from the moon, and their crimes, their agitation, their arson . . . and their black lackeys. Black Reds, you might call them, just for a laugh.

7. OF SHOES AND THORNS

LeRoi Jones and I were never really friends. I knew him very casually about 15 years ago when we both lived in Greenwich Village. I'd run into him in Washington Square Park or at one of the jazz clubs or at some party, and then we'd say Hello, and that was about it. And then, for a few months, I lived with a girl who had lived with LeRoi.

I don't know LeRoi Jones very well, and I don't pretend to know what goes on in black inner space. I don't know what is going on in the black community of Newark. I suspect that there is division, political fratricide, and all the usual agonies. I can say that justice has not been meted out to Jones; I can also say that Jones hasn't been very just to others.

But justice and Jones are strangers. America has kept them apart. Understand that, and you can understand Jones' indifference to the fate of white radicals and his cooperation with white racists, the Newark Police and, indirectly, with HUAC.

"The native is an oppressed person whose permanent dream is to become the persecutor," Frantz Fanon wrote in his *Wretched of the Earth*, and LeRoi Jones is living testimony to the dreadful truth. Never mind that he knows better; never mind that his appeal fund was organized and contributed to by the white radical intellectuals whom Jones circuituously finked out on. Forget your preconceptions of decency and justice; these qualities have nothing to do with Jones. Or did you think he'd be grateful?

I would only remind those who still can't reconcile Jones' perfidy with their image of a black poet-revolutionary that Roi never preached equality; he's never called for a united front, only for a black front. The fact that he is the poet laureate of this Black Revolution may confuse some hard-core innocents who still think that the Black Revolution has something to do with white justice. Or that poets can't be social perverts. Or that certain fanatics wouldn't sell their (white) brothers to save their (black) skin. That is what the color war is about. That is what fratricide is about.

Whether or not this is an exact description of LeRoi Jones, I can't say for certain. I can only suggest that if the shoe fits, Jones can wear it. Along with his crown of thorns.

BLACK MAN AS VICTIM*

Donald P. Costello

LeRoi Jones, in a 1962 address to the American Society for African Culture, insisted that the job of the Negro writer was to portray "the emotional history of the black man in this country: as its victim and its chronicler." Jones the dramatist has taken his own advice. The black man is the victim in Jones' plays, and Jones himself, with an increasingly strident voice, is the black man's chronicler, and, perhaps, America's chronicler.

The plays have been few. In 1961, 16 performances of Jones' *Dante* were presented at the Off-Bowery Theatre. This was a short dramatization, a modern parallel of the False Comforters theme, from *The Systems of Dante's Hell,* Jones' book of fiction. But 1964 was the big year for LeRoi Jones drama, with productions in New York of *The Baptism, The Toilet, Dutchman,* and *The Slave.*

The Baptism, presented at Writers' Stage Theatre off-Broadway in 1964, is not a racial play. It tries hard to be a comedy-of-cruelty, but it tries harder to be blasphemous. Most of the action takes place on the altar of a Baptist church, with characters including a homosexual in red leotards who does ballet steps, who sprinkles the assembly with confetti, and jokingly asserts that he is "the Son of Man." A 15-year-old girlishly handsome boy comes to be baptized, to be forgiven for 1,095 masturbations, one of which is described in detail, and for which Jones delights in finding synonyms. The minister claims at the altar that his usherettes are "the brides of the Lord's Son, our own Jesus Christ"; and they claim that the masturbating boy is actually the Lord's son because "it was he who popped us." After the boy admits that he *is* the Son of God, he kills the usherettes for "they had no charity." A motorcycle messenger from "The Man" comes to recall this Son of God who, although he was sent to save the earth, has been an absolute failure. God is tired of the world's mess, we are told, and plans to grenade the whole works. But the boy-Christ won't leave for his job is unfinished; so the messenger hits him with a tire iron and carries him off, home to God, on the back of the motorcycle. In a few hours before the grenade will destroy the world, the homosexual decides to cruise the bars,

* Reprinted from *Commonweal,* 88:436–40 (June 28, 1968), by permission of the editors.

wondering what happened "to that cute little religious fanatic." Jones strains to be shocking; and the play ends up to be incoherent and adolescent, with scatter-shot fury. In his racial plays, his fury finds its target.

The Toilet is an ugly but affecting racial play. It was presented at St. Mark's Playhouse in a double bill with *The Slave*. Jones tells us, in an "Introduction by the Playwright," that *"The Toilet* is about the lives of black people. White people tell me it is not. They have no way of knowing, but they insist they do."

In *The Toilet*, the victim—Jones again uses that word in his Introduction—is a black boy named Ray Foots who cannot express his love for a white boy named Karolis because of what Jones calls the "brutality" of the "social order." And one of the major achievements of the play is the stunning force with which that social order is shown to *be* brutal. The specific social order created by the play is that of high-school boys, most of them black. And the setting is a stinking "latrine of some institution." Throughout the play, comment is made on the social order by boys who turn their backs to the audience to urinate into one of the urinals which make up the visual line of the set, and by a boy who goes behind a toilet partition and is found "pulling his whatchamacallit," and by verbal obscenities, some trite and some imaginative.

When Karolis is dragged into the latrine by a group of black boys, he has been beat up, is "crying softly, with blood on his shirt and face." Karolis has been dragged to the toilet to fight Foots, the leader of the Negro gang, because of a homosexual love letter which Karolis has sent Foots, a letter in which Karolis said that Ray Foots was beautiful. Foots feels pity—and a kind of returned love—for Karolis, but because of social pressure from the gang, and because of Karolis' own insistence, Foots does fight the already-beaten Karolis. Eventually Karolis is jumped by all the gang and is left bleeding on the toilet floor, draped with wet toilet paper. Karolis, the white boy, is more obviously—but to Jones less profoundly—a victim than is Foots, the black boy. It is the white boy who is beaten. But the meaning of the play comes from Karolis' revelation that the black boy he really loves is a hidden beautiful boy named Ray, not the Foots of this stinking toilet who is visible to his gang members. "Did I call you Ray in that letter—or Foots? . . . That's who I want to kill. Foots . . . His name is Ray, not Foots. You stupid bastards. I love somebody you don't even know."

After Karolis is left bleeding on the toilet floor, Foots sneaks back in, kneels by Karolis' form and, weeping, cradles his head in his arms as he wipes the blood from Karolis' face. For all of its ugliness, *The Toilet* is, as Jones has written, "a play about love." It is a play about a love between a white boy and a black boy, a love which, because of the social order in which the black people live, cannot be expressed on any level. Brutality results, says Jones, in any social order, "if it is not an order which can admit of any man's beauty." The beauty of Foots remains hidden. Both the black and the white are therefore victims; and the chronicler, Jones, in this play talks—for the last time—about love.

The victim in *Dutchman* is Clay, and this is a play about hatred. *Dutchman* was produced off Broadway at the Cherry Lane Theatre, and it won the *Village Voice's* Obie Award for the Best American Play of the 1963–64 season. Subsequently it was presented at the Festival of Two Worlds, at Spoleto. It is the most widely known of Jones' works, primarily through the 1967 movie version directed by Anthony Harvey.

In *Dutchman*, Jones again, as he had in *The Toilet*, speaks through controlled dramatic art. He controls his form. He embodies his hatred in two characters; he is still a dramatist. In an interview, Jones said, "*Dutchman* is about the difficulty of becoming a man in America." The boy who is "desperately trying to become a man" is Clay, twenty-year-old Negro. Lula, beautiful young white woman on the make, sits next to Clay on the subway. In brilliant dialogue (by far the best art Jones has shown in any of his plays) Clay's lack of *place* is revealed to the audience. He doesn't belong, for he doesn't acknowledge his blackness. Lula has him pegged: "You're a well-known type," and "I know you like the back of my hand." He's a suburbanite, living in New Jersey with his parents; in college he thought of himself as Baudelaire. Never did he think of himself as a black nigger. He's a poser, not a man; he doesn't acknowledge what he *is*. Lula takes hold of his jacket and shouts: "Boy, those narrow shoulder clothes come from a tradition you ought to feel oppressed by. A three-button suit. What right do you have to be wearing a three-button suit and striped tie? Your grandfather was a slave, he didn't go to Harvard."

Scene I ends with Lula's insistence that she knows the truth about Clay. Ivy league clothes won't hide his blackness. And his submission is only a pretense. He cannot be free from his history, the heritage of slavery; and she cannot be free from her history, the heritage of oppression. And simmering under the pretense of Clay's submission to the white order is the necessity of the slave to murder his oppressor: "You're a murderer, Clay, and you know it."

By the end of Scene I the mood of the play is taut. The victim will not stay victimized peacefully. And by this time the observer hears obviously the voice of the chronicler, the tortured autobiographical gropings of LeRoi Jones himself, faced with "the difficulty of becoming a man in America." In a preface to a 1966 collection of essays, ironically called *Home*, Jones tells us something about that constant struggle of his own which, in *Dutchman*, is mirrored in the character of Clay: "One truth anyone reading these pieces ought to get is the sense of movement—the struggle, in myself, to understand where and who I am, and to move with that understanding." All these movements, Jones writes, "seem to me to have been always toward the thing that I had coming into the world, with no sweat: my blackness." And, he concludes, "by the time this book appears, I will be even blacker."

In Scene II, Clay becomes blacker. Lula goads him into it. She mocks him, wildly, dancing in the aisle: "You middle-class black bastard." "You liver-lipped white man." "You ain't no nigger, you're just a dirty white man." She commands Clay to do what Jones himself, in his dramatic career, has been doing: "Get up and scream at these people. Like scream meaningless shit in these hopeless faces." Clay finally answers back. He slaps her across the mouth as hard as he can, and announces: "Now shut up and let me talk." And then Clay launches into a long and obscene rage against Lula and against all whites who profess to understand the Negro. Lula cannot understand: "You great liberated whore! You fuck some black man, and right away you're an expert on black people." And neither can any whitey understand or help a black man come to an image of himself. So, Clay insists, through his teeth: "Let me be who I feel like being. Uncle Tom. Thomas. Whoever. It's none of your business." It's as simple as that. Whitey can tell the black man nothing because whitey can understand nothing. As early as 1961, Jones had written: "Liberals think that they are peculiarly qualified to tell American Negroes and the other oppressed peoples of the world how to wage their struggles." In *Dutchman*, the Jones reply to whitey is "It's none of your business."

Clay knows that it is insane to conceal his blackness, but Jones gives him only two alternatives. He can continue the insanity of living half-hidden in whitey's world; or he can relieve his insanity by asserting his blackness through murder: "Murder. Just murder! Would make us all sane." He warns Lula not to teach the black man the way of the white man, not to talk too much about the advantages of Western rationalism or the great intellectual legacy of the white man, because if the black man does learn the lesson of the white man, he will adopt his weapon: "All of those ex-coons will be stand-up Western men, with eyes for clean hard useful lives, sober, pious and sane, and they'll murder you." Clay chooses to avoid the easy, luxurious way of murder ("It takes no effort. To kill you soft idiots.") He chooses, instead, to stay in his insanity, to deny his blackness, to deny the murder that would liberate him: "Ahh, shit, who needs it? I'd rather be a fool. Insane. Safe with my words, and no deaths, and clean, hard thoughts."

But in the Jones world murder is inevitable once white and black confront each other. So, although Clay decides to remain insane by not murdering, Lula turns him into the complete victim by plunging a knife into his chest. In a ritual act, with the collaboration of the rest of the congregation in the subway, whitey kills the black man as indeed whitey has been doing all along. The black man who refuses to murder is himself murdered.

If Clay is the black man, if Clay is Jones (Jones has written often that everything he writes is necessarily written specifically *as* a black man), who is Lula? She is of course America, especially white liberal America who interferes with the black man, who professes friendship as it murders. Jones insists that Clay and Lula are not symbols; but then he goes on to talk of them as if they are. Lula, he insists, "does not represent anything—she is one. And perhaps that thing is America, or at least its spirit." When the critics complained that Lula is too crazy, extreme, neurotic, Jones replied, "You remember America, don't you, where they have unsolved murders happening before your eyes on television? How crazy, extreme, neurotic, does that sound? Lula, for all her alleged insanity, just barely reflects the insanity of this hideous place."

Harold Clurman has pointed out that if *Dutchman* is angry, *The Slave* is rabid. Anger, he says, has a definite form; rage only smolders and explodes. The form of *The Slave* is supposedly a fable in which a debate takes place. But rather it is a tirade delivered by Walker, a Negro who is leading a violent murderous black rebellion which is in the midst of blowing up "this city . . . this country . . . or world." Walker talks at Easley, the white liberal intellectual who is now married to Walker's white ex-wife. But it is not a debate. It is merely pages of invective in which Walker speaks Jones' doctrine of race violence. "This hideous place" is no longer encompassed into a dramatic space small enough for Jones to control. Here he does not reflect America through a few boys in a toilet or through a white-black couple on a subway; he tries to reflect America in huge, amorphous, prophetic rhetoric. He ignores his own artistic principle that art must reflect man within a "defined world." The chronicler takes over from the artist. The chronicler takes up the role of self-conscious Prophet and shouts hatred.

The Slave holds dramatic interest only in the fact that Jones, as in his other plays, makes the black man a victim, this time—and Jones fully knows this—a victim of his own philosophy. Walker delivers a prologue during which he is dressed as an old field slave; and at the end of the play, as the city explodes, he is again a slave—enslaved by mutual hatred, hatred received and returned. All has been made rotten, we are told again, as we were in *Dutchman*, by the hatred of the heritage of slavery. The Negro writer is, Jones has written, "a chronicler of the Negro's movement from African slave to American slave." The central doctrine of the prologue is "We are liars, and we are murderers."

The slave, who is Walker, who is the black man, who is Jones, is destroyed as well as destroying. The wife knows that the black man has been robbed (like Clay in *Dutchman*) of his image of himself: "I don't even think you know who you are any more. No, I don't think you ever knew. . . . It must be a sick task keeping so many lying separate uglineses together . . . and pretending they're something you've made and understand."

However certain this black man is of his hatred, he is also certain what it has cost him. Hatred has cost the black man everything else that he has desired from life, and it has cost him all his art. The black man has chosen to promote "a bloody situation where white and black people are killing each other . . . despite the fact that I would rather argue politics, or literature, or boxing, or anything, with you, dear Easley, with you." And the black artist has chosen bloody rebellion knowing "I have killed for all time any creative impulses I will ever have by the depravity of my murderous philosophies."

The leader of the black rebellion knows that another tyranny will result after the rebellion; he is not the Marxist visionary preparing for the happy day after the revolution. The harvest of slavery, with so much hatred, must be bitter; the revolution is only a case of "you had your chance, darling, now these other folks have theirs." He knows it's ugly; but in "this hideous place" there is no alternative to murder and violence. Jones no longer admits Clay's alternative, no longer sees a possible alternative in choosing to remain insane by denying violence. The black man instead seeks the sanity that comes from murder. "God, what an ugly idea," says the white liberal; head in hands, the black man replies, "I know. I know."

Throughout the text of *The Slave*, Jones has the characters talk about "ritual drama." But the play never ascends to the level of ritual drama, to any cleansing emotion. It rants. It establishes no bond between author and audience. It speaks with only one human dimension, racial hatred: its people are partial. The play doesn't even have verisimilitude: Why do the white man and his wife leave their children in the midst of a bombardment? Why does Walker sit around and talk while he should be leading his troops? Why does Walker tell his wife that their children are dead although we hear them scream at the end of the play? Ritual drama affects one as a transcendent filling up, it exists throughout or even outside of time; this play freezes.

I don't think that *The Slave*, or the bigger question of LeRoi Jones the dramatist, can be understood without examination of Jones' dramatic credo, called "The Revolutionary Theatre," published in *Liberator*, the journal of the Afro-American Research Institute. In 1965, the year after his four off-Broadway productions, Jones reasserts that "Clay in *Dutchman*, Ray in *The Toilet*, Walker in *The Slave* are all victims." And because the black man is victimized by society, the role of black theatre is clear: "The Revolutionary Theatre must Accuse and Attack anything that can be accused and attacked. It must Accuse and Attack because it is a theatre of Victims." And that is the difference between *The Slave* on one hand and *Dutchman* and *The Toilet* on the other. In *The Slave*, Jones is writing "Revolutionary Theatre." Tension is gone because he has made up his mind to Attack and Accuse. *Dutchman* and *The Toilet* are controlled by containing form; Jones is still probing and the result is the tension that allows art. But in the Attacking and Accusing of *The Slave*, tension is relaxed, form is gone; and propaganda, the Revolutionary Theatre, takes over.

Jones' *Liberator* essay is itself incoherent, frantic, filled with sentences in upper case, with quintuple question marks and double exclamation points. Much of it is inexplicable: "The Revolutionary Theatre must function like an incendiary pencil planted in Curtis Lemay's cap. So that when the final curtain goes down brains are splattered over the seats and the floor, and bleeding nuns must wire SOS's to Belgians with gold teeth." But its central doctrine of hatred is clear enough: "White men will cower before this theatre because it hates them. . . . The Revolutionary Theatre must hate them for hating. . . . The Revolutionary Theatre must teach them their deaths." And clear, too, is its call for destruction: "It is a political theatre, a weapon to help in the slaughter of those dim-witted fat-bellied white guys who somehow believe that the rest of the world is here for them to slobber on. . . . It must crack their faces open to the mad cries of the poor. . . . Americans will hate the Revolutionary Theatre because it will be out to destroy them and whatever they believe is real. . . . The play that will split the heavens for us will be called *the destruction of America*."

If we are to believe our courts, Jones' life has followed both his art and his theatrical credo. For all of the certitude in *The Slave* that armed rebellion would ruin the artist, the hero-victim of that play took to the streets with guns. And, the courts tell us, so did Jones take to the streets with guns in Newark during last summer's black rebellion. In *The Slave*, the black man has made up his mind to pay a similar price; in the streets of Newark, Jones apparently made up his mind to pay the price. *The Slave* is fearful in its foretelling: in it Jones announces—before Watts and Newark—what will happen and what he will do. Before the riots, *Newsweek* concluded that LeRoi Jones "writes and harangues himself out of the company of civilized men." And, the magazine went on to say, he therefore "forfeits all claim to serious attention." It is, rather, because Jones has decided to leave the company of civilized men that he demands our attention, if not for our interest in art, then for our interest in humanity.

How can the white liberal critic—interested in art and humanity— react to the drama of LeRoi Jones? Jones certainly does not expect acceptance: "My ideas revolve around the rotting and destruction of America, so I can't really expect anyone who is part of that to accept my ideas." Jones intimidates. He predicts that the white liberal critic will attack him on aesthetic grounds. And he's right. That's just what any critic who refuses to abdicate his critical judgment must do in the face of Revolutionary Theatre like *The Slave*.

Jones further intimidates the white liberal critic by insisting—as do black revolutionists both literary and nonliterary—that whitey can never understand the black man. Again I suppose that Jones is right. When Jones says, "You cannot understand me," I will not deny it. I am afraid to be patronizing by saying, "I understand." I don't expect to come to understand the foul indignities heaped for centuries on the black man, nor to understand their result—for my skin is white. So how do we react, all boxed in, cowering like a Calvinist sinner before a God who has already decided he is damned? Can the critic do nothing but stand here and plead, "What do you want of me? You, LeRoi Jones, carry your heritage of slavery; I carry my heritage of guilt. Do we just stand here and stare at each other until the murder starts?"

The suffering involved in standing mute while Jones proposes mutual murder seems to be peculiarly the kind of suffering which many white liberals enjoy. When Jones singles out the white liberal as the black man's particular enemy, little response is heard from the self-flagellating liberal who thinks such suffering is good for us. We white liberals might indeed *need* the expiation which Jones offers for our guilt. But if we accept the inevitability of his prophesies, we will be as destructive as Jones.

I think that the white liberal who refuses to give up his rationality must see that Jones' art and philosophy are suicidal as well as murderous. His philosophy is ultimately a betrayal of all of humanity, and particularly of the black man. In fury and despair, Jones says that the black man must accept the white man's way of suppression and murder. This is a betrayal not only because it proceeds on the incredible assumption of *The Slave* that the black man could *win* an armed rebellion. (The white ghetto will not stand still, enjoying its punishment, as do the white liberals.) But the Jones philosophy is also a betrayal because it denies the black man the moral superiority over the white man, the moral superiority of nonviolence. The conclusion of *The Slave* is that the answer for the black man is to find himself, and at the same time destroy himself, through killing the white man. But there is no finding there. There is only loss, and a madness. The victim should remain a victim.

So, in spite of the fact that Jones has the power to intimidate into paralysis, the only sane response is to break out, to challenge the rules as Jones has laid them down. I will attack his art on aesthetic grounds, for when form is shattered in art, no shared experience results. And although admitting that full understanding between white and black may be impossible, movement toward the understanding must be continued, for we all know that it has been started. We *can* all still remember the "We Shall Overcome" days.

I don't think that Jones, deep down, believes himself when he insists that no understanding is possible. For he writes. He lets white men produce his plays for white audiences. If he truly felt that we could never come to know each other, he might as well talk to a tape recorder. He wears African robes; he insists on calling himself an Afro-American: but he has come to us in his writing. We must assume that he has something to say to us.

We hear obviously enough the hatred for which he has willingly sacrificed his art. Our human reaction is that his vision is so hate-ridden that it is insane, and that we must reject it, must not stand mute before it and watch racial hatred become a self-fulfilling prophesy. But after I reject him, I am still left with fear. *That* cannot be escaped or rejected. And maybe fear finally is the one shared experience that Jones communicates. Perhaps, at this point, poised for the horror which is promised for the summer, the shared experience of fear is what he has to say to us. Perhaps *it* can shake us into the doing—which could bring effective change within the political order.

Is there time for such change? Jones says that political change is only the liberal's game, "palliatives and symbols to remind him of his own good faith." So the fear remains. Is there time? And the prospect of mutual madness.

FROM "THE BLACK ARTS MOVEMENT"*

Larry Neal

IN THE SPRING of 1964, LeRoi Jones, Charles Patterson, William Patterson, Clarence Reed, Johnny Moore, and a number of other Black artists opened the Black Arts Repertoire Theatre School. They produced a number of plays including Jones' *Experimental Death Unit # One, Black Mass, Jello,* and *Dutchman.* They also initiated a series of poetry readings and concerts. These activities represented the most advanced tendencies in the movement and were of excellent artistic quality. The Black Arts School came under immediate attack by the New York power structure. The Establishment, fearing Black creativity, did exactly what it was expected to do— it attacked the theatre and all of its values. In the meantime, the school was granted funds by OEO (Office of Economic Opportunity) through HARYOU-ACT. Lacking a cultural program itself, HARYOU turned to the only organization which addressed itself to the needs of the comunity. In keeping with its "revolutionary" cultural ideas, the Black Arts Theatre took its programs into the streets of Harlem. For three months, the theatre presented plays, concerts, and poetry readings to the people of the community. Plays that shattered the illusions of the American body politic, and awakened Black People to the meaning of their lives.

Then the hawks from the OEO moved in and chopped off the funds. Again, this should have been expected. The Black Arts Theatre stood in radical opposition to the feeble attitudes about culture of the "War On Poverty" bureaucrats. And later, because of internal problems, the theatre was forced to close. But the Black Arts group proved that the community could be served by a valid and dynamic art. It also proved that there was a definite need for a cultural revolution in the Black community.

With the closing of the Black Arts Theatre, the implications of what Brother Jones and his colleagues were trying to do took on even more significance. Black Art groups sprang up on the West Coast and the idea spread to Detroit, Philadelphia, Jersey City, New Orleans, and Washing-

* Reprinted from *The Drama Review,* XII, No. 4 (T40) (Summer 1968), 32–37, by permission of the author and the editors.

ton, D. C. Black Arts movements began on the campuses of San Francisco State College, Fisk University, Lincoln University, Hunter College in the Bronx, Columbia University, and Oberlin College. In Watts, after the rebellion, Maulana Karenga welded the Black Arts Movement into a cohesive cultural ideology which owed much to the work of LeRoi Jones. Karenga sees culture as the most important element in the struggle for self-determination:

Culture is the basis of all ideas, images and actions. To move is to move culturally, i.e., by a set of values given to you by your culture.

Without a culture Negroes are only a set of reactions to white people.

The seven criteria for culture are:
1. Mythology
2. History
3. Social Organization
4. Political Organization
5. Economic Organization
6. Creative Motif
7. Ethos

In drama, LeRoi Jones represents the most advanced aspects of the movement. He is its prime mover and chief designer. In a poetic essay entitled "The Revolutionary Theatre," he outlines the iconology of the movement:

The Revolutionary Theatre should force change: it should be change. (All their faces turned into the lights and you work on them black nigger magic, and cleanse them at having seen the ugliness. And if the beautiful see themselves, they will love themselves.) We are preaching virtue again, but by that to mean NOW, toward what seems the most constructive use of the word.

The theatre that Jones proposes is inextricably linked to the Afro-American political dynamic. And such a link is perfectly consistent with Black America's contemporary demands. For theatre is potentially the most social of all the arts. It is an integral part of the socializing process. It exists in direct relationship to the audience it claims to serve. The decadence and inanity of the contemporary American theatre is an accurate reflection of the state of American society. Albee's *Who's Afraid of Virginia Woolf?* is very American: sick white lives in a homosexual hell hole. The theatre of white America is escapist, refusing to confront concrete reality. Into this cultural emptiness come the musicals, an up-tempo version of the same stale lives. And the use of Negroes in such plays as *Hello Dolly* and *Hallelujah Baby* does not alert their nature; it compounds the problem. These plays are simply hipper versions of the minstrel show. They present Negroes acting out the hangups of middle-class white America. Consequently, the American theatre is a palliative prescribed to bourgeois patients who refuse to see the world as it is. Or, more crucially, as the world sees them. It is no accident, therefore, that the most "important" plays come from Europe —Brecht, Weiss, and Ghelderode. And even these have begun to run dry.

The Black Arts Theatre, the theatre of LeRoi Jones, is a radical alternative to the sterility of the American theatre. It is primarily a theatre of the Spirit, confronting the Black man in his interaction with his brothers and with the white thing.

Our theatre will show victims so that their brothers in the audience will be better able to understand that they are the brothers of victims, and that they themselves are blood brothers. And what we show must cause the blood to rush, so that prerevolutionary temperaments will be bathed in this blood, and it will cause their deepest souls to move, and they will find themselves tensed and clenched, even ready to die, at what the soul has been taught. We will scream and cry, murder, run through the streets in agony, if it means some soul will be moved, moved to actual life understanding of what the world is, and what it ought to be. We are preaching virtue and feeling, and a natural sense of the self in the world. All men live in the world, and the world ought to be a place for them to live.

The victims in the world of Jones' early plays are Clay, murdered by the white bitch-goddess in *Dutchman*, and Walker Vessels, the revolutionary in *The Slave*. Both of these plays present Black men in transition. Clay, the middle-class Negro trying to get himself a little action from Lula, digs himself and his own truth only to get murdered after telling her like it really is:

Just let me bleed you, you loud whore, and one poem vanished. A whole people neurotics, struggling to keep from being sane. And the only thing that would cure the neurosis would be your murder. Simple as that. I mean if I murdered you, then other white people would understand me. You understand? No. I guess not. If Bessie Smith had killed some white people she wouldn't needed that music. She could have talked very straight and plain about the world. Just straight two and two are four. Money. Power. Luxury. Like that. All of them. Crazy niggers turning their back on sanity. When all it needs is that simple act. Just murder. Would make us all sane.

But Lula understands, and she kills Clay first. In a perverse way it is Clay's nascent knowledge of himself that threatens the existence of Lula's idea of the world. Symbolically, and in fact, the relationship between Clay (Black America) and Lula (white America) is rooted in the historical castration of black manhood. And in the twisted psyche of white America, the Black man is both an object of love and hate. Analogous attitudes exist in most Black Americans, but for decidedly different reasons. Clay is doomed when he allows himself to participate in Lula's "fantasy" in the first place.

It is the fantasy to which Frantz Fanon alludes in *The Wretched Of The Earth* and *Black Skins, White Mask*: the native's belief that he can acquire the oppressor's power by acquiring his symbols, one of which is the white woman. When Clay finally digs himself it is too late.

Walker Vessels, in *The Slave*, is Clay reincarnated as the revolutionary confronting problems inherited from his contact with white culture. He returns to the home of his ex-wife, a white woman, and her husband, a literary critic. The play is essentially about Walker's attempt to destroy his white past. For it is the past, with all of its painful memories, that is really the enemy of the revolutionary. It is impossible to move until history is either recreated or comprehended. Unlike Todd, in Ralph Ellison's *Invisible Man*, Walker cannot fall outside history. Instead, Walker demands a confrontation with history, a final shattering of bullshit illusions. His only salvation lies in confronting the physical and psychological forces that have made him and his people powerless. Therefore, he comes to understand that the world must be restructured along spiritual imperatives. But in the interim it is basically a question of *who* has power:

EASLEY: You're so wrong about everything. So terribly, sickeningly wrong. What can you change? What do you hope to change? Do you think Negroes are better people than whites . . . that they can govern a society *better* than whites? That they'll be more judicious or more tolerant? Do you think they'll make fewer mistakes? I mean really, if the Western white man has proved one thing . . . it's the futility of modern society. So the have-not peoples become the haves. Even so, will that change the essential functions of the world? Will there be more love or beauty in the world . . . more knowledge . . . because of it?

WALKER: Probably. Probably there will be more . . . if more people have a chance to understand what it is. But that's not even the point. It comes down to baser human endeavor than any social-political thinking. What does it matter if there's more love or beauty? Who the fuck cares? Is that what the Western ofay thought while he was ruling . . . that his role somehow brought more love and beauty into the world? Oh, he might have thought that concomitantly, while sipping a gin rickey and scratching his ass . . . but that was not ever the point. Not even on the Crusades. The point is that you had your chance, darling, now these other folks have theirs. *Quietly.* Now they have theirs.

EASLEY: God, what an ugly idea.

This confrontation between the black radical and the white liberal is symbolic of larger confrontations occurring between the Third World and Western society. It is a confrontation between the colonizer and the colonized, the slavemaster and the slave. Implicit in Easley's remarks is the belief that the white man is culturally and politically superior to the Black

Man. Even though Western society has been traditionally violent in its relation with the Third World, it sanctimoniously deplores violence or self-assertion on the part of the enslaved. And the Western mind, with clever rationalizations, equates the violence of the oppressed with the violence of the oppressor. So that when the native preaches self-determination, the Western white man cleverly misconstrues it to mean hate of *all* white men. When the Black political radical warns his people not to trust white politicians of the left and the right, but instead to organize separately on the basis of power, the white man cries: "racism in reverse." Or he will say, as many of them do today: "We deplore both white and black racism." As if the two could be equated.

There is a minor element in *The Slave* which assumes great importance in a later play entitled *Jello*. Here I refer to the emblem of Walker's army: a red-mouthed grinning field slave. The revolutionary army has taken one of the most hated symbols of the Afro-American past and radically altered its meaning.[1] This is the supreme act of freedom, available only to those who have liberated themselves psychically. Jones amplifies this inversion of emblem and symbol in *Jello* by making Rochester (Ratfester) of the old Jack Benny (Penny) program into a revolutionary nationalist. Ratfester, ordinarily the supreme embodiment of the Uncle Tom Clown, surprises Jack Penny by turning on the other side of the nature of the Black man. He skillfully, and with an evasive black humor, robs Penny of all of his money. But Ratfester's actions are "moral." That is to say, Ratfester is getting his back pay; payment of a long overdue debt to the Black man. Ratfester's sensibilities are different from Walker's. He is *blues people* smiling and shuffling while trying to figure out how to destroy the white thing. And like the blues man, he is the master of the understatement. Or in the Afro-American folk tradition, he is the Signifying Monkey, Shine, and Stagolee all rolled into one. There are no stereotypes any more. History has killed Uncle Tom. Because even Uncle Tom has a breaking point beyond which he will not be pushed. Cut deeply enough into the most docile Negro, and you will find a conscious murderer. Behind the lyrics of the blues and the shuffling porter loom visions of white throats being cut and cities burning.

Jones' particular power as a playwright does not rest solely on his revolu-

[1] In Jones' study of Afro-American music, *Blues People*, we find the following observation: ". . . Even the adjective *funky*, which once meant to many Negroes merely a stink (usually associated with sex), was used to qualify the music as meaningful (the word became fashionable and is now almost useless). The social implication, then, was that even the old stereotype of a distinctive Negro smell that white America subscribed to could be turned against white America. For this smell now, real or not, was made a valuable characteristic of 'Negro-ness.' And 'Negro-ness,' by the fifties, for many Negroes (and whites) was the only strength left to American culture."

tionary vision, but is instead derived from his deep lyricism and spiritual outlook. In many ways, he is fundamentally more a poet than a playwright. And it is his lyricism that gives body to his plays. Two important plays in this regard are *Black Mass* and *Slave Ship*. *Black Mass* is based on the Muslim myth of Yacub. According to this myth Yacub, a Black scientist, developed the means of grafting different colors of the Original Black Nation until a White Devil was created. In *Black Mass*, Yacub's experiments produce a raving White Beast who is condemned to the coldest regions of the North. The other magicians implore Yacub to cease his experiments. But he insists on claiming the primacy of scientific knowledge over spiritual knowledge. The sensibility of the White Devil is alien, informed by lust and sensuality. The Beast is the consummate embodiment of evil, the beginning of the historical subjugation of the spiritual world.

Black Mass takes place in some prehistorical time. In fact, the concept of time, we learn, is the creation of an alien sensibility, that of the Beast. This is a deeply weighted play, a colloquy on the nature of man, and the relationship between legitimate spiritual knowledge and scientific knowledge. It is LeRoi Jones' most important play mainly because it is informed by a mythology that is wholly the creation of the Afro-American sensibility.

Further, Yacub's creation is not merely a scientific exercise. More fundamentally, it is the aesthetic impulse gone astray. The Beast is created merely for the sake of creation. Some artists assert a similar claim about the nature of art. They argue that art need not have a function. It is against this decadent attitude toward art—ramified throughout most of Western society—that the play militates. Yacub's real crime, therefore, is the introduction of a meaningless evil into a harmonious universe. The evil of the Beast is pervasive, corrupting everything and everyone it touches. What was beautiful is twisted into an ugly screaming thing. The play ends with destruction of the holy place of the Black Magicians. Now the Beast and his descendants roam the earth. An off-stage voice chants a call for the Jihad to begin. It is then that myth merges into legitimate history, and we, the audience, come to understand that all history is merely someone's version of mythology.

Slave Ship presents a more immediate confrontation with history. In a series of expressionistic tableaux it depicts the horrors and the madness of the Middle Passage. It then moves through the period of slavery, early attempts at revolt, tendencies toward Uncle Tom-like reconciliation and betrayal, and the final act of liberation. There is no definite plot (LeRoi calls it a pageant), just a continuous rush of sound, groans, screams, and souls wailing for freedom and relief from suffering. This work has special affinities with the New Music of Sun Ra, John Coltrane, Albert Ayler, and Ornette Coleman. Events are blurred, rising and falling in a stream of sound. Almost cinematically, the images flicker and fade against a heavy back-drop of rhythm. The language is spare, stripped to the essential. It is a play which almost totally eliminates the need for a text. It functions on the basis of movement and energy—the dramatic equivalent of the New Music.

Slave Ship's essential energy is, at base, ritualistic. As a matter of fact to see the play in any other way is to miss the point. All of the New York reviewers, with the possible exception of John Lahr, were completely cut off from the central aspect of the play when it was performed at the Brooklyn Academy under the brilliant direction of Gilbert Moses. One of the prime motivations behind the work is to suck the audience into a unique and very precise universe. The episodes of this "pageant" do not appear as strict interpretations of history. Rather, what we are digging is ritualized history. That is, history that allows emotional and religious participation on the part of the audience. And, like all good ritual, its purpose is to make the audience stronger, more sensitive to the historical realities that have shaped our lives, and the lives of our ancestors. The play acts to extend memory. For Black people to forget the realities posed by *Slave Ship* is to fall prey to an existential paralysis. History, like the blues, demands that we witness the painful events of our prior lives and that we either confront these painful events or be destroyed by them.

The Writer and Social Responsibility

THE NEGRO ARTIST AND THE RACIAL MOUNTAIN*

Langston Hughes

ONE OF THE MOST PROMISING of the young Negro poets said to me once, "I want to be a poet—not a Negro poet," meaning, I believe, "I want to write like a white poet"; meaning subconsciously, "I would like to be a white poet"; meaning behind that, "I would like to be white." And I was sorry the young man said that, for no great poet has ever been afraid of being himself. And I doubted then that, with his desire to run away spiritually from his race, this boy would ever be a great poet. But this is the mountain standing in the way of any true Negro art in America—this urge within the race toward whiteness, the desire to pour racial individuality into the mold of American standardization, and to be as little Negro and as much American as possible.

But let us look at the immediate background of this young poet. His family is of what I suppose one would call the Negro middle class: people who are by no means rich yet never uncomfortable nor hungry—smug, contented, respectable folk, members of the Baptist church. The father goes to work every morning. He is a chief steward at a large white club. The mother sometimes does fancy sewing or supervises parties for the rich families of the town. The children go to a mixed school. In the home they read white papers and magazines. And the mother often says "Don't be like niggers" when the children are bad. A frequent phrase from the father is, "Look how well a white man does things." And so the word *white* comes to be unconsciously a symbol of all the virtues. It holds for the children beauty, morality, and money. The whisper of "I want to be white" runs silently through their minds. This young poet's home is, I believe, a fairly typical home of the colored middle class. One sees immediately how difficult it would be for an artist born in such a home to interest himself in interpreting the beauty of his own people. He is never taught to see that beauty. He is taught rather not to see it, or if he does, to be ashamed of it when it is not according to Caucasian patterns.

* Reprinted from the *Nation*, CXXII (1926), 692–94.

For racial culture the home of a self-styled "high-class" Negro has nothing better to offer. Instead there will perhaps be more aping of things white than in a less cultured or less wealthy home. The father is perhaps a doctor, lawyer, landowner, or politician. The mother may be a social worker, or a teacher, or she may do nothing and have a maid. Father is often dark but he has usually married the lightest woman he could find. The family attend a fashionable church where few really colored faces are to be found. And they themselves draw a color line. In the North they go to white theaters and white movies. And in the South they have at least two cars and a house "like white folks." Nordic manners, Nordic faces, Nordic hair, Nordic art (if any), and an Episcopal heaven. A very high mountain indeed for the would-be racial artist to climb in order to discover himself and his people.

But then there are the low-down folks, the so-called common element, and they are the majority—may the Lord be praised! The people who have their nip of gin on Saturday nights and are not too important to themselves or the community, or too well fed, or too learned to watch the lazy world go round. They live on Seventh Street in Washington or State Street in Chicago and they do not particularly care whether they are like white folks or anybody else. Their joy runs, bang! into ecstasy. Their religion soars to a shout. Work maybe a little today, rest a little tomorrow. Play awhile. Sing awhile. O, let's dance! These common people are not afraid of spirituals, as for a long time their more intellectual brethren were, and jazz is their child. They furnish a wealth of colorful, distinctive material for any artist because they still hold their own individuality in the face of American standardizations. And perhaps these common people will give to the world its truly great Negro artist, the one who is not afraid to be himself. Whereas the better-class Negro would tell the artist what to do, the people at least let him alone when he does appear. And they are not ashamed of him—if they know he exists at all. And they accept what beauty is their own without question.

Certainly there is, for the American Negro artist who can escape the restrictions the more advanced among his own group would put upon him, a great field of unused material ready for his art. Without going outside his race, and even among the better classes with their "white" culture and conscious American manners, but still Negro enough to be different, there is sufficient matter to furnish a black artist with a lifetime of creative work. And when he chooses to touch on the relations between Negroes and whites in this country with their innumerable overtones and undertones, surely, and especially for literature and the drama, there is an inexhaustible supply of themes at hand. To these the Negro artist can give his racial individuality, his heritage of rhythm and warmth, and his incongruous humor that so often, as in the Blues, becomes ironic laughter mixed with tears. But let us look again at the mountain.

A prominent Negro clubwoman in Philadelphia paid eleven dollars to hear Raquel Meller sing Andalusian popular songs. But she told me a few weeks before she would not think of going to hear "that woman," Clara Smith, a great black artist, sing Negro folksongs. And many an upper-class Negro church, even now, would not dream of employing a spiritual in its services. The drab melodies in white folks' hymnbooks are much to be preferred. "We want to worship the Lord correctly and quietly. We don't believe in 'shouting.' Let's be dull like the Nordics," they say, in effect.

The road for the serious black artist, then, who would produce a racial art is most certainly rocky and the mountain is high. Until recently he received almost no encouragement for his work from either white or colored people. The fine novels of Chesnutt go out of print with neither race noticing their passing. The quaint charm and humor of Dunbar's dialect verse brought to him, in his day, largely the same kind of encouragement one would give a sideshow freak (A colored man writing poetry! How odd!) or a clown (How amusing!).

The present vogue in things Negro, although it may do as much harm as good for the budding colored artist, has at least done this: it has brought him forcibly to the attention of his own people among whom for so long, unless the other race had noticed him beforehand, he was a prophet with little honor. I understand that Charles Gilpin acted for years in Negro theaters without any special acclaim from his own, but when Broadway gave him eight curtain calls, Negroes, too, began to beat a tin pan in his honor. I know a young colored writer, a manual worker by day, who had been writing well for the colored magazines for some years, but it was not until he recently broke into the white publications and his first book was accepted by a prominent New York publisher that the "best" Negroes in his city took the trouble to discover that he lived there. Then almost immediately they decided to give a grand dinner for him. But the society ladies were careful to whisper to his mother that perhaps she'd better not come. They were not sure she would have an evening gown.

The Negro artist works against an undertow of sharp criticism and misunderstanding from his own group and unintentional bribes from the whites. "O, be respectable, write about nice people, show how good we are," say the Negroes. "Be stereotyped, don't go too far, don't shatter our illusions about you, don't amuse us too seriously. We will pay you," say the whites. Both would have told Jean Toomer not to write *Cane*. The colored people did not praise it. The white people did not buy it. Most of the colored people who did read *Cane* hate it. They are afraid of it. Although the critics gave it good reviews the public remained indifferent. Yet (excepting the work of DuBois) *Cane* contains the finest prose written by a Negro in America. And like the singing of Robeson, it is truly racial.

But in spite of the Nordicized Negro intelligentsia and the desires of some white editors we have an honest American Negro literature already with us. Now I await the rise of the Negro theater. Our folk music, having achieved worldwide fame, offers itself to the genius of the great individual American Negro composer who is to come. And within the next decade I expect to see the work of a growing school of colored artists who paint and model the beauty of dark faces and create with new technique the expressions of their own soul-world. And the Negro dancers who will dance like flame and the singers who will continue to carry our songs to all who listen—they will be with us in even greater numbers tomorrow.

Most of my own poems are racial in theme and treatment, derived from the life I know. In many of them I try to grasp and hold some of the meanings and rhythms of jazz. I am sincere as I know how to be in these poems and yet after every reading I answer questions like these from my own people: Do you think Negroes should always write about Negroes? I wish you wouldn't read some of your poems to white folks. How do you find anything interesting in a place like a cabaret? Why do you write about black people? You aren't black. What makes you do so many jazz poems?

But jazz to me is one of the inherent expressions of Negro life in America: the eternal tom-tom beating in the Negro soul—the tom-tom of revolt against weariness in a white world, a world of subway trains, and work, work, work; the tom-tom of joy and laughter, and pain swallowed in a smile. Yet the Philadelphia clubwoman is ashamed to say that her race created it and she does not like me to write about it. The old subconscious "white is best" runs through her mind. Years of study under white teachers, a lifetime of white books, pictures, and papers, and white manners, morals, and Puritan standards made her dislike the spirituals. And now she turns up her nose at jazz and all its manifestations—likewise almost everything else distinctly racial. She doesn't care for the Winold Reiss portraits of Negroes because they are "too Negro." She does not want a true picture of herself from anybody. She wants the artist to flatter her, to make the white world believe that all Negroes are as smug and as near white in soul as she wants to be. But, to my mind, it is the duty of the younger Negro artist, if he accepts any duties at all from outsiders, to change through the force of his art that old whispering "I want to be white," hidden in the aspirations of his people, to "Why should I want to be white? I am a Negro—and beautiful!"

So I am ashamed for the black poet who says, "I want to be a poet, not a Negro poet," as though his own racial world were not as interesting as any other world. I am ashamed, too, for the colored artist who runs from the painting of Negro faces to the painting of sunsets after the manner of the academicians because he fears the strange unwhiteness of his own features. An artist must be free to choose what he does, certainly, but he must also never be afraid to do what he might choose.

Let the blare of Negro jazz bands and the bellowing voice of Bessie Smith singing Blues penetrate the closed ears of the colored near-intellectuals until they listen and perhaps understand. Let Paul Robeson singing Water Boy, and Rudolph Fisher writing about the streets of Harlem, and Jean Toomer holding the heart of Georgia in his hands, and Aaron Douglas drawing strange black fantasies cause the smug Negro middle class to turn from their white, respectable, ordinary books and papers to catch a glimmer of their own beauty. We younger Negro artists who create now intend to express our individual dark-skinned selves without fear or shame. If white people are pleased we are glad. If they are not, it doesn't matter. We know we are beautiful. And ugly too. The tom-tom cries and the tom-tom laughs. If colored people are pleased we are glad. If they are not, their displeasure doesn't matter either. We build our temples for tomorrow, strong as we know how, and we stand on top of the mountain, free within ourselves.

MANY THOUSANDS GONE*

James Baldwin

IT IS ONLY in his music, which Americans are able to admire because a protective sentimentality limits their understanding of it, that the Negro in America has been able to tell his story. It is a story which otherwise has yet to be told and which no American is prepared to hear. As is the inevitable result of things unsaid, we find ourselves until today oppressed with a dangerous and reverberating silence; and the story is told, compulsively, in symbols and signs, in hieroglyphics; it is revealed in Negro speech and in that of the white majority and in their different frames of reference. The ways in which the Negro has affected the American psychology are betrayed in our popular culture and in our morality; in our estrangement from him is the depth of our estrangement from ourselves. We cannot ask: what do we *really* feel about him—such a question merely opens the gates on chaos. What we really feel about him is involved with all that we feel about everything, about everyone, about ourselves.

The story of the Negro in America is the story of America—or, more precisely, it is the story of Americans. It is not a very pretty story: the story of a people is never very pretty. The Negro in America, gloomily referred to as that shadow which lies athwart our national life, is far more than that. He is a series of shadows, self-created, intertwining, which now we helplessly battle. One may say that the Negro in America does not really exist except in the darkness of our minds.

This is why his history and his progress, his relationship to all other Americans, has been kept in the social arena. He is a social and not a personal or a human problem; to think of him is to think of statistics, slums, rapes, injustices, remote violence; it is to be confronted with an endless cataloguing of losses, gains, skirmishes; it is to feel virtuous, outraged, helpless, as though his continuing status among us were somehow analogous to disease—cancer, perhaps, or tuberculosis—which must be checked, even though it cannot be cured. In this arena the black man acquires quite another aspect from that which he has in life. We do not know what to do with him in life; if he breaks our sociological and senti-

* Reprinted from *Notes of a Native Son* (Boston: Beacon Press, 1955), by permission of the author and publishers.

mental image of him we are panic-stricken and we feel ourselves betrayed. When he violates this image, therefore, he stands in the greatest danger (sensing which, we uneasily suspect that he is very often playing a part for our benefit); and, what is not always so apparent but is equally true, we are then in some danger ourselves—hence our retreat or our blind and immediate retaliation.

Our dehumanization of the Negro then is indivisible from our dehumanization of ourselves: the loss of our own identity is the price we pay for our annulment of his. Time and our own force act as our allies, creating an impossible, a fruitless tension between the traditional master and slave. Impossible and fruitless because, literal and visible as this tension has become, it has nothing to do with reality.

Time has made some changes in the Negro face. Nothing has succeeded in making it exactly like our own, though the general desire seems to be to make it blank if one cannot make it white. When it has become blank, the past as thoroughly washed from the black face as it has been from ours, our guilt will be finished—at least it will have ceased to be visible, which we imagine to be much the same thing. But, paradoxically, it is we who prevent this from happening; since it is we, who, every hour that we live, reinvest the black face with our guilt; and we do this—by a further paradox, no less ferocious—helplessly, passionately, out of an unrealized need to suffer absolution.

Today, to be sure, we know that the Negro is not biologically or mentally inferior; there is no truth in those rumors of his body odor or his incorrigible sexuality; or no more truth than can be easily explained or even defended by the social sciences. Yet, in our most recent war, his blood was segregated as was, for the most part, his person. Up to today we are set at a division, so that he may not marry our daughters or our sisters, nor may he—for the most part—eat at our tables or live in our houses. Moreover, those who do, do so at the grave expense of a double alienation: from their own people, whose fabled attributes they must either deny or, worse, cheapen and bring to market; from us, for we require of them, when we accept them, that they at once cease to be Negroes and yet not fail to remember what being a Negro means—to remember, that is, what it means to us. The threshold of insult is higher or lower, according to the people involved, from the bootblack in Atlanta to the celebrity in New York. One must travel very far, among saints with nothing to gain or outcasts with nothing to lose, to find a place where it does not matter—and perhaps a word or a gesture or simply a silence will testify that it matters even there.

For it means something to be a Negro, after all, as it means something to have been born in Ireland or in China, to live where one sees space and sky or to live where one sees nothing but rubble or nothing but high buildings. We cannot escape our origins, however hard we try, those origins which contain the key—could we but find it—to all that we later become. What it means to be a Negro is a good deal more than this essay can discover; what it means to be a Negro in America can perhaps be suggested by an examination of the myths we perpetuate about him.

Aunt Jemima and Uncle Tom are dead, their places taken by a group of amazingly well-adjusted young men and women, almost as dark, but ferociously literate, well-dressed and scrubbed, who are never laughed at, who are not likely ever to set foot in a cotton or tobacco field or in any but the most modern of kitchens. There are others who remain, in our odd idiom, "underprivileged"; some are bitter and these come to grief; some are unhappy, but, continually presented with the evidence of a better day soon to come, are speedily becoming less so. Most of them care nothing whatever about race. They want only their proper place in the sun and the right to be left alone, like any other citizen of the republic. We may all breathe more easily. Before, however, our joy at the demise of Aunt Jemima and Uncle Tom approaches the indecent, we had better ask whence they sprang, how they lived? Into what limbo have they vanished?

However inaccurate our portraits of them were, these portraits do suggest, not only the conditions, but the quality of their lives and the impact of this spectacle on our consciences. There was no one more forbearing than Aunt Jemima, no one stronger or more pious or more loyal or more wise; there was, at the same time, no one weaker or more faithless or more vicious and certainly no one more immoral. Uncle Tom, trustworthy and sexless, needed only to drop the title "Uncle" to become violent, crafty, and sullen, a menace to any white woman who passed by. They prepared our feast tables and our burial clothes; and, if we could boast that we understood them, it was far more to the point and far more true that they understood us. They were, moreover, the only people in the world who did; and not only did they know us better than we knew ourselves, but they knew us better than we knew them. This was the piquant flavoring to the national joke, it lay behind our uneasiness as it lay behind our benevolence: Aunt Jemima and Uncle Tom, our creations, at the last evaded us; they had a life—their own, perhaps a better life than ours—and they would never tell us what it was. At the point where we were driven most privately and painfully to conjecture what depths of contempt, what heights of indifference, what prodigies of resilience, what untamable superiority allowed them so vividly to endure, neither perishing nor rising up in a body to wipe us from the earth, the image perpetually shattered and the word failed. The black man in our midst carried murder in his heart, he wanted vengeance. We carried murder too, we wanted peace.

In our image of the Negro breathes the past we deny, not dead but living yet and powerful, the beast in our jungle of statistics. It is this which defeats us, which continues to defeat us, which lends to interracial cocktail parties their rattling, genteel, nervously smiling air: in any drawing room at such a gathering the beast may spring, filling the air with flying things and an unenlightened wailing. Wherever the problem touches there is confusion, there is danger. Wherever the Negro face appears a tension is created, the tension of a silence filled with things unutterable. It is a sentimental error, therefore, to believe that the past is dead; it means nothing to say that it is all forgotten, that the Negro himself has forgotten it. It is not a question of memory. Oedipus did not remember the thongs that bound his feet; nevertheless the marks they left testified to that doom toward which his feet were leading him. The man does not remember the hand that struck him, the darkness that frightened him, as a child; nevertheless, the hand and the darkness remain with him, indivisible from himself forever, part of the passion that drives him wherever he thinks to take flight.

The making of an American begins at that point where he himself rejects all other ties, any other history, and himself adopts the vesture of his adopted land. This problem has been faced by all Americans throughout our history—in a way it *is* our history—and it baffles the immigrant and sets on edge the second generation until today. In the case of the Negro the past was taken from him whether he would or no; yet to forswear it was meaningless and availed him nothing, since his shameful history was carried, quite literally, on his brow. Shameful; for he was heathen as well as black and would never have discovered the healing blood of Christ had not we braved the jungles to bring him these glad tidings. Shameful; for, since our role as missionary had not been wholly disinterested, it was necessary to recall the shame from which we had delivered him in order more easily to escape our own. As he accepted the alabaster Christ and the bloody cross—in the bearing of which he would find his redemption, as, indeed, to our outraged astonishment, he sometimes did—he must, henceforth, accept that image we then gave him of himself: having no other and standing, moreover, in danger of death should he fail to accept the dazzling light thus brought into such darkness. It is this quite simple dilemma that must be borne in mind if we wish to comprehend his psychology.

However we shift the light which beats so fiercely on his head, **or** *prove*, by victorious social analysis, how his lot has changed, how we have both improved, our uneasiness refuses to be exorcized. And nowhere is this more apparent than in our literature on the subject—"problem" literature when written by whites, "protest" literature when written by Negroes—and nothing is more striking than the tremendous disparity of tone between the two creations. *Kingsblood Royal* bears, for example, almost no kinship to *If He Hollers Let Him Go*, though the same reviewers praised them both for what were, at bottom, very much the same reasons. These reasons may be suggested, far too briefly but not at all unjustly, by observing that the presupposition is in both novels exactly the same: black is a terrible color with which to be born into the world.

Now the most powerful and celebrated statement we have yet had of what it means to be a Negro in America is unquestionably Richard Wright's *Native Son*. The feeling which prevailed at the time of its publication was that such a novel, bitter, uncompromising, shocking, gave proof, by its very existence, of what strides might be taken in a free democracy; and its indisputable success, proof that Americans were now able to look full in the face without flinching the dreadful facts. Americans, unhappily, have the most remarkable ability to alchemize all bitter truths into an innocuous but piquant confection and to transform their moral contradictions, or public discussion of such contradictions, into a proud decoration, such as are given for heroism on the field of battle. Such a book, we felt with pride, could never have been written before— which was true. Nor could it be written today. It bears already the aspect of a landmark; for Bigger and his brothers have undergone yet another metamorphosis; they have been accepted in baseball leagues and by colleges hitherto exclusive; and they have made a most favorable appearance on the national screen. We have yet to encounter, nevertheless, a report so indisputably authentic, or one that can begin to challenge this most significant novel.

It is, in a certain American tradition, the story of an unremarkable youth in battle with the force of circumstance; that force of circumstance which plays and which has played so important a part in the national fables of success or failure. In this case the force of circumstance is not poverty merely but color, a circumstance which cannot be overcome, against which the protagonist battles for his life and loses. It is, on the surface, remarkable that this book should have enjoyed among Americans the favor it did enjoy; no more remarkable, however, than that it should have been compared, exuberantly, to Dostoevski, though placed a shade below Dos Passos, Dreiser, and Steinbeck; and when the book is examined, its impact does not seem remarkable at all, but becomes, on the contrary, perfectly logical and inevitable.

We cannot, to begin with, divorce this book from the specific social climate of that time: it was one of the last of those angry productions, encountered in the late twenties and all through the thirties, dealing with the inequities of the social structure of America. It was published one year before our entry into the last world war—which is to say, very few years after the dissolution of the WPA and the end of the New Deal and at a time when bread lines and soup kitchens and bloody industrial battles were bright in everyone's memory. The rigors of that unexpected time filled us not only with a genuinely bewildered and despairing idealism—so that, because there at least was *something* to fight for, young men went off to die in Spain—but also with a genuinely bewildered self-consciousness. The Negro, who had been during the magnificent twenties a passionate and delightful primitive, now became, as one of the things we were most self-conscious about, our most oppressed minority. In the thirties, swallowing Marx whole, we discovered the Worker and realized—I should think with some relief—that the aims of the Worker and the aims of the Negro were one. This theorem—to which we shall return—seems now to leave rather too much out of account; it became, nevertheless, one of the slogans of the "class struggle" and the gospel of the New Negro.

As for this New Negro, it was Wright who became his most eloquent spokesman; and his work, from its beginning, is most clearly committed to the social struggle. Leaving aside the considerable question of what relationship precisely the artist bears to the revolutionary, the reality of man as a social being is not his only reality and that artist is strangled who is forced to deal with human beings solely in social terms; and who has, moreover, as Wright had, the necessity thrust on him of being the representative of some thirteen million people. It is a false responsibility (since writers are not congressmen) and impossible, by its nature, of fulfillment. The unlucky shepherd soon finds that, so far from being able to feed the hungry sheep, he has lost the wherewithal for his own nourishment: having not been allowed—so fearful was his burden, so present his audience!—to recreate his own experience. Further, the militant men and women of the thirties were not, upon examination, significantly emancipated from their antecedents, however bitterly they might consider themselves estranged or however gallantly they struggled to build a better world. However they might extol Russia, their concept of a better world was quite helplessly American and betrayed a certain thinness of imagination, a suspect reliance on suspect and badly digested formulae, and a positively fretful romantic haste. Finally, the relationship of the Negro to the Worker cannot be summed up, nor even greatly illuminated, by saying that their aims are one. It is true only insofar as they both desire better working conditions and useful only insofar as they unite their strength as workers to achieve these ends. Further than this we cannot in honesty go.

In this climate Wright's voice first was heard and the struggle which promised for a time to shape his work and give it purpose also fixed it in an ever more unrewarding rage. Recording his days of anger he has also nevertheless recorded, as no Negro before him had ever done, that fantasy Americans hold in their minds when they speak of the Negro: that fantastic and fearful image which we have lived with since the first slave fell beneath the lash. This is the significance of *Native Son* and also, unhappily, its overwhelming limitation.

Native Son begins with the *Brring!* of an alarm clock in the squalid Chicago tenement where Bigger and his family live. Rats live there too, feeding off the garbage, and we first encounter Bigger in the act of killing one. One may consider that the entire book, from that harsh *Brring!* to Bigger's weak "Good-by" as the lawyer, Max, leaves him in the death cell, is an extension, with the roles inverted, of this chilling metaphor. Bigger's situation and Bigger himself exert on the mind the same sort of fascination. The premise of the book is, as I take it, clearly conveyed in these first pages: we are confronting a monster created by the American republic and we are, through being made to share his experience, to receive illumination as regards the manner of his life and to feel both pity and horror at his awful and inevitable doom. This is an arresting and potentially rich idea and we would be discussing a very different novel if Wright's execution had been more perceptive and if he had not attempted to redeem a symbolical monster in social terms.

One may object that it was precisely Wright's intention to create in Bigger a social symbol, revelatory of social disease and prophetic of disaster. I think, however, that it is this assumption which we ought to examine more carefully. Bigger has no discernible relationship to himself, to his own life, to his own people, nor to any other people—in this respect, perhaps, he is most American—and his force comes, not from his significance as a social (or antisocial) unit, but from his significance as the incarnation of a myth. It is remarkable that, though we follow him step by step from the tenement room to the death cell, we know as little about him when this journey is ended as we did when it began; and, what is even more remarkable, we know almost as little about the social dynamic which we are to believe created him. Despite the details of slum life which we are given, I doubt that anyone who has thought about it, disengaging himself from sentimentality, can accept this most essential premise of the novel for a moment. Those Negroes who surround him, on the other hand, his hard-working mother, his ambitious sister, his poolroom cronies, Bessie, might be considered as far richer and far more subtle and accurate illustrations of the ways in which Negroes are controlled in our society and the complex techniques they have evolved for their survival. We are limited, however, to Bigger's view of them, part of a deliberate plan which might not have been disastrous if we were not also limited to Bigger's perceptions. What this means for the novel is that a necessary dimension has been cut away; this dimension being the relationship that Negroes bear to one another, that depth of involvement and unspoken recognition of shared experience which creates a way of life. What the novel reflects— and at no point interprets—is the isolation of the Negro within his own group and the resulting fury of impatient scorn. It is this which creates its climate of anarchy and unmotivated and unapprehended disaster; and it is this climate, common to most Negro protest novels, which has led us all to believe that in Negro life there exists no tradition, no field of manners, no possibility of ritual or intercourse, such as may, for example, sustain the Jew even after he has left his father's house. But the fact is not that the Negro has no tradition but that there has as yet arrived no sensibility sufficiently profound and tough to make this tradition articulate. For a tradition expresses, after all, nothing more than the long and painful experience of a people; it comes out of the battle waged to maintain their integrity or, to put it more simply, out of their struggle to survive. When we speak of the Jewish tradition we are speaking of centuries of exile and persecution, of the strength which endured and the sensibility which discovered in it the high possibility of the moral victory.

This sense of how Negroes live and how they have so long endured is hidden from us in part by the very speed of the Negro's public progress, a progress so heavy with complexity, so bewildering and kaleidoscopic, that he dare not pause to conjecture on the darkness which lies behind him; and by the nature of the American psychology which, in order to apprehend or be made able to accept it, must undergo a metamorphosis so profound as to be literally unthinkable and which there is no doubt we will resist until we are compelled to achieve our own identity by the rigors of a time that has yet to come. Bigger, in the meanwhile, and all his furious kin, serve only to whet the notorious national taste for the sensational and to reinforce all that we now find it necessary to believe. It is not Bigger whom we fear, since his appearance among us makes our victory certain. It is the others, who smile, who go to church, who give no cause for complaint, whom we sometimes consider with amusement, with pity, even with affection—and in whose faces we sometimes surprise the merest arrogant hint of hatred, the faintest, withdrawn, speculative shadow of contempt—who make us uneasy; whom we cajole, threaten, flatter, fear; who to us remain unknown, though we are not (we feel with both relief and hostility and with bottomless confusion) unknown to them. It is out of our reaction to these hewers of wood and drawers of water that our image of Bigger was created.

It is this image, living yet, which we perpetually seek to evade with good works; and this image which makes of all our good works an intolerable mockery. The "nigger," black, benighted, brutal, consumed with hatred as we are consumed with guilt, cannot be thus blotted out. He stands at our shoulders when we give our maid her wages, it is his hand which we fear we are taking when struggling to communicate with the current "intelligent" Negro, his stench, as it were, which fills our mouths with salt as the monument is unveiled in honor of the latest Negro leader. Each generation has shouted behind him, *Nigger!* as he walked our streets; it is he whom we would rather our sisters did not marry; he is banished into the vast and wailing outer darkness whenever we speak of the "purity" of our women, of the "sanctity" of our homes, of "American" ideals. What is more, he knows it. He is indeed the "native son": he is the "nigger." Let us refrain from inquiring at the moment whether or not he actually exists; for we *believe* that he exists. Whenever we encounter him amongst us in the flesh, our faith is made perfect and his necessary and bloody end is executed with a mystical ferocity of joy.

But there is a complementary faith among the damned which involves their gathering of the stones with which those who walk in the light shall stone them; or there exists among the intolerably degraded the perverse and powerful desire to force into the arena of the actual those fantastic crimes of which they have been accused, achieving their vengeance and their own destruction through making the nightmare real. The American image of the Negro lives also in the Negro's heart; and when he has surrendered to this image life has no other possible reality. Then he, like the white enemy with whom he will be locked one day in mortal struggle, has no means save this of asserting his identity. This is why Bigger's murder of Mary can be referred to as an "act of creation" and why, once this murder has been committed, he can feel for the first time that he is living fully and deeply as a man was meant to live. And there is, I should think, no Negro living in America who has not felt, briefly or for long periods, with anguish sharp or dull, in varying degrees and to varying effect, simple, naked and unanswerable hatred; who has not wanted to smash any white face he may encounter in a day, to violate, out of motives of the cruelest vengeance, their women, to break the bodies of all white people and bring them low, as low as that dust into which he himself has been and is being trampled; no Negro, finally, who has not had to make his own precarious adjustment to the "nigger" who surrounds him and to the "nigger" in himself.

Yet the adjustment must be made—rather, it must be attempted, the tension perpetually sustained—for without this he has surrendered his birthright as a man no less than his birthright as a black man. The entire universe is then peopled only with his enemies, who are not only white men armed with rope and rifle, but his own far-flung and contemptible kinsmen. Their blackness is his degradation and it is their stupid and passive endurance which makes his end inevitable.

Bigger dreams of some black man who will weld all blacks together into a mighty fist, and feels, in relation to his family, that perhaps they had to live as they did precisely because none of them had ever done anything, right or wrong, which mattered very much. It is only he who, by an act of murder, has burst the dungeon cell. He has made it manifest that *he* lives and that his despised blood nourishes the passions of a man. He has forced his oppressors to see the fruit of that oppression: and he feels, when his family and his friends come to visit him in the death cell, that they should not be weeping or frightened, that they should be happy, *proud* that he has dared, through murder and now through his own imminent destruction, to redeem their anger and humiliation, that he has hurled into the spiritless obscurity of their lives the lamp of his passionate life and death. Henceforth, they may remember Bigger—who has died, as we may conclude, for them. But they do not feel this; they only know that he has murdered two women and precipitated a reign of terror; and that now he is to die in the electric chair. They therefore weep and are honestly frightened—for which Bigger despises them and wishes to "blot" them out. What is missing in his situation and in the representation of his psychology—which makes his situation false and his psychology incapable of development—is any revelatory apprehension of Bigger as one of the Negro's realities or as one of the Negro's roles. This failure is part of the previously noted failure to convey any sense of Negro life as a continuing and complex group reality. Bigger, who cannot function therefore as a reflection of the social illness, having, as it were, no society to reflect, likewise refuses to function on the loftier level of the Christ-symbol. His kinsmen are quite right to weep and be frightened, even to be appalled: for it is not his love for them or for himself which causes him to die, but his hatred and his self-hatred; he does not redeem the pains of a despised people, but reveals, on the contrary, nothing more than his own fierce bitterness at having been born one of them. In this also he is the "native son," his progress determinable by the speed with which the distance increases between himself and the auction-block and all that the auction-block implies. To have penetrated this phenomenon, this inward contention of love and hatred, blackness and whiteness, would have given him a stature more nearly human and an end more nearly tragic; and would have given us a document more profoundly and genuinely bitter and less harsh with an anger which is, on the one hand, exhibited and, on the other hand, denied.

Native Son finds itself at length so trapped by the American image of Negro life and by the American necessity to find the ray of hope that it cannot pursue its own implications. This is why Bigger must be at the last redeemed, to be received, if only by rhetoric, into that community of phantoms which is our tenaciously held ideal of the happy social life. It is the socially conscious whites who receive him—the Negroes being capable of no such objectivity—and we have, by way of illustration, that lamentable scene in which Jan, Mary's lover, forgives him for her murder; and, carrying the explicit burden of the novel, Max's long speech to the jury. This speech, which really ends the book, is one of the most desperate performances in American fiction. It is the question of Bigger's humanity which is at stake, the relationship in which he stands to all other Americans—and, by implication, to all people—and it is precisely this question which it cannot clarify, with which it cannot, in fact, come to any coherent terms. He is the monster created by the American republic, the present awful sum of generations of oppression; but to say that he is a monster is to fall into the trap of making him subhuman and he must, therefore, be made representative of a way of life which is real and human in precise ratio to the degree to which it seems to us monstrous and strange. It seems to me that this idea carries, implicitly, a most remarkable confession: that is, that Negro life is in fact as debased and impoverished as our theology claims; and, further, that the use to which Wright puts this idea can only proceed from the assumption—not entirely unsound—that Americans, who evade, so far as possible, all genuine experience, have therefore no way of assessing the experience of others and no way of establishing themselves in relation to any way of life which is not their own. The privacy or obscurity of Negro life makes that life capable, in our imaginations, of producing anything at all; and thus the idea of Bigger's monstrosity can be presented without fear of contradiction, since no American has the knowledge or authority to contest it and no Negro has the voice. It is an idea, which, in the framework of the novel, is dignified by the possibility it promptly affords of presenting Bigger as the herald of disaster, the danger signal of a more bitter time to come when not Bigger alone but all his kindred will rise, in the name of the many thousands who have perished in fire and flood and by rope and torture, to demand their rightful vengeance.

But it is not quite fair, it seems to me, to exploit the national innocence in this way. The idea of Bigger as a warning boomerangs not only because it is quite beyond the limit of probability that Negroes in America will ever achieve the means of wreaking vengeance upon the state but also because it cannot be said that they have any desire to do so. Native Son does not convey the altogether savage paradox of the American Negro's situation, of which the social reality which we prefer with such hopeful superficiality to study is but, as it were, the shadow. It is not simply the relationship of oppressed to oppressor, of master to slave, nor is it motivated merely by hatred; it is also, literally and morally, a *blood* relationship, perhaps the most profound reality of the American experience, and we cannot begin to unlock it until we accept how very much it contains of the force and anguish and terror of love.

Negroes are Americans and their destiny is the country's destiny. They have no other experience besides their experience on this continent and it is an experience which cannot be rejected, which yet remains to be embraced. If, as I believe, no American Negro exists who does not have his private Bigger Thomas living in the skull, then what most significantly fails to be illuminated here is the paradoxical adjustment which is perpetually made, the Negro being compelled to accept the fact that this dark and dangerous and unloved stranger is part of himself forever. Only this recognition sets him in any wise free and it is this, this necessary ability to contain and even, in the most honorable sense of the word, to *exploit* the "nigger," which lends to Negro life its high element of the ironic and which causes the most well-meaning of their American critics to make such exhilarating errors when attempting to understand them. To present Bigger as a warning is simply to reinforce the American guilt and fear concerning him, it is most forcefully to limit him to that previously mentioned social arena in which he has no human validity, it is simply to condemn him to death. For he has always been a warning, he represents the evil, the sin and suffering which we are compelled to reject. It is useless to say to the courtroom in which this heathen sits on trial that he is their responsiblity, their creation, and his crimes are theirs; and that they ought, therefore, to allow him to live, to make articulate to himself behind the walls of prison the meaning of his existence. The meaning of his existence has already been most adequately expressed, nor does anyone wish, particularly not in the name of democracy, to think of it any more; as for the possibility of articulation, it is this possibility which above all others we most dread. Moreover, the courtroom, judge, jury, witnesses and spectators, recognize immediately that Bigger is their creation and they recognize this not only with hatred and fear and guilt and the resulting fury of self-righteousness but also with that morbid fullness of pride mixed with horror with which one regards the extent and power of one's wickedness. They know that death is his portion, that he runs to death; coming from darkness and dwelling in darkness, he must be, as often as he rises, banished, lest the entire planet be engulfed. And they know, finally, that they do not wish to forgive him and that he does not wish to be forgiven; that he dies, hating them, scorning that appeal which they cannot make to that irrecoverable humanity of his which cannot hear it; and that he *wants* to die because he glories in his hatred and prefers, like Lucifer, rather to rule in hell than serve in heaven.

For, bearing in mind the premise on which the life of such a man is based, i.e., that black is the color of damnation, this is his only possible end. It is the only death which will allow him a kind of dignity or even, however horribly, a kind of beauty. To tell this story, no more than a single aspect of the story of the "nigger," is inevitably and richly to become involved with the force of life and legend, how each perpetually assumes the guise of the other, creating that dense, many-sided and shifting reality which is the world we live in and the world we make. To tell his story is to begin to liberate us from his image and it is, for the first time, to clothe this phantom with flesh and blood, to deepen, by our understanding of him and his relationship to us, our understanding of ourselves and of all men.

But this is not the story which *Native Son* tells, for we find here merely, repeated in anger, the story which we have told in pride. Nor, since the implications of this anger are evaded, are we ever confronted with the actual or potential significance of our pride; which is why we fall, with such a positive glow of recognition, upon Max's long and bitter summing up. It is addressed to those among us of good will and it seems to say that, though there are whites and blacks among us who hate each other, we will not; there are those who are betrayed by greed, by guilt, by blood lust, but not we; we will set our faces against them and join hands and walk together into that dazzling future when there will be no white or black. This is the dream of all liberal men, a dream not at all dishonorable, but, nevertheless, a dream. For, let us join hands on this mountain as we may, the battle is elsewhere. It proceeds far from us in the heat and horror and pain of life itself where all men are betrayed by greed and guilt and blood lust and where no one's hands are clean. Our good will, from which we yet expect such power to transform us, is thin, passionless, strident: its roots, examined, lead us back to our forebears, whose assumption it was that the black man, to become truly human and acceptable, must first become like us. This assumption once accepted, the Negro in America can only acquiesce in the obliteration of his own personality, the distortion and debasement of his own experience, surrendering to those forces which reduce the person to anonymity and which make themselves manifest daily all over the darkening world.

JAMES BALDWIN'S QUARREL
WITH RICHARD WRIGHT*

Maurice Charney

ONE OF THE best statements we have of the dilemma of the Negro writer in America may be found in James Baldwin's review of the *Selected Poems* of Langston Hughes. After taking Hughes severely to task for failing to transform his private experience as a Negro into art, Baldwin concludes: "Hughes is an American Negro poet and has no choice but to be acutely aware of it. He is not the first American Negro to find the war between his social and artistic responsibilities all but irreconcilable." [1] This statement goes to the heart of the quarrel between Baldwin and Wright, for Wright's failure, as Baldwin sees it, lay in a confusion of his social and artistic responsibilities, a distortion of artistic truth into protest and propaganda. When Baldwin was asked recently to explain his comment on Hughes, he ignored the literary implications and spoke only about how it feels to be a Negro in America: "to be a Negro in this country and to be relatively conscious, is to be in a rage almost all the time. So that the first problem is how to control that rage so that it won't destroy you." [2] Wright would certainly have agreed with the first part of Baldwin's statement, for Wright's whole career as a writer was devoted to expressing the violent rage and outrage of the native son who is doomed to be an outsider. But Wright would have earnestly rejected Baldwin's solution—"the first problem is how to control that rage"—as pusillanimity and compromise with reality.

It is interesting to note that Norman Mailer in *Advertisements for Myself* accuses Baldwin of a similar pusillanimity: he is fated to remain a charming minor writer because he is incapable of saying "Fuck you" to his

[1] James Baldwin, "Sermons and Blues," *The New York Times Book Review*, March 29, 1959, p. 6.

[2] "The Negro in American Culture," *Cross Currents*, XI (1961), 205. This is the text, with minor editing, of a symposium that was originally presented over WBAI. The participants were James Baldwin, Emile Capouya, Lorraine Hansberry, Langston Hughes and Alfred Kazin; Nat Hentoff was the moderator.

* Reprinted from the *American Quarterly*, XV (1963), 65–75, by permission of the author and editors.

readers (not one of Mailer's own failings).[3] But it is here precisely that the great temptation for the writer lies:

to simplify the issues under the illusion that if you simplify them enough, people will recognize them; and this illusion is very dangerous because that isn't the way it works. . . . As a writer, you have to decide that what is really important is not that the people you write about are Negroes, but that they are people, and the suffering of any person is really universal.[4]

Baldwin's quarrel with Wright, then, centers on the large issues of the intention and aim and values of the writer. Although both feel the inevitable rage of being a Negro in the United States, their ways of dealing with this rage are radically different. One makes fiction out of the rage itself, brutal, pure, violent and unconstrained, while the other tries to penetrate and analyze that rage and convert it into a recognizable human emotion.

In an essay on Wright written after his death in Paris in 1960, Baldwin tries to set forth their relationship. There is a remarkable blending of compassion and fierce candor in this essay and the portrait that emerges is a deeply ambivalent one: in his later years (he died at 52) Wright became a lonely, isolated, embittered and misunderstood man,[5] frequenting the

[3] Norman Mailer, *Advertisements for Myself* (New York, 1959), pp. 471–72. Baldwin answers Mailer and discusses their friendship in "The Black Boy Looks at the White Boy," *Nobody Knows My Name* (New York, 1961), pp. 216–41 (first published in *Esquire*, May 1961). There are some curious echoes of this essay in the relation of Rufus and Vivaldo in *Another Country* (New York, 1962), and Baldwin shows himself quite capable in this book of uttering every conceivable obscenity to his reader. But I think Mailer's comment still applies in the sense that Baldwin does not mean to taunt or flout his reader; his obscenities are not designed "*pour épater le bourgeois*" as some of Mailer's are.

[4] "The Negro in American Culture," p. 205.

[5] Wright's own defiant description of his personal life has an ill-concealed note of despair in it:

I'm a rootless man, but I'm neither psychologically distraught nor in any wise particularly perturbed because of it. Personally, I do not hanker after, and seem not to need, as many emotional attachments, sustaining roots, or idealistic allegiances as most people. I declare unabashedly that I like and even cherish the state of abandonment, of aloneness; it does not bother me; indeed, to me it seems the natural, inevitable condition of man, and I welcome it. I can make myself at home almost anywhere on this earth and can, if I've a mind to and when I'm attracted to a landscape or a mode of life, easily sink myself into the most alien and widely differing environments. I must confess that this is no personal achievement of mine; this attitude was never striven for. . . . I've been shaped to this mental stance by the kind of experiences that I have fallen heir to. [*White Man, Listen!*, New York, 1957, p. 17]

existentialist cafés of St. Germain where he was made to feel his utter estrangement from the new generation of American and African Negro writers and intellectuals. It is with deeply mixed feelings that Baldwin speaks his eulogy for Wright:

In the meantime, the man I fought so hard and who meant so much to me, is gone. First America, then Europe, then Africa failed him. He lived long enough to find all of the terms on which he had been born become obsolete; presently, all of his attitudes seemed to be historical.[6]

Baldwin's relation to Wright was complicated by Baldwin's own sense of the older writer as his mentor and spiritual father, from whom he needed to revolt in order to prove his own manhood and integrity and skill. He became Wright's protégé early in his career and it was Wright's support that helped Baldwin win his first writing fellowship. But the two were never destined to become friends. There was first the wide difference in age: Baldwin was born in 1924, Wright in 1908, and when they first met Baldwin was an aspiring writer of twenty and Wright a very successful novelist of thirty-six. This difference in generations is very significant. Wright's spiritual and intellectual outlook was molded by the Depression: he worked for the Federal Writers' Project, he was a member of the Communist Party,[7] and he shared in the acute social and political consciousness

This passage also reflects the pernicious influence on Wright of French existentialism seen at its worst in the novel *The Outsider* (New York, 1953). Wright is self-consciously representing himself as *"L'Etranger."* This is a far cry from the bitter rootlessness and isolation of Wright's autobiography, *Black Boy* (New York, 1945). Nelson Algren comes to a similar conclusion about Wright in his *Paris Review* interview (No. 11, Winter 1955). By refusing to admit that he writes out of passion, out of his belly, he made a tragic mistake. "He's trying to write as an intellectual which he isn't basically . . . he's trying his best to write like a Frenchman." (pp. 51–52)

   [6] James Baldwin, *Nobody Knows My Name: More Notes of a Native Son* (New York, 1961), pp. 188–89. But Baldwin sees in some of the stories of *Eight Men* (Cleveland, 1961) "a new power and a new tone," evidence that Wright "had survived, as it were, his own obsolescence. . . ." (p. 189) This statement needs to be qualified by the fact that most of the stories in *Eight Men* are old pieces previously published. There is also, however, Wright's last novel, *The Long Dream* (Garden City, 1958), which shows unmistakable signs of a new sensitivity and awareness.

   [7] Wright tells us in the preface to *Black Power* (New York, 1954, p. xi) that he was a member of the Communist Party from 1932–44, but left the party because he was convinced that Marxist Communism was changing the world in a manner that granted the Negro even less freedom than he had before. If Wright's report in *The God that Failed* (ed. Richard Crossman, New York, 1949) is any guide, he felt the conflict between party discipline and

of the times. His novel, *Native Son* (1940), vies with *The Grapes of Wrath* (1939) as the most characteristic expression of that period. Baldwin, however, came to maturity at the very end of the Depression and during the war years. He is also a product of a very different environment from Wright's. He was born and brought up in Harlem, while Wright was born in Natchez, Mississippi, and lived in the South for a good part of his earlier life (he did not go to Chicago until 1934). For Baldwin the South is the Egypt of his ancestors, a place that will always be remote and mythical, but for Wright the South was the living reality of his life even when loosely transposed to the South Side of Chicago.

The open quarrel between the two came in Paris in the spring of 1949 after Baldwin had published an essay called "Everybody's Protest Novel" in the first issue of *Zero*.[8] At the end of this essay, and almost as an afterthought, Baldwin adds a few damaging remarks about *Native Son*. Wright immediately felt betrayed by his spiritual son and a conflict arose between the two that could never be healed. To Baldwin the cause of this conflict is very simple:

I had used his work as a kind of springboard into my own. His work was a road-block in my road, the sphinx, really, whose riddles I had to answer before I could become myself. I thought confusedly then, and feel very definitely now, that this was the greatest tribute I could have paid him. [*Nobody Knows My Name*, p. 197]

It is just because Baldwin took Wright so seriously that the conflict he describes had to take place. Baldwin himself acknowledges:

In *Uncle Tom's Children*, in *Native Son*, and, above all, in *Black Boy*, I found expressed, for the first time in my life, the sorrow, the rage, and the murderous bitterness which was eating up my life and the lives of those around me. His work was an immense liberation and revelation for me. [*Nobody Knows My Name*, p. 191]

This reads like the crucial discovery of the hero of the *Bildungsroman* where the revolt of the son from the values of the father is the central act

his own will almost from the beginning and refused to submit to party dictation. Wright's novel, *The Outsider*, gives a full account of his disillusion with communism that is very close to Ralph Ellison's *Invisible Man* (New York, 1952). There is, by the way, a story in *Eight Men* (called "The Man Who Lived Underground" and first published in 1944) that must have influenced the conception of *Invisible Man*. "The Man Who Killed a Shadow" in *Eight Men* also deals with the theme of the Negro's invisibility.

    [8] *Zero*, I (Spring 1949), 54–58. This essay was reprinted in the June issue of the *Partisan Review*, XVI (1949), 578–85. In *Zero* Baldwin's essay follows immediately after Wright's "The Man Who Killed a Shadow," a brutal and violent story in the mood of *Native Son*.

of the book. Without any hypocrisy, Baldwin constantly testifies to the power of Wright as a novelist and as a spokesman for the Negro, and to the impact on him of *Native Son*:

Now the most powerful and celebrated statement we have yet had of what it means to be a Negro in America is unquestionably Richard Wright's *Native Son*. . . . We have yet to encounter . . . a report so indisputably authentic, or one that can begin to challenge this most significant novel.[9]

Baldwin's attack on *Native Son* is, therefore, deeply premeditated and deliberate; he uses it to define his own position as a novelist and critic, which is opposed to the values of naturalism and the naturalist view of reality.

In "Everybody's Protest Novel" the attack on *Native Son* is merely a brief appendix to a long and impassioned argument about the sentimentality and untruth of Harriet Beecher Stowe's *Uncle Tom's Cabin*. Uncle Tom, the only real black man in the novel, "has been robbed of his humanity and divested of his sex" in order that he may be clothed in the humility and forbearance necessary for his salvation. Since as a black man he will inevitably be damned, one can only arrange for his soul by making him into a simulacrum of a white man. Through a chain of argument about the nature of a literary character and the nature of reality, Baldwin arrives at the startling conclusion that Bigger, the ironic "native son,"

is Uncle Tom's descendant, flesh of his flesh, so exactly opposite a portrait that, when the books are placed together, it seems that the contemporary Negro novelist and the dead New England woman are locked together in a deadly, timeless battle; the one uttering merciless exhortations, the other shouting curses. [*Notes of a Native Son*, p. 22]

Both Mrs. Stowe and Richard Wright have refused to deal with man in his wholeness and complexity, but have been content to create stereotypes with a carefully defined social role.[10]

[9] James Baldwin, *Notes of a Native Son* (Boston, 1955), pp. 30–31. In *Another Country* the three books that Eric has with him in France are *An Actor Prepares*, *The Wings of the Dove* and *Native Son*. (p. 195)

[10] Wright's first published book was called *Uncle Tom's Children* (1938; enlarged 1940) and its epigraph shows his preoccupation with the "Uncle Tom" theme:

The post Civil War household word among Negroes—"He's an Uncle Tom!"—which denoted reluctant toleration for the cringing type who knew his place before white folk, has been supplanted by a new word from another generation which says:—"Uncle Tom is dead!"

If the Southern rural Negroes of these stories are not cringing, they are certainly cowed and beaten and full of despair. In the sense that they believe in a reality in which violence and prayer are the only means of protest—both equally futile for life on this earth—they are indeed Uncle Tom's children.

In this larger sense neither writer has tried to grapple with the nature of reality and the truth of human experience. Because "literature and sociology are not one and the same," the protest novel fails as a novel in the same measure as it succeeds as propaganda. Bigger Thomas is ultimately a failure as a character because he is a monster, a being deprived of all the attributes of human consciousness:

For Bigger's tragedy is not that he is cold or black or hungry, not even that he is American, black; but that he has accepted a theology that denies him life, that he admits the possibility of his being sub-human and feels constrained, therefore, to battle for his humanity according to those brutal criteria bequeathed him at his birth. [*Notes of a Native Son*, pp. 22–23]

It is this dependence of the novel on a set of abstract and impersonal ideas or principles, the subordination of art to ideology, that Baldwin is arguing against, whether it be the New England Calvinist philanthropy of Mrs. Stowe or the outraged sense of social justice of Richard Wright.

The very power of *Native Son* as a novel and its tremendous popular success served Baldwin as a way of defining his own ideas. He refers to this novel many times in his essays. In "Many Thousands Gone" he relates it to the traditional American story of "an unremarkable youth in battle with the force of circumstance"; in this case not merely poverty but color, "a circumstance which cannot be overcome, against which the protagonist battles for his life and loses." (*Notes of a Native Son*, p. 31) Bigger Thomas is foredoomed to failure and the pattern of chapters in the novel—Fear, Flight, Fate—makes this clear: the murder is a natural outcome of Bigger's fear, a way of exorcising that fear, a momentary triumph. But Bigger cannot win, and his flight and capture and death sentence are all part of a web of fate in which he is caught from the start. In the inevitable unfolding of events from that first sadistic killing of the rat, there is no way out for Bigger. It is in this sense of a preordained pattern set upon the living reality that *Native Son* resembles *Uncle Tom's Cabin*, although in the latter the web of fate is presented in theological terms.

To Baldwin the chief weakness in *Native Son* both artistically and humanly is its "unrewarding rage," and the most severe criticism he can level against Wright is that the violence in his work is "gratuitous and compulsive." Wright never examines the causes of this violence in the human soul, so that it remains merely brute violence and Bigger is merely subhuman and a monster. At its root in Wright "it is the rage, almost literally the howl, of a man who is being castrated." Thus, when Bigger "is found hacking a white woman to death, the very gusto with which this is done, and the great attention paid to the details of physical destruction reveal a terrible attempt to break out of the cage in which the American imagination has imprisoned him for so long." (*Nobody Knows My Name*, p. 188)

But Bigger for all of his rage remains only a social symbol without the consciousness of a human being, and therefore without any complexity or dimension:

Bigger has no discernible relationship to himself, to his own life, to his own people, nor to any other people. . . . It is remarkable that, though we follow him step by step from the tenement room to the death cell, we know as little about him when his journey is ended as we did when it began; and, what is even more remarkable, we know almost as little about the social dynamic which we are to believe created him. [*Notes of a Native Son*, pp. 34–35]

In this respect *Native Son* is a failure even as a social novel, for it gives the impression that the Negro has no real society and tradition about which one can write. A necessary dimension of life has been cut away, "this dimension being the relationship that Negroes bear to one another, that depth of involvement and unspoken recognition of shared experience which creates a way of life." (*Notes of a Native Son*, p. 35) This is a necessary limitation in all protest novels, of which *Native Son* is the most famous example in Negro literature.

The heart of Bigger's rage is not merely his hatred of whites but his self-hatred. He does not really become a Christ-like martyr for the Negro race, which he can redeem ritually by his act of murder. The truth of the matter is that he kills because of his own fierce bitterness at having been born a Negro. At the end of the novel Bigger *wants* to die because he glories in his hatred and prefers, like Lucifer, rather to rule in hell than serve in heaven." (*Notes of a Native Son*, p. 44) This is a powerful and heroic solution, but not a human one. Baldwin is preoccupied throughout his essays with this problem of the Negro's self-hatred, and in his tender and ambivalent eulogy for Wright he sees that lonely, exiled figure as someone who has deliberately cut himself off from the present complexities of the Negro problem, because "his real impulse toward American Negroes, individually, was to despise them." (*Nobody Knows My Name*, p. 212) This statement must have cost Baldwin great anguish to make, but it is part of his unflinching assumption that the Negro's hatred of the white man is always a manifestation of self-hatred. "Negroes in this country . . . are taught really to despise themselves from the moment their eyes open on the world. This world is white and they are black." [11]

[11] James Baldwin, "Letter from a Region in My Mind," *New Yorker*, November 17, 1962, p. 65. Wright's attitude to his own hate is very complex and deserves to be quoted at length. The last section of *Eight Men* is a long essay called "The Man Who Went to Chicago," which may be thought of

There are some splendid descriptive pages on the Harlem race riot of 1943 which support this conclusion. The underlying cause of this riot was the ghetto's chronic need to smash something: "Most of the time it is the members of the ghetto who smash each other, and themselves." (*Notes of a Native Son*, p. 111) Pure hatred like Bigger's is not viable because hate in such an extreme form is really a suicidal wish that destroys the man who hates. The race riot in Harlem in 1943 did not express any permanent attitude of blacks to whites but was merely a temporary escape valve for the frustrations of both Negroes and whites. The Negro's real relation to the white American prohibits "anything as uncomplicated and satisfactory as pure hatred. In order really to hate white people, one has to blot so much out of the mind—and the heart—that this hatred itself becomes an exhausting and self-destructive pose." (*Notes of a Native Son*, p. 112) In terms of his real psychological situation the Negro in America always faces a choice between the complicated alternatives of love and hate, he is always put in the position of having to decide between "amputation and gangrene." One is forced to make the choice that Bigger refused to make: to accept life as it is and to fight injustice without either hatred or despair.

In this sense the Negro problem is part of a more general injustice of man to man, perhaps a reflection of the capacity for evil in the nature of things that the innocently optimistic American refuses to see. Violence has an enormous primitive appeal because it seems so simple and final a solution to the problem of injustice: "And who has not dreamed of violence? That fantastical violence which will drown in blood, wash away in blood,

as a sequel to Wright's autobiography *Black Boy* (1945)—it was first published in 1945 with the title "Early Days in Chicago." Here Wright tries to define the strange interrelations of color-hate and self-hate:

Color-hate defined the place of black life as below that of white life; and the black man, responding to the same dreams as the white man, strove to bury within his heart his awareness of this difference because it made him lonely and afraid. Hated by whites and being an organic part of the culture that hated him, the black man grew in turn to hate in himself that which others hated in him. But pride would make him hate his self-hate, for he would not want whites to know that he was so thoroughly conquered by them that his total life was conditioned by their attitude but in the act of hiding his self-hate, he could not help but hate those who evoked his self-hate in him. So each part of his day would be consumed in a war with himself, a good part of his energy would be spent in keeping control of his unruly emotions, emotions which he had not wished to have, but could not help having. Held at bay by the hate of others, preoccupied with his own feelings, he was continuously at war with reality. He became inefficient, less able to see and judge the objective world. And when he reached that state, the white people looked at him and laughed and said:

"Look, didn't I tell you niggers were that way?" [pp. 213–14] not only generation upon generation of horror, but which will also release one from the individual horror, carried everywhere in the heart." (*Nobody Knows My Name*, p. 213) One must reject the romantic and heroic appeal of violence just because it is so simple and so personal and so unsatisfactory to the larger claims of justice. In one of his most eloquent passages, Baldwin refuses to separate the Negro past from the history of the human race, or to consider the Negro's fate apart from man's fate:

Which of us has overcome his past? And the past of a Negro is blood dripping down through leaves, gouged-out eyeballs, the sex torn from its socket and severed with a knife. But this past is not special to the Negro. This horror is also the past, and the everlasting potential, or temptation, of the human race. If we do not know this, it seems to me, we know nothing about ourselves, nothing about each other; to have accepted this is also to have found a source of strength—source of all our power. But one must first accept this paradox, with joy. [*Nobody Knows My Name*, p. 213]

Baldwin's fundamental argument against Wright, then, is that he has refused to accept this paradox. Both Wright and the naturalists utterly reject such a noble and charitable view of man's potentialities, while Baldwin cannot accept the will-less paradigm of *Native Son*—Fear, Flight, Fate —or the Dread, Dream, Descent, Despair, Decision sequence of *The Outsider* as an accurate description of reality.

Baldwin wants to get rid of Bigger Thomas not because he is not vividly real and present, but because he is only one part of a larger reality. There is, in fact, one incident in *Notes of a Native Son* in which Baldwin shows himself remarkably like Bigger. In 1942 he had been working in defense plants in New Jersey and discovering with shock and outrage the realities of race relations. On his last night in New Jersey, he went to the movies in Trenton with a white friend. After seeing "This Land is Mine" they went on to the "American Diner," where they were refused service— the ironies of the names are all underscored by Baldwin. This refusal set off a sort of hysteria in him, "like a physical sensation, a click at the nape of my neck as though some interior string connecting my head to my body had been cut." He went blindly into "an enormous, glittering, and fashionable restaurant in which I knew not even the intercession of the Virgin would cause me to be served." (*Notes of a Native Son*, pp. 95–96) He then experienced that sense of blind rage and impotence that Bigger felt in the presence of Mary and the Daltons, and suddenly hurled a half-filled water-pitcher at a white waitress with intent to kill. Luckily, with the aid of his friend, he was able to escape unscathed, but the incident preyed on his mind and he drew from it a conclusion exactly opposite to Wright's:

I could not get over two facts, both equally difficult for the imagination to grasp, and one was that I could have been murdered. But the other was that I had been ready to commit murder. I saw nothing very clearly but I did see this: that my life, my *real* life was in danger, and not from anything other people might do but from the hatred I carried in my own heart. [*Notes of a Native Son*, pp. 97–98]

This incident supports very well Baldwin's thesis that the Negro's hatred for the white man is always self-hatred and always self-destructive.

But more important, I think, is the distinction he makes between his *real* life as a human being and his social and mythic and fantasy life as a Negro. There is a dangerous conflict between the two which can never be resolved. As Baldwin admits, "no American Negro exists who does not have his private Bigger Thomas living in the skull," but a "paradoxical adjustment" comes when the Negro is compelled "to accept the fact that this dark and dangerous and unloved stranger is part of himself forever." And Baldwin adds significantly: "Only this recognition sets him in any wise free. . . ." (*Notes of a Native Son*, p. 42) This is the sort of freedom that Bigger never had and Baldwin's insistence on this freedom constitutes one of his major themes. He is willing to accept the reality of being an American and to return from his exile in France (as Wright never did) to continue the search for his own identity. It is therefore no mere bravado when, in the preface to *Nobody Knows My Name*, he takes as a motto for his work the great Socratic dictum: "the unexamined life is not worth living." The same impulse lies behind his constant concern for "human weight and complexity" and the full human reality. It is from this vantage point that Baldwin launches his attack on the protest novel, which is, as I have been trying to show, really an attack on the assumptions of naturalism.

Baldwin's central beliefs about man and the purpose of the novel are surprisingly close to those of Faulkner's Nobel Prize Acceptance Speech; man is

something resolutely indefinable, unpredictable. In overlooking, denying, evading his complexity—which is nothing more than the disquieting complexity of ourselves—we are diminished and we perish; only within this web of ambiguity, paradox, this hunger, danger, darkness, can we find at once ourselves and the power that will free us from ourselves. It is this power of revelation which is the business of the novelist, this journey toward a more vast reality which must take precedence over all other claims. [*Notes of a Native Son*, p. 15]

In this statement Baldwin as a Negro resolutely affirms his concern with man, black or white, in all of his complexity. The hard, deterministic world of *Native Son* denies this complexity and must be rejected. As a critic of naturalism Baldwin allies himself with Ralph Ellison, who, in his National Book Award speech, tried to define the sense of reality that governs his *Invisible Man* (1952):

Thus to see America with an awareness of its rich diversity and its almost magical fluidity and freedom, I was forced to conceive of a novel unburdened by the narrow naturalism which has led after so many triumphs to the final and unrelieved despair which marks so much of our current fiction.[12]

Neither Baldwin nor Ellison is a writer of despair: *Invisible Man* is a comic masterpiece like *The Adventures of Augie March* (1953), and its author, as Baldwin sees him, is "the first Negro novelist I have ever read to utilize in language, and brilliantly, some of the ambiguity and irony of Negro life." (*Notes of a Native Son*, p. 8)

Although the blackness of the human heart, the inability to love, the sense of emptiness and waste in modern life are Baldwin's major concerns in his novels, he ends not in despair but in a tragic paradox: "How's one going to get through it all? How can you live if you can't love? And how can you live if you *do*?" (*Another Country*, p. 340) But the possibility of love, no matter how brief or futile, defines the characters' being and makes war on the chaos of despair. Despite the fact that *Another Country*, Baldwin's latest and best novel, does not have the narrative compulsion of *Native Son*, it does have a turbulence and a passionate eloquence that Wright could never achieve, and the seriousness of its concern about love and chaos and the loss of innocence is foreign to Wright's work. Baldwin's earlier novels, *Go Tell It on the Mountain* (1953) and *Giovanni's Room* (1956), are sensitive and troubled, but it is not until *Another Country* that he speaks with full assurance in style and theme.[13] It is, in its way, a remarkable novel, and it begins to realize Baldwin's powers as a writer of fiction; he has already given us a set of essays of incredible lucidity and intelligence.

[12] Quoted in Robert A. Bone, *The Negro Novel in America* (New Haven, 1958), p. 198.
[13] *Another Country* is, in part, a very successful rewriting of the sterile and ingrown novel, *Giovanni's Room*. Some of its success comes from balancing the homosexual theme against the heterosexual and the androgynous; it is one kind of love in a world in which all kinds of love are equally difficult and perilous.

BLACK BOYS AND NATIVE SONS*

Irving Howe

JAMES BALDWIN first came to the notice of the American literary public
not through his own fiction but as author of an impassioned criticism of
the conventional Negro novel. In 1949 he published in *Partisan Review* an
essay called "Everybody's Protest Novel," attacking the kind of fiction,
from *Uncle Tom's Cabin* to *Native Son*, that had been written about the
ordeal of the American Negroes; and two years later he printed in the
same magazine "Many Thousands Gone," a tougher and more explicit
polemic against Richard Wright and the school of naturalistic "protest"
fiction that Wright represented. The protest novel, wrote Baldwin, is
undertaken out of sympathy for the Negro, but through its need to present
him merely as a social victim or a mythic agent of sexual prowess, it has-
tens to confine the Negro to the very tones of violence he has known all
his life. Compulsively re-enacting and magnifying his trauma, the protest
novel proves unable to transcend it. So choked with rage has this kind of
writing become, it cannot show the Negro as a unique person or locate
him as a member of a community with its own traditions and values, its
own "unspoken recognition of shared experience which creates a way of
life." The failure of the protest novel "lies in its insistence that it is [man's]
categorization alone which is real and which cannot be transcended."

Like all attacks launched by young writers against their famous elders,
Baldwin's essays were also a kind of announcement of his own intentions.
He wrote admiringly about Wright's courage ("his work was an immense
liberation and revelation for me"), but now, precisely because Wright had
prepared the way for all the Negro writers to come, he, Baldwin, would
go further, transcending the sterile categories of "Negro-ness," whether
those enforced by the white world or those defensively erected by the
Negroes themselves. No longer mere victim or rebel, the Negro would stand
free in a self-achieved humanity. As Baldwin put it some years later, he
hoped "to prevent myself from becoming *merely* a Negro; or even, merely
a Negro writer." The world "tends to trap and immobilize you in the role

* Reprinted from *A World More Attractive* (New York: Horizon Press,
1963), by permission of the publishers.

you play," and for the Negro writer, if he is to be a writer at all, it hardly matters whether the trap is sprung from motives of hatred or condescension.

Baldwin's rebellion against the older Negro novelist who had served him as a model and had helped launch his career, was not of course an unprecedented event. The history of literature is full of such painful ruptures, and the issue Baldwin raised is one that keeps recurring, usually as an aftermath to a period of "socially engaged" writing. The novel is an inherently ambiguous genre: it strains toward formal autonomy and can seldom avoid being a public gesture. If it is true, as Baldwin said in "Everybody's Protest Novel," that "literature and sociology are not one and the same," it is equally true that such statements hardly begin to cope with the problem of how a writer's own experience affects his desire to represent human affairs in a work of fiction. Baldwin's formula evades, through rhetorical sweep, the genuinely difficult issue of the relationship between social experience and literature.

Yet in *Notes of a Native Son*, the book in which his remark appears, Baldwin could also say: "One writes out of one thing only—one's own experience." What, then, was the experience of a man with a black skin, what *could* it be in this country? How could a Negro put pen to paper, how could he so much as think or breathe, without some impulsion to protest, be it harsh or mild, political or private, released or buried? The "sociology" of his existence formed a constant pressure on his literary work, and not merely in the way this might be true for any writer, but with a pain and ferocity that nothing could remove.

James Baldwin's early essays are superbly eloquent, displaying virtually in full the gifts that would enable him to become one of the great American rhetoricians. But these essays, like some of the later ones, are marred by rifts in logic, so little noticed when one gets swept away by the brilliance of the language that it takes a special effort to attend their argument.

Later Baldwin would see the problems of the Negro writer with a greater charity and more mature doubt. Reviewing in 1959 a book of poems by Langston Hughes, he wrote: "Hughes is an American Negro poet and has no choice but to be acutely aware of it. He is not the first American Negro to find the war between his social and artistic responsibilities all but irreconcilable." All but irreconcilable: the phrase strikes a note sharply different from Baldwin's attack upon Wright in the early 'fifties. And it is not hard to surmise the reasons for this change. In the intervening years Baldwin had been living through some of the experiences that had goaded Richard Wright into rage and driven him into exile; he too, like Wright, had been to hell and back, many times over.

II

Gawd, Ah wish all them
white folks was dead.

The day *Native Son* appeared, American culture was changed forever. No matter how much qualifying the book might later need, it made impossible a repetition of the old lies. In all its crudeness, melodrama and claustrophobia of vision, Richard Wright's novel brought out into the open, as no one ever had before, the hatred, fear and violence that have crippled and may yet destroy our culture.

A blow at the white man, the novel forced him to recognize himself as an oppressor. A blow at the black man, the novel forced him to recognize the cost of his submission. *Native Son* assaulted the most cherished of American vanities: the hope that the accumulated injustice of the past would bring with it no lasting penalties, the fantasy that in his humiliation the Negro somehow retained a sexual potency—or was it a childlike goodnature?—that made it necessary to envy and still more to suppress him. Speaking from the black wrath of retribution, Wright insisted that history can be a punishment. He told us the one thing even the most liberal whites preferred not to hear: that Negroes were far from patient or forgiving, that they were scarred by fear, that they hated every moment of their suppression even when seeming most acquiescent, and that often enough they hated *us*, the decent and cultivated white men who from complicity or neglect shared in the responsibility for their plight. If such younger novelists as Baldwin and Ralph Ellison were able to move beyond Wright's harsh naturalism and toward more supple modes of fiction, that was possible only because Wright had been there first, courageous enough to release the full weight of his anger.

In *Black Boy*, the autobiographical narrative he published several years later, Wright would tell of an experience he had while working as a bellboy in the South. Many times he had come into a hotel room carrying luggage or food and seen naked white women lounging about, unmoved by shame at his presence, for "blacks were not considered human beings anyway . . . I was a non-man . . . I felt doubly cast out." With the publication of *Native Son*, however, Wright forced his readers to acknowledge his anger, and in that way, if none other, he wrested for himself a sense of dignity as a man. He forced his readers to confront the disease of our culture, and to one of its most terrifying symptoms he gave the name of Bigger Thomas.

Brutal and brutalized, lost forever to his unexpended hatred and his fear of the world, a numbed and illiterate black boy stumbling into a murder and never, not even at the edge of the electric chair, breaking through to an understanding of either his plight or himself, Bigger Thomas was a part of Richard Wright, a part even of the James Baldwin who stared with horror at Wright's Bigger, unable either to absorb him into his consciousness or eject him from it. Enormous courage, the discipline of self-conquest, was required to conceive Bigger Thomas, for this was no eloquent Negro spokesman, no admirable intellectual or formidable proletarian. Bigger was drawn—one would surmise, deliberately—from white fantasy and white contempt. Bigger was the worst of Negro life accepted, then rendered a trifle conscious and thrown back at those who had made him what he was. "No American Negro exists," Baldwin would later write, "who does not have his private Bigger Thomas living in the skull."

Wright drove his narrative to the very core of American phobia: sexual fright, sexual violation. He understood that the fantasy of rape is a consequence of guilt, what the whites suppose themselves to deserve. He understood that the white man's notion of uncontaminated Negro vitality, little as it had to do with the bitter realities of Negro life, reflected some ill-formed and buried feeling that our culture has run down, lost its blood, become febrile. And he grasped the way in which the sexual issue has been intertwined with social relationships, for even as the white people who hire Bigger as their chauffeur are decent and charitable, even as the girl he accidentally kills is a liberal of sorts, theirs is the power and the privilege. "We black and they white. They got things and we ain't. They do things and we can't."

The novel barely stops to provision a recognizable social world, often contenting itself with cartoon simplicities and yielding almost entirely to the nightmare incomprehension of Bigger Thomas. The mood is apocalyptic, the tone superbly aggressive. Wright was an existentialist long before he heard the name, for he was committed to the literature of extreme situations both through the pressures of his rage and the gasping hope of an ultimate catharsis.

Wright confronts both the violence and the crippling limitations of Bigger Thomas. For Bigger white people are not people at all, but something more, "a sort of great natural force, like a stormy sky looming overhead." And only through violence does he gather a little meaning in life, pitifully little: "he had murdered and created a new life for himself." Beyond that Bigger cannot go.

At first *Native Son* seems still another naturalistic novel: a novel of exposure and accumulation, charting the waste of the undersides of the American city. Behind the book one senses the molding influence of Theodore Dreiser, especially the Dreiser of *An American Tragedy* who knows there are situations so oppressive that only violence can provide their victims with the hope of dignity. Like Dreiser, Wright wished to pummel his readers into awareness; like Dreiser, to overpower them with the sense of society as an enclosing force. Yet the comparison is finally of limited value, and for the disconcerting reason that Dreiser had a white skin and Wright a black one.

The usual naturalistic novel is written with detachment, as if by a scientist surveying a field of operations; it is a novel in which the writer withdraws from a detested world and coldly piles up the evidence for detesting it. *Native Son*, though preserving some of the devices of the naturalistic novel, deviates sharply from its characteristic tone: a tone Wright could not possibly have maintained and which, it may be, no Negro novelist can really hold for long. *Native Son* is a work of assault rather than withdrawal; the author yields himself in part to a vision of nightmare. Bigger's cowering perception of the world becomes the most vivid and authentic component of the book. Naturalism pushed to an extreme turns here into something other than itself, a kind of expressionist outburst, no longer a replica of the familiar social world but a self-contained realm of grotesque emblems.

That *Native Son* has grave faults anyone can see. The language is often coarse, flat in rhythm, syntactically overburdened, heavy with journalistic slag. Apart from Bigger, who seems more a brute energy than a particularized figure, the characters have little reality, the Negroes being mere stock accessories and the whites either "agit-prop" villains or heroic Communists whom Wright finds it easier to admire from a distance than establish from the inside. The long speech by Bigger's radical lawyer Max (again a device apparently borrowed from Dreiser) is ill-related to the book itself: Wright had not achieved Dreiser's capacity for absorbing everything, even the most recalcitrant philosophical passages, into a unified vision of things. Between Wright's feelings as a Negro and his beliefs as a Communist there is hardly a genuine fusion, and it is through this gap that a good part of the novel's unreality pours in.

Yet it should be said that the endlessly repeated criticism that Wright caps his melodrama with a party-line oration tends to oversimplify the novel, for Wright is too honest simply to allow the propagandistic message to constitute the last word. Indeed, the last word is given not to Max but to Bigger. For at the end Bigger remains at the mercy of his hatred and fear, the lawyer retreats helplessly, the projected union between political consciousness and raw revolt has not been achieved—as if Wright were persuaded that, all ideology apart, there is for each Negro an ultimate trial that he can bear only by himself.

Black Boy, which appeared five years after *Native Son*, is a slighter but more skillful piece of writing. Richard Wright came from a broken home, and as he moved from his helpless mother to a grandmother whose religious fanaticism (she was a Seventh-day Adventist) proved utterly suffocating, he soon picked up a precocious knowledge of vice and a realistic awareness of social power. This autobiographical memoir, a small classic in the literature of self-discovery, is packed with harsh evocations of Negro adolescence in the South. The young Wright learns how wounding it is to wear the mask of a grinning niggerboy in order to keep a job. He examines the life of the Negroes and judges it without charity or idyllic compensation—for he already knows, in his heart and his bones, that to be oppressed means to lose out on human possibilities. By the time he is seventeen, preparing to leave for Chicago, where he will work on a WPA project, become a member of the Communist Party, and publish his first book of stories called *Uncle Tom's Children*, Wright has managed to achieve the beginnings of consciousness, through a slow and painful growth from the very bottom of deprivation to the threshold of artistic achievement and a glimpsed idea of freedom.

III

Baldwin's attack upon Wright had partly been anticipated by the more sophisticated American critics. Alfred Kazin, for example, had found in Wright a troubling obsession with violence:

If he chose to write the story of Bigger Thomas as a grotesque crime story, it is because his own indignation and the sickness of the age combined to make him dependent on violence and shock, to astonish the reader by torrential scenes of cruelty, hunger, rape, murder and flight, and then enlighten him by crude Stalinist homilies.

The last phrase apart, something quite similar could be said about the author of *Crime and Punishment*; it is disconcerting to reflect upon how few novelists, even the very greatest, could pass this kind of moral inspection. For the novel as a genre seems to have an inherent bias toward extreme effects, such as violence, cruelty and the like. More important, Kazin's judgment rests on the assumption that a critic can readily distinguish between the genuine need of a writer to cope with ugly realities and the damaging effect these realities may have upon his moral and psychic life. But in regard to contemporary writers one finds it very hard to distinguish between a valid portrayal of violence and an obsessive involvement with it. A certain amount of obsession may be necessary for the valid portrayal—writers devoted to themes of desperation cannot keep themselves morally intact. And when we come to a writer like Richard Wright, who deals with the most degraded and inarticulate sector of the Negro world, the distinction between objective rendering and subjective immersion becomes still more difficult, perhaps even impossible. For a novelist who

after so many triumphs to the final and unrelieved despair which marks so much of our current fiction." This note of willed affirmation—as if one could *decide* one's deepest and most authentic response to society!—was to be heard in many other works of the early fifties, most notably in Saul Bellow's *Adventures of Augie March*. Today it is likely to strike one as a note whistled in the dark. In response to Baldwin and Ellison, Wright would have said (I virtually quote the words he used in talking to me during the summer of 1958) that only through struggle could men with black skins, and for that matter, all the oppressed of the world, achieve their humanity. It was a lesson, said Wright with a touch of bitterness yet not without kindness, that the younger writers would have to learn in their own way and their own time. All that has happened since bears him out.

One criticism made by Baldwin in writing about *Native Son*, perhaps because it is the least ideological, remains important. He complained that in Wright's novel "a necessary dimension has been cut away; this dimension being the relationship that Negroes bear to one another, that depth of involvement and unspoken recognition of shared experience which creates a way of life." The climate of the book, "common to most Negro protest novels . . . has led us all to believe that in Negro life there exists no tradition, no field of manners, no possibility of ritual or intercourse, such as may, for example, sustain the Jew even after he has left his father's house." It could be urged, perhaps, that in composing a novel verging on expressionism Wright need not be expected to present the Negro world with fullness, balance or nuance; but there can be little doubt that in this respect Baldwin did score a major point: the posture of militancy, no matter how great the need for it, exacts a heavy price from the writer, as indeed from everyone else. For "Even the hatred of squalor / Makes the brow grow stern / Even anger against injustice / Makes the voice grow harsh . . . ." All one can ask, by way of reply, is whether the refusal to struggle may not exact a still greater price. It is a question that would soon be tormenting James Baldwin, and almost against his will.

IV

In his own novels Baldwin hoped to show the Negro world in its diversity and richness, not as a mere specter of protest; he wished to show it as a living culture of men and women who, even when deprived, share in the emotions and desires of common humanity. And he meant also to evoke something of the distinctiveness of Negro life in America, as evidence of its worth, moral tenacity and right to self-acceptance. How can one not sympathize with such a program? And how, precisely as one does sympathize, can one avoid the conclusion that in this effort Baldwin has thus far failed to register a major success?

His first novel, *Go Tell It on the Mountain,* is an enticing but minor work: it traces the growing-up of a Negro boy in the atmosphere of a repressive Calvinism, a Christianity stripped of grace and brutal with fantasies of submission and vengeance. No other work of American fiction reveals so graphically the way in which an oppressed minority aggravates its own oppression through the torments of religious fanaticism. The novel is also striking as a modest *Bildungsroman,* the education of an imaginative Negro boy caught in the heart-struggle between his need to revolt, which would probably lead to his destruction in the jungles of New York, and the miserly consolations of black Calvinism, which would signify that he accepts the denial of his personal needs. But it would be a mistake to claim too much for this first novel, in which a rhetorical flair and a conspicuous sincerity often eat away at the integrity of event and the substance of character. The novel is intense, and the intensity is due to Baldwin's absorption in that religion of denial which leads the boy to become a preacher in his father's church, to scream out God's word from "a merciless resolve to kill my father rather than allow my father to kill me." Religion has of course played a central role in Negro life, yet one may doubt that the special kind of religious experience dominating *Go Tell It on the Mountain* is any more representative of that life, any more advantageous a theme for gathering in the qualities of Negro culture, than the violence and outrage of *Native Son.* Like Wright before him, Baldwin wrote from the intolerable pressures of his own experience; there was no alternative; each had to release his own agony before he could regard Negro life with the beginnings of objectivity.

Baldwin's second novel, *Giovanni's Room,* seems to me a flat failure. It abandons Negro life entirely (not in itself a cause for judgment) and focuses upon the distraught personal relations of several young Americans adrift in Paris. The problem of homosexuality, which is to recur in Baldwin's fiction, is confronted with a notable courage, but also with a disconcerting kind of sentimentalism, a quavering and sophisticated submission to the ideology of love. It is one thing to call for the treatment of character as integral and unique; but quite another for a writer with Baldwin's background and passions to succeed in bringing together his sensibility as a Negro and his sense of personal trouble.

Baldwin has not yet managed—the irony is a stringent one—in composing the kind of novel he counterposed to the work of Richard Wright. He has written three essays, ranging in tone from disturbed affection to disturbing malice, in which he tries to break from his rebellious dependency upon Wright, but he remains tied to the memory of the older man. The Negro writer who has come closest to satisfying Baldwin's program is not Baldwin himself but Ralph Ellison, whose novel *Invisible Man* is a brilliant though flawed achievement, standing with *Native Son* as the major fiction thus far composed by American Negroes.

What astonishes one most about *Invisible Man* is the apparent freedom it displays from the ideological and emotional penalties suffered by Negroes in this country—I say "apparent" because the freedom is not quite so complete as the book's admirers like to suppose. Still, for long stretches *Invisible Man* does escape the formulas of protest, local color, genre quaintness and jazz chatter. No white man could have written it, since no white man could know with such intimacy the life of the Negroes from the inside; yet Ellison writes with an ease and humor which are now and again simply miraculous.

Invisible Man is a record of a Negro's journey through contemporary America, from South to North, province to city, naïve faith to disenchantment and perhaps beyond. There are clear allegorical intentions (Ellison is "literary" to a fault) but with a book so rich in talk and drama it would be a shame to neglect the fascinating surface for the mere depths. The beginning is both nightmare and farce. A timid Negro boy comes to a white smoker in a Southern town: he is to be awarded a scholarship. Together with several other Negro boys he is rushed to the front of the ballroom, where a sumptuous blonde tantalizes and frightens them by dancing in the nude. Blindfolded, the Negro boys stage a "battle royal," a free-for-all in which they pummel each other to the drunken shouts of the whites. Practical jokes, humiliations, terror—and then the boy delivers a prepared speech of gratitude to his white benefactors. At the end of this section, the boy dreams that he has opened the briefcase given him together with his scholarship to a Negro college and that he finds an inscription reading: "To Whom It May Concern: Keep This Nigger-Boy Running."

He keeps running. He goes to his college and is expelled for having innocently taken a white donor through a Negro ginmill which also happens to be a brothel. His whole experience is to follow this pattern. Strip down a pretense, whether by choice or accident, and you will suffer penalties, since the rickety structure of Negro respectability rests upon pretense and those who profit from it cannot bear to have the reality exposed (in this case, that the college is dependent upon the Northern white millionaire). The boy then leaves for New York, where he works in a white-paint factory, becomes a soapboxer for the Harlem Communists, the darling of the fellow-traveling bohemia, and a big wheel in the Negro world. At the end, after witnessing a frenzied race riot in Harlem, he "finds himself" in some not entirely specified way, and his odyssey from submission to autonomy is complete.

Ellison has an abundance of that primary talent without which neither craft nor intelligence can save a novelist: he is richly, wildly inventive; his scenes rise and dip with tension, his people bleed, his language sings. No other writer has captured so much of the hidden gloom and surface gaiety of Negro life.

There is an abundance of superbly rendered speech: a West Indian woman inciting her men to resist an eviction, a Southern sharecropper calmly describing how he seduced his daughter, a Harlem street-vender spinning jive. The rhythm of Ellison's prose is harsh and nervous, like a beat of harried alertness. The observation is expert: he knows exactly how zootsuiters walk, making stylization their principle of life, and exactly how the antagonism between American and West Indian Negroes works itself out in speech and humor. He can accept his people as they are, in their blindness and hope: here, finally, the Negro world does exist, seemingly apart from plight or protest. And in the final scene Ellison has created an unforgettable image: "Ras the Destroyer," a Negro nationalist, appears on a horse dressed in the costume of an Abyssinian chieftain, carrying spear and shield, and charging wildly into the police—a black Quixote, mad, absurd, unbearably pathetic.

But even Ellison cannot help being caught up with *the idea* of the Negro. To write simply about "Negro experience" with the esthetic distance urged by the critics of the 'fifties, is a moral and psychological impossibility, for plight and protest are inseparable from that experience, and even if less political than Wright and less prophetic than Baldwin, Ellison knows this quite as well as they do.

If *Native Son* is marred by the ideological delusions of the 'thirties, *Invisible Man* is marred, less grossly, by those of the 'fifties. The middle section of Ellison's novel, dealing with the Harlem Communists, does not ring quite true, in the way a good portion of the writings on this theme during the postwar years does not ring quite true. Ellison makes his Stalinist figures so vicious and stupid that one cannot understand how they could ever have attracted him or any other Negro. That the party leadership manipulated members with deliberate cynicism is beyond doubt, but this cynicism was surely more complex and guarded than Ellison shows it to be. No party leader would ever tell a prominent Negro Communist, as one of them does in *Invisible Man*: "You were not hired [as a functionary] to think"—even if that were what he felt. Such passages are almost as damaging as the propagandist outbursts in *Native Son*.

Still more troublesome, both as it breaks the coherence of the novel and reveals Ellison's dependence on the postwar *Zeitgeist*, is the sudden, unprepared and implausible assertion of unconditioned freedom with which the novel ends. As the hero abandons the Communist Party he wonders, "Could politics ever be an expression of love?" This question, more portentous than profound, cannot easily be reconciled to a character who has been presented mainly as a passive victim of his experience. Nor is one easily persuaded by the hero's discovery that "my world has become one of infinite possibilities," his refusal to be the "invisible man" whose body is manipulated by various social groups. Though the unqualified assertion of self-liberation was a favorite strategy among American literary people in the 'fifties, it is also vapid and insubstantial. It violates the reality of social life, the interplay between external conditions and personal will, quite as much as the determinism of the 'thirties. The unfortunate fact remains that to define one's individuality is to stumble upon social barriers which stand in the way, all too much in the way, of "infinite possibilities." Freedom can be fought for, but it cannot always be willed or asserted into existence. And it seems hardly an accident that even as Ellison's hero asserts the "infinite possibilities" he makes no attempt to specify them.

Throughout the 'fifties Richard Wright was struggling to find his place in a world he knew to be changing but could not grasp with the assurance he had felt in his earlier years. He had resigned with some bitterness from the Communist Party, though he tried to preserve an independent radical outlook, tinged occasionally with black nationalism. He became absorbed in the politics and literature of the rising African nations, but when visiting them he felt hurt at how great was the distance between an American Negro and an African. He found life in America intolerable, and he spent his last fourteen years in Paris, somewhat friendly with the intellectual group around Jean-Paul Sartre but finally a loner, a man who stood by the pride of his rootlessness. And he kept writing, steadily experimenting, partly, it may be, in response to the younger men who had taken his place in the limelight and partly because he was truly a dedicated writer.

These last years were difficult for Wright, since he neither made a true home in Paris nor kept in imaginative touch with the changing life of the United States. In the early 'fifties he published a very poor novel, *The Outsider*, full of existentialist jargon applied but not really absorbed to the Negro theme. He was a writer in limbo, and his better fiction, such as the novelette "The Man Who Lived Underground," is a projection of that state.

In the late 'fifties Wright published another novel, *The Long Dream*, which is set in Mississippi and displays a considerable recovery of his powers. This book has been criticized for presenting Negro life in the South through "old-fashioned" images of violence, but one ought to hesitate before denying the relevance of such images or joining in the criticism of their use. For Wright was perhaps justified in not paying attention to the changes that have occurred in the South these past few decades. When Negro liberals write that despite the prevalence of bias there has been an improvement in the life of their people, such statements are reasonable and necessary. But what have these to do with the way Negroes feel, with the power of the memories they must surely retain? About this we know very little and would be well advised not to nourish preconceptions, for their feelings may be much closer to Wright's rasping outbursts than to the more modulated tones of the younger Negro novelists. *Wright remembered*, and what he remembered other Negroes must also have remembered. And in that way he kept faith with the experience of the boy who had fought his way out of the depths, to speak for those who remained there.

His most interesting fiction after *Native Son* is to be found in a posthumous collection of stories, *Eight Men*, written during the last 25 years of his life. Though they fail to yield any clear line of chronological development, these stories give evidence of Wright's literary restlessness, his often clumsy efforts to break out of the naturalism which was his first and, I think, necessary mode of expression. The unevenness of his writing is highly disturbing: one finds it hard to understand how the same man, from paragraph to paragraph, can be so brilliant and inept. Time after time the narrative texture is broken by a passage of sociological or psychological jargon; perhaps the later Wright tried too hard, read too much, failed to remain sufficiently loyal to the limits of his talent.

Some of the stories, such as "Big Black Good Man," are enlivened by Wright's sardonic humor, the humor of a man who has known and released the full measure of his despair but finds that neither knowledge nor release matters in a world of despair. In "The Man Who Lived Underground," Wright shows a sense of narrative rhythm which is superior to anything in his full-length novels and evidence of the seriousness with which he kept working.

The main literary problem that troubled Wright in recent years was that of rendering his naturalism a more terse and supple instrument. I think he went astray whenever he abandoned naturalism entirely: there are a few embarrassingly bad experiments with stories employing self-consciously Freudian symbolism. Wright needed the accumulated material of circumstance which naturalistic detail provided his fiction; it was as essential to his ultimate effect of shock and bruise as dialogue to Hemingway's ultimate effect of irony and loss. But Wright was correct in thinking that the problem of detail is the most vexing technical problem the naturalist writer must face, since the accumulation that makes for depth and solidity can also create a pall of tedium. In "The Man Who Lived Underground" Wright came close to solving this problem, for here the naturalistic detail is put at the service of a radical projective image—a Negro trapped in a sewer; and despite some flaws, the story is satisfying both for its tense surface and elasticity of suggestion.

Richard Wright died at 52, full of hopes and projects. Like many of us, he had somewhat lost his intellectual way but he kept struggling toward the perfection of his craft and toward a comprehension of the strange world that in his last years was coming into birth. In the most fundamental sense, however, he had done his work: he had told his contemporaries a truth so bitter, they paid him the tribute of trying to forget it.

V

Looking back to the early essays and fiction of James Baldwin, one wishes to see a little further than they at first invite: to see past their brilliance of gesture, by which older writers could be dismissed, and past their aura of gravity, by which a generation of intellectuals could be enticed. After this hard and dismal decade, what strikes one most of all is the sheer pathos of these early writings, the way they reveal the desire of a greatly talented young man to escape the scars—and why should he not have wished to escape them?—which he had found upon the faces of his elders and knew to be gratuitous and unlovely.

Chekhov once said that what the aristocratic Russian writers assumed as their birthright, the writers who came from the lower orders had to pay for with their youth. James Baldwin did not want to pay with his youth, as Richard Wright had paid so dearly. He wanted to move, as Wright had not been able to, beyond the burden or bravado of his stigma; he wanted to enter the world of freedom, grace, and self-creation. One would need a heart of stone, or to be a brutal moralist, to feel anything but sympathy for this desire. But we do not make our circumstances; we can, at best, try to remake them. And all the recent writing of Baldwin indicates that the wishes of his youth could not be realized, not in *this* country. The sentiments of humanity which had made him rebel against Richard Wright have now driven him back to a position close to Wright's rebellion.

Baldwin's most recent novel, *Another Country*, is a "protest novel" quite as much as *Native Son*, and anyone vindictive enough to make the effort, could score against it the points Baldwin scored against Wright. No longer is Baldwin's prose so elegant or suave as it was once; in this book it is harsh, clumsy, heavy-breathing with the pant of suppressed bitterness. In about half of *Another Country*—the best half, I would judge—the material is handled in a manner somewhat reminiscent of Wright's naturalism: a piling on of the details of victimization, as the jazz musician Rufus Scott, a sophisticated distant cousin of Bigger Thomas, goes steadily down the path of self-destruction, worn out in the effort to survive in the white man's jungle and consumed by a rage too extreme to articulate yet too amorphous to act upon. The narrative voice is a voice of anger, rasping and thrusting, not at all "literary" in the somewhat lacquered way the earlier Baldwin was able to achieve. And what that voice says, no longer held back by the proprieties of literature, is that the nightmare of the history we have made allows us no immediate escape. Even if all the visible tokens of injustice were erased, the Negroes would retain their hatred and the whites their fear and guilt. Forgiveness cannot be speedily willed, if willed at all, and before it can even be imagined there will have to be a fuller discharge of those violent feelings that have so long been suppressed. It is not a pretty thought, but neither is it a mere "unrewarding rage"; and it has the sad advantage of being true, first as Baldwin embodies it in the disintegration of Rufus, which he portrays with a ferocity quite new in his fiction, and then as he embodies it in the hard-driving ambition of Rufus' sister Ida, who means to climb up to success even if she has to bloody a good many people, whites preferably, in order to do it.

Another Country has within it another novel: a nagging portrayal of that entanglement of personal relationships—sterile, involuted, grindingly rehearsed, pursued with quasi-religious fervor, and cut off from any dense context of social life—which has come to be a standard element in contemporary fiction. The author of *this* novel is caught up with the problem of communication, the emptiness that seeps through the lives of many cultivated persons and in response to which he can only reiterate the saving value of true and lonely love. These portions of *Another Country* tend to be abstract, without the veined milieu, the filled-out world, a novel needs: as if Baldwin, once he moves away from the Negro theme, finds it quite as hard to lay hold of contemporary experience as do most other novelists. The two pulls upon his attention are difficult to reconcile, and Baldwin's future as a novelist is decidely uncertain.

During the last few years James Baldwin has emerged as a national figure, the leading intellectual spokesman for the Negroes, whose recent essays, as in *The Fire Next Time,* reach heights of passionate exhortation unmatched in modern American writing. Whatever his ultimate success or failure as a novelist, Baldwin has already secured his place as one of the two or three greatest essayists this country has ever produced. He has brought a new luster to the essay as an art form, a form with possibilities for discursive reflection and concrete drama which make it a serious competitor to the novel, until recently almost unchallenged as the dominant literary genre in our time. Apparently drawing upon Baldwin's youthful experience as the son of a Negro preacher, the style of these essays is a remarkable instance of the way in which a grave and sustained eloquence— the rhythm of oratory, but that rhythm held firm and hard—can be employed in an age deeply suspicious of rhetorical prowess. And in pieces like the reports on Harlem and the account of his first visit South, Baldwin realizes far better than in his novel the goal he had set himself of pre-

senting Negro life through an "unspoken recognition of shared experience."
Yet it should also be recognized that these essays gain at least some of
their resonance from the tone of unrelenting protest in which they are
written, from the very anger, even the violence Baldwin had begun by
rejecting.

Like Richard Wright before him, Baldwin has discovered that to assert
his humanity he must release his rage. But if rage makes for power it does
not always encourage clarity, and the truth is that Baldwin's most recent
essays are shot through with intellectual confusions, torn by the conflict
between his assumption that the Negro must find an honorable place in the
life of American society and his apocalyptic sense, mostly fear but just a
little hope, that this society is beyond salvation, doomed with the sickness
of the West. And again like Wright, he gives way on occasion to the lure
of black nationalism. Its formal creed does not interest him, for he knows
it to be shoddy, but he is impressed by its capacity to evoke norms of
discipline from followers at a time when the Negro community is threatened by a serious inner demoralization.

In his role as spokesman, Baldwin must pronounce with certainty and
struggle with militancy; he has at the moment no other choice; yet whatever may have been the objective inadequacy of his polemic against Wright
a decade ago, there can be no question but that the refusal he then made
of the role of protest reflected faithfully some of his deepest needs and
desires. But we do not make our circumstances; we can, at best, try to
remake them; and the arena of choice and action always proves to be a
little narrower than we had supposed. One generation passes its dilemmas
to the next, black boys on to native sons.

"It is in revolt that man goes beyond himself to discover other people,
and from this point of view, human solidarity is a philosophical certainty."
The words come from Camus: they might easily have been echoed by
Richard Wright: and today one can imagine them being repeated, with
a kind of rueful passion, by James Baldwin. No more important words
could be spoken in our century, but it would be foolish, and impudent,
not to recognize that for the men who must live by them the cost is heavy.

THE WORLD AND THE JUG*

Ralph Ellison

"The World and the Jug" is actually a combination of two separate pieces. The first, bearing the original title, was written at the suggestion of Myron Kolatch of *The New Leader*, who was interested in my reactions, via telephone, to an essay by Irving Howe titled "Black Boys and Native Sons," which appeared in the Autumn 1963 issue of Howe's magazine, *Dissent*.

Usually such a reply would have appeared in the same magazine in which the original essay was published, but in this instance, and since it hadn't occurred to me to commit my reactions to paper, they went to the editor who asked for them. The second section of the essay, originally entitled, "A Rejoinder," was written after Irving Howe had consented to reply, in *The New Leader*, of February 3, 1964, to my attack. There is, unfortunately, too little space here to do justice to Howe's arguments, and it is recommended that the interested reader consult Mr. Howe's book of essays, *A World More Attractive*—a book worthy of his attention far beyond the limits of our exchange—published by Horizon Press in 1963.

> What runs counter to the revolutionary convention is, in revolutionary histories, suppressed more imperiously than embarrassing episodes in private memoirs, and by the same obscure forces. . . .
> —André Malraux

I

First, three questions: Why is it so often true that when critics confront the American as *Negro* they suddenly drop their advanced critical armament and revert with an air of confident superiority to quite primitive modes of analysis? Why is it that sociology-oriented critics seem to rate literature so far below politics and ideology that they would rather kill a novel than modify their presumptions concerning a given reality which it seeks in its own terms to project? Finally, why is it that so many of those

* Reprinted from *Shadow and Act* (New York: Random House, 1964) by permission of the publishers.

271

who would tell us the meaning of Negro life never bother to learn how varied it really is?

These questions are aroused by "Black Boys and Native Sons," an essay by Irving Howe, the well-known critic and editor of *Dissent*, in the Autumn 1963 issue of that magazine. It is a lively piece, written with something of the Olympian authority that characterized Hannah Arendt's "Reflections on Little Rock" in the Winter 1959 *Dissent* (a dark foreshadowing of the Eichmann blowup). And in addition to a hero, Richard Wright, it has two villains, James Baldwin and Ralph Ellison, who are seen as "Black boys" masquerading as false, self-deceived "native sons." Wright himself is given a diversity of roles (all conceived by Howe): He is not only the archetypal and true-blue black boy—the "honesty" of his famous autobiography established this for Howe—but the spiritual father of Ellison, Baldwin and all other Negroes of literary bent to come. Further, in the platonic sense he is his own father and the culture hero who freed Ellison and Baldwin to write more "modulated" prose.

Howe admires Wright's accomplishments, and is frankly annoyed by the more favorable evaluation currently placed upon the works of the younger men. His claims for *Native Son* are quite broad:

The day [it] appeared, American culture was changed forever. . . . it made impossible a repetition of the old lies. . . . [it] brought out into the open . . . the fear and violence that have crippled and may yet destroy our culture. . . . A blow at the white man, the novel forced him to recognize himself as an oppressor. A blow at the black man, the novel forced him to recognize the cost of his submission. *Native Son* assaulted the most cherished of American vanities: the hope that the accumulated injustice of the past would bring with it no lasting penalties, the fantasy that in his humiliation the Negro somehow retained a sexual potency . . . that made it necessary to envy and still more to suppress him. Speaking from the black wrath of retribution, Wright insisted that history can be a punishment. He told us the one thing even the most liberal whites preferred not to hear: that Negroes were far from patient or forgiving, that they were scarred by fear, that they hated every moment of their suppression even when seeming most acquiescent, and that often enough they hated *us*, the decent and cultivated white men who from complicity or neglect shared in the responsibility for their plight. . . .

There are also negative criticisms: that the book is "crude," "melodramatic" and marred by "claustrophobia" of vision, that its characters are "cartoons," etc. But these defects Howe forgives because of the book's "clenched militancy." One wishes he had stopped there. For in his zeal to champion Wright, it is as though he felt it necessary to stage a modern version of the Biblical myth of Noah, Ham, Shem and Japheth (based originally, I'm told, on a castration ritual), with first Baldwin and then

Ellison acting out the impious role of Ham: Baldwin by calling attention to Noah-Wright's artistic nakedness in his famous essays, "Everybody's Protest Novel" (1949) and "Many Thousands Gone" (1951); Ellison by rejecting "narrow naturalism" as a fictional method, and by alluding to the "diversity, fluidity and magical freedom of American life" on that (for him at least) rather magical occasion when he was awarded the National Book Award. Ellison also offends by having the narrator of *Invisible Man* speak of his life (Howe either missing the irony or assuming that *I* did) as one of "infinite possibilities" while living in a hole in the ground.

Howe begins by attacking Baldwin's rejection in "Everybody's Protest Novel" of the type of literature he labeled "protest fiction" (*Uncle Tom's Cabin* and *Native Son* being prime examples), and which he considered incapable of dealing adequately with the complexity of Negro experience. Howe, noting that this was the beginning of Baldwin's career, sees the essay's underlying motive as a declaration of Baldwin's intention to transcend "the sterile categories of 'Negro-ness,' whether those enforced by the white world or those defensively erected by the Negroes themselves. No longer mere victim or rebel, the Negro would stand free in a self-achieved humanity. As Baldwin put it some years later, he hoped to prevent himself 'from becoming *merely* a Negro; or even, merely a Negro writer.' " Baldwin's elected agency for self-achievement would be the novel—as it turns out, it was the essay *and* the novel—but the novel, states Howe, "is an inherently ambiguous genre: it strains toward formal autonomy and can seldom avoid being a public gesture."

I would have said that it is *always* a public gesture, though not necessarily a political one. I would also have pointed out that the American Negro novelist is himself "inherently ambiguous." As he strains toward self-achievement as artist (and here he can only "integrate" and free himself), he moves toward fulfilling his dual potentialities as Negro and American. While Howe agrees with Baldwin that "literature and sociology are not one and the same," he notes nevertheless that, "it is equally true that such statements hardly begin to cope with the problem of how a writer's own experience affects his desire to represent human affairs in a work of fiction." Thus Baldwin's formula evades "through rhetorical sweep, the genuinely difficult issue of the relationship between social experience and literature." And to Baldwin's statement that one writes "out of one thing only—one's own experience" (I would have added, for the novelist, this qualification: one's own experience as understood and ordered through one's knowledge of self, culture and literature), Howe, appearing suddenly in blackface, replies with a rhetorical sweep of his own:

What, then, was the experience of a man with a black skin, what *could* it be here in this country? How could a Negro put pen to paper, how could he so much as think or breathe, without some impulsion to protest, be it harsh or mild, political or private, released or buried? . . . The "sociology" of his existence forms a constant pressure on his literary work, and not merely in the way this might be true of any writer, but with a pain and ferocity that nothing could remove.

I must say that this brought a shock of recognition. Some twelve years ago, a friend argued with me for hours that I could not possibly write a novel because my experience as a Negro had been too excruciating to allow me to achieve that psychological and emotional distance necessary to artistic creation. Since he "knew" Negro experience better than I, I could not convince him that he might be wrong. Evidently Howe feels that unrelieved suffering is the only "real" Negro experience, and that the true Negro writer must be ferocious.

But there is also an American Negro tradition which teaches one to deflect racial provocation and to master and contain pain. It is a tradition which abhors as obscene any trading on one's own anguish for gain or sympathy; which springs not from a desire to deny the harshness of existence but from a will to deal with it as men at their best have always done. It takes fortitude to be a man and no less to be an artist. Perhaps it takes even more if the black man would be an artist. If so, there are no exemptions. It would seem to me, therefore, that the question of how the "sociology of his existence" presses upon a Negro writer's work depends upon how much of his life the individual writer is able to transform into art. What moves a writer to eloquence is less meaningful than what he makes of it. How much, by the way, do we know of Sophocles' wounds?

One unfamiliar with what Howe stands for would get the impression that when he looks at a Negro he sees not a human being but an abstract embodiment of living hell. He seems never to have considered that American Negro life (and here he is encouraged by certain Negro "spokesmen") is, for the Negro who must live it, not only a burden (and not always that) but also a *discipline*—just as any human life which has endured so long is a discipline teaching its own insights into the human condition, its own strategies of survival. There is a fullness, even a richness here; and here *despite* the realities of politics, perhaps, but nevertheless here and real. Because it is *human* life. And Wright, for all of his indictments, was no less its product than that other talented Mississippian, Leontyne Price. To deny in the interest of revolutionary posture that such possibilities of human richness exist for others, even in Mississippi, is not only to deny us our humanity but to betray the critic's commitment to social reality. Critics who do so should abandon literature for politics.

For even as his life toughens the Negro, even as it brutalizes him, sensitizes him, dulls him, goads him to anger, moves him to irony, sometimes fracturing and sometimes affirming his hopes; even as it shapes his attitudes toward family, sex, love, religion; even as it modulates his humor, tempers his joy—it *conditions* him to deal with his life and with himself. Because it is *his* life and no mere abstraction in someone's head. He must live it and try consciously to grasp its complexity until he can change it; must live it *as* he changes it. He is no mere product of his sociopolitical predicament. He is a product of the interaction between his racial predicament, his individual will and the broader American cultural freedom in which he finds his ambiguous existence. Thus he, too, in a limited way, is his own creation.

In his loyalty to Richard Wright, Howe considers Ellison and Baldwin guilty of filial betrayal because, in their own work, they have rejected the path laid down by *Native Son*, phonies because, while actually "black boys," they pretend to be mere American writers trying to react to something of the pluralism of their predicament.

In his myth Howe takes the roles of both Shem and Japheth, trying mightily (his face turned backward so as not to see what it is he's veiling) to cover the old man's bare belly, and then becoming Wright's voice from beyond the grave by uttering the curses which Wright was too ironic or too proud to have uttered himself, at least in print:

In response to Baldwin and Ellison, Wright would have said (I virtually quote the words he used in talking to me during the summer of 1958) that only through struggle could men with black skins, and for that matter, all the oppressed of the world, achieve their humanity. It was a lesson, said Wright with a touch of bitterness yet not without kindness, that the younger writers would have to learn in their own way and their own time. All that has happened since bears him out.

What, coming eighteen years after *Native Son* and thirteen years after World War II, does this rather limp cliché mean? Nor is it clear what is meant by the last sentence—or is it that today Baldwin has come to out-Wrighting Richard? The real questions seem to be: How does the Negro writer participate *as a writer* in the struggle for human freedom? To whom does he address his work? What values emerging from Negro experience does he try to affirm?

I started with the primary assumption that men with black skins, having retained their humanity before all of the conscious efforts made to dehumanize them, especially following the Reconstruction, are unquestionably human. Thus they have the obligation of freeing themselves—whoever their allies might be—by depending upon the validity of their own experience for an accurate picture of the reality which they seek to change, and for a gauge of the values they would see made manifest. Crucial to this view is the belief that their resistance to provocation, their coolness under pressure, their sense of timing and their tenacious hold on the ideal of their ultimate freedom are indispensable values in the struggle, and are at least as characteristic of American Negroes as the hatred, fear and vindictiveness which Wright chose to emphasize.

Wright believed in the much abused idea that novels are "weapons"—the counterpart of the dreary notion, common among most minority groups, that novels are instruments of good public relations. But I believe that true novels, even when most pessimistic and bitter, arise out of an impulse to celebrate human life and therefore are ritualistic and ceremonial at their core. Thus they would preserve as they destroy, affirm as they reject.

In *Native Son*, Wright began with the ideological proposition that what whites think of the Negro's reality is more important than what Negroes themselves know it to be. Hence Bigger Thomas was presented as a near-subhuman indictment of white oppression. He was designed to shock whites out of their apathy and end the circumstances out of which Wright insisted Bigger emerged. Here environment is all—and interestingly enough, environment conceived solely in terms of the physical, the nonconscious. Well, cut off my legs and call me Shorty! Kill my parents and throw me on the mercy of the court as an orphan! Wright could imagine Bigger, but Bigger could not possibly imagine Richard Wright. Wright saw to that.

But without arguing Wright's right to his personal vision, I would say that he was himself a better argument for my approach than Bigger was for his. And so, to be fair and as inclusive as Howe, is James Baldwin. Both are true Negro Americans, and both affirm the broad possibility of personal realization which I see as a saving aspect of American life. Surely, this much can be admitted without denying the injustice which all three of us have protested.

Howe is impressed by Wright's pioneering role and by the "enormous courage, the discipline of self-conquest, required to conceive Bigger Thomas. . . ." And earlier: "If such younger novelists as Baldwin and Ralph Ellison were able to move beyond Wright's harsh naturalism toward more supple modes of fiction, that was only possible because Wright had been there first, courageous enough to release the full weight of his anger."

It is not for me to judge Wright's courage, but I must ask just why it was possible for me to write as I write "only" because Wright released his anger? Can't I be allowed to release my own? What does Howe know of my acquaintance with violence, or the shape of my courage or the intensity of my anger? I suggest that my credentials are at least as valid as Wright's, even though he began writing long before I did, and it is possible that I have lived through and committed even more violence than he.

Howe must wait for an autobiography before he can be responsibly certain. Everybody wants to tell us what a Negro is, yet few wish, even in a joke, to be one. But if you would tell me who I am, at least take the trouble to discover what I have been.

Which brings me to the most distressing aspect of Howe's thinking: his Northern white liberal version of the white Southern myth of absolute separation of the races. He implies that Negroes can only aspire to contest other Negroes (this at a time when Baldwin has been taking on just about everyone, including Hemingway, Faulkner and the United States Attorney General!), and must wait for the appearance of a Black Hope before they have the courage to move. Howe is so committed to a sociological vision of society that he apparently cannot see (perhaps because he is dealing with Negroes—although not because he would suppress us socially or politically for in fact he is anxious to end such suppression) that whatever the efficiency of segregation as a sociopolitical arrangement, it has been far from absolute on the level of *culture*. Southern whites cannot walk, talk, sing, conceive of laws or justice, think of sex, love, the family or freedom without responding to the presence of Negroes.

Similarly, no matter how strictly Negroes are segregated socially and politically, on the level of the imagination their ability to achieve freedom is limited only by their individual aspiration, insight, energy and will. Wright was able to free himself in Mississippi because he had the imagination and the will to do so. He was as much a product of his reading as of his painful experiences, and he made himself a writer by subjecting himself to the writer's discipline—as he understood it. The same is true of James Baldwin, who is not the product of Negro storefront church but of the library, and the same is true of me.

Howe seems to see segregation as an opaque steel jug with the Negroes inside waiting for some black messiah to come along and blow the cork. Wright is his hero and he sticks with him loyally. But if we are in a jug it is transparent, not opaque, and one is allowed not only to see outside but to read what is going on out there; to make identifications as to values and human quality. So in Macon County, Alabama, I read Marx, Freud, T. S. Eliot, Pound, Gertrude Stein and Hemingway. Books which seldom, if ever, mentioned Negroes were to release me from whatever "segregated" idea I might have had of my human possibilities. I was freed not by propagandists or by the example of Wright—I did not know him at the time and was earnestly trying to learn enough to write a symphony and have it performed by the time I was twenty-six, because Wagner had done so and I admired his music—but by composers, novelists, and poets who spoke to me of more interesting and freer ways of life.

These were works which, by fulfilling themselves as works of art, by being satisfied to deal with life in terms of their own sources of power, were able to give me a broader sense of life and possibility. Indeed, I understand a bit more about myself as Negro because literature has taught me something of my identity as Western man, as political being. It has also taught me something of the cost of being an individual who aspires to conscious eloquence. It requires real poverty of the imagination to think that this can come to a Negro *only* through the example of *other Negroes*, especially after the performance of the slaves in re-creating themselves, in good part, out of the images and myths of the Old Testament Jews.

No, Wright was no spiritual father of mine, certainly in no sense I recognize—nor did he pretend to be, since he felt that I had started writing too late. It was Baldwin's career, not mine, that Wright proudly advanced by helping him attain the Eugene Saxton Fellowship, and it was Baldwin who found Wright a lion in his path. Being older and familiar with quite different lions in quite different paths, I simply stepped around him.

But Wright was a friend for whose magazine I wrote my first book review and short story, and a personal hero in the same way Hot Lips Paige and Jimmy Rushing were friends and heroes. I felt no need to attack what I considered the limitations of his vision because I was quite impressed by what he had achieved. And in this, although I saw with the black vision of Ham, I was, I suppose, as pious as Shem and Japheth. Still I would write my own books and they would be in themselves, implicitly, criticisms of Wright's; just as all novels of a given historical moment form an argument over the nature of reality and are, to an extent, criticisms each of the other.

While I rejected Bigger Thomas as any *final* image of Negro personality, I recognized *Native Son* as an achievement; as one man's essay in defining the human condition as seen from a specific Negro perspective at a given time in a given place. And I was proud to have known Wright and happy for the impact he had made upon our apathy. But Howe's ideas notwithstanding, history is history, cultural contacts ever mysterious, and taste exasperatingly personal. Two days after arriving in New York I was to read Malraux's *Man's Fate* and *The Days of Wrath*, and after these how could I be impressed by Wright as an ideological novelist? Need my skin blind me to all other values? Yet Howe writes:

When Negro liberals write that despite the prevalence of bias there has been an improvement in the life of their people, such statements are reasonable and necessary. But what have these to do with the way Negroes feel, with the power of the memories they must surely retain? About this we know very little and would be well advised not to nourish preconceptions, for their feelings may well be closer to Wright's rasping outbursts than to the more modulated tones of the younger Negro novelists. *Wright remembered, and* what he remembered other Negroes must also have remembered. And in that way he kept faith with the experience of the boy who had fought his way out of the depths, to speak for those who remained there.

Wright, for Howe, is the genuine article, the authentic Negro writer, and his tone the only authentic tone. But why strip Wright of his individuality in order to criticize other writers? He had his memories and I have mine, just as I suppose Irving Howe has his—or has Marx spoken the final word for him? Indeed, very early in *Black Boy*, Wright's memory and his contact with literature come together in a way revealing, at least to the eye concerned with Wright the literary man, that his manner of keeping faith with the Negroes who remained in the depths is quite interesting:

(After I had outlived the shocks of childhood, after the habit of reflection had been born in me, I used to mull over the strange absence of real kindness in Negroes, how unstable was our tenderness, how lacking in genuine passion we were, how void of great hope, how timid our joy, how bare our traditions, how hollow our memories, how lacking we were in those intangible sentiments that bind man to man and how shallow was even our despair. After I had learned other ways of life I used to brood upon the unconscious irony of those who felt that Negroes led so passional an existence! I saw that what had been taken for our emotional strength was our negative confusions, our flights, our fears, our frenzy under pressure.

(Whenever I thought of the essential bleakness of black life in America, I knew that Negroes had never been allowed to catch the full spirit of Western civilization, that they lived somehow in it but not of it. And when I brooded upon the cultural barrenness of black life, I wondered if clean, positive tenderness, love, honor, loyalty and the capacity to remember was native with man. I asked myself if these human qualities were not fostered, won, struggled and suffered for, preserved in ritual from one generation to another.)

Must I be condemned because my sense of Negro life was quite different? Or because for me keeping faith would never allow me to even raise such a question about any segment of humanity? *Black Boy* is not a sociological case history but an autobiography, and therefore a work of art shaped by a writer bent upon making an ideological point. Doubtlessly, this was the beginning of Wright's exile, the making of a decision which was to shape his life and writing thereafter. And it is precisely at this point that Wright is being what I would call, in Howe's words, "literary to a fault."

For just as *How Bigger Was Born* is Wright's Jamesian preface to *Native Son*, the passage quoted above is his paraphrase of Henry James's catalogue of those items of a high civilization which were absent from American life during Hawthorne's day, and which seemed so necessary in order for the novelist to function. This, then, was Wright's list of those items of high humanity which he found missing among Negroes. Thank God, I have never been quite that literary.

How awful that Wright found the facile answers of Marxism before he learned to use literature as a means for discovering the forms of American Negro humanity. I could not and cannot question their existence, I can only seek again and again to project that humanity as I see it and feel it. To me Wright as *writer* was less interesting than the enigma he personified: that he could so dissociate himself from the complexity of his background while trying so hard to improve the condition of black men everywhere; that he could be so wonderful an example of human possibility but could not for ideological reasons depict a Negro as intelligent, as creative or as dedicated as himself.

In his effort to resuscitate Wright, Irving Howe would designate the role which Negro writers are to play more rigidly than any Southern politician—and for the best of reasons. We must express "black" anger and "clenched militancy"; most of all we should not become too interested in the problems of the art of literature, even though it is through these that we seek our individual identities. And between writing well and being ideologically militant, we must choose militancy.

Well, it all sounds quite familiar and I fear the social order which it forecasts more than I do that of Mississippi. Ironically, during the 1940s it was one of the main sources of Wright's rage and frustration.

II

I am sorry Irving Howe got the impression that I was throwing beanballs when I only meant to pitch him a hyperbole. It would seem, however, that he approves of angry Negro writers only until one questions his ideas; then he reaches for his honor, cries "misrepresentation" and "distortion," and charges the writer with being both out of control of himself and with fashioning a "strategy calculated to appeal, ready-made, to the preconceptions of the liberal audience." Howe implies that there are differences between us which I disguised in my essay, yet whatever the validity of this attempt at long-distance psychoanalysis, it was not his honor which I questioned but his thinking; not his good faith but his critical method.

And the major differences which these raised between us I tried to describe. They are to be seen by anyone who reads Howe's "Black Boys and Native Sons" not as a collection of thematically related fragments but as the literary exposition of a considered point of view. I tried to interpret this essay in the light of the impact it made upon my sense of life and literature, and I judged it through its total form—just as I would have Howe base his judgments of writers and their circumstances on as much of what we know about the actual complexity of men living in a highly pluralistic society as is possible. I realize that the *uncommon* sense of a critic, his special genius, is a gift to be thankful for whenever we find it. The very least I expected of Howe, though, was that he would remember his *common* sense, that he would not be carried away by that intellectual abandon, that lack of restraint, which seizes those who regard blackness as an absolute and who see in it a release from the complications of the real world.

Howe is interested in militant confrontation and suffering, yet evidently he recognizes neither when they involve some act of his own. He *really* did not know the subject was loaded. Very well, but I was brought into the booby-trapped field of his assumptions and finding myself in pain, I did not choose to "hold back from the suffering" inflicted upon me there. Out of an old habit I yelled—without seeking Howe's permission, it is true—where it hurt the most. For oddly enough, I found it far less painful to have to move to the back of a Southern bus, or climb to the peanut gallery of a movie house—matters about which I could do nothing except walk, read, hunt, dance, sculpt, cultivate ideas, or seek other uses for my time—than to tolerate concepts which distorted the actual reality of my situation or my reactions to it.

I could escape the reduction imposed by unjust laws and customs, but not that imposed by ideas which defined me as no more than the *sum* of those laws and customs. I learned to outmaneuver those who interpreted my silence as submission, my efforts at self-control as fear, my contempt as awe before superior status, my dreams of faraway places and room at the top of the heap as defeat before the barriers of their stifling, provincial world. And my struggle became a desperate battle which was usually fought, though not always, in silence; a guerrilla action in a larger war in which I found some of the most treacherous assaults against me committed by those who regarded themselves either as neutrals, as sympathizers, or as disinterested military advisers.

I recall this not in complaint, for thus was I disciplined to endure the absurdities of both conscious and unconscious prejudice, to resist racial provocation and, before the ready violence of brutal policemen, railroad "bulls," and casual white citizens, to hold my peace and bide my time. Thus was I forced to evaluate my own self-worth, and the narrow freedom in which it existed, against the power of those who would destroy me. In time I was to leave the South, although it has never left me, and the interests which I discovered there became my life.

But having left the South I did not leave the battle—for how could I leave Howe? He is a man of words and ideas, and since I, too, find my identity in the world of ideas and words, where would I flee? I still endure the nonsense of fools with a certain patience, but when a respected critic distorts my situation in order to feel comfortable in the abstractions he would impose upon American reality, then it is indeed "in accordance with my nature" to protest. Ideas are important in themselves, perhaps, but when they are interposed between me and my sense of reality I feel threatened; they are too elusive, they move with missile speed and are too often fired from altitudes rising high above the cluttered terrain upon which I struggle. And too often those with a facility for ideas find themselves in the councils of power representing me at the double distance of racial alienation and inexperience.

Taking leave of Howe for a moment—for his lapse is merely symptomatic—let me speak generally. Many of those who write of Negro life today seem to assume that as long as their hearts are in the right place they can be as arbitrary as they wish in their formulations. Others seem to feel that they can air with impunity their most private Freudian fantasies as long as they are given the slightest camouflage of intellectuality and projected as "Negro." They have made of the no-man's-land created by segregation a territory for infantile self-expression and intellectual anarchy. They write as though Negro life exists only in light of their belated regard, and they publish interpretations of Negro experience which would not hold true for their own or for any other form of human life.

Here the basic unity of human experience that assures us of some possibility of empathic and symbolic identification with those of other backgrounds is blasted in the interest of specious political and philosophical conceits. Prefabricated Negroes are sketched on sheets of paper and superimposed upon the Negro community; then when someone thrusts his head through the page and yells, "Watch out there, Jack, there're people living under here," they are shocked and indignant. I am afraid, however, that we shall hear much more of such protest as these interpositions continue. And I predict this, not out of any easy gesture of militancy (and what an easy con-game for ambitious, publicity-hungry Negroes this stance of "militancy" has become!) but because as Negroes express increasingly their irritation in this critical area, many of those who make so lightly with our image shall find their own subjected to a most devastating scrutiny.

One of the most insidious crimes occurring in this democracy is that of designating another, politically weaker, less socially acceptable, people as the receptacle for one's own self-disgust, for one's own infantile rebellions, for one's own fears of, and retreats from, reality. It is the crime of reducing the humanity of others to that of a mere convenience, a counter in a banal game which involves no apparent risk to ourselves. With us

Negroes it started with the appropriation of our freedom and our labor; then it was our music, our speech, our dance and the comic distortion of our image by burnt-corked, cotton-gloved corn-balls yelling, "Mammy!" And while it would be futile, nontragic, and un-Negro American to complain over the processes through which we have become who and what we are, it is perhaps permissible to say that the time for such misappropriations ran out long ago.

For one thing, Negro American consciousness is not a product (as so often seems true of so many American groups) of a will to historical forgetfulness. It is a product of our memory, sustained and constantly reinforced by events, by our watchful waiting, and by our hopeful suspension of final judgment as to the meaning of our grievances. For another, most Negroes recognize themselves as themselves despite what others might believe them to be. Thus, although the sociologists tell us that thousands of light-skinned Negroes become white each year undetected, most Negroes can spot a paper-thin "white Negro" every time simply because those who masquerade missed what others were forced to pick up along the way: discipline—a discipline which these heavy thinkers would not undergo even if guaranteed that combined with their own heritage it would make of them the freest of spirits, the wisest of men and the most sublime of heroes.

The rhetorical strategy of my original reply was not meant, as Howe interprets it, to strike the stance of a "free artist" against the "ideological critic," although I *do* recognize that I can be free only to the extent that I detect error and grasp the complex reality of my circumstances and work to dominate it through the techniques which are my means of confronting the world. Perhaps I am only free enough to recognize those tendencies of thought which, actualized, would render me even less free.

Even so, I did not intend to take the stance of the "knowing Negro writer" against the "presuming white intellectual." While I am without doubt a Negro, and a writer, I am also an *American* writer, and while I am more knowing than Howe where my own life and its influences are concerned, I took the time to question his presumptions as one responsible for contributing as much as he is capable to the clear perception of American social reality. For to think unclearly about that segment of reality in which I find my existence is to do myself violence. To allow others to go unchallenged when they distort that reality is to participate not only in that distortion but to accept, as in this instance, a violence inflicted upon the art of criticism. And if I am to recognize those aspects of my role as writer which do not depend primarily upon my racial identity, if I am to fulfill the writer's basic responsibilities to his craft, then surely I must insist upon the maintenance of a certain level of precision in language, a maximum correspondence between the form of a piece of writing and its content, and between words and ideas and the things and processes of this world.

Whatever my role as "race man" (and it knocks me out whenever anyone, black or white, tries to tell me—and the white Southerners have no monopoly here—how to become their conception of a "good Negro"), I am as writer no less a custodian of the American language than is Irving Howe. Indeed, to the extent that I am a writer—I lay no claims to being a thinker—the American language, including the Negro idiom, is all that I have. So let me emphasize that my reply to Howe was neither motivated by racial defensiveness nor addressed to his own racial identity.

It is fortunate that it was not, for considering how Howe identifies himself in this instance, I would have missed the target, which would have been embarrassing. Yet it would have been an innocent mistake, because in situations such as this many Negroes, like myself, make a positive distinction between "whites" and "Jews." Not to do so could be either offensive, embarrassing, unjust or even dangerous. If I would know who I am and preserve who I am, then I must see others distinctly whether they see me so or no. Thus I feel uncomfortable whenever I discover Jewish intellectuals writing as though *they* were guilty of enslaving my grandparents, or as though the *Jews* were responsible for the system of segregation. Not only do they have enough troubles of their own, as the saying goes, but Negroes know this only too well.

The real guilt of such Jewish intellectuals lies in their facile, perhaps unconscious, but certainly unrealistic, identification with what is called the "power structure." Negroes call that "passing for white." Speaking personally, both as writer and as Negro American, I would like to see the more positive distinctions between whites and Jewish Americans maintained. Not only does it make for a necessary bit of historical and social clarity, at least where Negroes are concerned, but I consider the United States freer politically and richer culturally because there are Jewish Americans to bring it the benefit of their special forms of dissent, their humor and their gift for ideas which are based upon the uniqueness of their experience. The diversity of American life is often painful, frequently burdensome and always a source of conflict, but in it lies our fate and our hope.

To Howe's charge that I found his exaggerated claims for Richard Wright's influence upon my own work presumptuous, I plead guilty. Was it necessary to impose a line of succession upon Negro writers simply because Howe identified with Wright's cause? And why, since he grasps so readily the intentional absurdity of my question regarding his relationship to Marx, couldn't he see that the notion of an intellectual or artistic succession based upon color or racial background is no less absurd than one based upon a common religious background? (*Of course, Irving, I know that you haven't believed in final words for twenty years—not even your own—and I know, too, that the line from Marx to Howe is as complex and as dialectical as that from Wright to Ellison. My point was to try to see to it that certain lapses in your thinking did not become final.*) In fact, this whole exchange would never have started had I not been dragged into the discussion. Still, if Howe could take on the role of man with a "black skin," why shouldn't I assume the role of critic-of-critics?

But how surprising are Howe's ideas concerning the ways of controversy. Why, unless of course he holds no respect for his opponent, should a polemicist be expected to make things *hard* for himself? As for the "preconceptions of the liberal audience," I had not considered them, actually, except as they appear in Howe's own thinking. Beyond this I wrote for anyone who might hesitate to question his formulations, especially very young Negro writers who might be bewildered by the incongruity of such ideas coming from such an authority. Howe himself rendered complicated rhetorical strategies unnecessary by lunging into questionable territory with his flanks left so unprotected that any schoolboy sniper could have routed him with a bird gun. Indeed, his reaction to my reply reminds me of an incident which occurred during the 1937 Recession when a companion and I were hunting the country outside Dayton, Ohio.

There had been a heavy snowfall and we had just put up a covey of quail from a thicket which edged a field when, through the rising whirr of the rocketing, snow-shattering birds, we saw, emerging from a clump of trees across the field, a large, red-faced, mackinawed farmer, who came running toward us shouting and brandishing a rifle. I could see strands of moisture tearing from his working mouth as he came on, running like a bear across the whiteness, the brown birds veering and scattering before him; and standing there against the snow, a white hill behind me and with no tree nor foxhole for cover I felt as exposed as a Black Muslim caught at a meeting of the K.K.K.

He had appeared as suddenly as the quail, and although the rifle was not yet to his shoulder, I was transfixed, watching him zooming up to become the largest, loudest, most aggressive-sounding white man I'd seen in my life, and I was, quite frankly, afraid. Then I was measuring his aproach to the crunching tempo of his running and praying silently that he'd come within range of my shotgun before he fired; that I would be able to do what seemed necessary for me to do; that, shooting from the hip with an old twelve-gauge shotgun, I could stop him before he could shoot either me or my companion; and that, though stopped effectively, he would be neither killed, nor blinded, nor maimed.

It was a mixed-up prayer in an icy interval which ended in a smoking fury of cursing, when, at a warning from my companion, the farmer suddenly halted. Then we learned that the reckless man had meant only to warn us off of land which was not even his but that of a neighbor—my companion's foster father. He stood there between the two shotguns pointing short-ranged at his middle, his face quite drained of color now by the realization of how close to death he'd come, sputtering indignantly that we'd interpreted his rifle, which wasn't loaded, in a manner other than he'd intended. He truly did not realize that situations can be more loaded than guns and gestures more eloquent than words.

Fortunately, words are not rifles, but perhaps Howe is just as innocent of the rhetorical eloquence of situations as the farmer. He does not see that the meaning which emerges from his essay is not determined by isolated statements, but by the juxtaposition of those statements in a context which creates a larger statement. Or that contributing to the judgment rendered by that larger statement is the tone in which it is uttered. When Howe pits Baldwin and Ellison against Wright and then gives Wright the better of the argument by using such emotionally weighted terms as "remembered" and "kept faith," the implication to me is that Baldwin and Ellison did *not* remember or keep faith with those who remained behind. If this be true, then I think that in this instance "villain" is not too strong a term.

Howe is not the first writer given to sociological categories who has had unconscious value judgments slip into his "analytical" or "scientific" descriptions. Thus I can believe that his approach was meant to be "analytic, not exhortatory; descriptive, not prescriptive." The results, however, are something else again. And are we to believe that he simply does not recognize rhetoric when he practices it? That when he asks, "what *could* [his italics] the experience of a man with a black skin be . . ." etc., he thinks he is describing a situation as viewed by each and every Negro writer rather than expressing, yes, and in the mode of "exhortation," the views of Irving Howe? Doesn't he recognize that just as the anti-Negro stereotype is a command to Negroes to mold themselves in its image, there sounds through his descriptive "thus it is" the command "thus you become"? And doesn't he realize that in this emotion-charged area definitive description is, in effect, prescription? If he does not, how then can we depend upon his "analysis" of politics or his reading of fiction?

Perhaps Howe could relax his views concerning the situation of the writers with a "black skin" if he examined some of the meanings which he gives to the word "Negro." He contends that I "cannot help being caught up with *the idea* of the Negro," but I have never said that I could or wished to do so—only Howe makes a problem for me here. When he uses the term "Negro" he speaks of it as a "stigma," and again, he speaks of "Negro-ness" as a "sterile category." He sees the Negro writer as experiencing a "constant pressure upon his literary work" from the "sociology of his existence . . . not merely in the way this might be true of any writer, but with a *pain* and *ferocity* that nothing could remove."[1]

Note that this is a condition arising from a *collective* experience which leaves no room for the individual writer's unique existence. It leaves no room for that intensity of personal anguish which compels the artist to seek relief by projecting it into the world in conjunction with other things; that anguish which might take the form of an acute sense of inferiority for one, homosexuality for another, an overwhelming sense of the absurdity of human life for still another. Nor does it leave room for the experience that might be caused by humiliation, by a harelip, by a stutter, by epilepsy— indeed, by any and everything in this life which plunges the talented individual into solitude while leaving him the will to transcend his condition through art. The individual Negro writer must create out of his own special needs and through his own sensibilities, and these alone. Otherwise, all those who suffer in anonymity would be creators.

Howe makes of "Negro-ness" a metaphysical condition, one that is a state of irremediable agony which all but engulfs the mind. Happily, the view from inside the skin is not so dark as it appears to be from Howe's remote position, and therefore my view of "Negro-ness" is neither his nor that of the exponents of *negritude*. It is not skin color which makes a Negro American but cultural heritage as shaped by the American experience, the social and political predicament; a sharing of that "concord of sensibilities" which the group expresses through historical circumstances and through which it has come to constitute a subdivision of the larger American culture. Being a Negro American has to do with the memory of slavery and the hope of emancipation and the betrayal by allies and the revenge and contempt inflicted by our former masters after the Reconstruction, and the myths, both Northern and Southern, which are propagated in justification of that betrayal. It involves, too, a special attitude toward the waves of immigrants who have come later and passed us by.

It has to do with a special perspective on the national ideals and the national conduct, and with a tragicomic attitude toward the universe. It has to do with special emotions evoked by the details of cities and countrysides, with forms of labor and with forms of pleasure; with sex and with love, with food and with drink, with machines and with animals; with climates and with dwellings, with places of worship and places of entertainment; with garments and dreams and idioms of speech; with manners and customs, with religion and art, with life styles and hoping, and with that special sense of predicament and fate which gives direction and resonance to the Freedom Movement. It involves a rugged initiation into

[1] Italics mine.

the mysteries and rites of color which makes it possible for Negro Americans to suffer the injustice which race and color are used to excuse without losing sight of either the humanity of those who inflict that injustice or the motives, rational or irrational, out of which they act. It imposes the uneasy burden and occasional joy of a complex double vision, a fluid, ambivalent response to men and events which represents, at its finest, a profoundly civilized adjustment to the cost of being human in this modern world.

More important, perhaps, being a Negro American involves a *willed* (who wills to be a Negro? I do!) affirmation of self as against all outside pressures—an indentification with the group as extended through the individual self which rejects all possibilities of escape that do not involve a basic resuscitation of the original American ideals of social and political justice. And those white Negroes (and I do not mean Norman Mailer's dream creatures) are Negroes too—if they wish to be.

Howe's defense against my charge that he sees unrelieved suffering as the basic reality of Negro life is to quote favorable comments from his review of *Invisible Man*. But this does not cancel out the restricted meaning which he gives to "Negro-ness," or his statement that "the sociology of [the Negro writer's] existence forms a constant pressure with a *pain* and *ferocity* that nothing could remove." He charges me with unfairness for writing that he believes ideological militancy is more important than writing well, yet he tells us that "there may of course be times when one's obligation as a human being supersedes one's obligation as a writer. . . ." I think that the writer's obligation in a struggle as broad and abiding as the one we are engaged in, which involves not merely Negroes but all Americans, is best carried out through his role as writer. And if he chooses to stop writing and take to the platform, then it should be out of personal choice and not under pressure from would-be managers of society.

Howe plays a game of pitty-pat with Baldwin and Ellison. First he throws them into the pit for lacking Wright's "pain," "ferocity," "memory," "faithfulness" and "clenched militance," then he pats them on the head for the quality of their writing. If he would see evidence of his statement, let him observe how these terms come up in his original essay when he traces Baldwin's move toward Wright's position. Howe's rhetoric is weighted against "more modulated tones" in favor of "rasping outbursts," the Baldwin of *Another Country* becomes "a voice of anger, rasping and thrusting," and he is no longer "held back" by the "proprieties of literature." The character of Rufus in that novel displays a "ferocity" quite new in Baldwin's fiction, and Baldwin's essays gain resonance from "the tone of unrelenting protest . . . from [their] very anger, even the violence," etc. I am afraid that these are "good" terms in Howe's essay and they led to part of my judgment.

In defense of Wright's novel *The Long Dream*, Howe can write:

. . . This book has been attacked for presenting Negro life in the South through "old-fashioned" images of violence, but [and now we have "prescription"] one ought to hesitate before denying the relevance of such images or joining in the criticism of their use. *For Wright was perhaps justified* in not paying attention to the changes that have occurred in the South these past few decades.[2]

If this isn't a defense, if not of bad writing at least of an irresponsible attitude toward good writing, I simply do not understand the language. I find it astonishing advice, since novels exist, since the fictional spell comes into existence precisely through the care which the novelist gives to selecting the details, the images, the tonalities, the specific social and psychological processes of specific characters in specific milieus at specific points in time. Indeed, it is one of the main tenets of the novelist's morality that he should write of that which he knows, and this is especially crucial for novelists who deal with a society as mobile and rapidly changing as ours. To justify ignoring this basic obligation is to encourage the downgrading of literature in favor of other values, in this instance "anger," "protest" and "clenched militancy." Novelists create not simply out of "memory" but out of memory modified, extended, transformed by social change. For a novelist to heed such advice as Howe's is to commit an act of artistic immorality. Amplify this back through society and the writer's failure could produce not order but chaos.

Yet Howe proceeds on the very next page of his essay to state, with no sense of contradiction, that Wright failed in some of the stories which comprise *Eight Men* ("The Man Who Lived Underground" was first published, by the way, in 1944) because he needed the "accumulated material of circumstance." If a novelist ignores social change, how can he come by the "accumulated material of circumstance"? Perhaps if Howe could grasp the full meaning of that phrase he would understand that Wright did not report in *Black Boy* much of his life in Mississippi, and he would see that Ross Barnett is not the whole state, that there is also a Negro Mississippi which is much more varied than that which Wright depicted.

For the critic there simply exists no substitute for the knowledge of history and literary tradition. Howe stresses Wright's comment that when he went into rooms where there were naked white women he felt like a

[2] Italics mine.

"non-man . . . doubly cast out." But had Howe thought about it he might have questioned this reaction, since most young men would have been delighted with the opportunity to study, at first hand, women usually cloaked in an armor of taboos. I wonder how Wright felt when he saw Negro women acting just as shamelessly? Clearly this was an ideological point, not a factual report. And anyone aware of the folk sources of Wright's efforts to create literature would recognize that the situation is identical with that of the countless stories which Negro men tell of the male slave called in to wash the mistress' back in the bath, of the Pullman porter invited in to share the beautiful white passenger's favors in the berth, of the bellhop seduced by the wealthy blond guest.

It is interesting that Howe should interpret my statement about Mississippi as evidence of a loss of self-control. So allow me to repeat it coldly: I fear the implications of Howe's ideas concerning the Negro writer's role as actionist more than I do the State of Mississippi. Which is not to deny the viciousness which exists there but to recognize the degree of freedom which also exists there precisely because the repression is relatively crude, or at least it was during Wright's time, and it left the world of literature alone. William Faulkner lived neither in Jefferson nor Frenchman's Bend but in Oxford. He, too, was a Mississippian, just as the boys who helped Wright leave Jackson were the sons of a Negro college president. Both Faulkner and these boys must be recognized as part of the social reality of Mississippi. I said nothing about Ross Barnett, and I certainly did not say that Howe was a "cultural authoritarian," so he should not spread his honor so thin. Rather, let him look to the implications of his thinking.

Yes, and let him learn more about the South and about Negro Americans if he would speak with authority. When he points out that "the young Ralph Ellison, even while reading these great writers, could not in Macon County attend the white man's school or movie house," he certainly appears to have me cornered. But here again he does not know the facts and he underplays choice and will. I rode freight trains to Macon County, Alabama, during the Scottsboro trial because I desired to study with the Negro conductor-composer William L. Dawson, who was, and probably still is, the greatest classical musician in that part of the country. I had no need to attend a white university when the master I wished to study with was available at Tuskegee. Besides, why should I have wished to attend the white state-controlled university where the works of the great writers might not have been so easily available?

As for the movie-going, it is ironic but nonetheless true that one of the few instances where "separate but equal" was truly separate and equal was in a double movie house in the town of Tuskegee, where Negroes and whites were accommodated in parallel theaters, entering from the

same street level through separate entrances and with the Negro side view-
ing the same pictures shortly after the showing for whites had begun. It
was a product of social absurdity and, of course, no real relief from our
resentment over the restriction of our freedom, but the movies were just
as enjoyable or boring. And yet, is not knowing the facts more interesting,
even as an isolated instance, and more stimulating to real thought than
making abstract assumptions? I went to the movies to see pictures, not
to be with whites. I attended a certain college because what I wanted was
there. What is more, I *never* attended a white school from kindergarten
through my three years of college, and yet, like Howe, I have taught and
lectured for some years now at Northern, predominantly white, colleges
and universities.

Perhaps this counts for little, changes little of the general condition of
society, but it *is* factual and it does form a part of my sense of reality because, though it was not a part of Wright's life, it is my own. And if Howe
thinks mine is an isolated instance, let him do a bit of research.

I do not really think that Howe can make a case for himself by bringing up the complimentary remarks which he made about *Invisible Man*.
I did not quarrel with them in 1952, when they were first published, and
I did not quarrel with them in my reply. His is the right of any critic to
make judgment of a novel, and I do not see the point of arguing that I
achieved an aesthetic goal if it did not work for him. I can only ask that
my fiction be judged as art; if it fails, it fails aesthetically, not because I
did or did not fight some ideological battle. I repeat, however, that Howe's
strategy of bringing me into the public quarrel between Baldwin and
Wright was inept. I simply did not belong in the conflict, since I knew,
even then, that protest is *not* the source of the inadequacy characteristic
of most novels by Negroes, but the simple failure of craft, bad writing;
the desire to have protest perform the difficult tasks of art; the belief that
racial suffering, social injustice or ideologies of whatever mammy-made
variety, is enough. I know, also, that when the work of Negro writers has
been rejected they have all too often protected their egos by blaming racial
discrimination, while turning away from the fairly obvious fact that good
art—and Negro musicians are ever present to demonstrate this—commands attention of itself, whatever the writer's politics or point of view.
And they forget that publishers will publish almost anything which is
written with even a minimum of competency, and that skill is developed
by hard work, study and a conscious assault upon one's own fear and
provincialism.

I agree with Howe that protest is an element of all art, though it does
not necessarily take the form of speaking for a political or social program.
It might appear in a novel as a technical assault against the styles which
have gone before, or as protest against the human condition. If *Invisible*

Man is even "apparently" free from "the ideological and emotional penalties suffered by Negroes in this country," it is because I tried to the best of my ability to transform these elements into art. My goal was not to escape, or hold back, but to work through; to transcend, as the blues transcend the painful conditions with which they deal. The protest is there, not because I was helpless before my racial condition, but because I *put* it there. If there is anything "miraculous" about the book it is the result of hard work undertaken in the belief that the work of art is important in itself, that it is a social action in itself.

I cannot hope to persuade Irving Howe to this view, for it seems quite obvious that he believes there are matters more important than artistic scrupulousness. I will point out, though, that the laws of literary form exert their validity upon all those who write, and that it is his slighting of the formal necessities of his essay which makes for some of our misunderstanding. After reading his reply, I gave in to my ear's suggestion that I had read certain of his phrases somewhere before, and I went to the library, where I discovered that much of his essay was taken verbatim from a review in the *Nation* of May 10, 1952, and that another section was published verbatim in the *New Republic* of February 13, 1962; the latter, by the way, being in its original context a balanced appraisal and warm farewell to Richard Wright.

But when Howe spliced these materials together with phrases from an old speech of mine, swipes at the critics of the *Sewanee* and *Kenyon* reviews (journals in which I have never published), and the Baldwin-Wright quarrel, the effect was something other than he must have intended. A dialectical transformation into a new quality took place and despite the intention of Howe's content, the form made its own statement. If he would find the absurdities he wants me to reduce to a quotation, he will really have to read his essay whole. One gets the impression that he did a paste-and-scissors job and, knowing what he intended, knowing how the separated pieces had operated by themselves, did not bother to read very carefully their combined effect. It could happen to anyone; nevertheless, I'm glad he is not a scientist or a social engineer.

I do not understand why Howe thinks I said anything on the subject of writing about "Negro experience" in a manner which excludes what he calls "plight and protest"; he must have gotten his Negroes mixed. But as to answering his question concerning the "ways a Negro writer can achieve personal realization apart from the common effort of his people to win their full freedom," I suggest that he ask himself in what way shall a Negro writer achieve personal realization (as writer) *after* his people shall have won their full freedom? The answer appears to be the same in both instances: He will have to go it alone! He must suffer alone even as he shares the suffering of his group, and he must write alone and pit his talents against the standards set by the best practitioners of the craft, both past and present, in any case. For the writer's real way of sharing the experience of his group is to convert its mutual suffering into lasting value. Is Howe suggesting, incidentally, that Heinrich Heine did not exist?

His question is silly, really, for there is no such thing as "full freedom" (Oh, how Howe thirsts and hungers for the absolute for *Negroes!*), just as the notion of an equality of talent is silly. I am a Negro who once played trumpet with certain skill, but alas, I am no Louis Armstrong or Clark Terry. Willie Mays has realized himself quite handsomely as an individual despite coming from an impoverished Negro background in oppressive Alabama; and Negro Americans, like most Americans who know the value of baseball, exult in his success. I am, after all, only a minor member, not the whole damned tribe; in fact, most Negroes have have never heard of me. I could shake the nation for a while with a crime or with indecent disclosures, but my pride lies in earning the right to call myself quite simply "writer." Perhaps if I write well enough the children of today's Negroes will be proud that I did, and so, perhaps, will Irving Howe's.

Let me end with a personal note: Dear Irving, I have no objections to being placed beside Richard Wright in any estimation which is based not upon the irremediable ground of our common racial identity, but upon the quality of our achievements as writers. I respected Wright's work and I knew him, but this is not to say that he "influenced" me as significantly as you assume. Consult the text! I *sought out* Wright because I had read Eliot, Pound, Gertrude Stein and Hemingway, and as early as 1940 Wright viewed me as a potential rival, partially, it is true, because he feared I would allow myself to be used against him by political manipulators who were not Negro and who envied and hated him. But perhaps you will understand when I say he did not influence me if I point out that while one can do nothing about choosing one's relatives, one can, as artist, choose one's "ancestors." Wright was, in this sense, a "relative"; Hemingway an "ancestor." Langston Hughes, whose work I knew in grade school and whom I knew before I knew Wright, was a "relative"; Eliot, whom I was to meet only many years later, and Malraux and Dostoevski and Faulkner, were "ancestors"—if you please or don't please!

Do you still ask why Hemingway was more important to me than Wright? Not because he was white, or more "accepted." But because he appreciated the things of this earth which I love and which Wright was too driven or deprived or inexperienced to know: weather, guns, dogs, horses, love *and* hate and impossible circumstances which to the courageous and dedicated could be turned into benefits and victories. Because he wrote with such precision about the processes and techniques of daily living that I could keep myself and my brother alive during the 1937 Recession by following his descriptions of wing-shooting; because he knew the difference between politics and art and something of their true relationship for the writer. Because all that he wrote—and this is very important—was imbued with a spirit beyond the tragic with which I could feel at home, for it was very close to the feeling of the blues, which are, perhaps, as close as Americans can come to expressing the spirit of tragedy. (And if you think Wright knew anything about the blues, listen to a "blues" he composed with Paul Robeson singing, a *most* unfortunate collaboration!; and read his introduction to Paul Oliver's *Blues Fell This Morning*.) But most important, because Hemingway was a greater artist than Wright, who although a Negro like myself, and perhaps a great man, understood little if anything of these, at least to me, important things. Because Hemingway loved the American language and the joy of writing, making the flight of birds, the loping of lions across an African plain, the mysteries of drink and moonlight, the unique styles of diverse peoples and individuals come alive on the page. Because he was in many ways the true father-as-artist of so many of us who came to writing during the late thirties.

I will not dwell upon Hemingway's activities in Spain or during the liberation in Paris, for you know all of that. I will remind you, however, that any writer takes what he needs to get his own work done from wherever he finds it. I did not need Wright to tell me how to be a Negro, or how to be angry or to express anger—Joe Louis was doing that very well—or even to teach me about socialism; my mother had canvassed for the socialists, not the communists, the year I was born. No, I had been a Negro for twenty-two or twenty-three years when I met Wright, and in more places and under a greater variety of circumstances than he had then known. He was generously helpful in sharing his ideas and information, but I needed instruction in other values and I found them in the works of other writers—Hemingway was one of them, T. S. Eliot initiated the search.

I like your part about Chekhov arising from his sickbed to visit the penal colony at Sakhalin Island. It was, as you say, a noble act. But shouldn't we remember that it was significant only because Chekhov was *Chekhov*, the great writer? You compliment me truly, but I have not written so much or so well, even though I *have* served a certain apprenticeship in the streets and even touch events in the Freedom Movement in a modest way. But I can also recall the story of a certain writer who succeeded with a great fanfare of publicity in having a talented murderer released from prison. It made for another very short story which ended quite tragically—though not for the writer: A few months after his release the man killed the mother of two young children. I also know of another really quite brilliant writer who, under the advice of certain wise men who were then managing the consciences of artists, abandoned the prison of his writing to go to Spain, where he was allowed to throw away his life defending a worthless hill. I have not heard his name in years but I remember it vividly; it was Christopher Cauldwell, *né* Christopher St. John Sprigg. There are many such stories, Irving. It's heads you win, tails you lose, and you are quite right about my not following Baldwin, who is urged on by a nobility—or is it a demon—quite different from my own. It has cost me quite a pretty penny, indeed, but then I was always poor and not (and I know this is a sin in our America) too uncomfortable.

Dear Irving, I am still yakking on and there's many a thousand gone, but I assure you that no Negroes are beating down my door, putting pressure on me to join the Negro Freedom Movement, for the simple reason that they realize that I am enlisted for the duration. Such pressure is coming only from a few disinterested "military advisers," since Negroes want no more fairly articulate would-be Negro leaders cluttering up the airways. For, you see, my Negro friends recognize a certain division of labor among the members of the tribe. Their demands, like that of many whites, are that I publish more novels—and here I am remiss and vulnerable perhaps. You will recall what the Talmud has to say about the trees of the forest and the making of books, etc. But then, Irving, they recognize what you have not allowed yourself to see; namely, that my reply to your essay is in itself a small though necessary action in the Negro struggle for freedom. You should not feel unhappy about this or think that I regard you either as dishonorable or an enemy. I hope, rather, that you will come to view this exchange as an act of, shall we say, "antagonistic co-operation"?

BLACK MAGIC, BLACK ART[*]

Ronald Miller

RECENTLY in New York a friend of mine handed me an advertisement for a poetry reading, a card, which declared in bold letters: BLACK MAGIC, BLACK ART, WILL TOPPLE THE CITADEL OF WHITE RACIST AMERICA! He smirked as I looked at the card, and told me that Art wasn't gonna' do sh—! My friend is one of those who believe we black artists should beat our saxophones and typewriters into spears and daggers, and each pick out a white pelt and be recorded in History as The Black Assassin Saints. Which isn't what Stokely means by Black Power.

But, getting back to the card, my buddy had picked the wrong time to try to rile me into an argument on the relevance of art: One, the New York critical establishment had just hung my play out for target-practice;[1] two, in this same day, I had seen two brilliant, black poet-playwrights, of two widely separated generations, both of whom were struggling through New York like crippled lizards. So, rather than going a few verbal rounds with him, I told my friend something vulgar and sat down. He respected my mood and just shut-up and let Charlie Parker talk.

Well, we sat there with Bird playing, and me wishing for my wife— she was here on campus—or maybe a whole harem, or some religion I could believe in, or—something.

And I kept looking at this card: Black Art Will Destroy White Racist America. I thought about the work of the two writers I had seen earlier. Of men like Richard Wright, James Baldwin, and Ralph Ellison. And there was Charlie Parker on the box—a black man with his art: Was all that flowing, convoluted beauty Charlie was pushing considered black magic too? Would it topple white racist America?

I remembered a white guy, Dave, let's say, in Detroit, telling me that when he started listening to Parker, Clifford Brown, and others, he knew he couldn't keep on being scared of "black cats" and, in his words, "protecting myself with the stereotypes"; so he started making the jazz-sets

[1] *Who's Got His Own*, produced by the American Place Theatre, New York.

[*] Reprinted from *Negro Digest*, XVI (1967), 9–12 +, by permission of the author and editors.

and introduced himself to some black people. I think he even, eventually, went South with one of the Rights groups. So when Charlie led Dave to shake hands with black-folks, something had toppled, right? Some preconceptions and stereotypes, certainly. Dave had at least stepped toward that frenetic, frightening darkness from which all that music was being shaped. Good!

But suppose—and it occurred to me because he had all the makings—Dave turned out to be one of those Quixote-Lone Ranger-complexed ones who couldn't stand reprimands and commands from the supposed Sanchoes and Tontoes who were now asserting themselves and their own directions, and so found it easier to protest for the Vietnamese who would not try to regulate methods or positions in the protest? One of those totally committed, as long as the means and ends fit the terms of their own vision of things; but completely unable to understand it when a Malcolm X, or Stokely C, tells them that their physical, psychological image goes counter to the needed impact on ripped and self-doubting black minds! that at best he can be a silent partner, plotting with black men around conference tables, but having his true—real—work to do, alone, in places like Cicero, Illinois, and hillbilly country southern America, where at least he can order a cup of coffee and begin to talk to people before trouble starts, can even move in and start a club or something? Suppose Dave was one of those who would rather try to protest across oceans than have black men point directions for him? Still good. Charlie had still helped topple something within Dave—broken the God-is-always-on-our-side idea; inspired the step that led to protest. Yeh, still a score for Black Art, Black Magic, if you will. I intended to run that point down to my friend.

But I stopped myself as I anticipated a possible, and very disturbing, reaction of his. There is a bitter line in my play: "Fightin' or fussin', beggin' or cussin', you always gotta' go through Chuck." And here, immediately, I had jumped to that side of the fence to prove a point, to establish validity; unconsciously, automatically. Damn! It's enough to make you go vomiting through the house breaking all the mirrors!

Now it is *white racist* America which must be toppled, destroyed. The one which exploits race and class denies the truth of man's sameness to all men. Not that ideal racial-rainbow that now and again incredibly peeps through and has set forth ideas and methods to better man's people-to-people relationships. But that greenbacked, red, white, and blue-bellied snake. That's the one that has to go! Now it sits heaviest on the heads of black men. And to speak of the black artist's power to topple it is to get into the whole idea of black men's self-assertion, of black men going and doing for themselves. If I were going to say something, I had to talk first of what black men's art did to and for black men; what it made them feel and want to assert. I had to get to why the two of us were sitting there listening to Bird as though the room were suddenly a mosque and this music was the chant of the true believers.

I don't know about my friend Ray, but when I first heard Charlie it was like . . . well, let me put it just like it was: Like all boys, I depended on the things I saw and heard around me for self-clarification, for reaffirmations of my urges and longings, intuitions and impulses; to give me some idea of my way of being. So I went along finger-popping, shaking my hips, doing the chicken, getting some little Mama's skirt dirty as we rubbed bellies against the wall to one of those syrupy beats, you know. And in that Detroit, Hastings Street environment everything was about like that kind of music—in that register, with that kind of focus-point: bluesy and groovy, you know. I dug it. It was cool. But always I had this frustrated, intuitive vibration; this sense of never really hearing or seeing anything truly indicative of all that was me, or nearly all. That foot-patting, shoulder-dipping, pelvic-evoluting groove was all right. But I needed some more image, some further, higher points of self-reflection. Then I stumbled onto what Charlie Parker, Bud Powell and others were doing!

And lo, affirmations, affirmations, affirmations! Those quick changing rhythms! That involved lyricism! The shifting harmonies! The speaking not only in two or three shouted words, but in long flowing complex sentences. How can I tell you about the sudden possibilities this music brought to me? The ceiling lifted, and out went my sense of freakishness. Here was what I could not get from white movies, no matter how good they were. Here was that intangible difference in the way Ernie Wagner moved up the basketball court for Northeastern High and the way Karl Kawalski came down for Denby High. In what seemed so strange and exotic to others—and so real and natural to me—in this music, was something of the reason why I could hardly get a new hat out of the store before I had to break it down and put that particular pointed—jitterbug, if you must—crease in it. You see that hat had to start right away looking like where it had to live and whom it had to suit, not some designer in some factory.

Yes, affirmations and possibilities. Charlie told me by the particular points and creases that he put to old standards like "In the Still of the Night" that I could wear my felt crown to the White House and not have to stumble all over myself trying to act and sound like I was a fourth-generation graduate from Harvard. He crystallized a nuance of being that was very necessary to me: I needed that crease in my hat. He, along with others, updated the sound of things; added intellect to sensuality; sped up the beat so that the foot-patting was still there but now it was like the way you stomp out a cigarette when you've got to clear your mouth because you've got something to say and Life is racing. And, most important, I say once more, that this music was one of the things that convinced me that I could be as black as night and Hastings Street and still be whatever in life I wanted, if only I did it well enough. They might not play my music on the radio, and try to make a joke out of me, but someone, somewhere, would react if I did it well.

Affirmations and inspiration, that is what the black artist must mean to the black man. Speaking of the qualities of himself and his living-place as truthfully and artistically as he can with no one's standards or acceptance in mind but his own, the artist strikes empathy and identification; there is the reaction of acknowledgement, and the changing and toppling—first inner, with the body personal, then outward through the bodies social, political, etc.—is on its way.

And if you think that all this sounds very romantic, you are right. In any revolution, or evolution—if you'd rather—there must be the romantic art: The wishes and longings must be symbolized and projected; the pains and transgressions must be fixed in hated pictures. Jazz—so far, the blackest of the arts—is probably the most romantic music since brother Beethoven gave up the ghost. And that is as it should be.

There is a peculiarly ironic reason for Jazz, America's most indigenous and significant contribution to art, being basically and mainly the work of black men, and for jazz-men being far ahead of all other black artists in true self-expression and assertion. That reason is that only in music were our slave forefathers allowed to retain and nurture anything of Africa—of blackness. *You see, me being white, and the slave-master and all, I ain't about to let you talk in no old tribal language. Naw, no tellin' what you might be gettin' those black heads together on, when I can't understand you. So no story-telling; no passing down traditions, and all that. You'll learn this here language and the right stories outta' this Good-Book, and the lies I got to tell you, and enforce upon you, so's I can sleep at night. That's all. And none of that foolin' roun' with your hands either. You might call it sculpturing and painting, but it looks like Voodoo signs to me. You gonna' paint, paint Christ like Michelangelo and them did. You gonna' make figures out of wood and stone, then put some clothes on 'em and make 'em look more like me than they do, so's I can trust 'em. But, boy, that rhythm you all got with them drums!! And oh, those deep, soulful voices!! I want you to go sing outside the big-house, and out in the fields while you're working—keeps your mind occupied, and it makes everything sound and look and feel so peaceful!*

Yes. That is why the jazz-man is the furthest along in self-assertion and unrestrained, unaccommodating self-expression. Because the slave-master understood the danger in education, but had never gotten to Socrates' warning about the song-makers. So, since music is the most abstract, least concrete or plastic of the arts, the jazz-maker never had to waste precious time proving how well he knew the language and forms of Western man, but went right ahead and bent that European scale to fit his own impulses.

Had jazz-men been using words, or readily definable images, like our writers and painters, then they too would be just now emerging in their true colors; would have been squelched by editors, publishers, and critics. For John Coltrane is a man who, through his saxophone, before your eyes and ears, completely annihilates every single Western influence, and longs and strains so totally, so desperately for the Asian-African nuance that soon he is actually there in his playing—as a man who calls on his Gods and lo! they appear. This is the same thing as the Afro-haircuts and clothes worn by people who have never been further East than Boston—a rejection and a yearning. It may seem all a ridiculous joke to you. But it's no less an effective and important joke than the one which was once recorded as law in this country: that two Indians and one African—or vice-versa, I'm not sure—constituted, legally, one human being. Yeh, funny, huh?

Now, getting back to the music. There is another saxophonist named Pharaoh Saunders who plays horrible lynch-scenes with barking dogs and all coming out of his horn, and then—to my strange mind, at least—goes into the massacre of the resultant retaliation, with the bleeding screams of men, women, and children. When he finishes, you don't know whether to applaud or go ask for an aspirin and a boat-ticket to somewhere else. But it is Truth! As he has witnessed and visualizes it. It is an artful projection.

There are other men, like Sonny Rollins and Ornette Coleman, who play so starkly, freely personal, that one knows that somehow they have felt nearly all the stimuli and hangups of this place and this time; have gone into themselves somewhere and found new scales; new harmonies— a new religion, in fact. Now isn't that frighteningly interesting? And what would it sound like in words; appear as in definite symbols and images? Would it affect the Selective-Service Draft, do you think? Make for further boycotts and rejections?

With verbal jazz-men, like LeRoi Jones, adding and explaining dimensions, what will this yearning for the destruction of things Western and the exulting of things Eastern, and this other personal insulation, come to mean when it has all hit earth and settled? I honestly do not know. I only know that, at least psychically, there will be changes, good changes. It is as I eventually answered my friend: "Black Art can do a lot to topple white, racist America, if it is *black* enough."

What do I mean by black enough? Well, let me try to give some examples of what I mean by Black Art, or more specifically black literature.

I mean, when a black writer really works inside that 60-year-old Sister Sadie who has been a rock of her church for some thirty years and finds that she is a black nun, loving and giving herself to her—"her"—Jesus with a passion and a need that Catholics only dream guiltily about; that there are such things in that African-Baptist dance she does when the "spirit" hits her that are hardly imaginable to most people.

I mean, when a writer looks into one of those housing projects and sees Anna Karenina, or a Madame Bovary—with a different hue, tone, and manner of course—and just when the world-reader is panting for her and hoping that her plans work out, the writer drops in the bigoted white cop of this black ghetto setting, like a filthy stink-bomb, and splatters the love story all to hell with a quick trigger-finger. That's more like what blackness in this country is like: Life being stopped because its covering, its skin, is taboo.

I mean, putting John Henry on the stage with his pride and hammers and wife, family, neighbors; and have him go roaring against automation and the enslavement of the human spirit; cussing, fighting, loving and hating all the way—coming down hard on anybody and anything standing against his simple truth: "Aw, a man ain't nothin' but a man!"

I mean, a writer examining that crude, but almost reflexive phrase, the big MF, and seeing it in Matriarch Feeding Oedipus Complex coming out of the emasculation of the Black Male and Father Image and the Historic Rape of the Black Woman; and finding the way to explode that phrase into full meaning and consciousness. I mean, a writer sitting the late and great Malcolm X down with us and letting us hear the to-be's and not-to-be's of a more modern and unique Hamlet. I mean seeing on paper how a black ghetto organizes politically and otherwise against the pressures of government, police, landlords, and Mafia. The fictionist is free to project never-before-seen times, places, and circumstances. He's the one who's supposed to be sitting up all night talking on and raking over the sins of the world, is he not?

I mean, a way of literarily stylizing that little bounce-dip in the walks, those creases and points in those hats. I mean, a literature knowing that, since it deals with human beings, the universals will fall no matter what, if the reader's lap is open, so concerning itself with colloquials, the little shades and nuances that come out of unique life-experiences, and environmental influences. A literature that asserts rather than reacts; states rather than explains. That is what I mean by black literature, and when this literature—as did Irish, Russian, French, and earlier American literature—finally comes into being, adding its weight to all the other force factors in the air, there will be a change in the consciousness, the self-sense, of this country, this people; and something must topple, must give way to the changes.

Bibliography

THE FOLLOWING BIBLIOGRAPHY is intended to be reasonably complete though by no means exhaustive. It makes no attempt, for example, to include the numerous reviews of the works of these authors nor to include articles which would not be of obvious use to the critic and scholar. There has been no attempt to list books which mention these writers unless the comment is extensive.

RICHARD WRIGHT

Baldwin, James. "Many Thousands Gone." *Partisan Review*, XVII, 665–80. Reprinted in *Notes of a Native Son*. Boston: Beacon Press, 1955.

———. "Richard Wright." *Encounter*, XVI, 58–60.

Bone, Robert A. *The Negro Novel in America*. New Haven: Yale University Press, 1958.

Brignano, Russell C. "Richard Wright: The Major Themes, Ideas and Attitudes in His Work." *Dissertation Abstracts*, XVIII, 666A–7A (University of Wisconsin).

Burgum, Edwin Berry. "The Art of Richard Wright's Short Stories." *The Novel and the World's Dilemma*. New York: Oxford University Press, 1947. Reissued by Russell and Russell, 1963.

———. "The Promise of Democracy in Richard Wright's *Native Son*." *The Novel and the World's Dilemma*. New York: Oxford University Press, 1947. Reissued by Russell and Russell, 1963.

Cayton, Horace. "Frightened Children of Frightened Parents." *Twice A Year*, XII–XIII, 262–9.

Cohn, David L. "The Negro Novel: Richard Wright." *Atlantic Monthly*, CLXV, 659–61.

Creekmore, Hubert. "Social Factors in *Native Son*." *University of Kansas City Review*, VIII, 136–43.

Davis, Arthur P. "*The Outsider* as a Novel of Race." *Midwest Journal*, VII, 320–6.

Dempsey, David. "Uncle Tom's Ghost and the Literary Abolitionists." *Antioch Review*, VI, 442–8.

Ellison, Ralph. "Richard Wright's Blues." *Antioch Review*, V, 198–211.

Fabre, Michel and Edward Margolies. "Richard Wright (1908–1960)." *Bulletin of Bibliography*, XXIV, 131–3, 137.

Ford, Nick Aaron. "The Ordeal of Richard Wright." *College English*, XV, 87–94.

———. "Richard Wright, a Profile." *Chicago Jewish Forum*, XXI, 26–30.

Gibson, Donald B. "Richard Wright and the Tyranny of Convention." *CLA Journal*, XII, 344–57.

———. "Richard Wright: A Bibliographical Essay." *CLA Journal*, XII, 360–65.

Glicksberg, Charles I. "Existentialism in *The Outsider.*" *Four Quarters*, VII, 17–26.

———. "Negro Fiction in America." *South Atlantic Quarterly*, XLV, 477–88.

Gloster, Hugh. *Negro Voices in American Fiction*. Chapel Hill: University of North Carolina Press, 1948.

Gray, Yohma. "An American Metaphor: The Novels of Richard Wright." *Dissertation Abstracts*, XXVIII, 4175A (Yale).

Green, Gerald. "Back to Bigger." *Proletarian Writers of the Thirties*. David Madden, ed. Carbondale: Southern Illinois University Press, 1968.

Hand, Clifford. "The Struggle to Create Life in the Fiction of Richard Wright." *The Thirties: Fiction, Poetry, Drama*. Warren French, ed. DeLand, Florida: Everett Edwards, Inc., 1967, pp. 81–7.

Hill, Herbert, moderator. "Reflections on Richard Wright: A Symposium on an Exiled Native Son." *Anger and Beyond*. New York: Harper & Row, Publishers, 1966.

Hughes, Carl Milton. *The Negro Novelist*. New York: Citadel Press, 1953.

Isaacs, Harold R. "Five Writers and Their African Ancestors." *Phylon*, XXI, 243–65.

Jackson, Blyden. "Richard Wright: Black Boy from America's Black Belt and Urban Ghetto." *CLA Journal*, XII, 287–309.

Kent, George. "Richard Wright: Blackness and the Adventure of Western Culture." *CLA Journal*, XII, 322–43.

———. "On the Future Study of Richard Wright." *CLA Journal*, XII, 366–70.

Kinnamon, Kenneth. "Richard Wright Items in the Fales Collection." *Bulletin of the Society for the Libraries of New York University*, No. 66, p. 4.

———. "Richard Wright's Use of *Othello* in *Native Son.*" *CLA Journal*, XII, 358–59.

Knipp, Thomas, ed. *Richard Wright: Letters to Joe C. Brown*. With an Introduction. Kent, Ohio: Kent State University Library Occasional Papers, 1968.

Knox, George. "The Negro Novelist's Sensibility and the Outsider Theme." *Western Humanities Review*, XI, 137–48.

Lehan, Richard. "Existentialism in Recent American Fiction: The Demonic Quest." *Texas Studies in Literature and Language*, I, 181–202.

Lewis, Theophilus. "Saga of Bigger Thomas." *Catholic World*, CLIII, 201–6.

McCall, Dan. *The Example of Richard Wright*. New York: Harcourt, Brace & World, 1969.

Margolies, Edward. *The Art of Richard Wright*. Carbondale, Illinois: Southern Illinois University Press, 1969.

———. "A Critical Analysis of the Works of Richard Wright." *Dissertation Abstracts*, XXVII, 1829A–30A (New York University).

———. "Richard Wright: *Native Son* and Three Kinds of Revolution." *Native Sons*. New York: J. B. Lippincott Co., 1969.

———. *See* Fabre, Michel.

Rascoe, Burton. "Negro Novel and White Reviewers: Richard Wright's *Native Son.*" *American Mercury*, L, 113–17.

Redding, Saunders. "The Alien Land of Richard Wright." *Soon, One Morning: New Writing by American Negroes*. Herbert Hill, ed. New York: Alfred A. Knopf, 1963.

Reilly, John. "Afterword" in Richard Wright, *Native Son*. New York: Perennial Classics, 1966.

———. "Insight and Protest in the Works of Richard Wright." *Dissertation Abstracts*, XXVIII, 4185A–6A (Washington University).

Riesman, David. "Marginality, Conformity, and Insight." *Phylon*, XIV, 241–57.

Scott, Nathan A., Jr. "The Dark and Haunted Tower of Richard Wright." *Graduate Comment* (Wayne State University), VII, 93–9.

———. "Search for Beliefs: The Fiction of Richard Wright." *University of Kansas City Review*, XXIII (1924), 19–24.

———. "Search for Beliefs: Richard Wright." *University of Kansas City Review*, XXIII, 131–8.

Slochower, Harry. *No Voice is Wholly Lost*. New York: Creative Age Press, 1945.

Stillen, Samuel. "The Meaning of Bigger Thomas." *New Masses*, XXXV, 13–21.

Sullivan, Richard. "Afterword" in Richard Wright, *Native Son*. New York: Signet, 1950.

Turner, Darwin. "*The Outsider*: Revision of an Idea." *CLA Journal*, XII, 310–21.

Webb, Constance. *Richard Wright*. New York: George Putnam's Sons, 1968.

———. "What Next for Richard Wright?" *Phylon*, II, 161–6.

White, Ralph. "Black Boy: A Value Analysis." *Journal of Abnormal Psychology*, XLII, 440–61.

Zietlow, Edward R. "Wright to Hansberry: The Evolution of Outlook in Four Negro Writers." *Dissertation Abstracts*, XXVIII, 701A (University of Washington). [Wright, Ellison, Baldwin, Hansberry].

RALPH ELLISON

Baumbach, Jonathan. "Nightmare of a Native Son: Ellison's *Invisible Man*." *Criticism*, VI, 48–65. Reprinted in *The Landscape of Nightmare*. New York: New York University Press, 1965.

Bennett, John Z. "The Race and the Runner: Ellison's *Invisible Man*." *Xavier University Studies*, V, 12–26.

Bloch, Alice. "Sight Imagery in *Invisible Man*." *English Journal*, LV, 1019–21, 1024.

Bone, Robert. *The Negro Novel in America*. New Haven: Yale University Press, 1958, pp. 196–212.

———. "Ralph Ellison and the Uses of Imagination." *Anger and Beyond: The Negro Writer in the United States*. Herbert Hill, ed. New York: Harper & Row, Publishers, 1966. Reprinted in *The Tri-Quarterly*, No. 6, pp. 39–54.

Ellison, Ralph. "Light on *Invisible Man*." *Crisis*, LX, 154–6.

———. *Shadow and Act*. New York: Random House, 1964.

Geller, Allen. "An Interview with Ralph Ellison." *Tamarack Review*, No. 32, pp. 3–24.

Glicksberg, Charles. "The Symbolism of Vision." *Southwest Review*, XXXIX, 259–65.

Horowitz, Ellin. "The Rebirth of the Artist." *On Contemporary Literature*. Richard Kostelanetz, ed. New York: Avon, 1964.

Horowitz, Floyd Ross. "The Enigma of Ellison's Intellectual Man." *CLA Journal*, VII, 126–32.

——. "Ralph Ellison's Modern Version of Brer Bear and Brer Rabbit in *Invisible Man*." *Mid-Continent American Studies Journal*, IV, ii, 21–7.

Klein, Marcus. "Ralph Ellison." *After Alienation.* Cleveland: World Publishing Company, 1964.

Kostelanetz, Richard. "The Negro Genius." *Twentieth Century*, MXXXIII, 49–50.

——. "The Politics of Ellison's Booker: *Invisible Man* as Symbolic History." *Chicago Review*, 19, ii, 5–26.

Lehan, Richard. "The Strange Silence of Ralph Ellison." *California English Journal*, I, ii, 63–8.

Mengeling, Marvin E. "Whitman and Ellison: Older Symbols in a Modern Mainstream." *Walt Whitman Review*, XII, 67–70.

O'Daniel, Therman B. "The Image of Man Portrayed by Ralph Ellison." *CLA Journal*, X, 272–84.

Olderman, Raymond M. "Ralph Ellison's Blues and *Invisible Man*." *Wisconsin Studies in Contemporary Literature*, VIII, 142–59.

Rovit, Earl. "Ralph Ellison and the American Comic Tradition." *Wisconsin Studies in Contemporary Literature*, I 34–42.

Schafer, William J. "Ralph Ellison and the Birth of the Anti-Hero." *Critique*, X, ii, 81–93.

Thompson, James, Lennox Raphael, and Steve Cannon. "A Very Stern Discipline: An Interview with Ralph Ellison." *Harper's* Magazine, CCXXXIV (March), 76–95.

Warren, Robert Penn. "The Unity of Experience." *Commentary*, XXXIX, 91–6.

JAMES BALDWIN

Bigsby, C. W. "The Committed Writer: James Baldwin as Dramatist." *Twentieth Century Literature*, XIII, 39–48.

Blount, Trevor. "A Slight Error in Continuity in James Baldwin's *Another Country*." *Notes and Queries*, XIII, 102–3.

Bone, Robert A. "The Novels of James Baldwin." *Tri-Quarterly*, No. 2 (1965), pp. 3–20. Reprinted in Seymour L. Gross and John Edward Hardy, *Images of the Negro in American Literature.* Chicago: University of Chicago Press, 1966.

Bonosky, Phillip. "The Negro Writer and Commitment." *Mainstream*, XV, ii, 16–22.

Boyle, Kay. "Introducing James Baldwin." *Contemporary American Novelists.* Harry T. Moore, ed. Carbondale: Southern Illinois University Press, 1964.

Breit, Harvey. "James Baldwin and Two Footnotes." *The Creative Present: Notes on Contemporary American Fiction.* Nona Balakian and Charles Simmons, eds. Garden City: Doubleday and Co., 1967.

Charney, Maurice. "James Baldwin's Quarrel with Richard Wright." *American Quarterly*, XV, 65–75.

Coles, Robert. "Baldwin's Burden." *Partisan Review*, XXXI, 409–16.

Collier, Eugenia W. "The Phrase Unbearably Repeated." *Phylon*, XXV, 288–96.

Cox, C. B., and A. R. Jones. "After the Tranquilized Fifties: Notes on Sylvia Plath and James Baldwin." *Critical Quarterly*, VI, 107–22.

Eckman, Fern Marja. *The Furious Passage of James Baldwin*. New York: Popular Library, 1966.

Elkoff, Marvin. "Everybody Knows His Name." *Esquire*, LXII, ii, 59–64, 120–3.

Featherstone, J. "Blues for Mr. Baldwin." *New Republic*, CLIII (Nov. 27, 1965), 34–6.

Finn, James. "The Identity of James Baldwin." *Commonweal*, LXXVII, 113–6.

———. "James Baldwin's Vision." *Commonweal*, LXXVII, 447–9.

Fischer, Russell G. "James Baldwin: A Bibliography, 1947–1962." *Bulletin of Bibliography*, XXIV, 127–30.

Foote, Dorothy N. "James Baldwin's 'Holler Books.' " *College English Association Critic*, XXV, viii, 8, 11.

Friedman, Neil. "James Baldwin and Psychotherapy." *Psychotherapy*, III, 177–83.

Gayle, Addison, Jr. "A Defense of James Baldwin." *CLA Journal*, X, 201–8.

Graves, Wallace. "The Question of Moral Energy in James Baldwin's *Go Tell It on the Mountain*." *CLA Journal*, VIII, 215–23.

Gross, Theodore. "The World of James Baldwin." *Critique*, VII, 139–49.

Hagopian, John V. "James Baldwin: The Black and the Red-White-and-Blue." *CLA Journal*, VII, 133–40.

Hassan, Ihab. *Radical Innocence*. Princeton: Princeton University Press, 1961.

Howe, Irving, "James Baldwin: At Ease in Apocalypse." *Harper's* Magazine, 237 (Sept.), 92–100.

Jacobson, Dan. "James Baldwin as Spokesman." *Commentary*, XXXII, 497–502.

Jones, A. R. *See* Cox, C. B.

Kent, George. "Baldwin and the Problem of Being." *CLA Journal*, VII, 202–14.

Kindt, Kathleen A. "James Baldwin: A Checklist, 1947–1962." *Bulletin of Bibliography*, XXIV, 123–6.

Klein, Marcus. "James Baldwin." *After Alienation*. Cleveland: World Publishing Co., 1964.

Lash, John S. "Baldwin Beside Himself: A Study in Modern Phallicism." *CLA Journal*, VIII, 132–40.

Levin, David. "Baldwin's Autobiographical Essays: The Problem of Negro Identity." *Massachusetts Review*, V, 239–47.

Moore, John Rees. "An Embarrassment of Riches: Baldwin's *Going to Meet the Man*." *The Hollins Critic*, II, v, 1–12.

Newman, Charles. "The Lesson of the Master: Henry James and James Baldwin." *Yale Review*, LVI, 45–59.

O'Daniel, Therman. "James Baldwin: An Interpretive Study." *CLA Journal*, VII, 37–47.

Peterson, Fred. "James Baldwin and Eduardo Mallea: Two Essayists' Search for Identity." *Discourse*, X, 97–107.

Phillips, Louis. "The Novelist as Playwright: Baldwin, McCullers, and Bellow" in *Modern American Drama: Essays in Criticism*. DeLand, Florida: Everett Edwards, 1968

Podhoretz, Norman. "In Defense of James Baldwin." *Doings and Undoings*. New York: Farrar, Straus and Company, 1964.

Potter, Vilma. "Baldwin and Odets: The High Cost of 'Crossing.'" *California English Journal*, I, iii, 37–41.

Sayre, Robert F. "James Baldwin's Other Country." *Contemporary American Novelists*. Harry T. Moore, ed. Carbondale: Southern Illinois University Press, 1964.

Schroth, Raymond A., S.J. "James Baldwin's Search." *Catholic World*, CXLVIII, 288–94.

Spender, Stephen. "James Baldwin: Voice of a Revolution." *Partisan Review*, XXX, 256–60.

Standley, Fred L. "James Baldwin: A Checklist, 1963–1967." *Bulletin of Bibliography*, XXV, 135–37, 160.

———. "James Baldwin: The Crucial Situation." *South Atlantic Quarterly*, LXV, 371–81.

Strout, Cushing. "*Uncle Tom's Cabin* and the Portent of Millenium." *Yale Review*, LVII, 375–85.

Watson, Edward A. "The Novels of James Baldwin: Case Book of a 'Lover's War' with the United States." *Queens Quarterly*, LXXII, 385–402.

LANGSTON HUGHES

Arvey, Verna. "Langston Hughes, Crusader." *Opportunity*, XVII, 363–4.

Bontemps, Arna. "Langston Hughes: He Spoke of Rivers." *Freedomways*, VIII, 140–3.

Carmen, Y. "Langston Hughes, Poet of the People." *International Literature*, 1939, No. 1, 192–4.

Clarke, John Hendrick. "Langston Hughes & Jesse B. Semple." *Freedomways*, VIII, 167–9.

Davis, Arthur P. "The Harlem of Langston Hughes' Poetry." *Phylon*, XIII, 276–83. Reprinted in Seymour L. Gross and John Edward Hardy, *Images of the Negro in American Literature*. Chicago: University of Chicago Press, 1966.

———. "Jesse B. Semple: Negro American." *Phylon*, XV, 21–8.

———. "Langston Hughes: Cool Poet." *CLA Journal*, XI, 280–96.

———. "The Tragic Mulatto Theme in Six Works of Langston Hughes." *Phylon*, XVI, 195–204.

Dickinson, Donald Charles. "A Bio-Bibliography of Langston Hughes, 1920–1960." *Dissertation Abstracts*, XXV, 7282–3 (University of Michigan).

Emanuel, James A. *Langston Hughes*. New York: Twayne, 1967.

———. "The Literary Experiments of Langston Hughes." *CLA Journal*, XI, 335–44.

———. "The Short Stories of Langston Hughes." *Dissertation Abstracts*, XXVII, 474A–75A (Columbia University).

———. "Langston Hughes' First Short Story: 'Mary Winosky.'" *Phylon*, XXII, 267–72.

Filatova, Lydia. "Langston Hughes: American Writer." *International Literature*, 1933, No. 2, pp. 103–5.

Holmes, Eugene C. "Langston Hughes: Philosopher Poet." *Freedomways*, VIII, 144–51.

Hudson, Theodore R. "Langston Hughes' Last Volume of Verse." *CLA Journal*, XI, 345–8.

Jackson, Blyden. "A Word About Simple." *CLA Journal*, XI, 310–18.

Jones, Eldred. " 'Laughing to Keep from Crying': A Tribute to Langston Hughes." *Présence Africaine*, LXIV, 51–5.

Jones, Harry L. "A Danish Tribute to Langston Hughes." *CLA Journal*, XI, 331–4.

Kaiser, Ernest. "Selected Bibliography of the Published Writings of Langston Hughes." *Freedomways*, VIII, 185–91.

Kramer, Aaron. "Robert Burns & Langston Hughes." *Freedomways*, VIII, 159–66.

Larkin, Margaret. "A Poet for the People." *Opportunity*, V, 84–5.

MacLeod, Norman. "The Poetry and Argument of Langston Hughes." *Crisis*, XLV, 358–9.

Matheus, John F. "Langston Hughes as Translator." *CLA Journal*, XI, 319–30.

O'Daniel, Therman. "Langston Hughes: A Selected Classified Bibliography." *CLA Journal*, XI, 349–66.

———. "Lincoln's Man of Letters." *Lincoln University Bulletin*, LXVII, 9–12.

Parker, John W. "Tomorrow in the Writing of Langston Hughes." *College English*, V, 438–41.

Patterson, Lindsay. "Langston Hughes: An Inspirer of Young Writers." *Freedomways*, VIII, 179–81.

Patterson, Louise Thompson. "With Langston Hughes in the U.S.S.R." *Freedomways*, VIII, 152–8.

Peterkin, Julia. "Negro Blue and Gold." *Poetry*, XXXI, 44–7.

Presley, James. "The American Dream of Langston Hughes." *Southwest Review*, XLVIII, 380–6.

Rive, Richard. "Taos in Harlem: An Interview with Langston Hughes," *Contrast*, XIV, 33–9.

Rivers, Clarence. *See* Spencer, T. J.

Spencer, T. J. and Clarence Rivers. "Langston Hughes: His Style and Optimism." *Drama Critique: A Critical Review of Theatre Arts & Literature*, VII (Spring 1964), 99–102.

Turner, Darwin T. "Langston Hughes as Playwright." *CLA Journal*, XI, 297–309.

LEROI JONES

Costello, Donald P. "LeRoi Jones: Black Man as Victim." *Commonweal*, LXXXVIII, 436–40.

Dennison, George. "The Demagogy of LeRoi Jones." *Commentary*, XXVIII, 4.

Howard, R. "Two Against Chaos." *Nation*, CC, 289–90.

Jones, LeRoi. "In Search of the Revolutionary Theatre." *Negro Digest*, XVI, No. 6 (April 1966), 20.

Jouffroy, Alain. "LeRoi Jones, Théâtre de la révolution noire." *Cahiers de la compagnie Madeleine Renaud-Jean Louis Barrault*, LXIII, 44–53.

Neal, Lawrence P. "Development of LeRoi Jones." *Liberator*, VI, No. 1 (January 1966), 20 (Part 1): VI No. 2 (February 1966), 18 (Part 2).

Nelson, Hugh. "LeRoi Jones' *Dutchman*: A Brief Ride on a Doomed Ship." *Educational Theatre Journal*, XX, 53–9.

Resnik, H. S. "Brave New Words." *Saturday Review*, L. (Dec. 9, 1967), 28–9.
Richardson, J. "Blues for Mr. Jones." *Esquire*, LXV (June 1966), 106–8.
Russell, Charlie. "LeRoi Jones Will Get Us All in Trouble." *Liberator*, IV, No. 8 (August 1964), p. 18.
Velde, Paul. "LeRoi Jones: Pursued by the Furies." *Commonweal*, LXXXVIII, 440–1.